Beyond Sovereignty

Issues for a Global Agenda

Beyond Sovereignty

Issues for a Global Agenda

Maryann K. Cusimano

The Catholic University of America

Bedford/St. Martin's
Boston • New York

For Bedford/St. Martin's

Political Science Editor: James R. Headley
Senior Editor, Publishing Services: Douglas Bell
Production Supervisor: Joe Ford
Project Management: Stratford Publishing Services, Inc.
Text Design: Paul Lacy
Cover Design: Lucy Krikorian
Cover Art: Copyright © Tom Sciacca/The Stock Illustration Source, Inc.
Composition: Stratford Publishing Services, Inc.
Printing and Binding: Haddon Craftsman, an R.R. Donnelley & Sons Company

President: Charles H. Christensen
Editorial Director: Joan E. Feinberg
Director of Editing, Design, and Production: Marcia Cohen
Manager, Publishing Services: Emily Berleth

Library of Congress Catalog Card Number: 98-85002

Manufactured in the United States of America.

5 4 3 2 1 0
f e d c b a

For information write: Bedford/St. Martin's, 75 Arlington Street, Boston, MA 02116
(617-426-7440)

ISBN: 1-57259-751-8 (paperback)
        0-312-21951-2 (hardcover)

To my family, who taught me anything was possible,
and who loved me enough to make it so.

Preface

Government and private sector officials from Lagos to London have noted that the pressing international relations issues of the post–Cold War era are transsovereign challenges. These issues "have no passports" and are difficult, if not impossible, for states to solve alone.

Often missed in an examination of transsovereign problems is the understanding that we are not adrift in a strange new world; we are in a world of our own making. Transsovereign problems are not unfathomable and irksome coincidences of bad luck or bad policy; they are the unintended consequences of decades of sustained and deliberate Western policies aimed at opening markets; encouraging open, democratic societies; and spreading open, modern technologies. By our very success in these endeavors, we have created the infrastructure that makes transsovereign problems possible.

Transsovereign problems are difficult to solve for a number of reasons. First, states and the private sector have to figure out how to control or contain them without moving to close off economies, societies, or technologies. Second, because their very nature precludes unilateral solutions, transsovereign problems are harder to tackle because they require the cooperation of a greater number of actors. Third, they are complex because they entail state as well as nonstate actors. Fourth, transsovereign problems are challenging because they often take place in the economic and social spheres, where the arm of liberal capitalist states has the shortest reach. Finally, they are challenging because efforts to combat or contain transsovereign problems may further undermine sovereignty.

Beyond Sovereignty: Issues for a Global Agenda begins with an outline of the rise of transsovereign problems, open markets, open societies, and open economies, a historical description of sovereignty, as well as a review of current theories concerning whether sovereignty is receding, changing, or remaining as powerful as ever. The chapters that follow, written by noted academics and expert practitioners, consider various transsovereign issues; their connections with open economies, societies, and technologies; and potential policy solutions. These issue chapters are followed by ones that describe the changing roles of nonstate actors, such as intergovernmental and nongovernmental organizations and multinational corporations. For new problems to be dealt with adequately institutions must change; therefore, Chapter 11 considers the obstacles and the promise of institutional change to meet transsovereign challenges. The concluding chapter reviews the various policy proposals to combat transsovereign problems, noting the variety of responses, some which focus on the state as savior, others which regard states as ill-positioned to deal with transsovereign problems and therefore suggest looking to private actors instead. The volume concludes by returning to the theoretical arguments about the future of sovereignty. Do the issue areas discussed offer supportive or undermining evidence for the various theories on the future of the state? If sovereignty has not yet been dethroned by some competing organizational form, does that mean that it remains unchanged and unscathed by current developments?

Beyond Sovereignty is written with students in introductory courses in international relations, U.S. foreign policy, global issues, or globalization in mind. The book grew out of my own frustrations in looking for material for such courses. In discussing the need for a fresh interpretation of post–Cold War global issues, editors at Bedford/St. Martin's suggested I write this book—that as an author who came through graduate school after the Cold War had ended, they felt I might approach the material with a different perspective.

Beyond Sovereignty differs from other issue texts. The chapters were written explicitly for this volume, revolving around the common themes of open economies, societies, and technologies. The issues are not presented in an ad hoc, disconnected fashion, as occurs with many "issues" readers which present descriptive accounts (usually reprinted from journals), without providing the theoretical or historical context that unites current challenges. Many of these books have the "and now this!" organizational framework of TV journalism. Readers may be left with little understanding of how these issues intersect, why it is no accident that they are on the rise simultaneously, what are the origins of these issues, and what are the theoretical as well as practical problems in policy solutions. These books can leave readers with the mistaken impression that we are adrift in a dangerous world we don't understand and can do little about.

This book benefitted from conversations and input from many individuals, although any errors or omissions are purely my own. Discussions with other Pew Faculty Fellows in International Affairs, particularly Stephen Flynn of the U.S. Coast Guard Academy, Ivo Daalder of the University of Maryland, Deborah Gerner of the University of Kansas, and William LeoGrande of American University, encouraged me to go forward with these ideas. Sessions of the WITS (Washington International Theory Seminars) group, especially comments by Deborah Avant, Martha Finnemore, James Goldgeier, and James Rosenau, all of George Washington University, Virginia Haufler of the University of Maryland, and Anne Florini and P. J. Simmons of the Carnegie Endowment for International Peace, cross-fertilized ideas and also encouraged me to proceed.

Graduate research assistants Leslie Rodriguez, Mark Hensman, and Michelle Boomgaard of the Catholic University of America provided valuable assistance (supported by faculty development grants). My undergraduate and graduate students at the Catholic University of America and at the Pentagon, especially those in my introduction to international relations, global issues, U.S. foreign policy, and the problem of sovereignty courses were guinea pigs for early drafts, and provided useful feedback and lively discussions. Special thanks go to graduate students Peter Howard, Rob Connallon, Charles Pierce, Ahmed Elbashari, and Sara Johnson for their enthusiastic comments.

The editorial and production staff at Bedford/St. Martin's, especially editors James Headley and Beth Gillett, were very encouraging, and the manuscript was also helped by the reviewer comments of Wes Chapin, University of Wisconsin, River Falls; Ralph DiMuccio, University of Florida; Michael Erisman, Indiana State University; Roger Hamburg, Indiana University, South Bend; Joseph Lepgold, Georgeown University; Pernilla M. Neal, Dickinson College; George Quester, University of Maryland; Carolyn Rhodes, Utah State University; and Raymond Tarter, University of Michigan.

Last but not least, my family and friends, especially at St. Aloyius Gonzaga Parish, PeaceKids, SAIC, Women in International Security, USIP, Habitat for Humanity, Greenhome, and the Jesuit order, helped buoy my spirits and keep me sane throughout. A portion of the proceeds from this book will go to the Francis Cusimano S. J. Scholarship Fund to support the education of children in Nigeria.

Maryann K. Cusimano

Contents

Contents

About the Editor

Maryann K. Cusimano is assistant professor of politics at the Catholic University of America in Washington, D.C. She teaches graduate and undergraduate courses on international relations and U.S. foreign policy at both Catholic University and the Pentagon. She is also author of *Unplugging the Cold War Machine: Rethinking U.S. Foreign Policy Institutions,* which is forthcoming from Sage Publications. She holds a B.A. degree from St. Joseph's University in Philadelphia, and a Ph.D. from Johns Hopkins University.

About the Contributors

Stephen E. Flynn is associate professor of international relations at the U.S. Coast Guard Academy in New London, Connecticut. He is a commander in the U.S. Coast Guard and has served in command of two cutters. He has been engaged in policy-oriented research on the illicit drug trade and international organized crime since 1991 when he was selected as the Coast Guard's first Council on Foreign Relations' International Affairs Fellow. A 1982 graduate of the Coast Guard Academy, he holds the M.A.L.D. and Ph.D. degrees from the Fletcher School of Law and Diplomacy.

James L. Ford is director of planning and applications in the Office of Safeguards and Security, Department of Energy, Germantown, Maryland. He is coauthor of *Controlling Threats to Nuclear Security,* and author of two monographs on *Nuclear Smuggling: How Serious a Threat* and *Radiological Dispersal Devices: Assessing the Transnational Threat* (all from National Defense University Press, Washington, D.C.). He holds B.A. and M.A. degrees from Louisiana State University, and a second M.A. from the University of Kansas.

Roy Godson is a professor of government at Georgetown University. He has written, coauthored, or edited nineteen books and numerous articles on a variety of security-related subjects. His most recent books include *Dirty Tricks or Trump Cards* (1995) and *Security Studies for the Twenty-First Century* (1998). He is editor of the quarterly journal *Trends in Organized Crime.*

Hal Kane is a writer and consultant in San Francisco, and a Senior Fellow at Redefining Progress, a public-policy think tank. He is author or coauthor of nine books about international environmental issues, hunger, and economic development, many of them written for the Worldwatch Institute in Washington, D.C. He holds his M.A. degree from Johns Hopkins University School of Advanced International Studies.

Rensselaer W. Lee is president of Global Advisory Services in Mclean, Virginia, and author of *Smuggling Armageddon: the Nuclear Black Market in the Former Soviet Union and Europe* (New York: St. Martin's, 1998).

David E. Long is a scholar, author, and former diplomat specializing in terrorism and Middle East politics. He is a former deputy director of the State Department's Office of Counterterrorism and author of *The Anatomy of Terrorism* (Free Press, 1990).

Dennis Pirages is professor of government and politics and director of the Harrison Program on the Future Global Agenda at the University of Maryland, College Park. He is the author or editor of several books on international relations and environmental politics including *Building Sustainable Societies* (M. E. Sharpe, 1996), *Transformations in the Global Political Economy* (St. Martin's, 1990), and *Global Technopolitics* (Brooks Cole, 1989). Dr. Pirages holds a Ph.D. in political science from Stanford University.

Leslie Rodrigues is an intelligence operations specialist in the Domestic Terrorism/Weapons of Mass Destruction Operations Unit in the Federal Bureau of Investigation (FBI) in Washington, D.C. She is also coauthor of Jane's Defense's *Jane's U.S. Chemical/Biological Defense Guidebook.* She holds a M.A. from the University of San Diego and is completing her Ph.D. at the Catholic University of America.

Paul Runci is a researcher with the Global Climate Change Group of the Pacific Northwest National Laboratory in Washington, D.C. He is also currently a doctoral candidate in the Department of Government and Politics at the University of Maryland, College Park.

Ursula C. Tafe is a Ph.D. candidate in the department of politics at the Catholic University of America. She is presently completing her dissertation, "International Organizations and the Legitimation of Governments: The Role of Electoral Observation." Ursula received a B.A. from the University of Massachusetts at Amherst and an M.A. from Northeastern University.

Phil Williams is director of the Ridgway Center for International Security Studies, and professor in the graduate school of public and international affairs at the University of Pittsburgh, Pennsylvania. He is the founder and editor of the journal *Transnational Organized Crime.* Dr. Williams has published extensively on transnational crime, and he is a consultant to the United Nations Drug Control Programme.

David A. Wirth is a professor of law at Boston College Law School in Newton, Massachusetts. The author was formerly attorney-adviser for Oceans and International Environmental and Scientific Affairs in the U.S. Department of State and senior attorney and co-director of international programs at the Natural Resources Defense Council. This work draws on the author's research as a Fulbright scholar through the Organization for Security and Cooperation in Europe Regional Research Program.

Beyond Sovereignty

Issues for a Global Agenda

Chapter One

Beyond Sovereignty

The Rise of Transsovereign Problems

Maryann K. Cusimano

AMIDST THE SMOKE AND CONFUSION

Dean Acheson, in his memoir *Present at the Creation,* recalled what it was like to witness the end of the age of empires after World War II, and to usher in a new bipolar international system of U.S.-Soviet/Communist confrontation. As President Truman's secretary of state, Acheson was a key architect of the defining features of the Cold War world. Acheson helped create the Truman Doctrine to contain communism, the Marshall Plan to rebuild Europe, international institutions (such as the UN), and U.S. foreign policy institutions (such as the National Security Council).

For over forty years the world was organized around the battle lines that Acheson and his cohorts drew. Then, with amazing speed, the Berlin Wall fell in 1989, the Soviet Union fell in 1991, and our ways of thinking about the world have been falling ever since. The end of the Cold War has also meant the end of clarity and consensus about the nature of the international system and the United States' role in it. Since 1991 a misplaced nostalgia for the Cold War has been growing, a yearning for the supposed simpler times of great resolve against a clear and common enemy.[1] But this halcyon view of Cold War clarity and deliberate resolve is *not* how Acheson recalls it. Acheson remembers the years following the end of World War II as a period of "ignorance of the true situation," of "smoke and confusion," in which a sense of hope and opportunity was mixed with "a sense of disappointment and frustration."[2]

> Many times in the course of this book I have remarked upon our misconceptions of the state of the world around us, both in anticipating postwar conditions and in recognizing what they actually were when we came face to face with them. This was true not only of the extent of physical destruction, damage, and loss caused by the war, but even more of social, economic, and

political dislocations undermining the very continuance of great states and empires. Only slowly did it dawn upon us that the whole world structure and order that we had inherited from the nineteenth century was gone . . . as we looked further into political and economic problems, and particularly as we began to meet them, our preliminary ideas appeared more and more irrelevant to the developing facts and the attitudes, purposes, and capabilities of other actors on the scene.[3]

Since the fall of the Soviet empire, we are experiencing a similar period of slow and uncertain awakening to the different dynamics of the post–Cold War world. Twentieth-century international relations were epic battles of behemoth states, bent on capturing the hearts, minds, and sovereign territories of other men. It was a century of "heroic warfare" among strong, competing states; in contrast, the dawn of the twenty-first century marks a period of "post-heroic warfare."[4] International relations challenges now come not from battles among strong states, but from the problems posed by weak or disintegrating states (Humpty Dumpty wars in which all the kings forces and men may not be able to put the fractured states back together again), and from the growing activities of nonstate actors.[5] International relations problems now move *beyond sovereignty*, yet the machinery we have to combat these problems are wired for the sovereign military confrontations of a bygone era.

Sovereignty is the form of political organization that has dominated the international system since the Treaty of Westphalia in 1648. Sovereign states have exclusive and final jurisdiction over territory, as well as the resources and populations that lie within that territory. A system based on sovereignty is one that acknowledges only one political authority over a particular territory, and looks to that authority as final arbiter to solve problems that occur within its borders. In theory, the sovereign state has a monopoly on the use of force within that territory. Outside a state's territory, states may voluntarily band together in treaties or alliances to try to solve particular problems, but only state actors are accorded international legal recognition and standing in a system based on sovereignty. The origins, definitions, and challenges to sovereignty will be discussed later in this chapter.

This volume will trace the rise of an important new class of international relations problems—transsovereign issues—that move beyond sovereignty and traditional, state responses. As Gillian Sorenson of the UN describes it, "Disease and pollution cross borders without passports."[6] The transsovereign challenges from international criminal organizations, narcotics and weapons proliferation, terrorism, environmental degradation, infectious disease, and refugee flows, transcend state borders and are not responsive to traditional, unilateral state policy actions.[7] How can transsovereign issues be tackled in a system based on sovereignty? The volume will discuss the nonstate actors (such as multinational corporations, nongovernmental organizations, and intergovernmental organizations) that play an important role in both generating and resolving transsovereign issues. The volume will investigate the institutional challenges that transsovereign issues raise. Our international and U.S. foreign policy institutions were not built with these changed international circumstances in mind. How can and are institutions changing to meet a changed international environment? Finally, the volume will review various theories on the status and future of sovereignty, and assess whether the empirical evidence on transsovereign problems undercuts or corroborates the various ideas about where sovereignty is heading.

THE RISE OF TRANSSOVEREIGN PROBLEMS

Transsovereign problems fill the international relations agenda of the post–Cold War world and make a mockery of state borders and unilateral state responses. Environmental threats,[8] refugee flows,[9] contagious diseases,[10] drug trafficking, terrorism, nuclear smuggling, and international criminal activities[11] defy traditional ideas of sovereignty. Transsovereign problems are "problems which transcend state boundaries in ways over which states have little control and which cannot be solved by individual state actions alone."[12] Nonstate actors, such as NGOs (nongovernmental organizations), IGOs (intergovernmental organizations), MNCs (multinational corporations), and international crime cartels, are important players both in creating and responding to transsovereign issues.

Although many policymakers (and sometimes even scholars) use the term "transnational" problems, this volume will instead use the more accurate name "transsovereign" problems. The term "nation" is *not* synonymous with the term "sovereign state." A nation is a group with a common cultural, linguistic, ethnic, racial, or religious identity, such as the Sioux nation in North Dakota, or the Moluccans in Northern Europe. A sovereign state, however, is an internationally recognized unit of political authority over a given territory, such as the United States of America or the Netherlands. National boundaries—where various ethnic or linguistic groups are located—often do not coincide with sovereign state boundaries. For example, the Basques live on either side of the border between Spain and France, and the Kurds live in Iraq, Iran, Turkey, and Afghanistan. There are by some counts over 8,000 national groups, while there are only 185 sovereign states.[13] Since most states internally comprise many national groups, virtually all the domestic affairs of sovereign states are actually "transnational" issues. In contrast, the issues considered here transcend international, sovereign, territorial borders, so we will use the term "transsovereign" in order to keep clear the distinction between sovereign states and national groups.

The rise of transsovereign problems is made possible by the very changes hoped for by Acheson and his colleagues, changes heralded since the end of the Cold War: the opening of societies, economies, and technologies. Transsovereign issues represent the downside, or at least the challenge, to what are otherwise thought of as good, progressive, and liberalizing international trends: the rise of democracies and liberal, capitalist economies, and advances in technology, transportation, and communication. Thus, the rise of transsovereign problems is wrought with irony. Problems such as nuclear and drug trafficking, and refugee movements, are *made possible* by the very open market and open society forces[14] that Western and U.S. foreign policies seek to promote. International and U.S. foreign policy institutions will be challenged increasingly by the conflict between promoting free trade, free-market capitalism, and free, democratic societies, while restricting or limiting the flow of people (be they legal or illegal immigrants, terrorists, drug traffickers, or refugees), and limiting the flow of particular materials (such as narcotics, nuclear materials, and dual-use technologies). It is physically difficult to limit the flow of particular peoples and goods at a time when technological, market, and societal forces make such movement easier than ever before. As President Clinton recognizes,

> The world we live in is going through profound and fast-paced change, perhaps the fastest pace of change in all human history. In so many ways this change is clearly for the good. . . . Democracy and free markets are on the march; the laptops, the CD-ROMS, the satellites that are second nature to all of you send ideas, products, money, all across our planet in a matter of seconds. Political, economic, and technological revolutions are bringing us all closer together, and bringing with them extraordinary opportunities for all to share in humanity's genius for progress. But we know that these same forces also pose new challenges. The end of communism has opened the door to the spread of weapons of mass destruction and lifted the lid on ethnic and religious conflicts. The growing openness that we so cherish also benefits a host of equal opportunity destroyers—terrorists, international criminals, drug traffickers, and those who do environmental damage that cross national borders. None of these problems has any particular respect for the borders of the nation. . . . Because the Cold War is over, some of these challenges are underestimated.[15]

Further, the post–Cold War era is witness to the collapse of many weak states, previously kept afloat by Cold War aid and alliances.[16] These same trends of open societies, open economies, and open technologies can further erode already weak state institutions in many "quasi-states," pushing them closer to collapse. Failed states provide a natural breeding ground for transsovereign problems such as international criminal activity, refugee flows, the spread of contagious disease, nuclear and drug trafficking, etc. In a world primarily organized around state sovereignty, world politics practitioners are challenged by a double bind. How can transsovereign issues be dealt with effectively in a world of sovereign states? Simultaneously, how can democratization and economic liberalization be promoted in ways that do not undermine already fragile state institutions to the point of collapse, thus further increasing the spread and intensity of transsovereign problems?

THE DIFFICULTIES IN ADDRESSING TRANSSOVEREIGN PROBLEMS

Of course, value trade-offs are nothing new in foreign policy. For example, although Cold War presidents routinely professed an interest in promoting democracy, freedom, and human rights, these concerns often took a back seat to containing Soviet or communist forces. Jeanne Kirkpatrick explained this necessity in her article "Dictatorships and Double Standards," in which she argued that repressive, nondemocratic regimes must sometimes be supported in the larger battle against Communism. During the Cold War, foreign policy values were prioritized, and military containment of Soviet and communist forces was the agreed-upon trump card in the West. During the post–Cold War era, threats to security in the West are more diffuse, disputed, and less intense than during the Cold War period; thus, there is now less consensus about the goals of foreign policy, and there is no agreed trump card.

Transsovereign issues, however, present an even more difficult dilemma for policymakers. Policymakers still face the perennial and painful question of prioritizing foreign policy goals, such as in determining whether promoting free trade and liberal, capitalist economic forms is more important than promoting democracy and human rights (in China, for example). Yet in addition to the traditional value trade-off questions, transsovereign issues present another difficult bind: the very same policies that work to bring about open markets and open societies also make transsovereign problems possible. Drug smuggling illegally piggybacks on the very same international financial networks that free trade and capitalist economic policies create. Liberal political reforms allow people to move freely within and across state borders, but refugees and diseases may move more easily as well. Transsovereign problems raise the ante for foreign policy value trade-offs. Policymakers not only have to decide "which value do I want to pursue most?," but also, "Am I willing to accept the costs (in transsovereign problems and weakened states) that pursuing this policy may entail?"

Transsovereign problems cross state boundaries in ways over which states have little control and which cannot be solved by unilateral state actions alone,[17] and involve the heavy participation of nonstate actors. Thus, transsovereign problems can be difficult for states to address because effective action requires greater coordination among states, NGOs, IGOs, MNCs, and other nonstate actors, groups which have different interests, capabilities, and constituencies. Coordinating action among a larger number and variety of players makes responding to transsovereign issues more difficult and complex, with more opportunities for policy to go awry. As Michael Meacher, the United Kingdom's minister for the environment, explains,

> We face new dilemmas—of problems that cross boundaries, of issues that no single government can control, of shared risk. Nowhere is this collectivity more true than with the environment. Pollution, global warming, ozone depletion, and loss of species do not respect borders. . . . Globalization—in the form of increasing trade, the communications revolution, and increasing cultural exchanges—means that nation states and their governments have less influence over activities and economic sectors that were formerly under their control. . . . Some people refer to the effect this has on governments as "loss of agency." But the need for intervention in the public interest has not diminished—it is just that the locus has changed. Activities that were formerly national are now international, but the institutional capacity to deal with them has yet to evolve . . . we must manage the changing responsibilities of governments, business and civil society, forming new partnerships, learning from each other, finding new ways of harnessing the expertise and legitimate concerns and aspirations of each.[18]

Additionally, addressing transsovereign problems can be difficult for states because these issues blur the conventional concepts of domestic versus foreign policy. As President Clinton describes it,

> The once bright line between domestic and foreign policy is blurring. If I could do anything to change the speech patterns of those of us in public life, I would almost like to stop hearing people talk about foreign policy and domestic policy, and instead start discussing economic policy, security policy, environmental policy— you name it. . . . When the President of Mexico comes here . . . and we talk about drug problems, are we talking about domestic problems or foreign problems? If we talk about immigration, are we discussing a domestic issue or a foreign issue? If we talk about NAFTA and trade, is it their foreign politics or our domestic economics? We have to understand this in a totally different way.[19]

Because transsovereign issues transcend the border between domestic and foreign policy, state action again can be more difficult. As domestic constituencies become mobilized over transsovereign issues, policymakers find their tasks complicated, as they have to address and try to coordinate the interests of additional groups. Domestic labor, environmental, and industry groups mobilize for international discussions of acid rain, for example, whereas in many Cold War foreign policy debates such domestic constituencies would generally not get involved, and politics was thought to stop at "the water's edge."

Ambassador Craig Johnstone, director of the Office of Resources, Plans, and Policy at the U.S. State Department, believes transsovereign issues signal a fundamental change in foreign policy.

> Foreign policy as we have known it is dead . . . because it is no longer foreign. The world has invaded us and we have invaded it. . . . The distinctions between domestic and foreign are gone. Look at the issues: The principal preoccupation of Americans is on drugs and crime. And the fight against drugs and crime has major international components. Our stolen cars end up in El Salvador or Guatemala, or Poland. Our drugs come from Peru or Pakistan or Burma or elsewhere and transit almost anywhere. Crime cartels spread tentacles from Nigeria or Russia or Columbia. Today it is inconceivable to consider a coordinated attack on crime without working a part of the strategy in the international arena. . . . International terrorism has reached our shores. . . . We cannot deal with the threats to our environment, to assaults on biodiversity with domestic policy. Ozone layer depletion and global warming cannot be addressed by domestic environmental regulations alone. Over and over again we find issues that are domestic in consequence but international in scope. These are the consuming issues of the twenty-first century.[20]

As "intermestic" (*inter*national-do*mestic*) issues, transsovereign problems are also difficult for policymakers to address because they are linked to contentious and often unsettled domestic policy debates, such as the proper regulatory relationship between the federal government and industry in environmental matters, for example.

Finally, transsovereign problems can be difficult for states to address because the existing foreign policy bureaucracies were not created or structured to deal with these problems. Bureaucracies are slow to change and resist taking on new functions that may divert resources from their traditional missions. For example, the U.S. Department of Defense (DOD) was created at the beginning of the Cold War to work to unify the armed services and strengthen the military in peacetime in order to contain the communist Soviet threat. DOD organized quite effectively to deter an armed invasion of Europe by the Soviet army. But this organization, set up to deter and fight aggressive states, is somewhat befuddled by how to respond when the threat to U.S. territory and citizens comes not from aggressive invaders but from drug trafficking, refugee flows, greenhouse gases or acid rain, which are neither directly caused by or containable by any one state. Thus, transsovereign problems frequently fall through the cracks of foreign policy organizations, which were designed to contain strong, aggressive states, not to attend to the problems associated with weakened sovereignties and nonstate actors.

YESTERDAY: WHERE SOVEREIGNTY CAME FROM

The international system has not always been organized around sovereignty. Prior to the Treaty of Westphalia in 1648, there were overlapping jurisdictions of political authority with no clear hierarchy or pecking order among them. In this feudal system, claims to authority were diffuse, decentralized, and based on personal ties, not territory. Medieval subjects faced simultaneous and competing claims for allegiance to the pope, the king or the emperor, the bishop, and the local feudal princes, dukes, counts, and lords, etc.[21] Taxes and military service could be required of a person from several different authorities within the same territory. A person's bonds to an authority figure were based on personal ties and agreements, and "political authority was treated as a private possession."[22] Since ties were personal, secession was problematic, and contractual obligations might not survive a person's death.

Rather than land, authority claims were based on the divine, on spiritual connections or the legitimacy of lineage to the Church (and in the days before the Reformation, that meant the Roman Catholic Church). Secular and spiritual authority were intertwined; kings were anointed with holy insignia (British monarchs took the title "Defender of the Faith"), emperors were crowned as "servants of the apostles," and popes and bishops needed the support of non-clerical leaders to gain and retain power. Both the Church and the Holy Roman Empire sought to fill the vacuum left by the fall of the Roman Empire, and both made universal claims of authority over all Christians. People were the primary object of rule, not territory, and "rule was per definition spiritual,"[23] not spatial. In the struggle between the papacy and the Holy Roman Empire for control, both institutions were weakened in ways that helped new forms of political organization to emerge.

There were many reasons why the feudal system declined and the sovereign state emerged. According to scholar Hendrik Spruyt, the rise of long-distance trade in the late Middle Ages created both a new merchant class of elites and the need for a new political system that could better accommodate the mercantilist economic system. The Church was against the exchange and loan of money and the taking of oaths, but currency and contracts were crucial to long-distance trade. Trade also required more precise and consistent measurements of time, weights, jurisdiction, and property.

> The result of this economic dynamism was that a social group, the town dwellers, came into existence with new sources of revenue and power, which did not fit the old feudal order. This new social group had various incentives to search for political allies who were willing to change the existing order. The new trading and commercial classes of the towns could not settle into the straightjacket of the feudal order, and the towns became a chief agent in its final disruption. . . . Business activity could not be organized according to

the . . . system of personal bonds. The businessperson depersonalizes ties. . . . Business contracts are upheld merely for the exchange of commodities, not because they signify some deeper bond. If service is required, it is depersonalized, circumscribed for a particular time and amount. . . . The necessity to have circumscribed areas of clear jurisdiction, and the desire to substantiate private property combined with the necessity of more formalized interaction which could exist independent of the specific actors, renewed interest in Roman law. There was the attraction—especially felt by merchants—of more convenient and rational procedures. . . . Contracts could not depend on the initiating actors. Sometimes these contracts might have to carry through beyond the death of the original contractors.[24]

The rise of a new economic system with its own needs, however, was not enough to bring about the rise of the sovereign state. The currency of other ideas aided the development of the concept of sovereignty. Martin Luther and the Protestant Reformation, Henry VIII and his Anglican separatists, the rise of scientific knowledge and explorations, along with the new merchant elites, challenged the authority and legitimacy of the Church in Rome. Roman ideas of property rights were on the rise, which stressed exclusive control over territory.[25] Ideas of individual autonomy and freedom from outside interference, later captured by Immanual Kant, were important in the development of sovereignty.[26] Nicholas Onuf cites three conceptual antecedents as crucial to the genesis of sovereignty: *majestas*—that institutions inspire respect; *potestus imperiandi,* or the ability to coerce and enforce rules; and the protestant idea of stewardship, or rule on behalf of the citizens of the body politic, not the personal rule of the Middle Ages.[27]

Besides conceptual changes, sovereignty also emerged because of changes in practical political balances. Sovereign states were more effective and efficient at waging war[28] and conducting trade than were competing political organizations. Elites that benefitted from the new form of organization sought to delegitimize actors who were not like them (who were not organized as sovereign states) by excluding them from the international system.

There were other forms of political organization that competed with the sovereign state to be the successor to the feudal system: the city-state, the urban league, the empire. Hendrik Spruyt believes that the sovereign state eventually won out for several reasons. First, states were better able to extract resources and rationalize their economies than other forms of political organization. Second, states were more efficient and effective than medieval forms of organization, especially at being able to "speak with one voice" and make external commitments necessary to the new trading system. And finally, social choice and institutional mimicry meant that sovereign states selected out and delegitimized other actors who were not sovereign states.[29]

Out of these changes in economics, in political balances, and in conceptual frameworks came the eventual acceptance of the sovereign state. Sovereignty cut the cord between church and state, between secular and religious authority. Only one political authority could claim people's taxes or military service, and that political authority no longer necessarily rested on sanction or indirect acceptance by God or the Church. Authority was now based on exclusive jurisdiction over territory. Identity became based on geography; you were where you lived, a citizen of French territory, not primarily a member of the Holy Roman Empire or the community of Christians or the Celtic or Norman clans.

Sovereignty entailed a one-to-one correspondence between territory and political authority. The sovereign state had a monopoly on the legitimate use of force within a territory. Sovereignty was reciprocal: You recognized other states' exclusive jurisdiction over their territories and the populations and resources that resided on their land, and in return they recognized your exclusive jurisdiction over your territory and everything located on your land.[30] So from the beginning, sovereignty was based in part on a social compact—in order to be a sovereign state the other sovereign states had to accept you as such. Sovereignty never meant that all states had equal power or resources—some had vast lands, populations, and resources, while the capabilities of other states were meager. But sovereignty meant that legally only other sovereigns had standing in international agreements; states were the main unit of the international system.

From its origins in Europe, the idea and practice of sovereignty spread around the globe as Europeans conquered and carved up the planet into colonial territories. Sovereignty (with its territorial limits) came into conflict with the unlimited, universal empires of China, Japan, and the Ottoman Empire, but eventually sovereignty was either forced upon or acceded to worldwide. When the European colonies became independent after World War II, and when the Soviet block disintegrated between 1989 and 1991, the political units that emerged sought sovereign statehood, not recognition of some other form of political organization.

Sovereignty is an equalizing concept. Internally, governments organize themselves in whatever fashion they choose: monarchy; republican constitutional parliamentary systems; autocracy; theocracy; etc. But externally, all a state needs is international recognition as a sovereign state that has a set territory, population, and a government with authority over that territory and population.

TODAY: SOVEREIGNTY CHALLENGED

Since the Treaty of Westphalia in 1648, international relations have been the province of sovereign states. The modern international system is built on the foundation of sovereignty. Today, sovereignty is under siege.

While there have always been weak states, and distinctions between the theory and the practice of sovereignty, both de jure and de facto sovereignty are now under more challenge than ever. While the sovereign state will likely continue to be the main unit in the international system for some time, the operation and the legitimacy of sovereignty are being undermined by both external and internal dynamics.

The *principle* of sovereignty is under siege by those who contend that in grave humanitarian crises the international community (of NGOs, IGOs, and states) has a right to intervene to aid citizens whom the state is not protecting. In Somalia, Bosnia, and Rwanda, the international community has intervened in the internal affairs of states to distribute aid directly to individuals in a time of grave humanitarian crisis without either the invitation or consent of the sovereignties involved. It used to be that only sovereign states, not individuals, had standing in international law, and that within sovereign borders a polity could do whatever it pleased with its citizens, even if that meant abusing their human rights or neglecting basic human needs.

Now that thinking is changing (among some) to consider the responsibilities of sovereignties to provide for their citizens. As Boutros Boutros-Ghali, former Secretary-General of the United Nations put it, "Sovereignty is no longer absolute. . . . Sovereignty must be kept in its place."[31] These are strong words from the director of an organization founded on the principle of sovereign states, and comprised solely of sovereign states as voting members.

The *Wall Street Journal* editorialized in a similar vein, saying that sovereignty is not an absolute right because starvation and wanton killing are "everybody's business," and that in cases like Somalia or Rwanda "any absolute principle of nonintervention becomes a cruel abstraction indeed."[32] Editorial writers at the *Economist* agreed, noting that we "are increasingly concerned not just to see countries well governed but also to ensure that the world is not irreparably damaged—whether by global warming, by the loss of species, by famine or by war. . . . Increasingly, world opinion, when confronted by television pictures of genocide or starvation is unimpressed by those who say 'We cannot get involved. National sovereignty must be respected.' . . . National sovereignty be damned."[33]

Principles of sovereignty took centuries to become established and are not in danger of dissolving entirely any time soon. However, perhaps we ought to take notice anytime the more liberal Boutros-Ghali, the conservative *Wall Street Journal,* and the moderate *Economist* agree that the principle of sovereignty is under challenge, and that individuals in need might seek international redress if states are unable or unwilling to carry out basic duties to their citizens.

Besides the theory of sovereignty being challenged, sovereignty is also under siege *in practice.* Sovereignty is challenged *externally* by the globalizing dynamics of open markets, open societies, and open technologies, which make the borders of even strong states permeable by outside forces. Sovereignty is also under siege *internally,* from the rise of internal conflicts and subnational movements, as well as from the reinforcing crises of economic development (resource scarcity, environmental degradation, population growth) which undermine the international and internal legitimacy on which sovereignty stands. Both these dynamics have led to a growing number of collapsed and collapsing states.

In his book *Collapsed States,* I. William Zartman notes that half of the states in Africa may be in serious or maximum "danger of collapse, if not already gone."[34] (Not coincidentally, Africa is also the "most warring region on the planet, currently hosting fourteen major armed conflicts."[35]) All of the thirty-five major armed conflicts taking place on the globe today are primarily internal conflicts, showing that sovereign states beyond Africa are feeling the effects of substate challenges.

When sovereign states collapse, the international system feels the shock waves. According to Zartman, a state is in a process of collapse when its institutions and leaders lose control of political and economic space. When state authorities can no longer provide security, law and order, an economic infrastructure, or other services for citizens, government retracts and the countryside is left on its own. Political space broadens as outside actors usurp (as in Lebanon) and intervene (as IGOs and NGOs do, to provide relief services necessitated by state breakdown). Economic space contracts as the informal economy takes over beyond state control, and as localities resort to barter, as occurred in Somalia.[36] In the power vacuum left by state collapse, transsovereign problems thrive. Refugee flows, disease, ethnic conflict, crime, drug smuggling, and civil war all thrive as the state recedes.

When states implode more than the residents are affected; the shrapnel can hurt distant international as well as immediate local actors. In an interdependent world, flows of refugees, market disruptions, environmental degradation, contagious diseases, and violence spurred on by state collapse spread beyond state borders. Drug smugglers, terrorists, nuclear smugglers, and international criminal organizations look to set up shop where state control is weak or nonexistent, yet clearly the threats they pose move beyond state borders.

Robert Jackson, in his book *Quasi-States,* notes that the international system used to be based primarily on "positive sovereignty," the actual, empirical ability of a state to control its political and economic space, to "provide political goods for its citizens . . . the sociological, economic, technological, psychological, and similar wherewithal to declare, implement, and enforce public policy both domestically and internationally."[37] Weak states existed (despite difficulty controlling their political and economic space), but not for long, as it was considered perfectly legitimate for an outside power to conquer and absorb a weak state. The "old sovereignty game" recognized but did not protect weak sovereignties. They were vulnerable links in the international system's food chain; their digestion by more powerful states was internationally sanctioned behavior.

This changed with the rise of Woodrow Wilson's idea of self-determination, with the discrediting of the concept of "salt-water colonialism"[38] and the end of colonial empires, and with the rise of democracy. The "new sovereignty game," Jackson contends, is increasingly based on "negative sovereignty," the formal-legal entitlement to freedom from outside interference and the "de jure" norm of nonintervention.[39] Thus, the current norms and practices of the international system create conditions that allow weak, ineffectual "quasi-states" to exist.

Sovereignty is under siege from *internal* pressures. As stated previously, internal conflict is growing in the world today, weakening state institutions. Many states in the developing world are undergoing related crises of economic development, environmental degradation, and internal conflict. GNP per capita in Africa, for example, has stagnated or declined since the 1970s, and per capita grain production is lower than it was in 1950.[40] Population continues to increase, intensifying environmental degradation as trees are felled, topsoil is eroded, water supplies become fouled, and air is polluted in a desperate attempt to provide economic sustenance for the growing population.[41] The opportunity for conflict among societal groups increases as resources shrink.

Reinforcing economic and political crises are not restricted to Africa. GNP in the former Soviet states fell by as much as 30 percent after the Cold War, while major armed conflicts in the region quadrupled.[42] Pressure on (and disillusionment with) fragile state institutions grows, as the state fails to break (or contributes to) the scarcity cycle, and as the chasm between the lesser developed and the developed states grows. States confronted with reinforcing crises can "harden," resorting to increased repression in an attempt to establish control.[43] Repressive tactics are costly, however. Civil institutions of the state atrophy (and economic and social performance often suffer) as power and resources concentrate in the military and police. State legitimacy and authority is further undermined and opposition increases with the increase in repressive tactics.

The result is not just a crisis of a particular regime but of the sovereign state itself. Any regime that wins power will face extremely denigrated (to nonexistent) state institutions and societal bases of state power. Thus, the related crises of economic development and internal conflict are increasingly undermining the foundations of sovereign power.

Additionally, sovereignty is undermined by *external* trends which have been heralded since the end of the Cold War: the opening of societies, economies, and technologies. For the United States, the irony is that problems such as nuclear and drug trafficking, and refugee movements, are *made possible* by the very open market and open society forces which U.S. foreign policy seeks to promote. For developing states, the irony is that state institutions and leaders are caught in a bind: they are attracted to the prospect of wealth that democracy, capitalism, and technology promise (which can strengthen the state), yet they fear the loss of control and the decentralization of power that these processes entail (which can weaken the state). Capitalism, democracy, and technology can devolve power away from central state institutions, and undermine the state's ability to control its borders.[44] Many developing states desire the end result of a stable, prosperous, modern democratic state, attractive to international capital and taking part in the international system. However, the process of liberalizing economic and political systems can be quite destabilizing. The job of government and citizen demands on government cannot wait until new institutions are built and put into place. So developing states are put in the challenging position of trying to modernize and democratize their institutions while these same institutions are trying to solve critical problems. As Jack Snyder and Edward Mansfield describe the dangers of democratization, it is like changing the steering wheel while driving the car.[45]

The end of the superpower conflict has also increased the pressure on many weak states. During the Cold War, many quasi-states were propped up by economic and military aid, alliance, and sponsorship from the United States and the USSR, as the superpowers enlisted proxies in their conflict. U.S. and Russian foreign aid has fallen dramatically since the end of the Cold War (especially to weak states in Africa and the developing world),[46] as have arms deliveries to the Third World.[47] Without Cold War aid and allies, many sovereign states are literally coming apart at the seams. The standard of living has dropped precipitously in many states, such as in Cuba, and in North Korea (where the UN is now providing food aid to stave off famine). The underlying ineffectiveness of state political and economic institutions becomes clear (without the mask of Cold War aid and alliances). The incapacity of state institutions also intensifies as the authority and legitimacy of the state suffer, because the state cannot meet citizen expectations and living standards decline.

It is not just the case, as Max Singer and Aaron Wildavsky argue, that the post–Cold War world is increasingly segregated into two camps, zones of peace and zones of turmoil, with a widening gap between the advanced capitalist democracies and the underdeveloped, nondemocratic states. According to Singer and Wildavsky, the stabilizing solution to this dilemma was the advancement of democratization, economic liberalization and development, so that more states would move from the "zone of turmoil" to the "zone of peace."[48]

However, it is not that simple. Democratization and economic liberalization can undermine already fragile state institutions;[49] during the transition period, attempts to establish open societies and markets can further move a quasi-state into the zone of turmoil. Even if a state survives the transition and becomes a peaceful and wealthy market democracy, open societies, markets, and technologies make a state vulnerable to transsovereign problems. While Singer and Wildavsky might have argued that the zone of peace (even with its problems of drugs and crime) is preferable to the zone of turmoil (with its starvation and war), surely their argument is in need of some qualification, at least to check the expectations of fledgling democracies. Singer and Wildavsky's zone of peace is not the promised land. Democratization and economic liberalization carry with them their own costs, in terms of transsovereign problems. Even strong, wealthy states with healthy internal institutions cannot unilaterally defeat transsovereign problems.

Open Economies

The United States has long been a proponent of spreading capitalist, liberal, free market and free trade economic systems around the world.[50] One of the instigating incidents triggering the American Revolutionary War with Britain was the Boston Tea Party, a protest against British anti–free trade policies of granting a monopoly to the British East India Company, and imposing tariffs on commerce. Squabbles with the Barbary pirates, who were supported by the pasha of Tripoli (present day Libya—even in the 1790s the United States had poor relations with Libya due to a form of state-sponsored terrorism), led to the formation of the U.S. Navy and the beginnings of the president's ability to commit troops abroad without a formal declaration of war by Congress. These landmarks in U.S. foreign policy came about because of the government's desire to protect commercial shipping engaged in free trade abroad.

In the war of 1812 with Britain, the U.S. capital was burned; the British used books from the Library of Congress, including Thomas Jefferson's collection, to light the Capitol building on fire. Outside of the Civil War and the Revolution, this was the only war in which U.S. territory was significantly damaged from fighting. This war was fought in opposition to British policies of embargoing U.S. trade, and seizing U.S. ships, goods, and seamen. Similarly, U.S. tensions with China and Japan in the nineteenth and twentieth centuries centered on opening of the Asian market to U.S. goods.

Ironically, U.S. imperialism in Latin America and the Pacific was done in the name of promoting free trade and opening commerce. The American empire, in the form of U.S. protectorates in Puerto Rico, Guam, Samoa, Hawaii, etc., was acquired largely to assist U.S. commercial interests in their efforts to expand foreign trade. The creation of the country of Panama (by seizing territory from Columbia) and the building of the Panama Canal was accomplished to facilitate free trade. Military intervention in Guatemala in 1954 was done largely to protect the interests of the United Fruit Company. Former Under Secretary of Commerce for International Trade Jeffrey E. Garten argues that "For most of America's history, foreign policy has reflected an obsession with open markets for American business. . . . Business expansion abroad was often seen as an extension of the American frontier, part of the nation's manifest destiny."[51]

Some historians argue that the Cold War was caused by U.S. opposition to the Soviets closing off Eastern European markets to Western goods and trade.

During the Cold War, many believed that the superior economic performance of capitalist, free-market systems would eventually bring state-controlled, communist economic systems to their knees. George Kennan predicted that the demise of the Soviet sphere would come about *not* through the external, military confrontation of a globalized and militarized U.S. containment policy, which the United States could not afford. Instead, Kennan presciently predicted that if the West built strong, internal open societies and open markets, eventually the Soviet bloc would be "unable to stand the comparison."[52]

> If economic recovery could be brought about and public confidence restored in Western Europe—if Western Europe, in other words, could be made the home of a vigorous, prosperous and forward-looking civilization—the communist regime in Eastern Europe . . . would never be able to stand the comparison, and the spectacle of a happier and more successful life just across the fence . . . would be bound in the end to have a disintegrating and eroding effect on the communist world.[53]

This thesis appeared to be confirmed at the Cold War's end. The Marshall Plan and forty-five years of concerted policy of building open economic and political institutions in Western Europe succeeded in rebuilding a continent destroyed by war. Such rebuilding never took place in Eastern Europe, where an oppressive Nazi regime was replaced by a repressive Soviet regime. Eventually, even the top leaders of the Soviet Union were forced to admit that their economic system was in need of reform when Gorbachev came to power in the 1980s.

Gorbachev's reforms began as attempts to improve the productivity and efficiency of the state-controlled economy: cutting down on vodka abuse on the job, decreasing bureaucratic red tape, and increasing worker and industry accountability. Quickly, these internal attempts to reform and strengthen the communist system unleashed massive dissatisfaction with the existing system. Gorbachev's reforms tapped into consumer and social unrest over shortages and poor economic performance (for example, exploding television sets in Moscow were a common cause of hospital emergency room visits), including the Chernobyl nuclear disaster. The legitimacy of the communist model was undermined, accelerating the pace of Gorbachev's initially modest reforms into the eventual overthrow of the entire system.[54] Gorbachev soon learned (what the Chinese are now grappling with) that it is difficult to uncork just a little economic freedom.

With the demise of communist regimes in Eastern Europe and the former Soviet Union, and with the demise of state-controlled economies and authoritarian regimes in Latin America, many assumed that the United States had won the Cold War's economic battle. As Paul Krugman put it, "Governments that had spent half a century pursuing statist, protectionist policies suddenly got free market religion. It was . . . the dawn of a new golden age for global capitalism." Additionally, there "was a sea change in the intellectual Zeitgeist: the almost universal acceptance, by governments and markets alike, of a new view about what it takes to develop. This view has come to be widely known as the 'Washington Consensus'. . . . It is the belief that . . . free markets and sound money [are] the key to economic development. Liberalize trade, privatize state enterprises, balance the budget, peg the exchange rate, and one will have laid the foundations for an economic takeoff."[55]

Of course, while many states "talk the talk" of capitalism, "free market religion" has not been established universally. There are still some states, like North Korea, with closed economies. Some states, such as North Vietnam, Cuba, and China, are trying to attract foreign capital and investment and encourage some privatization of the economy, but the central government still owns and plays a key role in many industries. Many countries, such as Mexico, are in the process of privatizing state-owned industries, but the transition to free market economies is still underway. This is the case in Eastern Europe, where formerly communist states are still constructing the institutions that support free markets, such as laws which allow and protect the private ownership of property, stock exchanges, and the laws governing investment.

John Ikenberry contends that the triumph of U.S. Cold War policy toward economic openness is so thorough that we often forget that "America is not adrift in uncharted seas. It is at the center of a world of its own making."[56] As free trade agreements expand, such as NAFTA and the European Union treaties, and as the liberalization and privatization of economic spheres increases, with governments selling off state-run industries, relations with the United States and access to international loans and aid are often contingent upon progress in privatization and economic reform.[57]

However, while open economies often perform better than state-run counterparts, they also carry costs.[58] The transition to capitalist economic structures can destabilize states, and provide openings for organized crime to step into the vacuum, as has occurred in Russia. The old order has been pulled down, but new laws and institutions supporting free market economies are still being built, and much turmoil can result in the interim. Decreased regulation and increased transborder trade decreases the opportunities for shipments to be searched or monitored; thus, states lose significant control over borders, one of the hallmarks of sovereignty.

The same emerging, global financial infrastructure useful to legal businesses (such as free-trade zones, opening markets and decreased regulatory barriers to trade and international investment, instant global capital flows, etc.) also increases the opportunity and ease of conducting and covering illicit economic activities, such as narcotic and nuclear smuggling. Open, intertwined, interdependent economies make it very easy for money and goods (of any sort) to move quickly and freely across borders and across financial instruments. The profits from illicit activities can be hidden in legal investments, sprinkled into front companies, bank accounts, and small investments across a range of industries and states; with the Internet and Ecash, the money trail can be moved around quickly and erased, as investments can be changed and moved with a keystroke.

Additionally, open economies decentralize power, as more and more actors have autonomous economic power and the central government's ability to control economic activities in a global marketplace wanes. Microsoft President Bill Gates' annual income is more than the annual GNP of many states. The income of prominent drug lords often overwhelms and distorts the legal economy in a state, and is difficult for states to control or regulate. Especially where state institutions are already fragile, open markets can undermine sovereignty, and transitions to open markets can undermine state institutions, further creating the opportunity for transsovereign problems to arise. The transsovereign problems we face are as much a part of this "world of our own making" (even if unintentionally) as the open economies the United States and the West have worked hard to create since the end of World War II.

Open Societies

Francis Fukuyama argues that the end of the Cold War also signaled the end of history, by which he means that "a remarkable consensus concerning the legitimacy of liberal democracy as a system of government has emerged throughout the world over the past few years, as it conquered rival ideologies like hereditary monarchy, fascism, and most recently communism."[59] While certainly liberal democracy has not (and may not) triumph in all areas of the globe, Fukuyama contends that the twentieth century has been marked by great battles of competing ideologies, and that now no alternative ideology of consequence exists to challenge liberal democracy. Liberal democracy "gives fullest scope" to satisfying "all three parts of the soul [desire, reason, and spirit] simultaneously."[60]

Even analysts less optimistic about the liberal democratic form agree that "We are currently witnessing the fourth historical wave of democratization . . . more global in its reach . . . affecting far more countries and more thorough than its predecessors."[61] Certainly, democracy is not new and has been around in one form or another since the ancient Greeks. What is new, however, is the number of states which are turning to representative government forms with free multiparty elections and the protection of individual and minority rights including free speech and free press, freedom of association, freedom of movement, and freedom of religion.

In the "first wave" of democratization in the 1800s, universal suffrage was extended in states committed to democratic principles, so that more than white male property owners could vote. This movement toward democracy ended as monarchies and authoritarian rulers sought to reestablish control in many states after the "Springtime of Freedom" in Europe in 1848 to 1849. Ironically, while the first wave expanded democracy within societies and sought to spread democracy in Western Europe and North America, these same states were involved simultaneously in carving up the non-Western world into colonial empires in a very nondemocratic way.

The second wave of democratization occurred with World War I and its aftermath, as many states believed that autocracies were more to blame for starting the war than were democratic states. However, many of the democracies established after World War I were weak, such as the Weimar Republic, and many of these states again reverted to authoritarianism as fascism swept the globe.

The third wave of democratization occurred with World War II, as the colonial powers were no longer able or willing to hold on to their overseas possessions, and a tidal wave of decolonization swept the globe. The number of independent states tripled from 1945 to 1979, and many of these former colonies turned to democratic government forms. Once again, however, this wave of democratization was followed by reversals. As Haitian leader Jean-Bertrande Aristide likes to say, it is easy to have the first democratic election; it is difficult to have the peaceful transfer of power to a second democratic election. "By some counts, one-third of the globe's democracies had fallen under authoritarian rule by the late 1970s,"[62] as personal rule, military rule, or single party autocracy replaced democratic political participation and institutions in developing states. Even though there were reverses, with each wave the number of democracies overall increased, as states like India joined and stayed in the community of democracies.

The fourth wave of democratization differs from previous eras in a number of respects. First, it was not due to a single external event such as World War I or World War II. Instead, a variety of factors, including the internal failures of existing authoritarian regimes, led to the rising number of democracies in the 1980s and 1990s. While the end of the Soviet empire led a number of Eastern European states into the democratic experiment, other states such as Portugal, Spain, and South Africa, turned to democracy for reasons other than (and prior to) the end of the Cold War.

Secondly, the most recent wave of democratization differs from its predecessors in scope and intensity. More states on more continents are becoming more democratic than ever before. This wave is not restricted to Europe or to former colonial empires, and this wave is more intensive, entailing a wholesale rebuilding of political institutions from the ground up, not a mere facelift or grafting of liberal political reforms onto basically illiberal political structures.

While the fate of these newly emerging democracies is by no means secure from retrenchment, the fourth wave of democratization has some advantages the previous movements could not claim. The simultaneous trends of open markets and open technologies support and facilitate political openings. Previous reformers did not have CNN looking in, reporting advances or backsliding immediately to an international audience. Previous reformers also did not have to liberalize political institutions as a prerequisite to receiving international capital investments, be they from international lending institutions like the World Bank or the International Monetary Fund (IMF), or from private investors who believe the rule of law as practiced in democratic societies secures a better business environment.

This opening of societies represents more than Acheson and his Cold War colleagues, or even policymakers a few short years ago, could have hoped to imagine. The opening of societies tends to lend itself to more open economic systems, as people with some say in their political futures tend to desire a say in their economic futures as well, and vice versa.[63] Of course, movement toward open societies is not complete. Some states, such as China, are trying to open up the economic system to achieve prosperity and development without allowing significant political freedoms. Many states, particularly in Africa and the Middle East, retain authoritarian political systems.

There are a number of reasons why most states favor the opening of societies to democratic political reforms in general (of course, there are significant disagreements over how best to promote democracy specifically). Democracies are more likely to have free-market, free-trade, capitalist economies, and to have more prosperity and better records of economic development. Democratic protections of property rights and individual liberties provide a rule of law which fosters a more stable investment and business climate and better protects the larger number of citizens now traveling abroad, taking advantage of more advanced transportation and communication links. Perhaps most importantly, developed democracies tend not to go to war with one another.[64] Democracies are not more peaceful overall; they tend to go to war with nondemocracies, and the transition period of democratization can be wrought with conflict. But for now, at least, the empirical record of democracies not warring with other democracies is strong. For these reasons, enlargement of the sphere of market democracies is a key component of the Clinton administration's national security strategy.[65]

However, democratization carries costs. Transitions to democracy can be destabilizing in the short run, as "Democratization typically creates a syndrome of weak central authority, unstable domestic coalitions, and high-energy mass politics."[66] During democratic transitions, the old, centralized order has been dismantled or delegitimized, but strong, new state institutions have not yet grown up to take their place. "Democratization weakens the central government's ability to keep policy coherent and consistent. Governing a society that is democratizing is like driving a car while throwing away the steering wheel, stepping on the gas, and fighting over which passenger will be in the driver's seat."[67] If privatization and liberalization of the economy are occurring simultaneously with democratization efforts (as is often the case), powerful corporate or criminal organizations may gain assets and influence before the civic institutions of public control and accountability are established (many argue this is the case in Russia). Any one of these transitions would be highly complex and destabilizing for a society. The simultaneous and often sudden overlapping of these transitions only increases the level of difficulty for polities, increasing the pressures for fragmentation which can undermine states.

Even in mature, stable democracies, power is decentralized, as government officials are held accountable for their actions by voters, interest groups, and an independent judiciary. Because central governments in open societies must respect individual rights and freedoms such as free speech, free movement, free association, property rights, privacy rights, and freedom from arbitrary search and seizure, democracy creates an infrastructure which not only allows but also promotes the free movement of people, property, and ideas. However, this same infrastructure creates an environment in which transsovereign challenges such as international crime and narcotics smuggling can prosper. For example, democratic government agents cannot trammel individual rights and liberties, privacy of person, property, or freedom of association in investigating or prosecuting criminal cases without just cause and prior evidence assembled according to the rule of law. They cannot randomly burst into your bedroom to search for drugs without following lawful search and seizure practices. Authoritarian states have no such qualms. Criminals may take advantage of this protection of rights, and authoritarian states may be more efficient in prosecuting criminals. In democracies, however, the protection of individual rights and liberties is thought to outweigh considerations of efficiency. However, the rise in crime and drug smuggling may further undermine the authority of state institutions, and can cause disenchantment with open societies, and nostalgia for authoritarian order.

Open Technologies

Americans tend to be enamored of technological advances, and it is easy to understand why. Technology made possible the settlement of the American continent. Technological innovations fueled expansion of the economy and of living standards. Advances in transportation and communication keep this geographically huge and diverse Atlantic and Pacific state functioning. Superior military technology won World War II, guaranteed the U.S. position as a global power, and still undergirds the military's preeminent position in the world today.

Americans own more computers and televisions than any other nation. Of 64 million Internet users worldwide, 41 million are in the United States. Sixty-eight percent of Internet hosts stem from North America.[68] U.S. scientists and the U.S. government invented the computer and the Internet.

But "the information revolution" is profoundly changing the way all states do their business. "Today all of humankind is linked by almost instantaneous communications. There is no corner of the globe that is not accessible to us, or us to them. Marshall McLuhan's global village is upon us with profound consequences . . . a market crash in Hong Kong is felt immediately by pensioners in Dubuque (Iowa)."[69]

Technological advances have been dramatically spurred by advances in computers. The first modern computer, developed in 1946 to calculate firing trajectories for artillery shells, "could execute the then-astonishing number of 5,000 arithmetic operations per second . . . weighed 30 tons, filled an enormous room at the University of Pennsylvania, consumed 150,000 watts of power, and used 18,000 vacuum tubes."[70] The term "bugs in the system" literally referred to getting the insects out of these huge machines, which interfered with operations. Today a Pentium chip is built on a thumbnail-sized piece of silicon. Laptop computers are smaller than a briefcase, weigh four pounds, and are capable of executing over 200 million instructions per second.[71]

Many argue that openings in technology drove the interpenetration of economies and the openings of societies. Computers, faxes, cellular phones, and air travel shrunk the planet and made sovereign borders less important for economic transactions. Television, radio, video cameras, and computers made sovereign authorities less able to control the flow of information and ideas, thus making authoritarian control more expensive and difficult to maintain. Anyone with a concealed, handheld video camera can record government abuses and instantly transmit these images via the Internet to place international pressure on the offending regime. Technological openings in essence undermined sovereign authority, decentralized power, and opened markets and societies.[72]

To some extent, this is a "chicken or the egg" question. While technological openings may in some sense have "driven" the process of opening markets and societies, technological advances do not occur in an economic or political vacuum. Sustained political and investment decisions drive technological advances. Scientists did not happen upon the discovery of powerful supercomputers, tiny microchips, and fiberoptic telecommunications links by accident. These advancements came about through sustained investment, political, and social policy that harnessed resources in pursuit of technological progress, and pursued technological innovation as a tool to advance economic and political goals. The first mainframe computer and the Internet were developed by the U.S. Department of Defense working in close connection with universities. Both were invented originally for military purposes; the predecessor to the modern Internet was created to maintain communications in the event of a nuclear attack.

Causality flows in all directions, but together the trends of open economies, open societies, and open markets substantially reinforce each other, and combined they equal more than the sum of their parts. Technological advances facilitate the opening of markets and of societies, and vice versa.

However, like its counterparts, open technologies also undermine sovereignty and make transsovereign challenges possible. The intensified spread of drugs, disease, criminal activities, and nuclear proliferation is made possible by technology that moves information, people, and goods more quickly and efficiently than ever before across borders without the consent or even knowledge of sovereign authorities. Drug traffickers and international businessmen alike use cell phones, Ecash, and computers to track their product, storage, billing, and profit investment information, and to instantly reroute shipments or profit.

Noting that open societies, economies, and technologies have their downsides, however, should not be interpreted as declaring the nation-state dead, or advocating movement toward state-controlled economies and authoritarian societies, free of advanced technologies. Sovereignty carries many benefits, but there is nothing sacrosanct about sovereignty. Human history is the unfolding story of numerous and varying social organizing frameworks. The nation-state has had a good, 350-year-long run as an organizing unit, and while it is in no imminent danger of disappearing, there is no reason to expect that the sovereign state in the form we know it will continue to exist 350 years from now. But just as advances in medicine create lifesaving benefits as well as new legal, ethical, and practical challenges, so open economies, societies, and technologies create both practical and civilizational benefits as well as carry costs for established sovereign orders.

TOMORROW: DEBATES ABOUT THE FUTURE OF SOVEREIGNTY

Scholars disagree about how much change the sovereign state is presently undergoing, and therefore, over whether sovereignty will continue in its present form, mutate, or disappear. Susan Strange believes that the sovereign state continues to be an important actor on the world scene, especially in the military security realm, but that the state is increasingly losing power to markets and nonstate actors. Strange argues that power is moving vertically from weak states to strong states (as many states collapse into internal conflict or limp along as "quasi-states"); power is moving sideways from states to markets; and some power is evaporating, as states abandon certain functions that no new actor assumes.[73]

Specifically, Strange discusses ten important powers or authorities claimed by states that are on the decline, that nonstate actors fulfill, or that no state does anymore. First, the state is responsible to defend national territory against foreign invasion, but in developed countries the threat of foreign invasion is declining and/or minimal, thereby eroding this source of state authority. Second, the state is responsible to maintain the value of its currency, but inflation in one country can spread to others, revealing that this responsibility is now a more collective one.

Third, the state used to choose the appropriate form of economic development, but open economies now allow market pressures from the IMF, World Bank, and private investors to limit state choice and force convergence on a narrow range of development models (Paul Krugman's aforementioned "Washington Consensus"). Fourth, the state used to be responsible for correcting the booms and busts of market economies through state spending to infuse money into public works or other state enterprises. Franklin Delano Roosevelt combated the Great Depression in the 1930s in the United States by initiating large public works projects, building national parks, the Hoover Dam, highways and bridges, to put people back to work and get the economy moving again. But this option is no longer open to governments, given the market pressures to keep government spending at a minimum. Fifth, states used to provide a social safety net for those least able to survive in a market economy by providing assistance to the very old or young, sick, disabled, or unemployed. Today, market pressures are leading states to cut back on their social welfare benefits and protective regulations. Sixth, states used to have the ability to set tax rates appropriately in order to pay for whatever government public works or social benefits spending in which the state wanted to engage. Today, all states are pressured by international market forces to keep tax rates to a minimum, thereby limiting its autonomy and authority to raise funds.

Seventh, states used to have great autonomy in control over foreign trade, especially imports. Today government intervention can only impact the margins, because most of the decisions concerning trade flows are the "aggregate result of multiple corporate decisions."[74] Strong international market forces pressure governments to reduce obstacles to cross-border trade.

Eighth, governments used to take responsibility for building the economic infrastructure of the state "from ports and roads to posts and telegraphs. . . . Even where governments, as in the United States, looked to private enterprise to find the necessary capital, they never hesitated in revising the laws on landed property so that landowners could not easily obstruct the infrastructural investment."[75] Today, public utilities are being privatized, and the key infrastructure needed in modern economies are communications technology, most of which do not depend on government's control over territory. "This time, governments are in a weaker bargaining position in dealing with private interests." Most infrastructure development decisions are being made in corporate boardrooms, not state offices. Eastern European states are being integrated into the modern telecommunications grid not by governments, primarily, but by private corporations who recognize the profit margins open to the corporation that gets there first. Microsoft, not the Russian state, is computerizing Russia. States may have built the infrastructure of highways, but firms and private actors are building and extending the information superhighways.

Ninth, states used to be able to create or allow public or private monopolies to dominate the local market, often as part of the government's economic development strategies. Today, competitiveness in the world market requires an increasingly competitive local market. International market pressures now impose greater costs on state governments that try to maintain monopolies.

Finally, states used to entertain one "special kind of monopoly—that of the legitimate use of violence against the citizen or any group of citizens."[76] Now, international market forces and technological advances make the means of violence more readily available to nonstate actors. Strong and weak states alike are losing their monopolies on force. The chemical attack on the Japanese subway, and the bombing of the World Trade Center in the United States, show that it is not only weak states like Columbia or states in transition such as Russia that face challenges from nonstate actors who possess increasingly destructive firepower.

From these examples, Strange concludes that "the domain of state authority in society and economy is shrinking; and/or that what were once domains of authority exclusive to state authority are now being shared with other loci or sources of authority. . . . If indeed, the state's provision of military security is no longer considered crucial and is therefore likely to decline, while its provision of economic security has reached its highest point, it could be that the net value of national government to society is headed for decline."[77] States continue to exist, but their powers are not as extensive as they used to be. Nonstate actors, including private firms, international organized crime, and civic groups, increasingly take or share power with states over key functions or sectors. Other duties states used to assume are no longer exercised by anyone; for example, governments are getting out of the business of initiating large public works projects as a means to stimulate the economy, but no other actor is picking up this function. The result is "a ramshackle assembly of conflicting sources of authority," in which individuals' loyalties and identities will not necessarily lie with the sovereign state, but will spread among professions, civic groups, ethnic ties, firms, etc., just as state power is becoming diffused.[78] Strange describes but is not necessarily in favor of these changes. She points out that as more power shifts away from states and toward markets, accountability and democracy may decrease because corporate leaders are not subject to democratic accountability and market forces cannot be voted upon.

James Rosenau agrees with Strange's assessments that technological and market changes are bringing about political changes and changes in the sovereign state. "The boundaries of states no longer confine the flow of information, goods, money, and people . . . the authority of states has, like money, moved offshore. . . . Just as the foundations of sovereignty have been eroded by the centralizing processes of globalization, so have they been diminished by decentralizing tendencies wherein people are shrinking the definition of "we."[79]

Rosenau believes that sovereignty needs to be viewed as a continuous variable constantly in a process of flux and evolution, rather than as a fixed or dichotomous variable where sovereignty either exists or doesn't. We are in a period of transition or turbulence,[80] in which the sovereign state is increasingly under challenge but is not obsolete because alternatives to sovereignty have not yet established themselves. Rosenau tracks the changes occurring at three different parameters (or levels of analysis) which underpin global order.

At the micro level, Rosenau places greater emphasis than other scholars on individuals' growing skills and the changes these bring to loyalties, identities, and political structures. Whereas Strange argues that market forces are primarily responsible for the retreat of state power, Rosenau argues that increasingly skilled individuals are driving the changes. He believes access to the Internet, to personal computers, faxes, jet planes, etc., have led to a "skill revolution." People who are plugged in have become better able to assess, compare, and contrast large amounts of data, more sophisticated in critiquing the information provided to them by states and in seeking alternative information, and better able to articulate and mobilize around goals. "It is unimaginable that people have not learned and become more complex in order to adapt to an increasingly complicated world," says Rosenau.[81] In an evolutionary way, he believes that people are adapting to changes in their environment.[82] "People have become increasingly competent in assessing where they fit in international affairs and how their behavior can be aggregated into significant outcomes."[83] In his estimation, the fourth wave of democratization is no accident. Of course this wave of political change is global, because the telecommunications revolution which is fueling the skills revolution is global. A people plugged in are a people empowered to bring about change, to end apartheid in South Africa, to tear down the Berlin Wall and the Communist empire, and to challenge the dictatorship in Tiananmen Square. This view contrasts with that of scholars like Susan Strange. Rosenau believes the skills revolution makes governments more responsive to citizen needs and more democratic, whereas Strange and others believe that market forces reduce democratic processes and accountability.

Rosenau acknowledges that the skills revolution is proceeding at different rates for those in the developed world who have more access to advanced technologies and education than for those in the developing world. For example,[84] Cuba's telecommunications system is one of the least developed in the world, with only 39 telephones per 1,000 people; 40 percent of those lines are so old (installed in the 1930s) and poorly maintained as to make data transmission via fax or modem problematic. There are only four Cuban networks with international Internet connection capability and they are only operational a few times a day. During this time, two-way e-mail is exchanged in batches, but surfing the

Web is impossible. Poverty and the dearth of market forces, as well as control by the dictatorship of Fidel Castro, are responsible for Cubans' lack of access to modern telecommunications technologies. However, Rosenau notes that while "the information-rich are getting richer at a quicker rate than the information-poor, the trend line is conceived to slope in the same upward direction for both groups." Even citizens in lesser developed countries (where poverty and repressive regimes may limit access to technology) are becoming more skillful. For example, Haitians demonstrating to turn back the U.S. ship *Harlan County* from intervening in 1994, and Iranians demonstrating to denounce U.S. support of the Shah of Iran in 1979, carried signs in English and timed their protests to appear on the U.S. evening news broadcasts.

At the micro-macro parameter, which focuses on the authority structures that link macro collectivities to individuals, Rosenau also believes fundamental transformations are underway. How do organizations achieve and sustain the cooperation and compliance of their members? Traditionally, legitimacy and compliance "derived from constitutional and legal sources. Under these circumstances individuals were habituated to compliance with the directives issued by higher authorities. They did what they were told to do because . . . that is what one did. As a consequence, authority structures remained in place for decades even centuries as people unquestioningly yielded to the dictates of governments." Today, because of the skills revolution, there is a pervasive "authority crises," as people are increasingly inclined to and have the means to question. Legitimacy now derives not from tradition but from performance. "The more the performance record is considered appropriate—in terms of satisfying needs, moving toward goals, and providing stability—the more likely it becomes that individuals will cooperate and comply. The less they approve of the performance record, the more likely they are to withhold their compliance or otherwise complicate the efforts of macro authorities."[85]

At the macro level, which looks to the overall structures of global politics, Rosenau believes the "state-centric world is no longer predominant. Owing to the skills revolution, the worldwide spread of authority crises, the globalization of national economies, and a variety of exogenous sources of turbulence, it has undergone bifurcation. A complex world of diverse, relatively autonomous actors has emerged. . . . Multinational corporations, ethnic minorities, subnational governments and bureaucracies, professional societies, political parties, transnational organizations, broadly based social movements . . . compete, conflict, cooperate, or otherwise interact with the sovereignty-bound actors of the state-centric world. . . . States are no longer the only key actors. Now they are faced with the new task of coping with disparate rivals from another world as well as with the challenges posed by counterparts in their own world."[86] Sovereignty continues to limp along, not because of its strength but because none of these new organizations has delivered a knockout blow. Existing states resist change, and we are unable to imagine a world organized around other lines than sovereignty. Sovereignty's continuation says less about its strengths than about our weaknesses. "History is replete with bureaucracies that survive even though their original purposes have been rendered obsolete by transformations of their environments and functions."[87]

Richard Rosecrance agrees that sovereignty has been changed but not made obsolete by market forces. Like Strange, Rosecrance argues that "the powers of existing states are becoming circumscribed" and "the market fills the vacuum, gaining power. . . . The state will become just one of many players in the international marketplace and will have to negotiate directly with foreign factors of production to solve domestic economic problems."[88]

Rosecrance places greater emphasis on territorial change than Strange or Rosenau. Sovereignty is losing its identification with territory. "In economies where capital, labor, and information are mobile and have risen to predominance, no land fetish remains. Developed countries would rather plumb the world market than acquire territory. The virtual state—a state that has downsized its territorially based production capability—is the logical consequence of this emancipation from the land."[89]

For Rosecrance, small is better; by shedding outmoded functions to nonstate actors and by downsizing territory, states are becoming lean and mean, more prosperous and powerful. States are adapting their logic to market forces. States aren't retreating; they are evolving. "The nation-state is becoming a tighter, more vigorous unit capable of sustaining the pressures of worldwide competition."[90]

When the Treaty of Westphalia was signed, the economic system was mercantilist and land based. Wealth and power depended on the control of land, to access to raw materials and the means of production. In a world of slow-moving ships and horseback messengers, capital and labor were fixed in place, not mobile. Increasing power meant increasing land, and thus the European colonial empires were born. It is no accident that under this economic system, the political organization that developed—sovereignty—directly correlated authority to territory.

Rosecrance argues that the economy has changed and states are changing to reflect the new reality. The new economic system is based on information, technology, and services—none of which depends on the control of land. In a world of open borders and economic flows, equipped with computers, faxes, phones, the Internet, E-cash, and other advanced technologies, the means of production, capital, and labor are mobile rather than fixed. States have access to raw materials through trade, not conquest. Thus, for states with modern, information-based economies, territory becomes passé—as does conflict over territory.

Rosecrance qualifies that for states with less developed economies which are still land based (primarily dependent on natural resource extraction or agricultural exports) territory will not become passé and may still be a source of conflict. A population explosion might make land important again. But Rose-crance argues that these trends are not sustainable in the long term, because land does not produce a better return than knowledge. Knowledge allows more extraction and more efficient and effective utilization of resources. States recognize the success of "virtual" states like Japan, and will try to emulate them, to develop modern economies that are less shackled to land.

The virtual state that emerges from these changes in economic structure serves different functions. "As more production by domestic industries takes place abroad and land becomes less valuable than technology, knowledge, and direct investment, the function of the state is being further redefined. The state no longer commands resources as it did in mercantilist yesteryear; it negotiates with foreign and domestic capital and labor to lure them into its own economic sphere and stimulate its growth. A nation's economic strategy is now at least as important as its military strategy; its ambassadors have become foreign trade and investment representatives."[91] The virtual state is a negotiating state that derives its power from direct foreign investment, an educated workforce, and market savvy, not from military superiority or control over territory.

Like Strange, Rosecrance believes "the rise of the virtual state portends a crisis for democratic politics. . . . Domestic political change does not suffice because it has insufficient jurisdiction to deal with global problems. The people in a particular state cannot determine international outcomes by holding an election."[92] States lose some of their autonomy over selecting and enforcing policy to nonelected, nonstate actors.

Rosecrance argues this need not be problematic if citizens stop expecting the state to take care of them in a globalized economy where a state cannot protect its citizens from bumps in the road. He argues that citizens "expect too much and give and learn too little. . . . Displaced workers and businesspeople must be willing to look abroad for opportunities."[93] Unlike Rosenau, who believes that increasing skills of citizens are driving global changes, Rosecrance argues that citizens are not yet skillful enough. The key is increased international training and education. This would make citizens more skillful, as well as able to love their situation in their country or leave it. It would also make the state more skillful; in addition to being a negotiating state, the virtual state is also internationalized—"an agile entity operating in twin jurisdictions: abroad and at home."[94]

Thus, these authors agree that market forces are significantly downsizing the power of sovereign states, who can no longer act autonomously to solve many of their problems. Military problems—what states do best—are becoming less pressing, while economic issues—which states have the least ability to address—loom large. States will not become extinct anytime soon, but will continue as one of many actors on the global scene. The authors disagree on what role individuals play in bringing about these changes, what impact these changes will have on democratic accountability, whether the state that will emerge from the changes will be weaker or stronger than the old-style territorial state, and whether in some distant future the sovereign state will disappear altogether.

Other scholars, such as Stephen Krasner, William O'Neill, and Hendrik Spruyt, disagree with Strange, Rosenau, and Rosecrance about the extent of the challenges to sovereignty. Krasner argues that changes in the environment do not readily or easily translate into institutional changes. Sovereign states persist over time, even when their functions are not in sync with a changed international environment, because of vertical and horizontal linkages.

> Vertical depth refers to the extent to which the institutional structure defines the individual actors. Breadth refers to the number of links that a particular activity has with other activities, to the number of changes that would have to be made if a particular form of activity were altered. . . . With regard to both breadth and depth, sovereign states have become increasingly formidable institutions. They influence the self-image of those individuals within their territory through the concept of citizenship, as well as by exercising control, to one degree or another, over powerful instruments of socialization. With regard to breadth, states are the most densely linked institutions in the contemporary world. Change the nature of states and virtually everything else in human society would also have to be changed. Hence, even though environmental incentives have dramatically changed since the establishment of the state system in the seventeenth century, there is little reason to believe that it will be easy to replace sovereign states with some alternative structure for organizing human political life.[95]

For Krasner, the sovereign state is not retreating, not only because the costs of changing to an alternative system would be prohibitive, but also because people cannot even conceive of an alternative to sovereignty.

Hendrik Spruyt agrees. While he argues that a major transformation of the sovereign state system (due to changes in the international economy) should not be discounted, he believes that no such change is imminent because existing states have little incentive to alter the system. Because states are the gatekeepers to the international system, it is difficult for actors other than states to be accorded equal participation in that system. While the growth of the European Community is providing an alternative model to traditional sovereignty, other than that there are no serious challengers to sovereign arrangements. For sovereignty to be replaced, he argues, there must be competition among alternative models of organization, as there was at sovereignty's initiation after competition with the urban league and city-state. If anything, sovereignty is getting more entrenched, because ethnic and nationalist challenges to sovereignty reinforce the state as these groups fight for control over existing states or recognition of new states. While sovereignty is not the optimal institutional arrangement, new institutional challengers have to arise for the new economic forces to succeed in destabilizing the ideas and coalitions which reinforce sovereignty. This has not yet occurred. Sovereignty took centuries to emerge, Spruyt argues. It is too early to declare its demise.

William O'Neill agrees that the territorial state is being "buried too soon." Like Mark Twain's famous observation that news of his own demise had been much exaggerated, O'Neill believes that challenges to the existing sovereign state do not mean its death. He believes that many recent theories "deprive the territorial sovereign state of its pride of place among the overlapping loyalties and competing authorities that constitute the stuff of politics."[96] While states are challenged internally by ethnic and national conflict, and externally by the increasing role of international institutions, "the competition among all the diverse kinds of polity that they discovered will give pride of place to whatever authorities are able to organize and maintain superior armed force. This implies that their requiem for the Westphalian state is premature. So far, no promising alternative to the territorial organization of armed force has even begun to emerge."[97] To this, Strange, Rosenau, and Rosecrance would probably respond, yes but so what? If military power is less important in a world of interdependent economies, then the state may retain coercive powers that are less and less useful. The state still exists but is more compromised in its ability to act in the economic and social spheres which increasingly affect citizens' everyday lives.

Mapping out these debates in the scholarly literature helps establish some questions to consider in reading the chapters of this book. Do transsovereign problems challenge not only the interests of states (as traditional, realist International Relations theory stipulates), but also the very architecture of states? How can transsovereign problems be dealt with in a system of sovereign states, and do the responses to transsovereign problems (greater reliance on NGOs or IGOs, for example) undermine sovereignty? Are alternatives to sovereignty evolving as people struggle to respond to transsovereign problems? Or is the state becoming more entrenched as people rely on tried-and-true responses to combat new threats?

THE NEW SECURITY DILEMMA

Weakened sovereignty and transsovereign challenges have created a new security dilemma.[98] During the Cold War, the "security dilemma" was how to promote and protect Western military security against Soviet/Communist aggression, without provoking Soviet counteractions that would actually worsen the security of the West. Military capabilities had to be balanced in such a way that they would protect core interests without unduly aggravating enemy wrath. The dilemma was how to defend one's state without appearing offensive to other strong states, thus triggering a response from opponents that would further decrease one's own security. In a self-help international system of strong sovereign states, how could a state provide for its own military security against another state without setting off a self-defeating spiral of counteractions by other states? The dilemma was political—how best to communicate intentions—and military—what military hardware, equipment, training, and organization could best meet the threat?

But if the Cold War security dilemma was how to protect against strong states without triggering a dynamic that made the opponent more strong and threatening in the post–Cold War world, the new "security dilemma" is how to protect against transsovereign challenges and the implosion of weak states without taking actions that make weak states weaker and transsovereign problems more severe. For example, in the desire to contain the transsovereign threats of international crime, nuclear smuggling, etc., that come from the weakened states of the former Soviet Union, the United States pushes for rapid economic privatization, trade liberalization, and democratization. However, rapidly opening societies and economies can further destabilize states, further exacerbating the very transsovereign problems the United States wishes to contain. The post–Cold War security dilemma is how to open economies, societies, and technologies (in order to increase security) without making transsovereign problems worse (and thereby decrease security).

The new security dilemma is both political and military. Politically, it cuts to the heart of sovereignty—attempts to strengthen states by opening markets, expanding technology, and opening societies have the unintended effect of actually weakening states and facilitating transsovereign problems. How can threats that are nonstate-oriented be responded to by state architecture? Transsovereign problems increasingly occur in the economic and social spheres or are facilitated by economic and social dynamics—open societies, economies, and technologies. But the economic and social spheres are where the arm of the liberal, capitalist state has the least reach. The state operates primarily in the political and military realm, spheres which have less impact on transsovereign problems. As presently constructed, states have less ability to respond to transsovereign problems because their realm of activity and infrastructures do not fit neatly where the problems are.

Militarily, the problem is still how to equip, train, and organize forces to meet threats. Military power is easiest to use to repel or deter invasions of sovereign territory. The farther a state has to project military power, the less effective and costly it becomes. It also becomes more difficult to rally public support because the more distant a conflict appears from the homeland, the more remote the stakes seem from direct concerns that affect constituents.

In the United States, forces have been equipped, trained, and organized around sovereign threats to territory. The few experiences the U.S. military has had in fighting nonstate terrorist or guerrilla actors in Vietnam and Lebanon did not go well. Many states faced with military defeat, such as Germany after World War I, go back to the drawing board to learn how to better equip, train, and organize forces to win the type of battle they lost. The United States did the opposite. Rather than resolving to better learn how to fight nonstate actors in guerrilla war settings after Vietnam and Lebanon (and make appropriate changes in equipment, training, and organization), the United States instead devised the Weinberger Doctrine which resolved never to involve U.S. troops in those types of conflicts. Rather than revise the way it fights wars, the United States has chosen the strategy of avoiding the wars it is least equipped to fight.[99] The problem is that in the post–Cold War period, war is not an international conflict of competing states facing off over the borders of disputed territory. Instead, conflict is internal and the combatants are nonstate actors. Consequently, the military force the United States has amassed is less able to combat post–Cold War conflicts. But even if organization, training, and equipment priorities are changed to better prepare for the type of conflict that now predominates, military force is just not well suited to these conflicts, especially lacking a direct threat to U.S. territory, citizens, or institutions.

The new security dilemma is quite different and more complex than the Cold War security dilemma; it does not involve balancing along one (primarily military) dimension and against one enemy. Instead, the new security dilemma is how to balance, prioritize, promote, and protect interests along several different dimensions (economic, environmental, etc.), while military security against a powerful, aggressive sovereign state enemy is more assured than ever. Because the new security dilemma does not involve threats of direct attacks on U.S. territory by a strong sovereign enemy, the resources, political will, and political consensus available for the fight are greatly reduced. It is difficult for policymakers and the public to conceptualize the diffuse threats which transsovereign problems pose. It is hard for policymakers and the public to take seriously the threats which flow from weak states as opposed to strong states. Existing institutional frameworks don't lend themselves to addressing transsovereign problems systematically, and there is little will or wallet for building new organizational structures.

Finally, denial rules. It is almost unpatriotic for Westerners and Americans to consider the unintended and unanticipated ill effects of open society, open economy, and open technology forces. These trends are so closely associated with the ultimate embodiment of Western and U.S. ideals that it is difficult to get people to entertain the downside or challenges which these dynamics can entail. Attempts to open markets and open societies also create openings for international criminal organizations, for drug and nuclear trafficking, for environmental degradation, and for the free movement and organization of peoples, including refugees, terrorists, and infectious diseases. How can states protect territory, citizens, institutions, and core values from threats which are nonsovereign in nature, which travel across sovereign borders, and which are not resolvable by unilateral sovereign action alone, in an international system which is based on sovereignty? How can states provide for security when the basic building block, primary unit of the international system is being challenged from both without and within? President Clinton summarized the challenge when he said,

> We are going into a world of enormous possibility for our people, dominated by global trade, [democratization], and high technology. . . . But you also know that the more open our borders are, the more freely people can travel, the more freely money can move and information and technology can be transferred, the more vulnerable we are to people who would seek to undermine the very fabric of civilized life, whether through . . . the weapons of mass destruction, organized crime, or drugs—and sometimes through all of the above. So the great challenge we face, my fellow Americans, is how to get the benefits of this world toward which we are moving, and not be exposed to the forces that would undermine [us]."[100]

In the post–Cold War period, the security dilemma derives not from the dangers posed from strong states, but from the dangers stemming from weak and disintegrating states, and the transsovereign activities of nonstate actors. The theory of a sovereign-based system has not changed, while in practice sovereignty is being challenged and undermined from both within and without. Bureaucratic, organizational, political, and conceptual limitations hinder attempts to build new or change existing institutions. But sovereign organization has not been the only form of social organization in the history of the planet. If Machiavelli was right that change is the only constant in history, we can expect that international relations will not always be governed by the behavior of sovereign state units. An old folk saying notes that insanity is continually responding in the same ineffective mode and expecting different results. We keep responding to challenges that move beyond sovereignty with the same old state-centric institutions and response modes. So far this approach has been ineffectual. For saner heads to prevail and post–Cold War security dilemmas to be more effectively addressed, we must move our thinking about international problems and institutional responses beyond the conceptual and institutional prison of sovereignty. It is time to move beyond the transitional period of "smoke and confusion" described by Acheson, into a clear recognition of the new world which we face.

Notes

1. Richard N. Haas, "Paradigm Lost," *Foreign Affairs* 74 (January/February 1995): 43–58.
2. Dean Acheson, *Present at the Creation* (New York: W. W. Norton, 1969), 921–923.
3. Ibid., 922.

4. Edward Luttwak, "Toward Post-Heroic Warfare," *Foreign Affairs* 74 (May/June 1995): 109–122; Francis Fukuyama, *The End of History and the Last Man* (New York: Free Press, 1992).

5. Robert H. Jackson, *Quasi-States: Sovereignty, International Relations, and the Third World* (New York: Cambridge University Press, 1990); Ted Robert Gurr, "The State Failure Project: Early Warning Research for International Policy Planning" (paper presented at the International Studies Association Annual Meeting, Chicago, Ill., February 21–25, 1995); Stephen E. Flynn, "The Erosion of Sovereignty and the Emerging Global Drug Trade"(paper presented at the Annual Conference of the International Studies Association, Chicago, Ill., February 22, 1995); Maryann K. Cusimano, "Muddy in the Clay of Recreation: U.S. Military Intervention in the Post–Cold War World" (paper presented at the American Political Science Association Annual Meeting, New York City, September 2, 1994); Max Singer and Aaron Wildavsky, *The Real World Order: Zones of Peace and Zones of Turmoil* (Chatham, N.J.: Chatham House, 1993).

6. Gillian Sorensen, "The United Nations and Civil Societies: Redefining the Partnership for the 21st Century" (keynote address to Women in International Security [WIIS] Summer Symposium, Washington, D.C., June 15, 1998).

7. President Bill Clinton, "The UN at 50: A Pledge of Support by the White House," *New York Times,* October 23, 1995, A8; Alison Mitchell, "U.S. Freezes Assets of Cartel in New Effort Against Drugs," *New York Times,* October 23, 1995, A11.

8. Jessica Tuchman Mathews, "The Environment and International Security," 274–289, Thomas Homer-Dixon, "Environmental Scarcity and Intergroup Conflict," 290–313, and Dennis Pirages, "Demographic Change and Ecological Insecurity," 314–331, in *World Security: Challenges for a New Century,* eds. Michael T. Klare and Daniel C. Thomas (New York: St. Martin's Press, 1994); Thomas Homer-Dixon, "Environmental Changes as Causes of Acute Conflict," 425–441, and John K. Cooley, "The War Over Water," 413–424, in *Conflict after the Cold War: Arguments on the Causes of War and Peace,* ed. Richard Betts (New York: Macmillan Publishing Co., 1994); Michael Shuman, and Hal Harvey, "The Resource Roots of Conflict," 105–121, in *Security Without War: A Post–Cold War Foreign Policy* (Boulder, Colo.: Westview Press, 1993); Steven Greenhouse, "The Greening of U.S. Diplomacy: Focus on Ecology," *New York Times,* October 9, 1995.

9. Gil Loescher, *Beyond Charity: International Cooperation and the Global Refugee Crisis* (Oxford: Oxford University Press, 1993); Myron Weiner, "Security, Stability, and Migration," 394–411, in Richard Betts (ed.), *Conflict after the Cold War*; William LeoGrande, "The Cuban Refugee Crisis" (Washington, D.C.: Georgetown University Press, 1995, Case Program); Larry Minear and Thomas G. Weiss, *Mercy Under Fire* (Boulder, Colo.: Westview, 1995).

10. Tim Golden, "Patients Pay High Price in Cuba's War on AIDS," *New York Times,* October 16, 1995, A1, Foreign Policy Association, "The AIDS Pandemic, Global Scourge, U.S. Challenge," *Great Decisions* (Hanover, N.H.: Dartmouth Printing Co., 1992).

11. Flynn, "The Erosion of Sovereignty and the Emerging Global Drug Trade"; Phil Williams, "Transnational Criminal Organizations: Strategic Alliances," *Washington Quarterly* (Winter 1995): 57–72; United States Senate Permanent Subcommittee on Investigations, Committee on Governmental Affairs, Hearings on Global Proliferation of Weapons of Mass Destruction, March 20–21, 1996; James L. Ford, "Nuclear Smuggling: How Serious A Threat?" *Strategic Forum Bulletin* (Washington, D.C.: Institute for National Strategic Studies, January 1996); Paul Stares, *The Global Drug Problem in a Borderless World* (Washington, D.C.: Brookings, 1996); Zachary S. Davis, "Nuclear Proliferation and

Nonproliferation Policy in the 1990s," 106–133, in *World Security: Challenges for a New Century*; George H. Quester and Victor A. Utgoff, "U.S. Arms Reductions and Nuclear Nonproliferation: The Counterproductive Possibilities," 291–302, in Brad Roberts (ed.), *U.S. Security in an Uncertain Era* (Cambridge, Mass.: MIT Press, 1993); Charles A. Cerami, "Rogue States, Criminals and Terrorists Crash the Nuclear Club," *Insight* (June 20, 1994): 6–10.

12. Donald Snow and Eugene Brown, *Beyond the Water's Edge* (New York: St. Martin's Press, 1997).

13. Ernest Gellner, "Nations and Nationalism," in *Conflict After the Cold War*, 286.

14. Ralph C. Bryant, "Global Change: Increasing Economic Integration and Eroding Political Sovereignty," *Brookings Review* (Fall 1994): 42–45; Flynn, "The Erosion of Sovereignty and the Emerging Global Drug Trade"; Phil Williams, "Transnational Criminal Organizations: Strategic Alliances," *Washington Quarterly* (Winter 1995): 57–72; United States Senate Permanent Subcommittee on Investigations, Committee on Governmental Affairs, Hearings on Global Proliferation of Weapons of Mass Destruction; James L. Ford, "Nuclear Smuggling: How Serious A Threat?" *Strategic Forum Bulletin*; Paul Stares, *The Global Drug Problem in a Borderless World*; Sanger, "Trade's Bottom Line: Business Over Politics"; Sanger, "War. Peace. Aid. All Issues Are Trade Issues."

15. President Bill Clinton, "Remarks by the President at the United States Coast Guard Academy Commencement," White House Documents, Office of the Press Secretary, May 22, 1996.

16. I. William Zartman, *Collapsed States* (Boulder, Colo.: Lynn Reinner Publishers, 1995); Robert Jackson, *Quasi-States*; Maryann K. Cusimano, "The New Containment Doctrine," in *Unplugging the Cold War Machine* (Thousand Oaks, Calif.: Sage, forthcoming). Gerald B. Helman and Steven R. Ratner, "Saving Failed States," *Foreign Policy* (Winter 92/93): 3–20; Alex Rondos, "The Collapsing State and International Security," in *Global Engagement*, ed. Janne E. Nolan (Washington, D.C.: Brookings Institution, 1994), 481–503; Ted Robert Gurr, "The State Failure Project"; James C. Clad, "Old World Disorders," in *U.S. Security in an Uncertain World*, ed. Brad Roberts, 181–188; Chester Crocker, "The Global Law and Order Deficit: Is the West Ready to Police the World's Bad Neighborhoods?" *Washington Post* (December 20, 1992): C1; Michael Brown, "Introduction," *The International Dimensions of Internal Conflict* (Cambridge, Mass.: MIT Press, 1996); Pauline H. Baker and John A. Ausink, "State Collapse and Ethnic Violence: Toward a Predictive Model," *Parameters* (Spring 1996): 19–31.

17. Snow and Brown, *Beyond the Water's Edge*.

18. Michael Meacher, United Kingdom Minister for the Environment (speech at the Royal Society of Arts, April 1998).

19. President Bill Clinton, "Remarks by the President in Freedom House Speech," White House Documents, Office of the Press Secretary, October 6, 1995.

20. L. Craig Johnstone, "Strategic Planning and International Affairs in the 21st Century" (address to the Conference Series on International Affairs in the 21st Century, U.S. Department of State, Washington, D.C., November 18, 1997).

21. F. H. Hinsley, *Sovereignty* (London: C.A. Watts & Co. Ltd., 1966). The treaty of Westphalia is a commonly used, if somewhat controversial, marker for a historical process that took centuries. Some scholars, like Bruce Bueno de Mesquita, claim that the move toward sovereignty actually came much earlier, while others, such as Steven Krasner, point out that even after Westphalia there were struggles between religious and secular leaders, and contested and overlapping authority claims.

22. Hendrik Spruyt, *The Sovereign State and Its Competitors* (Princeton, N.J.: Princeton University Press), 40.

23. Ibid., 47.

24. Ibid., 62, 75.

25. Friedrich Kratochwil, "Sovereignty as Dominium: Is There a Right of Humanitarian Intervention?" in *Beyond Westphalia: State Sovereignty and International Intervention,* eds. Gene M. Lyons and Michael Mastanduno (Baltimore, Md.: Johns Hopkins University Press, 1995).

26. Nicholas Onuf, "Intervention for the Common Good," in *Beyond Westphalia: State Sovereignty and International Intervention,* 43.

27. Ibid.; Nicholas Onuf, "Sovereignty: Outline of a Conceptual History," *Alternatives* 16 (1991): 425–446.

28. Charles Tilly, *The Formation of National States in Western Europe* (Princeton, N.J.: Princeton University Press, 1975).

29. Spruyt, *The Sovereign State and Its Competitors.*

30. Michael Ross Fowler and Julie Marie Bunck, *Law, Power, and the Sovereign State: The Evolution and Application of the Concept of Sovereignty* (University Park, Pa.: Penn State University Press, 1995), 5–6.

31. Boutros Boutros-Ghali, *An Agenda for Peace* (New York: United Nations, 1992), 5.

32. "Everybody's Business," *Wall Street Journal,* August 24, 1992, A8.

33. "New Ways to Run the World," The *Economist* (November 5, 1991): 11.

34. Zartman, *Collapsed States,* 3.

35. Project Ploughshares, *Armed Conflicts Report 1995* (Waterloo, Ontario, Canada: Project Ploughshares Institute of Peace and Conflict Studies, Conrad Grebel College, 1995), 4.

36. Zartman, *Collapsed States,* 1–11. More than a succession struggle over which group will control the levers of state, state collapse is the failure of function of those very state institutions. While groups may be (and often are) involved in leadership contests, state collapse continues no matter who wins the helm, because state authority, legitimacy, and competence have badly disintegrated. States that have protracted or persistent leadership battles are vulnerable to state collapse, as state institutions atrophy during continued warfare, and as the legitimacy and authority which these institutions enjoy is undermined by the conflict. Civil war and state collapse are not synonymous terms, either. Internal war can occur in states which are not in the process or in danger of collapse, as is the case in Britain and Israel. More rarely, states can collapse without violence, as in the breakup of Czechoslovakia. Not surprisingly, state collapse is highly correlated with internal violence, however. Internal violence can weaken state institutions, preceding and contributing to state collapse. Alternatively, state collapse can provide the opportunity for groups to use violence, as they try to assert authority in the power vacuum left by state failure. See also Gerald B. Helman and Steven R. Ratner, "Saving Failed States," *Foreign Policy,* 3–20; Alex Rondos, "The Collapsing State and International Security," in *Global Engagement,* 481–503; Gurr, "The State Failure Project"; James C. Clad, "Old World Disorders," in *U.S. Security in an Uncertain World,* 181–188; Robert D. Kaplan, "The Coming Anarchy," *Atlantic Monthly* (February 1994): 44–76; and Jackson, *Quasi-States.*

37. Jackson, *Quasi-States,* 29.

38. Morton Halperin, *Self-Determination in the New World Order* (Washington, D.C.: The Carnegie Endowment for International Peace, 1992).

39. Jackson, *Quasi-States,* 27.

40. Hal Kane, *The Hour of Departure: Forces That Create Refugees and Migrants* (Washington, D.C.: Worldwatch Paper, 1995), 10–17.
41. Ibid.
42. Stockholm International Peace Research Institute, *SIPRI Yearbook 1995* (New York: Oxford University Press, 1995), 23–24.
43. Zartman, *Collapsed States,* 7–10.
44. Terry Lynn Karl and Philippe C. Schmitter, "Democratization around the Globe: Opportunities and Risks," in *World Security: Challenges for a New Century,* 43–62; Robert Rothstein, "Democracy, Conflict, and Development in the Third World," in *U.S. Foreign Policy after the Cold War,* ed. Brad Roberts (Cambridge, Mass.: MIT Press, 1992), 271–291; Roberts, "Democracy and World Order," in *U.S. Foreign Policy After the Cold War,* 293–307.
45. Edward D. Mansfield and Jack Snyder, "Democratization and War," *Foreign Affairs* (May/June 1995): 79–97.
46. United Nations Development Program (UNDP), *Human Development Report 1994* (New York: Oxford University Press, 1994); World Resources Institute, *World Resources 1994–95* (Washington, D.C., 1995).
47. Project Ploughshares, *Armed Conflicts Report 1995,* 4, 15.
48. Singer and Wildavsky, *The Real World Order.*
49. Edward Mansfield and Jack Snyder, "Democratization and War," 79–97; Susan Woodward, *Balkan Tragedy* (Washington, D.C.: Brookings Institution, 1995).
50. G. John Ikenberry, "The Myth of Post–Cold War Chaos," *Foreign Affairs* (May/June 1996), 79–91.
51. Jeffrey E. Garten, "Business and Foreign Policy," *Foreign Affairs* (May/June 1997): 68.
52. George Kennan, "Moscow Embassy Telegram #511: 'The Long Telegram,' February 22, 1946," *Foreign Relations of the United States: 1946, VI,* 696–709.
53. George Kennan, 1948, as quoted in John Lewis Gaddis, *Strategies of Containment,* 1982, 45.
54. Jessica Tuchman Matthews, "Lessons of Chernobyl," *Washington Post* (April 1996); "Sunshine and Shadow: The CIA and the Soviet Economy," John F. Kennedy School of Government, Case Program.
55. Paul Krugman, "Dutch Tulips and Emerging Markets," *Foreign Affairs* (July/August 1995).
56. Ikenberry, "The Myth of Post-Cold War Chaos," 91.
57. Paul W. Schroeder, "The New World Order: A Historical Perspective," in *Order and Disorder After the Cold War,* ed. Brad Roberts (Cambridge, Mass.: MIT Press, 1996), 367–386; John Stremlau, "Antidote to Anarchy," in *Order and Disorder After the Cold War,* 397–412.
58. John Lewis Gaddis, "Toward the Post Cold War World," in *At Issue: Politics in the World Arena,* eds. Steven L. Speigel and David J. Pervin (New York: St. Martin's Press, 1994), 27–42. There are clearly many more costs which have been attributed to global, open economies than those discussed here, such as exploitation of labor (Ethan Kapstein, "Workers and the World Economy," *Foreign Affairs* [May/June 1996]: 16–37); the exploitation (even the apartheid) of the developing South by the developed North (Richard Falk, "Democratizing, internationalizing, and globalizing," in *Global Transformation: Challenges to the State System,* ed. Yoshikazu Sakamoto [Tokyo: The United Nations University Press, 1994], 475–502); environmental degradation and endangerment of indigenous peoples and their civilizations (Richard Falk, "Democratizing, internationalizing, and globalizing," 475–502), etc.

59. Francis Fukuyama, *The End of History and the Last Man* (New York: The Free Press, 1992), xi.

60. Ibid., 337.

61. Terry Lynn Karl and Philippe C. Schmitter, "Democratization around the Globe: Opportunities and Risks," in *World Security: Challenges for a New Century,* 43–44. This description of the four waves of democratization is based on Karl and Schmitter's work. It should be noted that some theorists, such as Samuel Huntington, merge waves one and two into an overly long and undifferentiated category, and thus count only three waves of democratization.

62. Ibid., 60.

63. This has been a problematic point for states such as Singapore, which have tried to open up free market, capitalist economic systems while restricting political participation and democratic political reforms.

64. Michael Doyle, "Liberalism and World Politics," in *Conflict after the Cold War,* 263–279.

65. The White House, "A National Security Strategy of Engagement and Enlargement," July 1994.

66. Mansfield and Snyder, "Democratization and War," 88.

67. Ibid., 89.

68. Daniel F. Burton, Jr., "The Brave New Wired World," *Foreign Policy* (Spring 1997): 32.

69. Johnstone, "Strategic Planning and International Affairs in the 21st Century."

70. Burton, "The Brave New Wired World," 26.

71. Ibid.

72. Gaddis, "Toward the Post Cold War World," 27–42.

73. Susan Strange, *The Retreat of the State: The Diffusion of Power in the World Economy* (Cambridge: Cambridge University Press, 1996), 189.

74. Ibid., 78.

75. Ibid., 79.

76. Ibid., 81.

77. Ibid., 77, 82.

78. Ibid., 77, 199.

79. James N. Rosenau, "Sovereignty in a Turbulent World," in *Beyond Westphalia? State Sovereignty and International Intervention,* eds. Gene M. Lyons and Michael Mastanduno (Baltimore, Md.: Johns Hopkins University Press, 1995), 193.

80. James N. Rosenau, *Turbulence in World Politics* (Princeton, N.J.: Princeton University Press, 1990).

81. James N. Rosenau and W. Michael Fagen, "A New Dynamism in World Politics: Increasingly Skillful Individuals?" *International Studies Quarterly,* 41 (December 1997): 660.

82. Although he does not draw this comparison, Rosenau's arguments dovetail those of Neil Postman in *Amusing Ourselves to Death,* in which he maintains that the media technologies available to a generation affect not just the mode of their public discourse but its content, as well as the way they think about and interact with the world. Postman sees the move to a visual era as negative, reducing public discourse to soundbites, whereas Rosenau points up the positive effects that a skills revolution can have on political outcomes and dismembering repressive regimes.

83. Rosenau, "Sovereignty in a Turbulent World," 204.

84. This example does not come from Rosenau, but from the Central Intelligence Agency *1997 World Factbook* published on-line, and Larry Press "Cuban Computer Networks and Their Impact," and "Cuban Telecommunications Infrastructure and Investment," Association for the Study of the Cuban Economy, Florida International University, Proceedings

Volume VI, 1996, published on-line. This data was presented in Brad Millick, "Decentralization in Cuba?" (graduate student paper, Catholic University of America, Spring 1998).

85. Rosenau, "Sovereignty in a Turbulent World," 206–207; Rosenau, *Turbulence in World Politics,* 90–113.

86. Rosenau, "Sovereignty in a Turbulent World," 210; Rosenau, *Turbulence in World Politics,* 90–113.

87. Rosenau, "Sovereignty in a Turbulent World," 210; Rosenau, *Turbulence in World Politics,* 90–113.

88. Richard Rosecrance, "The Rise of the Virtual State," *Foreign Affairs* (July/August 1996): 59–60.

89. Ibid., 46.

90. Ibid., 45.

91. Ibid., 46.

92. Ibid., 59.

93. Ibid., 61.

94. Ibid., 61.

95. Stephen D. Krasner, "Sovereignty: An Institutional Perspective," *Comparative Political Studies* 21 (April 1988): 74.

96. William H. McNeill, "Territorial States Buried Too Soon," *Mershon International Studies Review* 41 (1997): 269.

97. Ibid.

98. President Bill Clinton, "The UN at 50: A Pledge of Support by the White House," A8; Alison Mitchell, "U.S. Freezes Assets of Cartel in New Effort Against Drugs," A11.

99. Andrew J. Bacevich, "The Limits of Orthodoxy: The Use of Force after the Cold War," in Aspen Strategy Group, *The United States and the Use of Force in the Post-Cold War Era* (Washington, D.C.: Brookings Institution, 1995), 171–190.

100. President Bill Clinton, "Remarks by the President Announcing the 1996 National Drug Control Strategy," White House Documents, Office of the Press Secretary, April 29, 1996.

Drug Trafficking

Despite the international "war on drugs," illegal narcotics are cheaper, more potent, and more readily available than ever before. The United Nations reports that "In recent years, illicit drug consumption has increased throughout the world . . . consumption has become a truly global phenomenon."[1]

This is not due to a failure of state will or attention, but instead to the success of policies to open economies, societies, and technologies. As societies democratize and liberalize their economies, they often find themselves facing serious problems with the abuse of illegal narcotics for the first time. In part, this is due to the greater free time and money provided by capitalist economies. Partly, it stems from an increase in individual rights and liberties which demarcates a private sphere relatively free from government control. The rise in drug problems in newly democratizing and liberalizing states is also due partly to the emergence of capitalist norms: Once entrepreneurial market forces have been released, they are mimicked in the creation of illicit as well as licit businesses. Supply follows demand, and markets are set up to cater to consumers, whether or not the consumer demand is a legal practice. The spread of technology also helps the drug trade, as drug traffickers use the latest cell phone, pager, fax, computer, and Internet technologies to track shipments and transactions, as would any international business.

Drug smuggling is also facilitated by state collapse prevalent in the post–Cold War era. Lieutenant Commander Stephen Flynn of the U.S. Coast Guard Academy notes,

> As governmental authority is everywhere sapped away by powerful globalizing and localizing forces, the global drug trade is growing and prospering and will continue to do so. The expansion of the drug trade not only reflects the general decline of governmental authority at the end of the millennium, but in growing measure, contributes directly to this trend. . . . The list of today's major producers of coca and opium reads like a "Who's Who" of failed states . . . seemingly validating the inverse relationship between production and viable national sovereignty. In all these countries: there has been a substantial decline in central governmental authority.[2]

Not only does drug trafficking occur where state control is weakest, but it also undermines state institutions. "Drug networks undermine the stability of political and financial institutions throughout the world. For example, countries formerly controlled by the Soviet Union in Central Asia and Eastern Europe, as well as Russia itself, are being weakened by the activities of transsovereign criminal drug syndicates. Many burgeoning entrepreneurs in the newly independent republics have learned that hard drugs are a ready substitute for hard currency in international markets. Opium production in Tajikistan, Turkmenistan, and Uzbekistan has doubled since 1990. Law enforcement in the former Soviet Union is now sporadic at best and is already riven by rampant corruption. In many areas, drug traffickers operate unchallenged."[3] In Columbia and Mexico, judges, police, and even Presidents are undermined by connections with the drug cartels. By bribing and assassinating public officials, and setting up huge economies beyond the reach of state control which dwarf and distort the legal economy, drug traffickers undermine state institutions.[4]

As the number of weak and collapsed states increases, so does international drug production. Since 1985 the worldwide production of opium poppy has more than tripled; the chief opium-producing countries, Afghanistan and Myanmar, are weak or failed states.[5] From 1985 to 1994, coca leaf production doubled, with the Andean countries of Peru, Columbia, and Bolivia accounting for 98 percent of world cocaine supplies.[6] Not surprisingly, the purity of drugs sold in the United States has dramatically increased during the same time period, while prices have dropped. Heroin is nine times more pure and half the price it was a decade ago; the price of cocaine has declined by two-thirds.[7]

Illegal drugs impose societal costs. The United Nations estimates that 22 percent of the world's HIV/AIDS population inject drugs.[8] While international figures are hard to come by, in the United States alone in 1996 over 1.5 million individuals were arrested for drug offenses.[9] Americans spent an estimated $49 billion in 1993 just on cocaine.[10] An estimated $20 billion in U.S. health care costs were related to illegal drug usage,[11] while the social and economic costs imposed by drug usage in the United States are estimated at between $69 and $300 billion.[12] Drug trafficking harms developed and developing states alike, however. While developed states are the largest drug consumers, and thus see the societal costs of drug usage, developing states are often producers and face the undermining of law and order and state institutions that result from powerful black market economies beyond the reach of the state.

In response, the Clinton administration announced its National Drug Control Strategy: (1) to reduce drug use, especially by young people in the United States; (2) to reduce drug-related crime and violence in the United States; (3) to reduce the social and economic costs of drug abuse to U.S. society; (4) to "shield America's air, land, and sea frontiers from the drug threat"; and (5) to break up the foreign and domestic sources of drug supply.[13] While the strategy does attempt to increase cooperation and coordination among the fifty U.S. agencies who work on drug control, it is still a heavily unilateral, state-centric, and law-enforcement approach to a transsovereign issue. The problem in combating drug smuggling, as in responding to many other transsovereign problems, is that the problem primarily takes place in the economic and social spheres where state control is weakest.

Additionally, as long as states continue to promote open economies, societies, and technologies, the infrastructure will be available for illicit use in the drug trade. The battle against drug trafficking, then, is not a "war" that can be won once and for all, but is a continuing problem which can be contained and managed if never entirely eliminated. "The metaphor of a 'war on drugs' is misleading. . . . Cancer is a more appropriate metaphor for the drug problem. Dealing with cancer is a long-term proposition. It requires the mobilization of support mechanisms—medical, educational, and societal—to check the spread of the disease and improve the prognosis. The symptoms of the illness must be managed while the root cause is attacked. The key to reducing both drug abuse and cancer is prevention coupled with treatment."[14]

Notes

1. United Nations, *1998 World Drug Report,* 29.
2. Stephen E. Flynn, "The Erosion of Sovereignty and the Emerging Global Drug Trade" (paper presented to the International Studies Association, February 22, 1995), 1–4.
3. Mathea Falco, "U.S. Drug Policy: Addicted to Failure," *Foreign Policy* (Spring 1996): 130.
4. "Memorandum for the Heads of Executive Departments and Agencies, Subject: Strengthening Drug Cooperation with Mexico," White House Documents, Office of the Press Secretary, April 8, 1996; "President's Message to the Congress re: Drug Trafficking," White House Documents, Office of the Press Secretary, April 23, 1996; "Contact Group with Mexico Regarding Drugs," White House Documents, Office of the Press Secretary, March 15, 1996.
5. UN, *1998 World Drug Report,* 17.
6. Ibid., 18.
7. Falco, "U.S. Drug Policy: Addicted to Failure," 124.
8. United Nations, *1998 World Drug Report,* 91.
9. Office of National Drug Control Policy (ONDCP), "Focus On: The Drug Problem," 1998, 1.
10. "President Message to the Congress re: Drug Trafficking."
11. Barry McCaffrey, "Press Briefing on Drug Strategy," White House Documents, Office of the Press Secretary, April 29, 1996.
12. President Bill Clinton, "Remarks by the President Announcing the 1996 National Drug Control Strategy," White House Documents, Office of the Press Secretary, April 29, 1996.
13. ONDCP, "1998 Drug-Control Strategy: An Overview," 3.
14. Ibid., 4.

The Global Drug Trade versus the Nation-State

Why the Thugs Are Winning

Stephen E. Flynn

Among the more disturbing new features of the emerging global landscape is the persistent growth and dramatic spread of illicit drug markets, most notably for heroin, cocaine, and synthetic drugs.* Over the past decade, the production of opium poppies has nearly tripled in Latin America and Southeast Asia, and climbed by 22 percent in Southwest Asia. Despite ten years of U.S.-sponsored eradication programs and aggressive enforcement efforts, there were at least 12,500 more metric tons of Andean coca leaf produced in 1996 than in 1987.[1] Internet users can readily surf the Net for formulas for preparing controlled substances and then order the chemical ingredients from a growing menu of on-line suppliers; the result, synthetic drugs like methamphetamine and LSD can be concocted by kitchen chemists around the globe.[2] The clandestine trafficking organizations that have evolved to link producers with distant consumers have also grown in number, size, and sophistication. Drug abuse and addiction, particularly near production areas and along the growing array of transit routes has expanded into areas that had hitherto remained largely unscathed.

This growth in the drug phenomenon has taken place despite a nearly century-old international prohibitionary regime designed to contain it. In the United States, even with a quarter trillion dollar investment in drug control programs by federal, state, and local governments since 1981,[3] the drug business continues to thrive. Indeed, for more than ten years suppliers have been compelled to lower wholesale and retail prices of cocaine and heroin and improve the street-level purity in order to stay competitive.[4] Around the world, drugs have become more available and affordable despite a rash of new multilateral

---

*The views expressed in this selection are those of the author and do not reflect the official policy or position of the U.S. Coast Guard, Department of Transportation, or the U.S. government.

initiatives that target not only illicit drugs, but the chemicals and money connected with them.

Today, drugs represent one of the world's largest—and perhaps most lucrative—commodities. As an illicit enterprise, it is impossible to establish the drug trade's total value with any precision. Estimates of its annual revenues range wildly from $100 billion to as high as $500 billion. The higher figure was cited in March 1995 by the head of the U.S. Drug Enforcement Administration (DEA), Thomas Constantine.[5] That figure would place drugs below only the global arms trade in a ranking of the world's largest industries. The lower estimate equates to a value greater than the GNP of the vast majority of the world's nations. A middle value of $300 billion would broach the size of the world petroleum industry.

That the marketing of drugs has become truly global is illustrated by the latest U.S. government estimates which maintain that Americans consume less than 40 percent of the cocaine manufactured in South America and just 1 to 4 percent of the world's opium supplies.[6] In 1995, the overwhelming majority of the heroin interdicted outside the production areas took place in Europe, with U.S. seizures equal to just 4 percent of the world total.[7] Virtually every nation is reporting that drugs are far more available than at any time in recent history.[8]

Why is the war on drugs going so badly? The answer lies in the fact that we continue to rely on tried-and-true approaches that are no longer true. Our drug control regime rests almost entirely on the coercive arm of the state, but the drug trade is a transsovereign problem that thrives in the dark corners of the international systems where traditional sovereign controls are weak or nonexistent. The end of the Cold War has dramatically expanded the realm where the writ of the state does not run. Thus, enforcement authorities intent on stemming the production, trafficking, and consumption of drugs often find themselves "all dressed up with nowhere to go." Because most of the world's illicit drug supply is cultivated within states that are weak or failing, international source control is a house built on the sand of local enforcement bodies that are too primitive or corrupt to take the actions to stop the cultivation of drug raw materials within their borders. Interdiction efforts face the improbable task of sifting contraband from the rising tide of legitimate goods, services, and people that now wash across state borders as a result of the explosive growth of the open global economy and the twin trends of liberalization and privatization. Finally, as democratization and open societies have taken root around the planet, the ability for police authorities to intrude into the lives of their citizens has been properly reigned in, leaving people with greater freedom to do more of what they please—including, inevitably, socially sanctioned activities like buying and consuming drugs—outside of the watchful eye of the state.

In short, the explosive rise of the global drug trade in the post–Cold War era highlights the fiction that the international system is the sum of its nation-states.

Drugs are produced and trafficked by nonstate actors who find borders essentially meaningless. In fact, the bad guys find the remaining vestiges of sovereignty to be largely an ally in their global enterprise. Because each state reserves for itself the right to draft laws, to establish rules and procedures for operating its criminal justice system, and to establish public policy priorities, drug control must be pursued against a backdrop of widely differing state jurisdictions. This lack of harmonization muddies the prospect for seamless multilateral cooperation among enforcement authorities. Whenever there is friction, there are "no-man's-lands" which drug traffickers can occupy. The bottom line is that while states must still be mindful of the sensibilities of their fellow sovereigns, traffickers need not. As a result, the legal barriers designed to prevent chemicals, drugs, and profits from circulating around the globe leak like a sieve.

The expansion of the drug trade not only reflects the unsteady state of states, but in growing measure, contributes to the turbulence. The enormous profits generated by drugs provide terrorists and insurgents with hard currency to purchase weapons. Drug moneys also make it possible for transsovereign criminal organizations to corrupt officials at every level of government, thereby undermining the legitimacy of political and judicial institutions. The billions of illegitimate dollars associated with the global drug trade are circulated within a shadow economy, providing a substantial impetus for its growth. Finally, a rise in participation in drug-related activities, particularly when concentrated among youth and minority ethnic populations, accentuates social cleavages already fueled by the pain and dislocations connected with modernization and post-communist and postindustrial societal transitions.

Acknowledging drugs as a phenomenon that lies *beyond sovereignty* achieves two ends. First, it helps explain why current U.S. and international drug control exertions are not working. Second, it points a way to a better approach. Ultimately, states must turn to the primary beneficiaries of globalization to redress its dark side. Because states have a declining presence in the economic and social spheres where the drug trade thrives, ultimately it is nongovernmental organizations, businesses, and community activists who are best positioned to create a climate less conducive to the rapid spread of drug supply and demand. In the end, it is not nation-states but nonstate actors who must be enlisted into tempering the forces that are motivating and facilitating drug-related activities.

THE RISE OF THE GLOBAL DRUG TRADE

The production and global distribution of drugs is by no means a new phenomenon. Turkish and Persian opium had been traded for centuries throughout the Middle East and in parts of Asia. By the latter part of the eighteenth century and throughout the nineteenth, large-scale production and worldwide distribution of opiates became systematically organized, often with the official sanction if not direct involvement of the major powers. On the eve of the twentieth century, legal markets in cocaine and opiates were flourishing within the United States, Europe, and the Far East, and the global drug trade could be characterized as a widely accepted sector of international commerce.

This would change beginning with the 1909 conference in Shanghai of the International Opium Commission. Growing concern over widespread drug abuse and addiction, primarily by religious missionaries serving overseas and a growing number of physicians and temperance organizations at home,[9] led the U.S. government to sponsor the Shanghai conference with the objective of convincing the principal producer countries to curtail the opium trade.[10] While this drug control agenda was slow to take root, following World War I the League of Nations did create mandatory international controls supervised by a newly created Opium Control Board. The opium trade was to be eliminated within fifteen years and restricted to government monopolies during the interim period. This regulatory body was later reconstituted as the Permanent Central Board and charged with creating a tighter world system of controls over a wider range of drugs to include cocaine and cannabis.

Resting as they did on the power and legitimacy of state authorities to enforce them, these initial steps to develop a global prohibition regime had the unsettling effect of displacing drug trafficking, production, and consumption into areas where state sovereignty was weakest if not non-existent.[11] Criminal suppliers stepped into the void left by long-standing government monopolies, initially basing their black market activities out of the cities of Istanbul and Shanghai. Thus began a trend that would gather force over the next five decades—the tendency for the chemicals, drugs, and money that sustain the drug trade to be concentrated in areas in the international system which offered the lowest level of regulatory resistance to international trade flows. During World War II, there were few such locales and the illicit traffic in drugs practically disappeared.[12] But following the war, as the number of these areas grew, so would the drug trade. Havana before Castro was the gateway to the Western Hemisphere. Marseilles served as a base for the famous French Connection until the early 1970s. Today, international drug criminals have a vast menu of havens for their activities, most notably, Caracas, Bogotá, Panama City, Karachi, Bangkok, Hong Kong, Lagos, Nairobi, Sofia, Moscow, St. Petersburg, and Warsaw.[13]

The tendency for trafficking activities to move toward cities where governmental authority is weakest paralleled a similar shift in production of the botanical ingredients. Over time, traditional cultivation areas once controlled by colonial monopolies were largely abandoned in favor of territories not under the effective control of any state authority. Nearly all coca is cultivated in remote regions in Peru, Bolivia, and Colombia, while Burma, Afghanistan, and Laos together account for 93 percent of opium poppy cultivation.[14] Newly emerging producers such as Kazakhstan, Kyrgyzstan, Uzbekistan, Turkmenistan, Tadjikistan, Ukraine, Azerbaijan, Georgia, Nigeria, Kenya, and Vietnam all share characteristics that seem to validate the inverse relationship between production and viable state sovereignty. All of these countries (1) have experienced a substantial decline in central governmental authority, (2) have recently established or enhanced ties to regional or global markets, and (3) contain vast remote areas where cultivation can take place largely undetected. Additionally, in several instances, production activities have been directly sponsored or protected by insurgent groups who resist, by force of arms, encroachments by the state into production regions.

While production and trafficking activities increasingly have been concentrated in the largely lawless corners of the global community, for much of the latter half of the twentieth century the end users of illicit drugs have resided largely in developed countries, with the United States serving as the primary market. Given the size and resources of the U.S. government, it would appear at first blush that if properly committed, the United States could insulate itself from the wholesale and retail activities of drug traffickers. But upon closer examination, it becomes clear that the government is not well positioned to do so. First, efforts to prevent retail transactions are necessarily hindered by basic civil liberty (open society) protections. While these protections obviously apply to all criminal investigations, what make drug crimes particularly difficult for law enforcement officials to pursue is that they rarely receive the cooperation of the victim. This is because, unlike crimes such as burglary or rape, the "victims" in drug transactions (the consumers) do not file police reports or make evidence available because they are also accomplices. Detecting drug retail crimes, therefore, generally must be accomplished unilaterally by state authorities. At the same time, these authorities must always be mindful not to interfere with the freedoms Americans enjoy to move when and where they please, to possess unfettered control over their disposable incomes, and most importantly, to be secure from the intrusiveness of the state in their private lives. In short, in supporting an essentially free and democratic society, Americans have imposed formidable constitutional limits on the sovereign prerogatives of their government to control wholesale or retail drug-related activities within its borders.

It is not only *within* their societies that advanced democratic countries are confronted with serious limits to their power to pursue drug crimes. The United States and Western European nations are also finding that they have a shrinking capacity to detect drug trafficking activities along their borders. This is in part due to conscious choices by governments to remove restrictions on cross-border flows of a growing volume of legal goods, capital, and services (open economies). Beginning in the 1970s, for instance, the U.S. Customs Service stopped stationing customs officers at international shipping piers and terminals where imported cargo is discharged and removed customs storekeepers from bonded warehouses. These traditional inspection controls were replaced with automated systems and audits in response to growing private-sector calls for reductions in domestic barriers to international commerce. New rules, which are in place today, allow foreign goods to transit throughout the United States without prior release authorization by customs officials. The carrier needs only to assure customs authorities that it will maintain custody over these imports until the goods reach their final destination. Officials then authorize release—in virtually all instances without an on-site inspection—upon receipt of accounting and importers documentation. If the Customs Service receives the appropriate paperwork in advance, it routinely authorizes release in advance. More recently, the U.S. Customs Service has adopted further liberalization procedures by relaxing requirements on labeling, cords, and seals, and has virtually eliminated spot inspections of bonded goods in transit.[15]

The member states of the European Community (EC) also have adopted new rules that have substantially liberalized their national transportation sectors. Beginning in 1988, for instance, the EC removed quotas and permits for transporters operating in a member country other than the hauler's own. In March 1991, the EC removed all restrictions on air cargo capacity, and authorized a carrier based in one country to pick up goods in another and deliver them to a third. Finally, on January 1, 1993, the community granted all EC shippers moving cargo by road, free access to any other EC country.[16]

These trends have not been restricted to the United States and Western Europe. Colombia, Venezuela, and Brazil are all engaged in efforts to deregulate maritime and land transport.[17] Mexico dramatically liberalized it regulations governing the trucking industry in June 1989, allowing any licensed truck to move freely within the country, and to load and unload in any city, port, or railway station.[18] In Panama, state control over the movement of goods through its major port all but disappeared with the creation of the Colon "free zone."[19] Having eliminated customs duties for most imports, the government possesses little incentive to inspect any cargo. Most recently, the Bahamian government authorized the construction and opening of a port terminal in a privately owned harbor in Freeport on Grand Bahama Island which can handle up to 500,000 containers annually.[20]

The advanced capitalist societies have also undertaken a number of steps to facilitate the flow of capital across state borders. Governments began to surrender regulatory control over cross-border investments with the creation of the Eurodollar market and off-shore banking centers in the late 1960s. The trend was given added impetus by the enactment of new laws that lowered the restrictions on foreign investment by pension funds, insurance companies, unit trusts, and mutual funds, giving rise to a proliferation of new players in international financial markets.[21] These concessions were inspired in part by the fallout from expansionary policies in the 1980s that produced large deficits in the Group of Seven countries. Confronted by the need to court foreign investors to help them finance bond issues, governments were inclined to eliminate barriers that might discourage would-be creditors. Pressures to ease reporting requirements and other controls came also from the banking and nonbanking industries. Given the volatility of exchange rates, competitive global bidding, and the explosive growth in clients attempting to make time-sensitive deals, financial institutions are finding that their survival is dependent on their ability to conclude transactions rapidly. They therefore tend to see government regulators almost exclusively in adversarial terms.

Deregulation of the transportation and financial sectors has been in part a reaction to the dictates of a global marketplace transformed by the extraordinary impact of the communications revolution (open technologies). The power of computers, computer software, satellites, fiber-optic cables, facsimile machines, modems, and wireless technology has effectively overcome most of the practical limitations connected with geographical distances. Communications technology has made it possible for financial markets to be truly globalized with around-the-clock trading in bonds, stocks, and exchanges conducted over 200,000 electronic monitors linked together in trading rooms all over the world.[22] Communications technology also provides manufacturers with the means to remotely coordinate distant operations, allowing them to disperse production activities to wherever the greatest value can be added to each stage of production. As multinational corporations deepen these international production-based linkages, their success in turn becomes increasingly tied to their access to open capital markets and a low-cost and smoothly functioning transportation and communications infrastructure. Thus, the incentives to lobby governments to deregulate their financial, transportation, and communications sectors only grows with time.

There is little question that these liberalization trends have served to stimulate the growth in world trade and investment over the past ten years. Since the early 1980s, world merchandise exports have grown in volume at twice the rate of gross domestic product. The Secretariat for the General Agreement on Trade and Tariffs (GATT) estimates that the 1993 Uruguay Round agreement will eventually generate an additional 25 percent growth on top of earlier rates. International direct investment has grown even faster than exports.[23] But these widely heralded outcomes have come at a cost—international markets have been made almost as accessible to illicit commercial activities as licit. A brief description of how trafficking organizations, based out of Cali, Colombia, service the U.S. cocaine market substantiates this finding.[24]

Contrary to popular conceptions encouraged by such television programs as *Miami Vice,* most cocaine does not find its way into the United States on low-flying Cessnas, fast-moving "cigarette" boats, or among the personal possessions of illegal immigrants.[25] The Cali organization prefers the more reliable forms of transportation provided by commercial sea, land, and air conveyances. International shipping centers in Central and South America, particularly in Brazil, Venezuela, Surinam, and Panama, are the preferred embarkation points to ship cocaine by sea. There, drugs are placed among containerized shipments and bulk cargo carried aboard large merchant ships. By land, most cocaine crosses the U.S.-Mexican border in the hidden compartments of tractor trailers and other vehicles or in commercial cargo itself. When commercial airlines are used, the drug is hidden on the plane, among perishable cargoes such as cut flowers or fruit pulp, or among passengers who conceal it by placing it in luggage with false bottoms or in hollowed-out sneakers, by taping it to their bodies, or by swallowing condoms filled with cocaine. Sometimes it is converted to liquid and smuggled in bottles of shampoo, mouthwash, and liquor. In most instances, these shipments are mixed in with legal cargo and are accompanied by complete documentation from licensed companies with legitimate destinations.

Once the drug arrives, it is distributed by one of the dozens of Cali distribution cells throughout the country. Each cell, made up of 10 to 15 Colombian employees who earn monthly salaries ranging from $2,000 to $7,500, conducts as much as $25 million of business a month. Each cell is self-contained, with information tightly compartmentalized; only a handful of managers know all the operatives. The cell typically has a leader, bookkeeper, money handler, cocaine handler, motor pool, and ten to fifteen apartments serving as stash houses.

Communications are conducted in code over facsimile machines, cellular phones, and pay phones. To eliminate any risk of interception, cellular phones are purchased and discarded, often weekly. When a wholesale customer wants to make a purchase, a cell member is notified by a pager system. That cell member proceeds to a public phone and arranges a rendezvous site. He then gets, from the motor pool, a rental car that is returned to the rental agency after the transaction. The transaction itself, including travel receipts, is logged by the bookkeeper, and the money is turned over to the money handler to be shipped to the financial network set up by the cartel to hide and invest it. One favored way to ship cash within the United States is by way of the U.S. Postal Service's Express Mail®.

The cartel moves the money from its drug sales into and through the legal financial system to conceal its origins. If a Cali cell broken up by federal authorities in December 1991 is representative, the Cali financial network must launder about $200 million each year per cell. Money laundering typically involves three independent phases. First, drug proceeds are "placed," that is, deposited in banks or used to purchase monetary instruments or securities that can be turned into cash elsewhere. This is often done by hiring individuals known as "smurfs" to deposit the money in small denominations in as many banks and financial institutions as possible so as to defeat currency reporting requirements.[26] Second, the money is "layered," or sent through multiple electronic transfers or other transactions to make it difficult to track and blur its illicit origin.[27] Finally, the source of the money disappears as it is "integrated," that is, invested into seemingly legitimate accounts and enterprises. To lower their exposure to law enforcement yet further, the Cali families increasingly have contracted out these last two phases, requiring money handlers in Colombia to provide them the money up front, less a 15 to 25 percent commission, in return for providing these handlers the opportunity to launder and keep the full amount.[28]

In essence, the Colombian drug organizations are mirroring the behaviors of the most successful multinational corporations. They have developed network structures that successfully support vertical and horizontal relationships with "contractors" across state borders. They have invested in the most advanced information technologies to maintain secure, real-time links over long distances to coordinate production and distribution activities under rapidly changing conditions and in a potentially adversarial environment. Most importantly, they have immersed their activities within parts of the global infrastructure that are virtually unregulated and perhaps may never be—commercial containers, air cargo, overland freight, rental cars, cellular phones, overnight mail, and electronic transfers.

Beginning with commercial containers, the problem for government regulators is all too apparent when one considers that, on average, five U.S. Customs agents must work for three full hours to thoroughly inspect a single maritime container[29]—and nearly 1.8 million containers moved through the port of Newark alone in 1996. By international standards, the task confronting the Newark officials is by no means extraordinary. For example, every *month* more than 1 million maritime containers transit through the port of Hong Kong and the port of Singapore. In Singapore, the average time between discharge and reloading an entire ship carrying as many as 3,000 containers is just eight hours.[30] Overall, 4 billion tons of goods plied the world waters in 1995 and the volume of seaborne trade is projected to rise by two-thirds over the next decade.[31]

Monitoring and inspecting commercial air traffic has become an equally formidable task for government regulators. Air carriers are not required to disclose to customs authorities the content of their cargo destined to U.S. airspace until they are at the start of their flight. This limited advance notice makes it extremely difficult for inspectors to target shipments. When these flights arrive in the United States, they are likely to land at a busy airport like Miami where more than 130 airlines moved millions of international travelers and 1.8 million tons of air cargo in 1996.[32] Frequently, the goods moved by air are perishable.[33] In Houston, for example, inspectors are confronted with shipments of 2 million plants from South America each month which they must process swiftly or risk generating huge spoilage losses for importers.[34]

Along the land borders of the United States, customs inspectors can find no relief for their overwhelming task of filtering the illicit traffic from the licit. A substantial proportion of the more than 430 million people who enter the United States each year do so in one of the 8 million automobiles, trucks, and buses that cross American borders. Along the Mexican border, to prevent mile-long traffic jams, U.S. customs officials in El Paso are directed to spend no more than one minute examining each northbound tractor trailer.[35]

Given what are quite clearly horrendous and diminishing odds for success-fully discovering drugs based on random border inspections, intelligence to support law enforcement operations would appear crucial to successful inter-diction of drugs along U.S. borders and in U.S. streets. Here, however, the traf-fickers' investment in state-of-the-art communications hardware and software has effectively defeated any hope of successful electronic surveillance by law enforcement officials. Communications via pagers and pay phones are, for all practical purposes, impossible to monitor. While it is possible to listen in on a cellular phone conversation, the interception technology is scarce and expen-sive. Further, a court order for electronic surveillance also takes time—generally longer than the very brief time span that a trafficker will use the phone before dumping it and getting a new one. Finally, the Internet makes it possible for traf-fickers to conduct completely secure communications. If the traffickers break their messages up into multiple subunits, send each unit through anonymous remailers that move the message through a large number of "routers" before it arrives at its final destination, and use widely available 128-bit encryption tech-nology such as PGP (Pretty Good Privacy), they can operate with virtually no risk from surveillance efforts by the law enforcement community.[36]

Because the prospects of interdicting drugs or investigating the trafficking organizations that move them appear to be so grim, one final temptation would be to target the money derived from this illicit business. The logic here is that because retail drug sales must be made in cash and the cash is actually far bulkier than the drugs for which it is sold, law enforcement should focus on keeping the money from finding its way back to Colombia or the other traffick-ing home bases. Unfortunately, given the liquidity of money and the globaliza-tion trends already outlined, this too is destined to prove illusive. There simply is no shortage of ways in which the money can be placed within the economy. Money launderers can and do use nonbank financial institutions such as exchange houses, check cashing services, and credit unions. They purchase instruments like postal money orders, cashier's checks, certificates of deposit, and even securities such as stocks and bonds. Proceeds are invested in legiti-mate businesses such as travel agencies, construction companies, casinos, secu-rities dealers, real estate agencies, jewelry shops, and antique dealers—that is, businesses with a high volume of cash transactions. Money managers may soon use microchip-based electronic money or cybercurrency, giving them the abil-ity to make instant and anonymous transfers of money around the globe.[37]

RECONSIDERING DRUG CONTROL

In sum, the drug trade has grown in recent years because changes within the international system have raised the fortunes of transsovereign actors while eroding the position of states.[38] Since the beginning of the post-colonial era, there has been an unparalleled growth in the number of state actors in the international system that lack the institutional capacity to exercise sovereignty over much of their territory. Actors within these new states have virtually unrestricted access to the global economy as a result of the worldwide trend towards economic liberalization. Wholesale privatization and deregulation within national economies has diminished the capacity of all states—developing, post-communist, and developed—to exercise control over production and distribution activities within and across their borders. As a result, the global economy has slid increasingly into a status of laissez-faire, creating little practical distinction between engaging in legitimate and illegitimate commercial activities. Traffickers in illicit narcotics merely merge with the legitimate flows of goods, capital, and services within the global marketplace, comfortable in the realization that governments have a shrinking capacity to separate the bad from the good.

The manifold factors influencing the growth of the global drug trade render impractical traditional supply-side policies. The drug problem cannot be solved by simply working harder at both eliminating drugs at their source or seizing them prior to their arrival in the United States. Policies enacted with these objectives in mind are fatally flawed for two reasons. First, the centrality of enforcement makes them an inherently reactive approach to an extremely dynamic phenomenon. Law enforcement by definition cannot be preemptive—rules must be broken *before* the legitimate coercive authority of the state can be brought to bear to impose sanctions. Second, these policies rest on the fallacious notion that drug production and trafficking activities can be somehow readily rooted out from the context in which they exist.

By defining drugs as "bad," drug control policies rest upon the normative presumption that the phenomenon is alien and "normalcy" can be restored by isolating and exorcizing it from the body politic. But the drug phenomenon cannot be exorcized precisely because it is deeply entrenched in so many of the activities that underlie modern life. Further, there is little agreement over exactly what constitutes the evil to be eradicated. While there is nearly universal acknowledgment that the abuse of drugs such as heroin and cocaine is a bad thing, it is difficult to formulate similar tidy judgments about the array of interwoven activities that ultimately supply addicts with their fix. Farmers, chemists, shippers, and bankers who are directly or indirectly involved in the drug trade rarely see themselves as criminals, but instead characterize themselves as "good" businessmen striving to embrace one of capitalism's chief tenets—a commitment to maximizing profits. The inventors and suppliers of new technologies that are exploited by organized criminal networks do not see themselves as accomplices to crime, but as purveyors of progress. Importers, exporters, tourists, and commercial carriers are acting in concert with the principles of economic liberalization when they strongly oppose the use of the intrusive border controls governments have traditionally relied upon to detect and stop contraband. Finally, civil libertarians are embracing the core ideals of democratic society when they fight to restrict the intrusiveness of governmental authority into the individual lives of their citizenry, even if it means that some drug crimes will go undetected.

So where does this leave policymakers committed to stemming the burgeoning global drug trade? Obviously it presents them with a far more complicated challenge than the one they have been willing to acknowledge up to this point for it is a challenge that cannot be reduced to a state-centric crusade against evil drug producers, traffickers, and consumers. Instead, it represents a vexing transsovereign problem of the first order.

By outlining the factors that motivate and facilitate drug production, it becomes self-evident why American- and UN-funded crop eradication, crop substitution, and alternative development programs are not working. Such programs are premised on the notion that if existing growers can be coerced or enticed to end drug cultivation, the void will remain unfilled. But the prevalence of only three rudimentary conditions render this approach unworkable: (1) the existence of suitable alternative sites for cultivation; (2) the greater appeal of profits from drug production vis-à-vis those of competing agricultural alternatives; and (3) the existence of jurisdictions where the host governments lack either the means or the will to end drug production. The first condition is a function of geography to which vast tracks of the global landscape are well suited. The second is a function of market demand that shows no signs of diminishing. And the third is dependent on political legitimacy and the effectiveness of regulatory and enforcement mechanisms, all of which are under significant strain in the post–Cold War era.

Similarly, it should be clear why interdiction initiatives that aim to stem the cross-border flows of processing chemicals, drugs, and drug moneys are ineffectual. As long as these activities can blend within the increasingly unregulated movements of people, goods, and services associated with an open global economy, enforcement efforts are reduced to futile "needle-in-the-haystack" exercises.

While begrudgingly acknowledging the dim prospect for real achievement, some might argue that these supply-side initiatives serve an important symbolic role, providing a tangible demonstration of national and international support for antidrug norms. This rationale is found wanting, however, once the costs of undertaking this essentially normative effort are considered. For example, crop eradication programs typically end up displacing production into more remote areas that are often environmentally sensitive public lands. Farmers neither own the land nor expect that their activities will go undetected over the long term, so they clear it with highly destructive slash-and-burn practices, plant and harvest a crop, and then move on. If these cultivation activities take place on mountainous terrain as is commonly the case in Southeast Asia and Latin America, erosion can produce irreversible harm to the surrounding area.[39]

In addition to displacement, some alternative development programs inadvertently facilitate the drug trade. This happens when assistance is provided to enhance the infrastructure of a drug-producing region so as to make the cultivation of other legitimate crops viable, but the farmers secretly continue to engage in illicit cultivation. The net result of these generous investments in new infrastructure is to lower the costs of moving chemicals and fertilizers into the region, and to ease the transportation burden of moving drugs to their downstream markets.

Pursuing interdiction efforts for largely symbolic reasons also can be largely counterproductive. Because criminal organizations are inherently more nimble than enforcement agencies constrained by resources and jurisdiction, new enforcement actions often end up generating incentives for traffickers to identify, exploit, and exacerbate new societal vulnerabilities. Investing in political corruption and immersing trafficking activities within the legitimate global transportation and financial sectors offer the greatest opportunities for avoiding the reach of state authorities. The consequences of these initiatives transcend drug smuggling. First, the legitimacy of governmental authority is eroded. Second, the credibility of the current global regulatory regimes that govern those sectors is undermined, inviting widespread rule-breaking. Third, the means and the incentives for drug trafficking organizations to diversify into an array of other nefarious commercial activities such as alien and weapons smuggling is ultimately enhanced.

Perhaps the greatest cost of pursuing inherently flawed supply-side policies is that it requires U.S. authorities to enter into an unholy alliance with governmental authorities who stand in direct opposition to many of the ideals Americans cherish. Undertaking antiproduction and antitrafficking initiatives mandate collaboration between U.S. officials and the host government. In the case of Burma, for example, this means cooperation with a military junta that seized power after firing on thousands of nonviolent demonstrators in 1988 and placed Nobel Prize winner Aung San Auu Kyi under house arrest for seven years. While human rights activists have strongly opposed any conciliatory gesture to the State Law and Order Restoration Council (SLORC), the DEA has lobbied hard for a relaxed official posture toward the government. The DEA's logic is straightforward: "Burma is home to most of the world's opium production. If drug control is a priority, you can't afford to be offended by the domestic policies of your enforcement allies." From a purely realist perspective, the DEA's position might be compelling if one could be confident that the SLORC leadership could end Burmese drug production with the assistance of the United States. Unfortunately, the evidence lies in the contrary direction,[40] but, despite this fact, the short-term drug policy imperatives have worked as a barrier to adopting a policy of aggressively isolating SLORC and supporting the democratic movement.

WHAT CAN BE DONE?

We need to rethink the drug war in light of the qualities of the drug trade illuminated by considering it a transsovereign problem. By overlooking its inherently transsovereign character, we overlook both a threat and an opportunity. Pursuing policies that treat the drug phenomenon primarily as an enforcement problem, we end up seeing only the proverbial tip of the iceberg as we steam at flank speed into the unfamiliar waters of the next millennium. At risk is an array of policies designed to smooth the international system's transition into the post–Cold War era. The drug issue inevitably complicates the process of modernization in the developing world; the painful political, economic, and social adjustments now underway in the post-communist world; and the difficult postindustrial transition in the developed world. While clearly not a causal variable, the drug issue also contributes to the challenges of ethnic conflict and civil war, weapons proliferation, and environmental devastation. To try to tackle all these problems without acknowledging the direct or indirect relationship of the burgeoning global drug trade seems wrong minded at best and possibly self-defeating at worse.

The opportunity lost is the chance that the drug issue provides to mobilize the general public to tackle a host of global challenges that it might otherwise be inclined to ignore. That is, to the extent that there is a growing consensus that drugs produce unacceptable levels of societal harm and human misery, there is a natural constituency for supporting programs that address the core causes of the problem that exist beyond one's national borders. The dynamic and global qualities of the drug issue make clear that a purely national response to the drug problem makes as much sense as a national response to ozone depletion. As with the rise in greenhouse emissions, a comprehensive and coordinated global response to its contributing causes is what is needed to spare the planet from the far reaching outcomes of an explosive growth in illicit drugs worldwide.

So what can be done? We must begin by completely revising the way we approach the drug control challenge. As with a growing number of other transsovereign threats such as the environment, weapons proliferation, terrorism, and disease control, our response to the emerging global drug trade must be guided by three general principles:

[1] *Coordinate drug control programs into a response that simultaneously targets all facets of the drug market.* Pursuing any one course without being mindful of

its impact on the others holds false promise. The U.S. government has been a particularly egregious practitioner of the piecemeal approach. With responsibility for drug control spread out among fifty-six departments, agencies, and bureaus, it should come as no surprise that communications and coordination between the various bureaucratic players is limited at best. The fact is that this division of labor approach has failed miserably. Each federal department or agency operates according to its own unique perspectives and policy priorities. There is a dearth of interagency input into the review process and the sum of the parts rarely equal the whole. Finally, the development of a coherent strategy has been hampered by a lack of sufficient, detailed information as to the breadth and depth of the globalization phenomenon itself. U.S. policymakers, and virtually everyone else, have been unable to see the forest for the trees. In short, we need an integrative understanding of what we are up against and an interagency process that spans the full range of governmental jurisdictions.

[2] *Embed drug control objectives within programs that redress the macro forces to which the drug phenomenon is tied.* Some possible examples: (a) Programs designed to deter the cultivation of drugs should be placed within a larger development context and programs designed to advance the development of the poorest countries should include elements that discourage the actual or potential cultivation of drugs. (b) Programs targeted at criminal drug organizations should be placed within a larger criminal justice institution-building context, and programs designed to advance institution-building in less developed or newly democratic countries should include elements that discourage the actual or potential corrosive effect of powerful organized criminal organizations. (c) Programs to combat money laundering should be lodged within regulatory conventions that increase the transparency of global financial markets and target shady financial schemes designed to evade national taxation laws or other financial regulatory regimes. (d) Programs designed to reduce consumption must be embedded in programs that promote general health and well-being and promote the protective societal factors that reduce the risk of widespread addiction to all drugs, including alcohol, nicotine, and pharmaceuticals.

[3] *Engage nonstate actors.* State-centric drug control regimes must give way to approaches that enlist the growing number of local, regional, and global actors who have a vested interest in minimizing the adverse consequences connected with the drug trade. International environmental groups, for instance, share an interest in restricting the expansion of drug production into vulnerable tropical forest lands, when cultivation is accomplished by slash-and-burn practices and when thousands of tons of refinement chemicals are dumped into local waterways. If the risk is the reintroduction of more intrusive government inspections and the associated rise in costs, transporters clearly posses a vested interest in working closely with government regulators to ensure that commercial air, land,

and sea carriers are not unwittingly used to transport contraband of all types. Finally, given the importance of the social setting in influencing drug consumption behaviors, demand reduction programs work best when they are community-based, tapping the energies of families, friends, and neighbors who share the commitment and the compassion to help prevent drug abuse in the first place and to assist in recovery in the second. As private voluntary organizations, businesses, and local, national, regional, and global nongovernmental organizations (NGOs) crowd their way onto the world stage, it seems only sensible that governments should share the burden with these nonstate actors of stemming threats that are inimical to a global community.

Any effort to engage nonstate actors must begin with a commitment to advancing public awareness of the methods of drug criminal enterprises. Law enforcement agencies instinctively tend to resist educating the public on the details of organized criminal activities. In part this is due to practical concerns of compromising an ongoing investigation or a prosecutory effort, and the pace of operations leaves little time or resources to commit to the task of education. Additionally, there are fears that publicity will compromise investigative techniques or generate imitation. While these inclinations are understandable, they need to be balanced with an appreciation of the costs associated with public ignorance. Such ignorance generates long shadows within the legitimate global economy in which organized crime can thrive. By casting a light on those shadows, vulnerable institutions and law-abiding citizens can act on their own to limit the chance that they will be victimized or inadvertently enlisted into supporting criminal activities.

A NEW TRANSSOVEREIGN FRAMEWORK

One way to work toward achieving the goals of better drug control coordination, integration, and engagement would be to form "Regional Drug Crime (RDC) Task Forces" with membership drawn from the private sector and NGO community, along with representatives from the enforcement, intelligence, financial, and judicial ministries of member nations. The RDC Task Forces would focus on identifying, promoting, and implementing private-sector initiatives and legislation throughout their respective regions with an eye toward enhancing the means to regulate domestic and international commercial activities that are currently vulnerable to organized crime. Among the initiatives the Task Forces could consider are:

[1] *Advance the adoption of a regional investment code.* Particular attention should be paid to developing meaningful and binding guidelines for trade and financial record-keeping, and these records should be made readily accessible

to enforcement authorities involved in investigative work. Specifically, access to international maritime transportation hubs should be restricted to those shippers who provide detailed manifests electronically to inspectors at transshipment points and the final destination. Additionally, no one should be allowed to make wire transfers through the interbank payment systems unless the originator and beneficiary of the transaction are documented. Enforcing this requirement would require some modification to how the transfer signal is currently constructed, but embedding this information into the message is technically feasible.

[2] *Establish guidelines and baseline information for a common global database on known criminals and their activities.* This information should be made widely available to travel agencies and financial institutions which should be called upon to conduct speedy background checks and to deny convicted criminals access to international travel and investment opportunities. Additionally, each member state should have a designated Organized Crime Intelligence Unit that is assigned the responsibility for coordinating crime intelligence collection and analysis within its borders and working with the intelligence units from other countries. Finally, the RDC Task Forces should regularly publish an "Accessories to Transsovereign Crime Report" that spotlights governments, business institutions, or individuals who routinely fail to abide by regional and international crime control conventions.

[3] *Work with private carriers and businesses to strengthen the capabilities of those involved in the international movement of legitimate goods to deter smugglers.* By developing adequate controls over the packing and shipping processes, these efforts should include providing training and technical assistance to the business community to adopt security procedures and participate in programs which deter illegal access to and use of their conveyances and cargo, their associated equipment, and company facilities located at ports and air terminals.

[4] *Actively advance legal reforms in transitional and developing countries that include sanctions against embezzlement, criminal conspiracies (RICO statutes), corruption, money laundering, and fraud.* Provide the technical and material support to build law libraries throughout the region, and to upgrade training for prosecutory work. Promote the drafting of common rules and provide training for conducting criminal investigative work including guidelines on using informants, conducting wire taps, and safeguarding evidence. Aggressively negotiate extradition treaties with all countries in the region, and adopt mutually agreeable procedures and a formula for sharing seized criminal assets.

[5] *Work to improve cultural understanding and linguistic abilities among the member nations.* This could be facilitated by establishing a common fund to train judicial, financial, intelligence, and law enforcement representatives and to support exchange programs.

Many may see the policy initiatives outlined above as impractical within the current political and budgetary environment. But if the skeptics ultimately carry the day, what alternatives remain? The projected rise of the global drug trade makes clear that one option which is unacceptable is continuing business as usual. Sticking to an approach that makes states the dominant players in drug control practically ensures that drugs will become even more widely available, and concurrently, that the criminal organizations that advance the trade will become increasingly powerful and corrosive. The only remaining logical course to pursue if we are unprepared to accept the proposals outlined above would be to consider dismantling the prohibitionary regime. In the final analysis, a failed prohibitionary approach to drug control does more harm than good because it ends up serving the interests of organized crime to a far greater extent than the interests of the collective society. If the global community is unprepared to redress the systemic weaknesses that are facilitating and motivating drug production, trafficking, and consumption, it should begin to accommodate itself to the fact that widespread drug use and its harmful social consequences are an unfortunate fact of life that is an inevitable byproduct of living in a global capitalist system.

CONCLUSION

Despite the long-standing national and international enforcement regimes designed to contain them, the persistent growth of the illicit drug trade offers a compelling case study in the precarious status of state sovereignty. The production of illicit narcotics has gravitated to areas where the writ of the state is weakest. Drug traffickers have benefitted from the same revolution in communications, transportation, trade, and finance that has made it possible for so many global businesses to pursue their ends with little concern for the traditional prerogatives of nation-states. Current and potential consumers of drugs are now free to use drugs with little or no risk of state intervention in a growing number of locales where there have been dramatic reductions in authoritarian social controls.

The success of drug traffickers reveals that there are widening holes within the global economy that are facilitating the free trade of an array of nefarious "commodities" of which drugs only rank among the more prominent. High-grade plutonium, hazardous waste, counterfeit credit cards and documents, pirated copyrighted materials, stolen vehicles, child pornography, aliens, and indentured teenage prostitutes can be found on that list. The fact is, as free trade zones and tax havens proliferate and new and largely lawless capitalist markets gain access to the international economy, global economic activity more and more has come to resemble the kind of capitalism familiar to industrialized countries at the turn of the century. Then, as today, national governments found themselves witnessing explosive economic growth largely from the sidelines. But the growth unleashed by the Industrial Revolution came at the cost of macroeconomic stability and led to widespread abuse of the environment, labor, and consumers. As the global community enters the new millennium, such negative externalities of capitalist activity cannot be absorbed as "the cost of doing business" without producing profound global dislocations.

There is a curious paradox embedded in the predicament of declining sovereignty that is playing an important role in fueling the drug trade. It is that in order to strengthen their role in the international system, states must agree to act less and less like states. That is, they must agree to embrace universal norms and empower an array of nonstate actors to advance common interests, even though these actions ultimately may limit their capacity to act independently in the pursuit of their own narrowly defined state interests. If they delay acknowledging this Faustian bargain and sovereignty continues to erode to the benefit of nonstate actors such as criminal organizations, the ailment may become terminal. The critical turning point will come when the power of criminal elements with a vested interest in an anarchical status quo co-opt some states altogether. Once that happens, the co-opted states will use their sovereign prerogatives to resist any meaningful multilateral regime that would endanger their nefarious interests.

Taking the necessary steps to prevent an irreversible erosion of the role of sovereign governments in the international system will require that the United States play a leadership role in promoting strategies of cooperative engagement, including a broad-based alliance of international and regional NGOs and the private business sector. Getting the United States to play such a role will require an antidote for the current contagion of unilateralism and isolationism afflicting the American polity. Ironically, the drug trade could potentially provide this antidote. Crime and drugs consistently rank at the very top of the list of domestic policy challenges that most worry U.S. voters. This is not surprising. Drug abuse has touched the lives of virtually every American family and it seems that each day we find ourselves confronted with the need to make new lifestyle adjustments to cope with the pervasive reach of nonviolent and violent crime. By outlining the clear linkages between forces acting well beyond our national territory and these "domestic" problems with all their local consequences, perhaps policymakers can begin to build the kind of necessary political support for sustained engagement in an array of transsovereign issues so important to the future of the United States and the global community at large.

Notes

1. More than twenty countries are now involved in the production of coca and opium. Total estimated worldwide opium gum production climbed from 2,242 metric tons in 1987 to 4,285 metric tons in 1996. Total coca leaf production grew from 291,100 metric tons to

303,600 metric tons. From U.S. Department of State, *International Narcotics Control Strategy Report (INCSR)—March 1997* (Washington, D.C.: Government Printing Office, 1997), 25.

2. "The Lycaeum" at <www.lycaem.org>, "Hyperreal" at <www.hyperreal.com>, and "Paranoia" at <www.paranoia.com> are three such sites that provide information on optimal drug dosages and "safe" administration methods, stories on drug experiences, and technical guidance on making drugs.

3. The federal drug budget has grown from $1.5 billion in 1981 to $15.2 billion in 1997 for a $128.5 billion total for that period. From Office of National Drug Control Policy, *National Drug Control Strategy—1996: Program, Resources, and Evaluation* (Washington, D.C.: Government Printing Office, 1996), 318–319. By one 1995 estimate, state and local governments spent an additional $150 billion over a fifteen-year period. See "Keeping Score: What We Are Getting for Our Federal Drug Control Dollars 1995," a report by Drugs Strategies (Washington, D.C. 1995), 1.

4. In most major American cities, heroin for a single "trip" can be purchased for $10 per bag, and a vial of crack can be had in New York City for $2. From Office of National Drug Control Policy, *Pulse Check: National Trends in Drug Abuse—Fall 1995* (Washington, D.C.: Government Printing Office, 1995), 19, 24. In 1995, the average purity for retail heroin was 39.7 percent nationwide, up from an average of 7 percent in 1985. Cocaine at the retail level had average purity levels of 61 percent and average wholesale purity levels of 83 percent in 1995. From Office of National Drug Control Policy, *National Drug Control Strategy—1997* (Washington, D.C.: Government Printing Office, 1997), 21.

5. Thomas A. Constantine, keynote address before the 17th Annual International Asian Organized Crime Conference, Boston, Massachusetts, March 8, 1995.

6. The Office of National Drug Control Policy (ONDCP) estimates that approximately 500 tons of cocaine are potentially available for consumption each year. Domestic consumption in the United States is estimated to be around 300 metric tons. This leaves about 200 metric tons available for consumers in source countries or in Europe. ONDCP also cites estimates of the amount of heroin available in the United States to range from 4 to 13 metric tons while potential global heroin production stands at 360 metric tons. From *National Drug Control Strategy—1997*, 10, 54–55.

7. U.S. seizures were 1.3 metric tons while worldwide seizures were 32 metric tons. From *National Drug Control Strategy—1997*, 54.

8. For a country-by-country breakdown, see *INCSR*, 59–492.

9. There was a substantial American missionary presence in China where, by 1906, over a quarter of all adult males were estimated to be regular opium smokers. See Arnold H. Taylor, *American Diplomacy and the Narcotics Traffic, 1900–1939* (Durham, N.C.: Duke University Press, 1969), 6. The advent of organic chemistry in the 1800s, along with the perfection of the hypodermic needle made it possible to isolate the active agents from drug plants and transform use patterns. By the mid-1890s, the United States was importing nearly eight pounds of opium per 1,000 people to be placed in a vast array of remedies ranging from cough syrup to pain relievers, mass produced by an astonishing growth in the pharmaceutical industry, and marketed aggressively through advertising. For example, the Bayer Company maintained that its heroin cough syrup, developed in 1898, "will suit the palate of the most exacting adult or the most capricious child." See David F. Musto, "Opium, Cocaine, and Marijuana in American History," *Scientific American* (July 1991): 40–47.

10. Peter D. Lowes, *The Genesis of International Narcotics Control* (New York: Arno Press, 1981), 199; and David F. Musto, *The American Disease: Origins of Narcotic Control* (New York: Oxford University Press, 1987), 35–37.

11. For a discussion of the evolution of global prohibition regimes and an evaluation of their successes and failures, see Ethan A. Nadelmann, "Global Prohibition Regimes: The Evolution of Norms in International Society," *International Organization* 44 (Autumn 1990): 479–526.

12. A *Time* editorial remarked in 1942, "The war is probably the best thing that ever happened to U.S. drug addicts." Quoted in James A. Inciardi, *The War on Drugs II: The Continuing Epic of Heroin, Cocaine, Crack, Crime, AIDS, and Public Policy* (Mountain View, Calif.: Mayfield, 1992), 24.

13. National Narcotics Intelligence Consumers Committee, *The Supply of Illicit Drugs to the United States—August 1995* (Washington, D.C.: Drug Enforcement Administration Pub. #95051, 1995), 3, 32.

14. *INCSR*, 25.

15. Kevin Monroy, "Customs Automation Captures the Imagination but Not the Crooks," *American Shipper* 35: 2 (February 1993): 42. These details were also drawn from site visits and interviews by the author with U.S. Customs Service inspectors at the Port of Newark, N.J., April 9, 1992.

16. Marcia MacLeod, "New Markets in the Old World," *Air Cargo World* 82 (July 1992): 20.

17. *Latin America and the Caribbean: A Decade After the Debt Crisis* (Washington, D.C.: World Bank, 1993), 90.

18. *Latin America*, 89–90.

19. *INCSR*, 155.

20. Craig Dunlap, "Freeport, Bahamas," *World Wide Shipping* 60 (June 1987), 32–35.

21. Foreign exchange turnover in international financial markets runs at over $1 trillion per day. The collective reserves of central banks were estimated at $565.6 billion in April 1992. From Philip Coggan, "Investment Institutions: More Power to Capital Markets," *Financial Times*, September 24, 1993.

22. Walter B. Wriston, *The Twilight of Sovereignty: How the Information Revolution Is Transforming Our World* (New York: Charles Scribner's Sons, 1992), 61.

23. Ernest H. Preeg, "The Post-Uruguay Free Trade Debate," *Washington Quarterly* 19 (Winter 1996): 230.

24. The details on the organization and operation of the Cali distribution cells were provided in a briefing to the author at Drug Enforcement Administration Headquarters on February 12, 1992 and a subsequent DEA briefing on May 18, 1994. These details were discovered after the arrest of an entire cell in New York City and the seizures of their records in December 1991. The narrative on the Cali organization draws heavily from my "Worldwide Drug Scourge: The Expanding Trade in Illicit Drugs," *Brookings Review* 11 (Winter 1993): 9–10.

25. The details of contemporary smuggling techniques were gathered from briefings provided to the author at the El Paso Intelligence Center (EPIC), December 7–8 1993; U.S. Customs field offices in Newark, N.J., April 9, 1992; and Customs and DEA field offices in Miami, January 11, 1994.

26. In one scheme, for instance, Cali cartel operatives recruit middle-aged Colombian couples to travel to Miami for short stays, provide them housing and a vehicle, and then send them on daily rounds to deposit money into banks in varying and uneven amounts under $5,000. On an average day, these couples may visit ten different branch offices, making deposits in the lobby in the morning, and then making deposits using

the drive-through windows in the afternoon (briefing to the author by DEA Field Office Miami, January 11, 1994). For a description of this and other "smurfing" activities run out of New York City, see Fredric Dannen, "Colombian Gold," *New Yorker*, (August 15, 1994): 26–31.

27. For a description of how globalization and technological change have facilitated the ease with which illegal drug profits can be laundered, see Jack A. Blum, *Enterprise Crime: Financial Fraud in International Interspace*, Working Group on Organized Crime (WGOC) Monograph Series, (Washington, D.C.: National Strategy Information Center, 1997). One example of layering practices was cited by the State Department in its 1994 International Narcotics Report: "An Asian trafficker operated more than 300 bank accounts in Hong Kong, the United States, and elsewhere in Asia. A number of these accounts were acquired when he purchased an established import/export firm, licensed in Africa, through a New York bank operating in Hong Kong. Because the shares were not publicly traded, there was no requirement to register the shares as sold, and as long as he used the same account signatories, usually nominees, none of the banks needed to be told of the change in ownership." U.S. Department of State, *International Narcotics Control Strategy Report—April 1994* (Washington, D.C.: Government Printing Office, 1994), 473.

28. Douglas Forsh and Steve Coll, "Cocaine Dollars Flow Via New Networks," *Washington Post*, September 19, 1993.

29. If this seems to be a surprising amount of time and manpower, it might be helpful to imagine how long it would take to inspect the contents of a fully loaded moving van.

30. Tony Carding, "Fastest Routes to Southeast Asia," *Intermodal Shipping* 30 (February 1995): 32.

31. Department of the Navy, The Office of Naval Intelligence, *Worldwide Maritime Challenges—1997* (Washington, D.C.: March 1997), 24.

32. Paul Scott Abbott, "Air Cargo Consolidation," *World Wide Shipping* 60 (July/August 1997): 41–42.

33. Drug traffickers are fully aware of the enormous pressure U.S. inspectors are under to facilitate the movement of goods, particularly seasonal, agricultural, and animal merchandise. One tactic they use is to smuggle the drugs among live animals. The U.S. Fish and Wildlife Administration upset one of these plans when an agent discovered 36 kgs of cocaine inside the stomachs of several dozen living boa constrictors shipped through Miami International Airport. From *ABC World News Tonight*, November 11, 1994.

34. Kathleen Walton, "Cargo Business is Hot at Sunbelt Airports," *Air Cargo World* 82 (May 1992): 30.

35. Interview by the author with U.S. Customs Service officials, El Paso, Tex., December 7–8, 1993. The U.S. Southwest Border Capital Improvement Program, which is now underway, will make road improvements to support more than twice the current traffic levels—up to 8.4 million trucks annually. From U.S. Department of Transportation, Federal Highway Administration, *Assessment of Border Crossing and Transportation Corridors for North American Trade: Report to Congress* (Washington, D.C.: Government Printing Office 1993), 7.

36. PGP is based on the RSA (Rivest-Shamir-Adleman) algorithm. "The basic mathematical idea behind public-key systems is that of the "one-way function." One-way functions are those that are much easier to perform in one direction than the other. . . . The simplest calculator can determine almost instantaneously that $987 \times 1,013 = 999,831$. But if a computer starts with the number 999,831, it will take time for the machine to

determine, through trial and error, that the number can be evenly divided by 987 and 1,013. As numbers become larger, this period of time becomes significant. . . . Finding the factors of a 200-digit number on a modern top-speed computer would require not milliseconds or minutes but at least several centuries. The task is, in computer terms, "computationally unfeasible." James Fallows, "Open Secrets," *Atlantic Monthly* (June 1994): 48.

37. *INCSR,* 512–527.
38. Portions of the next three sections of the chapter are drawn from my "Asian Drugs, Crime, and Control: Rethinking the War," in *Fires Across the Water: Transnational Problems in Asia,* ed. James Shinn (New York: Council on Foreign Relations, 1998), 18–44.
39. For an overview of the pernicious environmental effects of drug cultivation, see UN Drug Control Programme, "Illicit Narcotics Cultivation and Processing: The Ignored Environmental Drama" (Vienna, 1992).
40. The Was and Kokang in the northern Shan state signed cease-fire agreements in 1995 with SLORC and, as a result, the military reportedly does not interfere with their economic activity—which is mainly the cultivation, conversion, and sale of opium. See Josef Silverstein, "Change in Burma?" *Current History* (December 1995): 440–443. Burma's most notorious drug lord, Khun Sa, surrendered his Mong Tai Army and his Ho Mong headquarters to the military rulers in early January 1996. He traveled to Rangoon for meetings with the military in January, February, and March and negotiated an agreement that he would face neither a trial in Burma nor extradition to the United States. Foreign Broadcast Information Service, "Burma: Opposition Criticizes Government's Release of Khun Sa," FBIS-TDD-96–017-L (May 30, 1996): 73–74.

Nuclear Smuggling

Nuclear smuggling is another important transsovereign problem that is fueled by open market, open society, and open technology forces, as well as by state implosion. India and Pakistan have made public their status as nuclear states. Iraq, Iran, North Korea, and Libya have all tried or are still trying to develop nuclear weapons. But not only states are trying to buy nuclear materials, nuclear technologies, scientists, and secrets. Nonstate actors, specifically terrorist groups, have been trying to develop nuclear capacities. Aum Shinryko, the Japanese group that carried out a sarin gas attack on the Tokyo subway in 1995, was trying to obtain materials for a nuclear attack. While the bar for building a long-range nuclear weapon is still high because of the need for a reliable delivery vehicle (i.e., ballistic missile) capable of carrying a nuclear payload to its destination, the bar is low for acquiring a "dirty" nuclear device. A small amount of radioactive material, whether it is bomb grade or whether it is actually in the form of a bomb, could still wreak terror and havoc—the goal of terrorist organizations. In fact, a Chechyn separatist group has already left a small amount of radioactive material (taken from a nuclear lab in the former Soviet Union) in Gorky Park in Central Moscow, as a warning to Russian authorities to take autonomy for Chechnya seriously or they could decide to inflict more serious damage.

According to John Deutch, former director of central intelligence,

> The chilling reality is that nuclear materials and technologies are more accessible now than at any other time in history—due primarily to the dissolution of the former Soviet Union and the region's worsening economic conditions. This problem is exacerbated by the increasing diffusion of modern technology through the growth of the world market, making it harder to detect illicit diversions of materials and technologies relevant to a nuclear weapons program. . . . The protection of fissile material in the former Soviet Union has thus become even more critical at the same time that control has become more difficult . . . the breakup of the Soviet Union, the opening of Russian society, and its economic difficulties have subjected the security system to stresses and risks it was not designed to withstand.[1]

Organized crime has moved in as states have retreated, creating an active, black market in nuclear materials.[2] Highly enriched uranium and plutonium, beryllium, radium, palladium, and lithium are just some of the smuggled nuclear weapons component materials, which have been seized (often in Germany). So far the evidence shows the smuggling to be "supply-driven," prompted by the opportunity afforded by state collapse, rather than by the demand of a specific customer at the time of the theft. However, given the strains on Russian law enforcement and intelligence institutions, "officials readily admit"[3] that demand driven smuggling along traditional trade and smuggling routes (from Russia into Iran, for example) may also be taking place. While many reported nuclear smuggling attempts turn out to be frauds (in which criminals attempt to reap high profits for bogus nuclear materials), authentic smuggling cases are on the rise.[4]

Materials in civilian nuclear power and research facilities are the most vulnerable. Most facilities do not even have adequate inventories of the amount of nuclear materials they possess, making tracking and detection of theft difficult. Under the Soviet system of state- (not market-) imposed production quotas, it was not unusual for facility officials to deliberately withhold a secret cache of some of their nuclear stocks, so that if they ever had a shortfall, they could divert materials from their rainy day cache, and avoid penalties from their superiors for failure to meet state production quotas. For example, at one facility in the former Soviet Union officials noted that their accounting estimates "could be off by tens of thousands of elements."[5] Additionally, security measures at many facilities are poor to nonexistent. Sites may lack fences, guards, cameras, or sensors to detect nuclear theft. In addition to having ample opportunities for theft, many nuclear workers have increasing incentives for theft, as the Russian fiscal crisis leaves workers unpaid or underpaid.

The United States has responded with the Nunn-Lugar-Dominici Cooperative Threat Reduction Program, through which the U.S. military and the Department of Energy have been trying to contain this threat stemming from Soviet state collapse and the weakness of successor state institutions. The program has instituted direct government-to-government and nuclear lab-to-lab contacts to increase security and reduce proliferation of former Soviet nuclear materials. The primary focus of these efforts has been creating and improving nuclear material protection, control, and accounting (MPC&A) systems in the former Soviet Union. The program was slow to get underway given bureaucratic infighting in Washington, uncertain congressional support, and suspicion and difficulty dealing with the Russian nuclear energy ministries MINATOM and GAN. Although a great many of these start-up problems have been smoothed out, the program focuses entirely on the former Soviet Union, and primarily on bilateral relations with Russia. As a result, the United States knows practically nothing about nuclear materials smuggling taking place along traditional, and more likely smuggling routes along the Transcaucasus into Iran, Iraq, Afghanistan, Pakistan, etc. Many of the seizures of nuclear materials that have taken place have occurred purely by fortuitous accident, rather than through any strong or systematic multilateral efforts. United Nations efforts to stem nuclear proliferation through inspections by the International Atomic Energy Association (IAEA) have faltered due to chronic UN underfunding, as well as the inability of the monitoring agency to force states to allow them in for surprise inspections.

Notes

1. John Deutch, "Testimony to the Permanent Subcommittee on Investigations of the Senate Committee on Government Affairs," March 20, 1996, 1–2.

2. Tim Zimmerman, "The Russian Connection," *U.S. News and World Report,* October 21, 1995.

3. James L. Ford, "Nuclear Smuggling: How Serious A Threat?" *Strategic Forum* (Washington, D.C.: National Defense University Institute for National Strategic Studies, January 1996), 3.

4. Data drawn from James L. Ford, "Nuclear Smuggling: How Serious A Threat?" and testimony to the Permanent Subcommittee on Investigations of the Senate Committee on Governmental Affairs, March 20–21, 1996; United States General Accounting Office, "Nuclear Nonproliferation: Status of U.S. Efforts to Improve Nuclear Material Controls in Newly Independent States," March 1996; Center for Strategic and International Studies (CSIS), Global Organized Crime Project; and Greg Koblentz, "The Fissile Drizzle" (Washington, D.C.: Center for Defense Information, August 1994).

5. Minority Staff Statement, Permanent Subcommittee on Investigations of the Senate Committee on Government Affairs, Hearings on Global Proliferation of Weapons of Mass Destruction: Illicit Trafficking in Nuclear Materials, March 22, 1996, 5.

Chapter Three

Nuclear Smuggling

Rensselaer W. Lee and James L. Ford

THE NATURE OF NUCLEAR SMUGGLING

Cases of illicit transactions in nuclear materials, more often referred to as nuclear smuggling, have occurred over the last twenty-plus years virtually throughout the world, including the United States.[1] Of the 450 reported attempts of illegal trafficking recorded by the U.S. Department of Energy through 1994, most proved to be nothing more than profit-motivated scams involving bogus materials, such as "red mercury," and perpetrated by opportunists.[2]

But the end of the Cold War turned what had been a minor nuisance into a major transsovereign issue, as Dr. John Holdren, chairman of the President's Committee on Science and Technology, noted in August 1995. "There is now a clear and present danger that the essential ingredients of nuclear bombs could fall into the hands of radical states or terrorist groups."[3]

The unprecedented leakage of nuclear materials from the former Soviet Union in 1994 signaled a clear shift in the nature and significance of the nuclear smuggling problem. While Western and Central European government officials, including the Russians, recognized that the reporting of such incidents was incomplete and of mixed reliability, there were unmistakable new trends: increases observed in the numbers of attempted transactions, increases in the number of participants, and increases in the types and quantities of nuclear materials offered for sale.[4] The trafficking was no longer limited to bogus or nuclear-associated materials, such as beryllium or cesium, but included significant quantities of the core materials necessary for making nuclear weapons, highly enriched uranium and plutonium.[5]

Understanding the Threat: Not Just a Bomb

Experts agree that obtaining a sufficient amount of special nuclear material (SNM) is the single most difficult challenge in the construction of a nuclear weapon. The technical difficulty and expense of acquiring such material provided the principal barrier against the proliferation of nuclear weapons during the Cold War. Although still a significant challenge, that barrier has now been breached and is no longer as formidable as it once was.

John Sopko, deputy chief counsel to former Senator Sam Nunn of Georgia, noted several other significant changes to the mid-1990s proliferation threat: the actors themselves, the types of materials involved, and the means of delivery.[6]

No longer is the possibility of a rogue state, such as Iran, Iraq, or Libya, acquiring enough SNM to construct one or more rudimentary nuclear weapons the sole threat, nor perhaps is this scenario the most likely or worrisome. Other possibilities include substate groups or even disgruntled individuals using nuclear materials to construct an improvised nuclear device (IND) or a radiological dispersal device (RDD). An IND is designed to produce a nuclear explosion but has a lower yield, either by design or fault, and will greatly increase the radioactive fallout (a "dirty bomb"). An RDD produces a conventional explosion designed to scatter radioactive materials to contaminate an area, thus spreading fear and insecurity among inhabitants. These scenarios not only broaden the threat in terms of available materials and technologies, but also increase the pool of potential proliferators and the likelihood of an incident.

The dissolution of the former Soviet Union made large quantities of weapons-usable materials (not just radioactive medical isotopes or spent nuclear fuel) susceptible to theft or diversion while the security of at-risk facilities diminished, a paradox typical of transsovereign problems. Special nuclear material facilities and activities in the former Soviet Union no longer receive the same level of protection, control, and monitoring from the State Security Committee (KGB), the Russian Army, or other former Soviet control organs. In addition, there is no accurate and complete inventory of special nuclear materials in the former Soviet Union.

Delivery on target also has been simplified, especially in terms of an IND or RDD. It is not necessary to have sophisticated military aircraft or missile delivery systems. Terrorists can load one of these devices into a van and deliver it on target, in much the same manner as occurred at the World Trade Center in New York City or at the Federal Building in Oklahoma City.

In a Senate hearing in August 1995, Senator Sam Nunn described the nuclear threat emerging from the fall of the former Soviet Union as "creat[ing] scenarios that, even if anticipated, are unfathomable in their scope. Never before in history has an empire disintegrated while in possession of some 30,000 nuclear weapons, at least 40,000 tons of chemical weapons, significant biological weaponry capability, and thousands of weapons scientists and technicians unsure of how long they will receive salaries with which to feed their families. Let loose was a vast potential supermarket for nuclear weapons, weapons-grade uranium and plutonium, and equally deadly chemical and biological weapons."[7] Senator Nunn's concerns are echoed in findings from investigations of the nuclear black market conducted at Harvard[8] and at the Center for Strategic and International Studies, Washington, D.C.[9]

The threat is multifaceted. It can appear in many guises and be sustained by a multitude of motivations. While the supply of nuclear materials attractive to terrorist and criminal groups resides in a handful of states, the demand is more widespread and may very well include substate groups or even individuals, in addition to the so-called rogue states. Increasing amounts of nuclear material in the former Soviet Union are now more susceptible to theft. Meanwhile, political and social turmoil throughout the world increases the attractiveness of theft of nuclear material as a means to amassing power, exerting influence or seeking retribution.

Although policymakers and analysts are not in complete agreement about the severity of the nuclear smuggling threat, there does appear to be general consensus in the national security community that current patterns of nuclear smuggling may be a prelude to more serious episodes, including major covert exports of fissile material, weapon components, and even intact nuclear weapons. The current level of nuclear smuggling opens new criminal trade channels and increases opportunities for proliferation of weapons of mass destruction.[10]

How Serious Is the Problem?

The true dimensions of the current nuclear trafficking threat are not known with certainty. The handful of diversion incidents involving weapons-usable materials that have been recorded to date do not tell the whole story. Governments reveal little about nuclear theft and smuggling episodes, and government information channels themselves may be impaired. For example, the Russian government over the years has issued statements that "not a single gram of plutonium is moving from storage," and that no diversions of nuclear warheads or weapons-grade fissile materials have taken place in Russia. Yet, Western investigations indicate that the plutonium smuggled to Munich in August 1994 was from a Russian facility near Moscow. There is also reliable evidence that two nuclear warheads were stolen from a weapons assembly plant in the Urals in 1993 (fortunately, the warheads were later recovered). Furthermore, according to one credible Russian observer, criminal groups have been able to commandeer the isotope separation services of Russian nuclear plants and to export the products, including enriched reactor-grade and weapons-grade uranium, to various end-user countries in the Middle East and south Asia. The latter scenario is especially unsettling and points to a serious possible weakness, if not an outright breakdown, in Russia's nuclear control system.[11]

Law enforcement and security officials in the newly independent states (NISs) are able to intercept only a portion of materials diverted from criminal enterprises, some 30 to 40 percent in the Russian case according to an estimate by Russia's Federal Security Bureau (FSB); much of the rest is transported abroad or simply discarded.[12] Transstate smuggling chains have emerged to peddle stolen materials outside the NISs, principally in the Central European market. Although small compared to other illegal commodity flows (such as weapons or drugs), illegal global commerce in nuclear materials is hardly inconsequential, as different statistical indicators attest.

The UN's International Atomic Energy Agency (IAEA) database identifies 132 confirmed incidents of international nuclear smuggling, reflecting principally seizure data, between 1993 and 1996.[13] The German Federal Intelligence Service (BND), which also maintains a global database, reports more than five hundred cases of seizures, thefts, offers, or threats involving nuclear-related materials in the period 1992 through 1996. Within Germany, the principal Western European entrepôt for nuclear trafficking, the German Federal Criminal Police, the Bundeskriminalamt (BKA), recorded 84 actual seizures and more than 576 apparently genuine offers to sell nuclear materials between 1992 and 1996. In Poland, a key transit country for illegal nuclear commerce, border authorities detected an astounding 2,045 attempts to import radiation-causing substances between 1991 and 1996, mostly across the country's eastern frontier. In such cases, perpetrators were turned back at the border. How many such "turnbacks" were true smuggling events and how many were innocuous (involving, for example, persons wearing radium-dial wristwatches or radioactive surgical implants) cannot be determined from the data.[14]

BKA, BND, and IAEA data are highlighted in Tables 3–1 and 3–2. The data point in the same direction, indicating a marked decline in nuclear smuggling activity after 1994 or 1995. One possible explanation is that smugglers have learned the futility and nonprofitability of peddling stolen nuclear wares.

Qualitative factors such as the configuration of the nuclear "black market" and the sophistication of the actors involved in it are more difficult to measure.

Table 3–1

Trends in Nuclear Crime: Germany

Activity	1992	1993	1994	1995	1996	Totals
Fraudulent offers of nuclear materials	59	118	85	40	28	330
Cases of suspected trafficking in nuclear materials	99	123	182	123	49	576
Seizures	18	21	19	19	7	84

Source: German Federal Criminal Police.

Table 3–2						
Worldwide Nuclear Smuggling Incidents						
Source	1992	1993	1994	1995	1996	Total
BND	52	56	124	177	112	521
IAEA	NA	43	45	27	17	132[1]

[1] Only two trafficking incidents were reported by the IAEA in 1997, as of May of that year.
Sources: German Federal Intelligence Services, International Atomic Energy Agency.

Such factors are subjects of much controversy, both in the West and in Russia. Viable evidence from seizures and other law enforcement data suggests that the nuclear smuggling business qualifies more as a minor international nuisance rather than a world-class strategic threat.[15] Few weapon-usable materials are offered for sale, bona fide buyers seldom materialize, and amateur criminals and small-time traders rather than large underworld organizations dominate the supply chain for nuclear materials.

Yet such a view probably is incomplete and misleading. On the one hand, the traffic has considerable upside potential as a specialty business; this means that smugglers can learn from their mistakes, and increase the sophistication and lethality of their operations. As a recent report published by the National Defense University in Washington notes: "Current patterns of nuclear theft and smuggling may be a prelude to more serious episodes, including major covert exports of fissile material, weapons components and even intact nuclear weapons. The current level of nuclear smuggling opens new criminal trade channels and increases potential opportunities for proliferation of weapons of mass destruction."[16] Furthermore, unsettled political and economic conditions in the NISs, reflected in diminished security and controls in their nuclear establishments, contribute to the risk of nuclear breakout scenarios.

More ominously, some tantalizing evidence suggests that the nuclear smuggling business already may be evolving in new and dangerous directions and that sophisticated mechanisms for diverting sensitive nuclear materials are firmly in place, at least in Russia. A possible hypothesis is that two vastly different markets for nuclear materials coexist in post-communist Eurasia: one in the disorganized, supply-driven, and amateurish traffic pattern that is visible to Western analysts and policymakers; the other is a shadow market organized by professionals and brokered by criminals or corrupt officials that poses an immediate proliferation danger and a direct challenge to Western security. The shape and extent of the shadow market are difficult to ascertain; yet a few credible accounts of its functioning underscore the fragility of nuclear control systems in the NISs and the inherent limitations of Western counterproliferation policies and initiatives in these states.

As U.S. proliferation experts Barry Kellman and David Gualtieri noted, "The crucial truth about nuclear smuggling is that most of what is happening is covert and inferring the magnitude of the flow or the intentions of the actors from a small share of the known picture very likely is misleading."[17] Successful black market transactions are by their very nature likely to go unnoticed.[18]

THE PRICE OF A MORE OPEN SOCIETY

The collapse of the USSR was so swift and so complete that it left a void in the government, economic, and social infrastructure of Russia and other NISs. The transition to more open societies that is taking place there has made possible the soaring illegal trade in nuclear weapons materials. This unintended side effect constitutes a particularly alarming form of transsovereign criminality associated with the much-desired move toward greater political democratization and market-based economies.

The Impact of the Collapse of the Soviet Government

Nuclear crime was uncommon in the Soviet period. Although uranium thefts were reported at the Elektrostal Machine Building Plant in 1967 and at Krasnoyarsk-26, a fuel reprocessing facility, in 1971, the Russian criminal code did not incorporate laws against illegal acquisition, possession, transport, and use of radioactive materials until 1988.[19] Since the disintegration of the USSR, Russian and other NIS facilities-fuel cycle enterprises, research institutes, submarine bases, and even weapons assembly plants, have reported hundreds of thefts of such materials.

Modern-day nuclear criminality could not have existed within the framework of the Soviet totalitarian state. As a recent Harvard study notes, "one of the few benign results of that system was the unquestioned control of weapons-usable nuclear materials and nuclear weapons. The disappearance of the Soviet order and the collapse of communism, though, swept away this apparatus of repression exposing glaring weaknesses in NIS's nuclear security systems. As a result, "a vast potential supermarket" of nuclear wares is becoming increasingly accessible to would-be thieves and criminal proliferators.[20]

During the Soviet period, nuclear materials security focused on preventing outsiders from penetrating or spying on the nuclear complex, not on preventing knowledgeable insiders from taking radioactive and fissile materials out of enterprises and institutes. Essential features of Soviet nuclear security included multiple and overlapping internal controls (tightly guarded frontiers and remote

nuclear weapons complexes). Noteworthy centers of weapons design and production were the so-called secret cities, which were off limits to foreigners or to
anyone not cleared for access. The presence of the KGB was ubiquitous, even at
civilian nuclear facilities. For instance, the Kurchatov Institute in Moscow was
protected as a "special military object," and KGB guards were stationed on the
Institute's perimeter and within its buildings.[21]

Physical attributes of protection—fences, gates, locks, monitoring systems,
and the like—were modest, if not primitive by Western standards and by the late
Soviet period, were in a deteriorating state. Many enterprises were not equipped
with specialized equipment to deter employees from walking off the site with
nuclear materials. Yet in the authoritarian matrix of the Soviet Union, the nuclear
complex was practically secure against break-ins; moreover, isolation from the
outside world and the lack of buyers or brokers from nuclear substances practically eliminated incentives for insider thefts at enterprises at least until the late
Soviet period.

The collapse of the Soviet Union after August 1991 coincided with the disintegration of communist control structures and the opening of borders, as well
as with significant political and economic turmoil within the NISs. The impact
of these changes on civilian and defense nuclear enterprises in Russia and other
NISs was catastrophic. The system of physical protection which had depended
on pervasive direct control by the central government began to unravel. The
KGB was replaced by polyglot contingents of guards of uncertain reliability
operating under different auspices: Ministry of Atomic Energy (MINATOM)
and affiliated companies, the MVD, the KGB's successor agencies (the Federal
Counterintelligence Service and the Federal Security Service), and the individual enterprises themselves. The closed cities, which had no real raison d'être
other than the production of nuclear weapons became virtual economic "basket
cases" (in the words of one U.S. defense conversion expert).[22] At the same time
the overall security environment began to deteriorate in the cities. As the city
manager of one weapons development complex, Penza-19, noted, "The previous
system was based on regulations and ordinances which either no longer are in
place or [are] not effective and/or military discipline and a sense of responsibility which no longer exist."[23] Some cities experienced an influx of thieves, prof-
iteers, and criminals, which catalyzed the growth of nuclear-related crime. Thefts
(though not strategically significant ones) of nuclear and radioactive material
have been recorded at least at four locations—Arzamas-16, Chelyabinsk-70,
Chelyabinsk-65, and Sverdlovsk-45—during the 1992–1994 period. A potential exists for more serious episodes. Arzamas-16 (Sarov), where crime was virtually unknown in the Soviet period, reportedly housed 3,500 ex-convicts as of
1996. "Crime is worsening" at Arzamas, reads one assessment. "How can we
talk about physical protection at a nuclear facility," one Arzamas resident is

quoted as saying, "if criminals carrying firearms and terrorizing inhabitants with car bombings are freely walking the streets of the closed city?"[24]

The potential for thefts and illegal diversions of weapons-usable materials remains high in the secret cities. The bulk of reported incidents, though, occurred in civilian research institutes and fuel cycle enterprises and in the Russian Northern Fleet storage depots for submarine fuel; overall custodianship of nuclear materials at these sites tended to be weaker than in weapons complexes. Facilities such as the Chepetsk Mechanical Plant in Udmurtia, the Elektrostal Machine Building Plant and the Obninsk Institute of Physics and Power Engineering experienced multiple leakages in this period. In 1993 alone, according to the Russian MVD, employees of Russia's nuclear facilities made seven hundred attempts to "take out strictly protected materials and important technological documents." In the same year, the MVD recorded nine hundred attempts to gain unauthorized access to institutes and nuclear enterprises.[25] Internal controls and physical safeguards clearly had eroded to a dangerous extent.

The Impact of Open Society

Without the repressive controls of the Soviet period, the nuclear sectors of the NISs are painfully vulnerable both to penetration and theft. Activities that were once tightly monitored by the KGB and other control organs of the Soviet state are no longer watched over so carefully. This is the case with the protection, control, and accountability of the former Soviet Union's nuclear material, especially that outside the control of the military. Some of the old institutions have disappeared, the missions of others have changed, and some have suffered deep cutbacks in personnel and resources.

Physical safeguards such as radioactive monitoring devices and metal detectors, where they exist, are antiquated or defective. Perimeter walls and fences are frequently in disrepair. For example, according to Russian nuclear proliferation expert Vladimir Orlov, twenty-seven of thirty-seven kilometers of the guarded territory at the Elektrokhimpribor nuclear weapons plant (at Sverdlovsk-45) are "out of order," guaranteeing "practically free access" to the facility. Also, trucks that carry nuclear warheads out of the plant are able to "drive in without admittance documents."[26] In another case cited by a correspondent for *Obshchaya Gazeta*, a group of ecologists in the city of Perm (near the Urals) conducted an exercise to try to penetrate a nuclear weapons depot located in a forest outside the city. The "depot" proved to be ordinary aircraft hangars crammed with warheads. The mock "terrorists" encountered "no special difficulty" (according to *Obshchaya Gazeta*'s account) in crossing all the security barriers and within minutes had reached the hangars.[27] At the Sevmorput submarine base in Murmansk, the site of a diversion of 4.5 kilograms of highly enriched uranium (HEU) nuclear fuel in 1993, fences had holes and the alarms connecting the guard post to the storage building containing the uranium had rusted out.[28] Gaining access to the fuel storehouse was child's play, according to Mikhail Kulik of the Northern Fleet's Military Procuracy, who investigated the case.[29]

Following the Soviet government's collapse, storage conditions at many research facilities were extremely insecure. For example, at the Kurchatov Institute's Building-116—a research reactor site housing at least fifty kilograms of 96 percent HEU and a larger quantity of less-enriched uranium—no metal detectors existed to deter theft until 1994. Employees were not searched on entering or leaving the premises, and the fence surrounding the building reportedly "had holes in it that the staff often used as a shortcut to the cafeteria."[30] Similar conditions existed in Kazakstan and other NIS settings.[31]

Conditions in the larger society highlighted the threat posed by lax security safeguards at enterprises. In the post-Soviet (and post-KGB) era, individual security guards are open to bribes to permit nuclear materials to pass through checkpoints. "Guards will turn off any alarm system for a few moments for one thousand rubles," commented an unnamed nuclear dealer, referring to security conditions at Elektrostal' in mid-1993. "But if you have to bring out a kilo it will be much more expensive—and not in rubles."[32] Moreover, in the prevailing climate of crime and corruption, police officers, security operatives, and other officials might be tempted to accept payoffs or to dabble in trading radioactive materials themselves.

A further proliferation danger arises from inadequate accounting and control of nuclear materials in the NISs. Weapons-usable uranium and plutonium are stored at widely scattered sites. Principal locations include 80 to 100 facilities encompassing several institutes, fuel cycle enterprises, weapons assembly plants and naval fuel storehouses. Each facility, though, may comprise several storage areas; hence, in Russia, the State Atomic Inspection Agency Gosatomnadzor (GAN) estimates that the total number of individual locations with uranium and plutonium may be close to 1,000.[33] Because GAN currently enjoys little or no access to the defense nuclear sector (weapons assembly plants, plants producing nuclear explosives, naval fuel storehouses, and the like), the actual number is likely to be even higher. Introducing comprehensive and up-to-date control systems at such dispersed locations as these is a daunting challenge for Russia's nuclear containment policy.

Counting the material stored at different sites represents another challenge. Inventory control practices prevailing in Soviet times emphasized checking documents and containers rather than actual stocks. Because there is no state system for materials accounting in Russia or other NISs, managers of facilities housing large quantities of weapons-usable uranium or plutonium often do not know how much material they have, or whether any is missing. According to an American intelligence source cited in an August 29, 1994, *Newsweek* article, some Russian research laboratories "haven't opened up containers for decades to see if the nuclear material inside matches what was listed on their inventories."[34] Furthermore, according to a recent report by the National Research Council, some enterprises in Russia maintained stocks of material "off the books," which suggests that inventory records, where they exist, may be unreliable.[35] Currently, many NIS enterprises are beginning the laborious process of checking physical inventories at specific locations against the amounts that should be there according to documents.

A related problem concerned the Soviet practices of using standard estimates of rates of loss during fissile materials production instead of measuring actual losses. At the Luch' Scientific-Production Association in Podolsk, for example, an engineer removed 1.5 kilograms of weapons-grade uranium from the plant in twenty to twenty-five separate division episodes between May and September 1995. Laboratory procedures at Luch' allowed for a percentage of "irretrievable loss" in technical operations with the material; moreover, there were no radiation monitors at the doors of the plant. Hence, the theft went undetected (the thief was later arrested at the Podolsk railway station trying to carry the uranium to Moscow to look for a buyer).[36]

Also lacking in the Soviet period were material control systems to monitor and establish custody over nuclear material. According to U.S. nuclear experts, such a system comprises four main elements: equipping containers and vaults with seals that can indicate when tampering may have occurred, using badges and personnel identification equipment to control access to nuclear material areas, installing television cameras to maintain surveillance over nuclear inventories, and requiring two or more authorized persons to be present when materials are removed from storage.[37] Such procedures have just begun to be introduced at NIS nuclear facilities.

Most of the nuclear smuggling cases to date have involved opportunistic thieves, "insiders" within the vast Russian nuclear complex who took something of perceived value to which they had access, then tried to sell it for personal gain. Some acted individually, while others co-opted a small number of accomplices. Lacking a comprehensive analysis, it is difficult to say just what motivated these people to act—perhaps need in some cases, but most assuredly greed and the hope of making big money in others. One thing is certain: The collapse of the Soviet government had an impact on every facet of society in Russia and the other NISs. It made possible not only the betterment of many aspects of people's lives, but also the desperation felt by many as they struggle through the transition.

CONFLICTING GOALS OF OPEN SOCIETY VERSUS NUCLEAR SECURITY

Transsovereign problems often manifest themselves during a time of transition, which by its very nature can be characterized by crisis, or at a minimum, competing or even conflicting goals. Within Russia and the other NISs, those forces in support of the goals of more democratization and market-based economies in open societies must compete against those who would engage in, among other things, illicit trafficking in nuclear materials.

Open Society's Crisis

Proliferation dangers abound in the NISs, where countries undergoing difficult political and economic transitions face (in varying degrees) crises of authority and legitimacy. In Russia, the central government's control over nuclear weapons-usable materials and exports of sensitive nuclear goods appears increasingly problematic.[38] Strains of privatization and defense conversion are taking a toll on the nuclear establishments in the NIS, and are pushing many nuclear employees to the brink of economic ruin. Salaries in parts of the Russian nuclear establishment, especially in scientific research and weapons design facilities, fall well below the national average, and delays in payment of three to four months are common. A breakdown in discipline and moral standards coupled with a growing free-market mentality also creates an atmosphere conducive to nuclear materials trafficking. Powerful bureaucratic actors such as MINATOM are more interested in generating revenues and protecting the livelihood of employees (MINATOM reportedly employs or supports over 1 million people) than in promoting counterproliferation goals. Economically hard-pressed governments may "emphasize profits over nonproliferation" and turn a blind eye to violations of their own export control regimes.[39] In general, conditions in Russia and the NISs favor the growth of global black and gray markets that "could greatly accelerate the rate of proliferation by other states desiring nuclear arms."[40]

The former Soviet countries also appear to lack a nuclear security "culture" or philosophy, an internalized appreciation of the risks that proliferation entails.[41] A Russian observer, Valeriy Davydov of the Russian-American press information agency writes that "the Russian government has never paid serious attention to the illegal traffic in radioactive materials or to related issues of public health and nuclear proliferation." Western alarms following the Munich seizures, notes Davydov, produced strong diplomatic pressures that forced Moscow to take a "more cooperative stance" on countersmuggling issues.[42]

The Economy of the Nuclear Sector

Hard times befell the individual member states of the former USSR following the collapse of the Soviet order. In Russia, which contains the vast majority of nuclear sites housing weapons-grade materials, gross domestic product (GDP) has dropped 55 percent since 1992 and continued in a downward spiral through 1996, when GDP fell 7 percent. Russia's economy recorded a small gain of 0.4 percent in 1997. However, the industrial economy of Soviet times has almost collapsed. Defense orders in Russia dropped 68 percent from 1991 to 1992.[43] The machine-building industry shrank by more than 80 percent from 1992 to 1996.[44] General economic decline and the absence of new orders for nuclear weapons have forced a major downsizing of the atomic energy industry. As a result, the entire nuclear fuel cycle is paralyzed for lack of funds. According to a December 1996 report in the *Moscow Tribune,* Russia's nuclear complex (excepting power stations) still is owed $564 million for products already supplied to the state and other purchases; moreover, unpaid wages in the industry total $100 million.[45] At the Kurchatov Institute fully 73 percent of invoices were still outstanding as of late October 1996, and in many cases payments were received in the form of promissory notes rather than in cash.[46]

Downsizing of the nuclear complex and a generally poor economic outlook produced a catastrophic effect on employee well-being and morale. Scientists cleared for work in nuclear enterprises were once the cream of Soviet society, and enjoyed a higher standard of living than their colleagues in nonsecret lines of work. Now they are among the worst paid, receiving salaries as low as $50 per month. According to Vladimir Orlov, salaries of personnel working with nuclear weapons and weapons-grade materials at Arzamas-16 (Sarov) exceeded the minimum subsistence level by a factor of 4.5 in 1991, but averaged only one-third of the subsistence minimum throughout 1996. "And this is for people with nuclear bombs in their hands," commented Orlov.[47] In 1996, salaries at some MINATOM facilities were only one-third to three-fifths the national average; employees within the Ministry of Defense's direct chain of command fared somewhat better. The head of Russia's nuclear inspection agency stated in early 1994 that "highly qualified specialists who work in secret nuclear towns earn less than the cleaning women who work in the Moscow subway."[48] Payment of wages tends to be irregular, but this also is true of most of the rest of the Russian military-industrial complex. Reflecting these problems, monthly strikes and work stoppages have been reported in several of Russia's so-called secret cities.

Psychological factors—a sense of loss of function and purpose among enterprise employees—also exacerbate the soaring rate of nuclear crime. "Unneeded and unwanted, forlorn and forgotten" is how the Kurchatov Institute's security director, Nikolai Bondarev, describes nuclear workers.[49] "In just a few years, these people have gone from being valuable and respected members of society to being superfluous," Yevgeniy Korolev, a former nuclear scientist who heads a trading consortium in Ekaterinburg, declared in September 1994. "They are stealing not just to make a living, but also because they are angry."[50]

Further problems concern the quality and reliability of the nuclear workforce. Nuclear enterprises face a hemorrhaging of talent especially among younger people. Security clearances for new employees are perfunctory or are waived entirely (in the Soviet period, prospective employees underwent extensive background checks, carried out by the KGB).[51] Finally, discipline and control within the nuclear workforce have deteriorated because many employees hold down outside jobs to make ends meet. By 1994, fully half of the Kurchatov Institute's employees moonlighted in various commercial structures, joint ventures and laboratories, according to Kurchatov security chief Bondarev.[52]

The general malaise affecting NIS nuclear complexes has engendered criminality and corruption at higher levels of nuclear decision-making, clouding the lines between criminal behavior and deliberate state policy. "Because the materials that the Atomic Energy Ministry controls certainly is the goal of serious business deals—such deals are not always legal," says Aleksandr Emelyanenkov, deputy editor of the Moscow magazine *Observer*. Emelyanenkov and other observers suspect that ostensibly private companies set up under MINATOM's aegis have been conduits for undercover export of nuclear materials, technology, and know-how.[53]

In the view of U.S. specialists, MINATOM's insouciance about nuclear security and proliferation dangers is evident in the Ministry's nuclear cooperation agreements with Iran—a country that reportedly is actively procuring technology components for atomic weapons manufacture. In a 1995 protocol with Iran's Atomic Energy Organization, MINATOM agreed to an extensive nuclear cooperation package that included completion of a 1,000-megawatt nuclear reactor for a power plant in Bushehr and negotiations are underway to build three more. Estimates of the total value of signed contracts and planned deals with Iran range from $3 billion to $8 billion. Russia also plans to sell two light water reactors to India, an undeclared nuclear state that has refused to sign the nonproliferation treaty; the value of that deal is estimated at $3 to $4 million. In MINATOM's view, revenue streams from these arrangements clearly outweighed the risks of advancing Iran's or India's technology and skills for nuclear weapons-making.

Nuclear Smuggling's Appeal (Proximate Causes)

The various structural problems of Russian nuclear enterprises—weak physical safeguards, primitive accounting practices, and an economically desperate and an increasingly undisciplined workforce—create a fertile environment for insider thefts of nuclear material. Some anecdotal evidence, though, suggests that nuclear criminality among enterprise employees and their outside associates is aggravated by media hype about the escapades of nuclear criminals and about fabulous prices allegedly paid for stolen wares and by police intervention in the market to trap unwary thieves and smugglers. For instance, Yuriy Smirnov, the engineer who made off with 1.5 kilograms of weapons-grade uranium from the Luch' Scientific Production Association, recounted that articles in *Komsomolskaya Pravda* (a Moscow newspaper) about people who made big money from stolen uranium gave him the idea.[54] Certainly the media deserves a share of the blame, especially when guilty of arousing the expectations of prospective nuclear criminals.

Arranged purchases by law enforcement operatives are another proximate cause of nuclear theft and smuggling episodes. A classic Western sting operation culminated in the well-publicized seizure of plutonium in Munich in August 1996. BND and Bavarian land police operatives offered the suppliers a bank credit of $276 million to bring 4 kilograms of plutonium from Moscow to Munich, of which the confiscated 363 grams was the first installment. A MINATOM official initially described the Munich incident as a provocation designed to make Russian nuclear safeguards appear lax and to force Russia to accept Western specialists and technical assistance to plug the leak in MINATOM enterprises. "They want our nuclear industry to be under international control," said MINATOM public relations head Georgiy Kaurov.[55] Indeed, only one of the four main Western smuggling cases in 1994—the discovery of more than six grams of nearly pure plutonium-239 in a businessman's garage in Tengen Wiechs, Germany—was not attributable to a sting operation. In that case, police were investigating the businessman, Adolf Jaekle, for a totally unrelated crime, intent to distribute counterfeit money.

The absence of buyers has provoked commentaries contending that the police operations are creating an artificial demand for radioactive material and that the operations are driven by bureaucratic or political motives. In Munich, the 1994 plutonium seizure precipitated a full-blown investigation by the German Parliamentary Control Commission into the legality of offers of money to smugglers to buy foreign plutonium. The presiding judge handed out relatively light sentences to the three smugglers, concluding that they "were provoked to commit the crime."[56]

In Russia, bureaucratic warfare has erupted between MINATOM and law enforcement agencies over appropriate methods of controlling nuclear leakage from enterprises. MINATOM chief Viktor Mikhailov has bitterly denounced "provocateurs" within the MVD who prey on the economic vulnerabilities of nuclear workers. He cited a 1995 visit to the Chepetsk Machine Building Plant in Glazov, Udmurtia, where MVD officials offered workers large sums of money for the depleted waste uranium, in an ostensible effort "to identify possible channels," a clear provocation according to Mikhailov.[57]

RESOLVING THE NUCLEAR SMUGGLING PROBLEM

The IAEA has collected and analyzed the available data on nuclear smuggling incidents, and in some cases the actual nuclear material recovered from smuggling attempts. Nongovernmental organizations (NGOs), both in the United States and abroad, have also been active in publicizing the proliferation threats to national and international security, as well as the hazards to the world's environment and public health from trafficking in nuclear materials. These organizations range from the international press and more serious media to the U.S. National Academy of Science and the Union of Concerned Scientists. There is a role for all.

Yet, the IAEA and even more so the NGOs are limited in what assistance they can bring to bear on the transsovereign problem of nuclear smuggling. Unlike other transsovereign problems (drugs, disease, the environment, refugees) discussed in this volume, nuclear smuggling involves another dimension. Nuclear materials are manufactured in strictest secrecy and controlled by only a handful of states, the five announced nuclear powers of the United States, Russia, Great Britain, France, and China, and a few others (to include Israel, India, and Pakistan). There is, therefore, an understandable reluctance on the part of Russia as the primary inheritor of the Soviet nuclear complex and arsenal, as well as the other nuclear successor states of Belarus, Ukraine, and Kazakstan, to seek assistance from international organizations such as the IAEA. The IAEA's inspection teams could include members from nonnuclear powers. Ironically, to allow them access to highly classified processes of nuclear material protection, control and accountability (MPC&A) could conceivably have the undesirable effect of actually fostering proliferation. Therefore, the United States and other Western countries have provided the bulk of assistance to counter nuclear smuggling to Russia and other NISs on a bilateral basis.

Against this backdrop, serious efforts are underway to bolster the counterproliferation regime in Russia and other former Soviet states. Helped by the United States and other Western countries, the NISs are improving safeguards at enterprises housing sensitive nuclear materials, strengthening export control legislation, training law enforcement officials, and upgrading customs posts along NIS borders. (The United States spent approximately $140 to $150 million in fiscal year 1998 on such projects.) At year-end of 1997, the U.S. Department of Energy (DOE) and its national laboratories had agreements to implement new MPC&A systems at some forty-four civilian nuclear facilities in Russia and other former Soviet states. There are plans to extend MPC&A to naval fuel storehouses in Russia and to the Russian icebreaker fleet (which uses highly enriched uranium). DOE is cooperating with Russia's GAN to develop state systems for accounting and control over nuclear materials in that country. "Our multifaceted cooperation has resulted in impressive successes in the past two years," claims a 1997 DOE pamphlet describing the MPC&A program. Certainly the degree of U.S. access to NIS nuclear complexes gained under the MPC&A program represents an important accomplishment in itself.[58]

The regulatory framework governing legal and illegal transfer of nuclear material also shows progress in the NISs. Russia in 1996 revised its criminal law on nuclear offenses to impose especially harsh penalties when perpetrators are nuclear insiders and elements of conspiracy and planning are involved in the theft. Russia's licensing system for nuclear exports, which establishes an array of degrees and control, lists categories of fissile, radioactive, and dual-use materials, and increasingly is comparable to systems of Western states. (Kazakhstan introduced a comprehensive export control law in 1996, and Ukraine and

Belarus are contemplating enacting such legislation.[59]) Russia's State Customs Administration in 1995 set up a special operational unit charged with intercepting nuclear contraband at frontiers and at internal customs posts. However, only 25 percent of the customs checkpoints along Russia's 60,000-kilometer border are equipped with working radiation monitors—a daunting problem from an export control standpoint.[60]

A modest U.S. effort also focuses on strengthening antitrafficking responses of NIS authorities—that is, their ability to intercept stolen or illegally acquired materials (and to apprehend the smugglers) within their respective national territories. For example, the Department of Defense and the Federal Bureau of Investigation jointly run counterproliferation training seminars for NIS law enforcement. Two such seminars were held in Budapest in the summer of 1997. The U.S. Customs Service administers transfers of radioactive monitoring devices to the NISs. As of late 1996, nuclear-capable X-ray vans had been deployed in Belarus, Ukraine, and the Baltic states. Antitrafficking, though, still is a relatively low U.S. priority, receiving approximately $10 million in funding in fiscal year 1998 compared to $137 million allocated to the MPC&A program.[61]

Furthermore, the issue of nuclear materials security is acquiring a more prominent place on the agenda of international concern. At a Moscow summit meeting of the heads of state of the Group of Seven plus Russia in April 1996, participants agreed on a common "Program for Preventing and Combating Illicit Trafficking in Nuclear Material."[62] The program defined trafficking as a "global proliferation risk and a potential danger to public health and safety." The program identified as fundamental tasks the safe and secure storage of sensitive nuclear materials, international law enforcement and intelligence cooperation to intercept diverted materials, and joint efforts to suppress illicit demand for nuclear substances and to deter potential traffickers. President Boris Yeltsin's proposals at the conference to set up an "international nuclear counter terrorism center" and examine the possibility of concluding an international convention against nuclear smuggling represent Russia's apparent commitment to the counterproliferation objective.[63]

Such signs of cooperation and progress of course are encouraging. Nevertheless, conditions in the NISs still pose a clear threat to nuclear safety and stability globally. The real proliferation danger derives from systemic factors: diminished economic prospects in the military-industrial complex (including the nuclear sector), a weakening political control structure, an increasingly corrupt bureaucracy, and widening penetration of the economy by organized crime formations; such an environment increases the likelihood of exports of fissile materials and even weaponry to states or substate groups with goals inimical to the United States. Infusions of Western technical assistance, the NISs' own security and export control measures, improved East-West atmospherics, and what DOE calls "the spirit of mutual understanding partnership and respect between U.S. and Russian nuclear specialists"[64] can help to reduce nuclear leakages. Nevertheless, existing safeguards and controls can be circumvented easily—particularly in scenarios of collaboration between senior nuclear managers, corrupt officials, and professional underworld elements. The success of counterproliferation policies hinges ultimately on progress in stabilizing NIS economies and developing effective governing institutions and criminal justice systems in the new states, a process that could take years to accomplish.

CHALLENGE AND RESPONSE: POLICY SUGGESTIONS

Overall U.S. strategy emphasizes the containment of thefts at nuclear enterprises, but other promising lines of defense may be shortchanged as a consequence. For example, the more sophisticated collusive diversion scenarios outlined previously suggest that even well-guarded and upgraded facilities cannot prevent the eventual (and possibly even current) diversion of sensitive nuclear materials into international trafficking and marketing channels. Nonetheless, U.S. cooperation with, and support for, Russian law enforcement is languishing, beset by both insufficient funding and legal and bureaucratic wrangling. U.S. law enforcement and intelligence officers and their counterparts in the NISs have played little role in bilateral dialogues on counterproliferation—accentuating the one-sidedness of U.S. policy. Finally, U.S. programs in the NISs suffer from an insufficient focus on the core motivations that drive the supply side diversion of nuclear materials. Better and more comprehensive economic programs are needed to guarantee a decent livelihood for nuclear workers in post-Soviet states.

The Challenge

Containment of thefts—the rationale of the MPC&A programs—is a laudable and worthy objective. By the end of 1996, a total of forty-four NIS facilities had received U.S. technical assistance in upgrading MPC&A systems, an impressive success considering the legacy of hostilities in the Cold War and legendary Russian sensitivities about nuclear security and sovereignty. Whether strengthened MPC&A systems have reduced or will reduce significantly the risk of nuclear proliferation from the former Soviet Union is less clear. Certainly there are reasons to be skeptical. With few tangible achievements before 1995, MPC&A efforts may be too little, too late, and the task is obviously far from complete. According to 1996 testimony of an official of the General Accounting Office, the number of NIS facilities (excluding weapons storehouses) requiring MPC&A upgrades could be as high as 135.[65] Many of these facilities comprise multiple individual storage sites for nuclear materials, and additional sites continue to surface as the MPC&A program progresses; hence, the accomplishment of MPC&A can be described as partial at best, even at the enterprises covered under the program. As a sobering assessment by the National Research Council published in 1997 observed:

while significant improvements have been made at selected facilities the task has not been completed at any facility and has only begun at many. The DOE estimates that *tons* of direct-use materials are contained in internationally acceptable MPC&A systems and that *tens of tons* are in partially acceptable systems; but adequate MPC&A systems for hundreds of tons must still be installed.[66]

Furthermore, the new MPC&A technologies are an imperfect defense against the division-by-consensus scenarios discussed earlier in this study. Russian managers contend that well-placed insiders working in concert can defeat such systems. Lack of technical discipline and irresponsible work habits also work to undermine nuclear security at enterprises. As one astute observer noted, "An MPC&A system is only as good as the scientists, technicians, and guards in charge of running it. It will take years before we can accurately assess the extent to which Russia is able fully to integrate an MPC&A system jointly designed with U.S. engineers and scientists."[67]

Effective implementation of the new MPC&A safeguards will require monitoring and oversight from outside the MINATOM nuclear complex. The existing Russian oversight agency, GAN, lacks statutory authority to regulate facilities manufacturing nuclear weapons or explosive charges for such weapons, weapons storage sites, or naval bases storing submarine fuel. Furthermore, a report by the National Research Council notes, GAN "suffers from a shortage of well-trained inspectors, qualified staff, and necessary analytical and related equipment . . ."[68] GAN is a puny instrument in terms of resources and clout, compared to MINATOM, its principal object of control. GAN conducts inspections at civilian enterprises, where it found 29,000 violations of rules and norms in 1995. (The typical fine is $1 to $2 in such instances.) GAN also technically has the authority not to certify enterprises that stand in violation of safety regulations; not surprisingly this power has never been exercised. The overall organization is weak, and it is unlikely in the near term to play a major role in countering the pro-proliferation forces in Russia.[69]

The Response

Uncertainties and concerns about the MPC&A effort argue for shifts in the emphasis of U.S. counterproliferation policy in the NISs. One obvious recommendation is to devote more attention and resources to strengthening the new states' antitrafficking infrastructure—an important second line of defense against proliferation of nuclear materials. As noted, U.S. funding for antitrafficking, at $10 million in fiscal year 1998, is small—only 7 percent of the $137 million allocated to MPC&A projects in that year. A substantial risk exists that fissile materials will continue to escape from Russian enterprises for years to come, which means that law enforcement must assume a larger share of the counterproliferation burden. As the military prosecutor of the Northern Fleet, Mikhail Kulik, explained the issue to *Yaderny Kontrol:*

> For the time being we do not count on the improvement of the system for physical protection, control, and accounting—it seems that it could take many years to implement state programs. We rely on law enforcement bodies, primarily local ones . . . we find criminals and receive stolen materials.

A significantly larger share of total U.S. counterproliferation funding in the former Soviet Union probably should be devoted to second line activities—training and equipping law enforcement and security officials to interdict stolen nuclear materials and nuclear contraband. Police, prosecutors, security officials, and customs officers operating in the neighborhood of large nuclear complexes or secret cities (Obninsk, Mayak, Arzamas-16, Tomsk-7, and others) require special assistance and support. Officials of Russia's State Customs Committee, for example, want to deploy thirty to forty state-of-the-art gamma spectrometers (which can check the contents of radioactive cargoes) at internal customs posts that adjoin large nuclear enterprises. This equipment might help close "legal contraband" channels for diverting dangerous nuclear materials. So far, however, no funds are available for this purpose.[70]

Improving the ability of border agents and border guards to interdict contraband nuclear material at frontiers should receive increased attention. This is especially important with respect to states along Russia's southern periphery. Russia, as of late 1996, had deployed no radiation monitoring equipment along its borders with Transcaucasia or the Central Asian states, and these countries—except possibly Kazakhstan—lack such equipment of their own. No one knows just how much nuclear material might be illegally transiting the country's southern borders—the region is effectively a free zone for the smuggling of virtually any kind of contraband.

Additional concerns are the economic underpinnings and motivations of the illegal nuclear trade. MPC&A programs that construct increasingly sturdier walls around hungry and resentful employees will not eliminate the threat of nuclear theft and diversion in Russian facilities. Harvard scholar Graham Allison and his colleagues criticize U.S. programs for paying insufficient attention to the collapsing quality of life of nuclear workers. The authors contend that the real obstacle to removing the temptation of nuclear diversion lies in the unwillingness of the U.S. Congress to propose any support that might be construed as foreign aid or welfare spending for nuclear complexes and their employees in the former Soviet Union.[71]

Some funding in the U.S. government's MPC&A contracts with Russian facilities is earmarked for salary supplements of approximately $125 per month at Obninsk and a few other facilities. Because these funds are available only to participants in the cooperative MPC&A programs, even these small efforts may be creating a class system of sorts in Russian enterprises and fueling resentments that could increase the likelihood of nuclear theft scenarios.

Since 1994, the United States and other foreign donors have supported a program that provides salaries for unemployed or underemployed weapons technicians and scientists to work on nonmilitary projects. The program, managed by the International Science and Technology Center (ISTC) in Moscow and a parallel center in Ukraine, is intended partly to counter the "brain drain" of weapons specialists, but also is designed to reduce incentives to steal nuclear material. At the end of 1996, some 15,000 specialists in various weapons fields (nuclear, chemical, biological, and missile) in the former Soviet Union were receiving support. However, ISTC covers only a fraction of the hundreds of thousands of scientists and engineers associated with post-Soviet nuclear complexes. Furthermore, the ISTC "does little or nothing for the guards and administrators of nuclear installations who may also [be] a significant proliferation risk."[72] The ISTC is a temporary fix, not a permanent subsidy, and can only partially alleviate the sufferings of nuclear elites in the NIS.[73]

In summary, more comprehensive and broadly targeted efforts to improve the livelihood of nuclear workers need to be devised. Benefits should be distributed more equitably within enterprises and institutions participating in MPC&A programs. The composition of the assistance—the specific mix of salary supports and other items (food and medicines, for example)—perhaps could be worked out on a case-by-case basis. A more ambitious proposal, advanced by Allison, is "conversion and retraining" or enterprises and individuals suffering the aftershocks of nuclear dismantlement. A former member of the President's Committee of Advisors on Science and Technology, John Holdren, suggests a large international investment in developing business prospects to diversify the economic base of the former secret cities. "Major cultural changes and substantial subsidies will be required if these cities are to have any economic future independent of the production of nuclear weapons," says Holdren.[74] Such ideas perhaps are impractical given U.S. budgetary constraints and congressional aversion to "welfare" spending in the former USSR.[75] Nevertheless, as these and other observers note, U.S. counterproliferation strategy is likely to be more successful if accompanied by a broader effort to improve the economic conditions of people handling nuclear materials and weaponry.

Notes

1. Much of the material in this chapter was drawn from a book by Rensselaer W. Lee, *Smuggling Armageddon: The Nuclear Black Market in the Former Soviet Union and Europe*, (New York: St. Martin's Press, 1998).
2. *Special Report: Scams in the World of Nuclear Smuggling*, US. Department of Energy, Office of Nonproliferation and National Security (NN-62), May 1997.

3. Statement of John P. Holdren, Chairman, President's Committee of Advisors on Science and Technology, before the Senate Foreign Relations Committee Hearings, August 1995.

4. James L. Ford, "Nuclear Smuggling: How Serious a Threat," *National Defense University Strategic Forum* (January 1996).

5. William C Potter, "Before the Deluge? Assessing the Threat of Nuclear Leakage from the Post-Soviet States," *Arms Control Today*, October 1995, 9–16.

6. John Sopko, "The Changing Proliferation Threat," *Foreign Policy* (Winter 1996–97): 3.

7. Statement of Senator Sam Nunn, Hearing on Global Proliferation and Weapons of Mass Destruction, Permanent Subcommittee on Investigations, Senate Committee on Government Affairs, March 13, 1996.

8. Graham T. Allison, Owen R. Cote, Jr., Richard A. Falkenrath, and Steven E. Miller, *Avoiding Nuclear Anarchy: Containing the Threat of Loose Russian Nuclear Weapons and Fissile Material* (Cambridge, Mass.: The MIT Press, 1996).

9. Task Force of the Global Organized Crime Project, *The Nuclear Black Market* (Washington, D.C.: Center for Strategic International Studies, 1996).

10. Rensselaer W. Lee, "Recent Trends in Nuclear Smuggling" (speech at the Center for Strategic Leadership, U.S. Army War College, Carlisle Barracks, Pa., June 25, 1996).

11. Rensselaer W. Lee III, "Nuclear Crime in Russia: Causes, Dynamics, and Implications," draft report for the Foreign Policy Research Institute, Washington, D.C., October 1997.

12. Kirill Belyaninov, personal communications, March 27, 1997.

13. International Atomic Energy Agency, "INSIDE. Technical Cooperation, December 1996," 1.

14. Tadeusz Hadys and Slawomir Sterlinski, "Polish Prevention System Against Nuclear Trafficking of Radioactive Substances and Nuclear Materials," Central Laboratory for Radiological Protection and Border Guards Headquarters, 1997, 5.

15. See discussion in Phil Williams and Paul N. Woessner. "The Real Threat of Nuclear Smuggling," *Scientific American* 274 (January 1996): 40–41.

16. James L. Ford and C. Richard Schuller, *Nuclear Smuggling Pathways: A Holistic Perspective* (Washington, D.C.: National Defense University, December 1996), 7.

17. Barry Kellman and David S. Gualtieri, "Barricading the Nuclear Window: A Legal Regime to Curtail Nuclear Smuggling," *University of Illinois Law Review*, 3 (1966): 677.

18. Allison, et al., *Avoiding Nuclear Anarchy.*

19. *Ugolovny Kodeks Rossiiskoi Federatsii*, "Severozapad." St. Petersburg, 1994, 164–165; Article 223, sections 2 through 5, deals with nuclear-related offenses. Interestingly, the code fails to specify sale of nuclear materials as a crime, apparently not envisioning that possibility.

20. Allison et al., *Avoiding Nuclear Anarchy*, 2.

21. N. D. Bondarev, "Analez Kontseptsii RNTs 'Kurchatovskiy Institut,' " in *Proceedings. International Conference on Non-Proliferation and Safeguards in Russia*, Moscow, May 14–17, 1996, p. 146.

22. Holdren, "Reducing the Threat of Nuclear Theft in the Former Soviet Union," *Arms Control Today* (March 1996): 20.

23. Mark Hibbs, "Physical Protection Reportedly Evading at MINATOM's Ten Closed Cities in Russia," *Nuclear Fuel* (January 2, 1995): 13.

24. Cited in Vladimir Orlov, "Nuclear Blackmail Threats from Enemies Within More Disturbing than Conspiracies from Without," *Nezavisimaya Voennoye Obozreniye*, (August 29, 1997): 1, 7.

25. Nikolai Bondarev, "Background Report," The Kurchatov Institute, Moscow, November 1994, 8.

26. Vladimir Orlov, "Accounting, Control and Physical Protection of Fissile Materials and Nuclear Weapons in the Russian Federation: Current Situation and Main Concerns" (paper presented at the International Seminar on MPC&A in Russia and the NIS, Bonn, Germany, April 7–8, 1997), 9.

27. Alla Malakhova, "Nuclear Arsenals Kept in Ordinary Hangars," *Obshchaya Gazeta*, no. 30 (July 31–August 6, 1997): 2.

28. Oleg Bukharin and William Potter, "Potatoes Were Guarded Better," *The Bulletin of Atomic Scientists* (May–June 1995): 48–49.

29. Mikhail Kulik, "Nekotorye Problemy Khraneniya Yadernykh Materialov na Severnom Flote," *Yaderny Kontrol'*, no. 2 (February 1995): 12.

30. Allison, et al., *Avoiding Nuclear Anarchy*, 42–43; Jessica Stern, "U.S. Assistance Programs for Improving MPC&A in the Former Soviet Union," *The Non-Proliferation Review* 3 (Winter 1996): 25; Author interview, Kurchatov Institute, Moscow, October 25, 1996.

31. Emily Ewell, "Trip Report in Uzbekistan, Kazakhstan, Ukraine," Monterey Center for Non-Proliferation Studies, May 1996, 8.

32. Kirill Belyaninov, "Nuclear Nonsense Black-Market Bombs and Missile Flim-Flams," *Bulletin of the Atomic Scientists* (March–April 1994): 48.

33. Mark Hibbs, interview by Shelly Jones, "Loose Nukes," *Frontline*, Public Broadcasting System, November 20, 1996.

34. Tom Masland, et al., "For Sale," *Newsweek* (August 29, 1994): 32.

35. National Research Council, *Proliferation Control* (Washington, D.C.: National Academy Press, 1997), 13.

36. Yuriy Smirnov, interview by Shelly Jones, "Loose Nukes," *Frontline*, Public Broadcasting System, November 20, 1996.

37. U.S. General Accounting Office (GAO), "Nuclear Proliferation: Station of U.S. Efforts to Improve Nuclear Materials Control in Newly Independent States" (Washington, D.C.: GAO, March 1996), 13. (Hereafter the GAO Report).

38. Leonard S Spector, et al., *Tracking Nuclear Proliferation. A Guide in Maps and Charts, 1995* (Washington, D.C.: Carnegie Endowment for International Peace, 1995), 3.

39. William Potter "The Post-Soviet Proliferation Challenge," testimony prepared for the hearing on "Proliferation: Russian Case Studies," U.S. Senate Governmental Affairs Subcommittee on International Security Proliferation and Federal Service, June 5, 1997, 4.

40. Spector, et al., *Tracking Nuclear Proliferation*, 3.

41. William Potter, "The Post-Soviet Nuclear Proliferation Challenge" (paper prepared for the Aspen Strategy Group Meeting, August 10–15, 1996), 10.

42. Valeriy Davydov, "Nuclear Material in the Wrong Hands Pushes Russia to Cooperate With the West," *Christian Science Monitor* (April 26, 1996): 19.

43. *Proliferation Concerns*, 34.

44. Talk by Sergei Rogov, Director of U.S.A.-Canada Institute Moscow, at the Foreign Policy Research Institute (FPRI), Philadelphia, Pa., January 22, 1997.

45. Igor Zaslonov, "Nuclear Union Demands Wages," *Moscow Tribune* (December 10, 1996): 1.

46. Nikolai Kukharin, interviewed by Rensselaer W. Lee, Kurchatov Institute, October 25, 1996.

47. Orlov, "Nuclear Blackmail."

48. Olga Sitkova, "How About a Bomb," *Die Woche* (Hamburg), March 23, 1994, 14.

49. Nikolai Bondarev, interview by Shelly Jones, "Loose Nukes," *Frontline*, Public Broadcasting System, November 20, 1996.

50. Yevgeniy Korolev, interview by Rensselaer W. Lee, Yekaterinburg, Russia, September 10, 1994.

51. Kukharin interview, October 25, 1996.

52. Nikolai Bondarev, "Background Report," 13.
53. Aleksandr Emelyanenkov, interview by Shelly Jones, "Loose Nukes," *Frontline,* Public Broadcasting System, November 20, 1996.
54. Smirnov, "Loose Nukes."
55. Masland, et al., "For Sale," 3.
56. Mark Hibbs, "Agencies' Entrapment Justifies Mild Sentences in Munich Pu Case," *Nucleonic Week* (July 2, 1995): 2–3.
57. Viktor Mikhailov, "Intervia Mesyatsa," *Yaderny Kontrol* (February 1995): 9–10.
58. U.S. Department of Energy, *Partnership for Nuclear Materials Security* (Washington, D.C.: U.S. DOE January 1997), 1.
59. Personal communication with Professor Gary Bertsch, University of Georgia, Athens, Ga., September 25, 1997. The U.S. Department of Commerce plays a major role in helping the new states draft export control legislation.
60. Nikolai Kravchenko, "Interviu Mesyatsa," *Yaderny Kontrol* (August–September 1996), 8.
61. The rationale for emphasizing control of fissile materials at their sources, as one writer explains it, is that "once [nuclear] materials are stolen the difficulty of finding and recovering them before they can be used in weapons rises exponentially" See Holdren, "Reducing the Threat of Nuclaer Theft in the Former Soviet Union," 16.
62. Programs for Preventing and Combating Trafficking in Nuclear Material" (Moscow: Kremlin, April 19–20, 1996), 1.
63. Statement by Boris Yeltsin, Moscow Nuclear Safety and Security Summit, Moscow, "International Affairs," 1996, 38.
64. Nuclear Material Security Task Forces, "United States–Former Soviet Union Program of Cooperation on Nuclear Material Protection, Accounting, and Control," Washington, D.C.: U.S. DOE, December 1996).
65. Statement of Harold Johnson, "Nuclear Non-Proliferation. U.S. Efforts to Help Newly Independent States Improve Their Nuclear Material Controls," testimony before the Permanent Subcommittee on Investigations, Committee on Government Affairs, U.S. Senate, March 13, 1996, 5.
66. National Research Council, *Proliferation Concerns* (Washington, D.C.: National Academy Press, 1997), 69.
67. Jessica Stern, "Teaching Nuclear Custodians to Fish," unpublished paper draft, September 11, 1996, 8.
68. *Proliferation Concerns,* 13.
69. Nikolai Filonov, "O Deyatelnosti Gosatomnadzora v Oblasti Yadernoi i Radiyatsionnoi Bezopasnosti' Rossii v 1995 godu." *Yaderny Kontrol,* no. 20–21 (August–September 1996): 31; GAN, "*Otchet o Deyatelnosti Federal'nogo Nadzora Rossii po Yadernoi i Radiyatsionnoi Bezopasnost'* (Moscow: GAN, 1996), 149–150.
70. R. Lee's estimate of the total cost of this equipment is $750,000 to $1 million dollars. This would be a remarkably cheap and useful investment for the United States. See author interview, Russian State Customs Committee, Moscow, October 23, 1996. R. Lee interviews with delegation of Russia State Customs Committee, Washington, DC, June 14, 1996.
71. Allison, et al., *Avoiding Nuclear Anarchy,* 90, 150–151.
72. Ibid., 91.
73. Other problems mentioned by Russian authorities include a lengthy approval process for ISTC grants (which usually require a Western sponsor) and long delays in receiving funding for approved proposals.
74. Holdren, "Reducing the Threat," 19–20.
75. Allison, et al., *Avoiding Nuclear Anarchy,* 151.

Terrorism

International terrorism is somewhat unlike the other transsovereign issues discussed in this volume. Unlike the other trends, international terrorism is experiencing a downturn of sorts. In 1996 the number of international terrorist acts fell to 296, a twenty-five-year low and less than half the 665 terrorist acts which occurred in the peak year of 1987.[1] However, attacks increased again in 1997 to 304 acts of terrorism. Also, casualties remained high: in 1996 there were 314 killed and 2,912 people wounded by acts of terrorism; in 1997 there were 221 dead and 693 wounded;[2] and the August 7, 1998, terrorist attacks on U.S. embassy compounds in Kenya and Tanzania alone accounted for 312 dead and 5,000 wounded.[3]

Additionally, rather than going "beyond sovereignty," typically terrorist groups want in on the sovereignty game. They are generally state "wannabe's," often separatist or minority paramilitary groups who want to secede and set up their own autonomous state.

However, like drug traffickers, nuclear smugglers, and international crime cartels, terrorist groups take advantage of the infrastructure that open societies, open economies, and open technologies afford. They are more easily able to move people, money, and goods across international borders thanks to democratization, economic liberalization, and technological advancements. They rely on international telecommunications links to publicize their acts and their political demands. When Peru's Tupac Amaru Revolutionary Movement (MRTA) took over the Japanese ambassador's residence in Lima during a diplomatic reception in December 1996 and took five hundred people hostage, they kept talking with reporters throughout the months-long ordeal. The MRTA, along with many other terrorist organizations, has a home page on the World Wide Web to advertise their political philosophies and demands. While propaganda in defense of a cause is nothing new (American revolutionaries were prolific pamphleteers), tools such as Cable News Network (CNN) and the Internet dramatically extend the scope of a terrorist's reach.

Terrorists also take advantage of weaker or developing states to serve as base of operation for training and carrying out attacks against Western targets. For example, the terrorist network of Osama bin Laden which bombed U.S. embassy compounds in Nairobi, Kenya, and Dar es Salaam, Tanzania, operated from bases in Afghanistan.

While the number of terrorist attacks may be down from historic highs, the casualties caused by such attacks are on the rise thanks to the increase in destructive technologies and the increased availability of such technology and information via the Internet, free markets, and free societies. Terrorists now have more destructive biological, chemical, and even nuclear technologies available to them, and they are using them. When the Japanese terrorist group Aum Shinrikyo attacked the crowded Japanese subway system at rush hour in March 1995, they only needed to carry six small packages of lethal sarin gas onto the trains and puncture them with umbrella tips to kill twelve and injure more than five thousand. Chechen rebels left a package of nuclear materials on a park bench in Moscow's Gorky Park as a warning to Russian officials that if they wanted to, they could set off a low yield nuclear radioactive device. Such a device is easier to make and less lethal than a nuclear bomb, but thousands would still suffer from radioactive poisoning. It is not the case, as some alarmists say, that anyone can make a chemical, biological, or nuclear device at home. The scientific expertise needed to effectively complete such a task without self-harm is still quite high. Aum Shinrikyo has assembled a well-trained and well-funded scientific staff and has actively worked for years to set off a weapon of mass destruction before their sarin gas attack on the Japanese subway system. Fortunately, their efforts have been unsuccessful to date, underlining that while it is possible for terrorists to utilize highly destructive technologies, it is not necessarily easy.

Like international businessmen, terrorists are able to move their money, people, and products quickly across state borders. They are able to use the same financial instruments as legal businesses to hide the paper trail of money to their causes. Recognizing the increasing importance of economic targets, business facilities are by far the most popular target of terrorist attacks, as exemplified by the February 1993 bombing of the World Trade Center in New York City and the 1997 bombings of multinational oil pipelines in Columbia.[4]

Terrorists also take advantage of the legal protections of individual rights and liberties in open societies, to move people into position with less fear of search or seizure. Not coincidentally, as Europeans moved into closer economic, political, and technological integration in the 1990s, they suffered by far the largest number of terrorist attacks than any other region of the globe, with nearly one thousand acts of terrorism between 1991 and 1996.[5]

With terrorist organizations fully utilizing the international infrastructure of open markets, advanced technologies, and the freedoms associated with open societies, states cannot effectively combat terrorism alone. For this reason, states are trying to build multilateral efforts to combat international terrorism. More than ten international conventions address particular forms of terrorism. In the Ministerial Conference on Terrorism in Paris in July 1996, following the June 1996 bombing of the U.S. military's El Khobar barracks in Saudi Arabia, the United States, Britain, Canada, France, Germany, Italy, Japan, and Russia endorsed twenty-five measures to cooperate in fighting terrorism, including working to adopt strict international standards for detecting bombs at airports, tracking the manufacture and sale of explosives, and developing common standards for vehicle identification numbers and labeling parts, as well as for passenger and cargo manifests. However, due to differing legal standards and procedures from state to state, and the difficulties in information and intelligence sharing among states, terrorists can still take advantage of porous borders to escape detection and imprisonment. For example, while the notorious terrorist "Carlos the Jackal" was finally convicted by a French court and imprisoned for life in December 1997, he had slipped through the hands of the law for over twenty-two years.[6]

Notes

1. U.S. Department of State (DOS), "Patterns of Global Terrorism 1996," Washington, D.C., April 30, 1997.
2. DOS, "Patterns of Global Terrorism 1997," Washington, D.C., April 1998.
3. "Address to the Nation by the President," Office of the Press Secretary, the White House, August 20, 1998.
4. DOS, "Patterns of Global Terrorism 1997."
5. DOS, "Patterns of Global Terrorism 1996."
6. DOS, "Patterns of Global Terrorism 1997."

Countering Terrorism beyond Sovereignty

David. E. Long

The thesis of this book is that with the end of the Cold War finding foreign policy solutions to certain international problems such as terrorism has extended *beyond sovereignty*. At first glance, however, terrorism appears to be the exception that proves the rule. A good argument can be made that in recent years international terrorism has become more rooted in the sovereign state system rather than less. This is in sharp contrast to the Cold War years when there was a widely held assumption that terrorism was primarily a product of an international conspiracy created by the Soviet Union to spread communism and Soviet foreign policy.[1]

That assumption was never totally accurate even during the Cold War, and since then it has become clear that terrorism has always been motivated more by parochial ethnic, national, and religious loyalties than by universalist ideologies. Even the most prominent international terrorist threat of today, from radical Islamist political organizations, are in reality strongly rooted in the politics of individual sovereign political states. Islamist groups involved in terrorism in Egypt, Israel/Palestine, and Algeria, for example, are far more interested in creating revolutionary Islamic regimes in their own countries than in some utopian desire to submerge them into a larger Islamic political entity. In Iran, where there is already a radical Islamist regime, it is difficult to tell the difference between the regime's stated foreign policy goal of spreading their Islamic revolution and age-old Persian imperial political ambitions. Terrorism in the post–Cold War world is tied to the sovereign state system more than ever before.

How then can international terrorism be considered a problem beyond sovereignty? The answer lies more in state responses to terrorism than in the nature of the terrorism itself. It is not the motivations of terrorists per se that make terrorism a transsovereign problem, but rather the official policy responses of multiple sovereign states, each with only limited freedom of action to effect an outcome favorable to its interests. To the extent that terrorist activity crosses sovereign boundaries and that no single state can successfully contain international terrorism unilaterally, it is truly beyond sovereignty. Like other transsovereign problems, terrorism is facilitated by the very open market, open society, and open technology dynamics that allow the legal movement of goods, money, ideas, and people across borders. Before addressing policy responses to terrorism, however, it is important to look at the nature of terrorism to understand why unilateral state responses have had only moderate success in reducing terrorism to manageable proportions.

THE NATURE OF TERRORISM

Terrorism can be described as seeking political goals through psychological means by the use or threat of violence that is neither sanctioned under the criminal statutes of most states nor by international law. Understanding how and why this occurs—the nature of terrorism—is no easy matter. Of all the foreign policy problems facing the countries of the world in the post–Cold War era, terrorism is one of the most difficult to come to grips with conceptually. In the past twenty years or so, media sensationalism of terrorist acts and responses by politicians pandering to transient public opinion have so greatly distorted public perceptions of terrorist behavior that it is difficult to create common ground for informed discussion.

For example, there are a number of commonly held perceptions that simply have no basis in fact. One is that all terrorists are either evil or demented—either sociopaths or psychopaths or both. Studies of captured terrorists have produced a far different picture. According to one leading student of terrorist behavior, "the outstanding characteristic of terrorists is their normality."[2] On the subject of morality, there are few more moralistic people than fanatical followers of a radical political cause. It is not that they believe that terrorism itself is moral, but that they have convinced themselves that their cause is so sacred and so imperative that any means, including terrorism, no matter how reprehensible is justified in seeking to achieve their political ends.

A more sympathetic but no less simplistic perception is that terrorists are poor and downtrodden victims of economic, social, or political injustices. Although many are, this stereotype is no more accurate than the first. The vast majority of victims of such injustices do not resort to violence to assuage their sense of grievance, and many terrorists have never suffered personally but rather identify with others who they believe have. Moreover, the leaders of most known terrorist organizations are not economically or socially deprived but come from middle-class backgrounds and are relatively well educated with at least some college training. Without such training, it would be difficult to develop the political, organizational, and technical skills required to lead a successful terrorist group.

Two other traits appear to be prevalent among terrorists: low self-esteem and a predilection for risk-taking. People with low self-esteem tend to set unrealistically high goals for themselves; and when their goals are not met, they tend to raise rather than lower their aspirations. Bitter at failure, they are apt to blame external causes for their condition and join groups of others with similar feelings.

Beyond these generalizations, it is virtually impossible to stereotype terrorist behavior, particularly given the lack of meaningful social science research. Because most terrorist activity is covert, this kind of research is obviously very difficult to gather. Suffice it to say there are probably as many motives for becoming a member of a terrorist group as there are terrorists, underscoring individual psychology as a major motivating force.[3]

From the policymaker's point of view, there is an even greater constraint in combating international terrorism than public misperceptions of terrorists and their behavior—the absence of any international consensus of a legal definition of what terrorism is. It has often been claimed that the only difference between terrorists and freedom fighters is what side they are on. Cynical as that claim might appear, there is more than a little truth to it. Whereas most international terrorism consists of criminal acts—murder, arson, kidnapping, hijacking, sabotage, robbery, extortion—there is no existing criminal definition of terrorism itself. The reason for this is not hard to find. What sets terrorism apart from other international crimes of a similar nature is that it is essentially a political activity, and no country in the world is willing to have its sovereign right to respond to a foreign political act subordinated to a legal definition.

The political nature of determining under what circumstances a violent international political act should be considered terrorism is illustrated by U.S. State Department's official list of states supporting terrorism. The list was mandated by Congress in what was apparently an attempt to enable the United States to take the moral high ground against terrorism with little political cost. With no objective criteria for deciding when countries should be placed on or removed from the list, inclusion is a purely political decision. For example, Syria is still on the list although the State Department testified in 1995 that it had no evidence of Syrian involvement in terrorism since 1984.[4] Serbia, on the other hand, is not on the State Department list despite its support of Bosnian Serbs committing mass atrocities and terrorist acts in Bosnia.

Purely domestic terrorism does not usually encounter the same problem of definition as international terrorism, in large part because most terrorism involves some criminal act within virtually every criminal justice system, and each state reserves the sovereign right to determine what is and is not a political crime within its borders. If that right is challenged by a third country, it is ipso facto no longer purely a domestic matter. In states with democratic political systems and the rule of law, domestic terrorism is thus generally treated as a criminal rather that political matter.[5]

Even states that ignore the rule of law by conducting special trials for "political crimes" are constrained to some degree by international norms of civil and human rights. The risk they take in flouting those norms completely is that it could encourage other states to intervene in their domestic affairs which then transforms the problem into an international one.

CHARACTERISTICS OF TERRORISM

Despite the absence of an international consensus on how to define terrorism, there are a number of recognizable characteristics, some combination of which are inevitably present when particular countries characterize an act as terrorist. While they do not comprise a formal definition, they are sufficient to provide a reasonable description of what terrorism is. It is important to remember, however, that not all these characteristics are mutually exclusive from either nonterrorist acts of violence, such as murder, hijacking, or kidnapping, or other forms of non-sanctioned political violence such as insurgencies, revolutions, or rebellions.

The characteristics of terrorism can be grouped into five categories: goals, strategies, operations, organization, and ideology.[6]

Goals

As has already been mentioned, the ultimate goals of all international terrorism are political. This distinguishes it from nonpolitical violence by criminal elements or the emotionally disturbed. Most terrorist goals involve a sense of grievance, real or imagined, which the perpetrators seek to overcome either by forcing political authorities to accede to their demands or by forcing them from power entirely. Because the terrorists are almost always convinced that their political grievances cannot be assuaged by any other means, terrorism has been called a tactic of last resort, and by itself is almost never successful in attaining its perpetrators' stated goals.

Strategies

Terrorist strategy is basically psychological in nature. The first step is to create mass terror, not mass destruction. Worldwide, there are far more deaths each year attributed to hunting accidents that to terrorism. The second step is to manipulate political disaffection created by this psychological reaction either to intimidate governing authorities into acceding to specified political demands, or else to get rid of the government entirely.

To transform reasonable fear into irrational mass hysteria, it is also important for terrorists to generate the maximum possible publicity for their acts after the fact. The same principle applies as a tree falling in the forest; if there is no one there to hear it, it makes no sound. Some terrorist groups are quite adept at manipulating the news media, which unfortunately are often far too willing to be manipulated in order to arouse the prurient interests of their readers or listeners. The worldwide television coverage of the "Munich Massacre" at the 1972 Olympics, in which nine Israeli athletes were killed by Palestinian terrorists, helped to create a new dimension in terrorist strategy as obscure radical political groups around the world saw how they could get their message to a mass audience through media manipulation.

There are, however, parameters for media manipulation. The most extensive international news coverage comes from the largest Western media organizations, particularly those with worldwide coverage such as the Associated Press (AP) and Cable Network News (CNN) in the United States, Reuters and the British Broadcasting Corporation (BBC) in Great Britain, and their counterparts in other major Western European countries. Each news organization has its own priorities. Of course, government-owned media reflect the priorities if not necessarily the views of their governments, and private-sector organizations are influenced in what they cover by the interests of their audiences at least as much as they are able to influence those audiences by what they cover. Thus, it only makes good sense for a Third World terrorist group to choose European and, particularly, American targets if they want maximum international media coverage.

Operations

The basic characteristic of all terrorist operations is that they employ violence, either the use or threat thereof. Because terrorist violence is unsanctioned under the rule of law, terrorist operations are nearly always criminal in nature even though terrorism itself has no legal definition. Even terrorist acts sanctioned by state authorities, such as the aborted Israeli assassination attempt on a Hamas leader in Jordan on September 25, 1997, are criminal in nature because they are committed outside the law.

Another characteristic of terrorism is that it is generally noncombative. The distinction between terrorism and unconventional warfare is far from precise. Combatants can become targets of terrorist attacks and noncombatants can be targets of unconventional military forces (guerrillas and insurgents), or even of conventional forces, but by and large terrorist organizations have no military goals or objectives whereas regular and irregular military forces do. When terrorist organizations attack military targets, it is primarily to create fear among the general population, not to undermine the enemy's ability to fight.

Finally, despite a great deal of media publicity about the threat of terrorists acquiring nuclear, biological, and chemical weapons, which would require a very sophisticated organization with a great deal of money, most terrorist weapons are extremely cheap and easily available. With a basic knowledge of electronics and chemistry, an expert can manufacture a bomb powerful enough to blow up a city block with materials purchased at a local fertilizer store and electronics shop for a few hundred dollars. The implications of this are obvious: There is no practical way to deny to terrorists the raw materials required to carry out their acts. That explains why groups with limited means are attracted to terrorism to further their causes, and why governments support them as a cheap, deniable, covert means of furthering policy goals.

Organization

The most prevalent organizational characteristic of terrorism is that it is nearly always carried out by small groups. Occasionally, one or two individuals not affiliated with a larger group carry out random acts of terrorism, such as appears to have been the case in the Oklahoma City bombing, but this is comparatively rare. Because of the covert, criminal nature of terrorism, small groups are better suited for maintaining internal security and avoiding detection, and they also provide better environment for personal bonding among the members.

Independent small groups are often handicapped financially, however, lacking the means to raise operating expenses. Many of the most effective terrorist groups, therefore, are often cells or wings of or allied to larger political groups, blurring the relationship between terrorism and politics. For example, the Palestine Liberation Organization (PLO), headed by Yāsir Arafāt, though often branded a terrorist group, is in fact a purely political organization made up of many quasi-independent Palestinian groups. Some like al-Fatah, also headed by Arafat, were primarily political in nature, although al-Fatah created separate special units to conduct terrorism, including Force 17 and Black September (the latter name was also used as an alias by the Abu Nidal terrorist organization). Other member organizations of the PLO were almost entirely dedicated to terrorism, including the Popular Front for the Liberation of Palestine and its many spin-off groups. Now that the PLO has been granted a political role in the Palestinian Governing Authority, it is no longer involved in terrorist activities.

Similarly, the Stern Gang, and to a lesser extent the Irun, conducted terrorist activities as a relatively minor aspect of the Israeli military and political struggle for independence. Following the creation of Israel in 1949, their leaders also eschewed terrorist tactics.

An example of a terrorist organization having a political wing rather than the other way around is the Irish Republican Army (IRA), founded in 1916 to reunite (mostly Protestant) Northern Ireland with the rest of (Catholic) Ireland. The IRA created Sinn Fein as its political wing. In later years, however, the IRA became increasingly politically oriented, and in 1969 the Provisional Irish Republican Army (PIRA) broke off and has been responsible for most subsequent unionist terrorist activity in Northern Ireland, while Sinn Fein has steadily inched toward political legitimacy.

Ideology

We have seen that most individuals become involved and continue to be active in terrorist groups for highly personal reasons in reaction to some real or imagined political, economic, or social grievance. We have also noted that a major characteristic of individual terrorists is their normality and can conclude that with the exception of a few sociopaths, most members of terrorist groups consider terrorism to be morally reprehensible in itself, only justifiable as a means to a morally imperative end. To rationalize such a justification, nearly every terrorist group espouses some sort of ideology. These ideologies can be roughly divided into two categories: nationalistic and ethnic ideologies that seek independence or autonomy for a specific ethnic or national group, and universalist ideologies that seek political conformity to a specific religious or secular political dogma or creed.

These categories are not mutually exclusive. For example, Hamas is a radical Islamist organization that has employed terrorism in the cause of creating an independent Islamic Palestinian state. Moreover, the two greatest proponents of universalist doctrinal terrorism in recent times, the former Soviet Union and republican Iran, used the export of communist and radical Islamic doctrines respectively as tools of their foreign policies.

With the end of the Cold War, communist terrorism has ceased to be a major international threat, though left-wing groups still exist. There is a substantial body of opinion, including those in the U.S. foreign policy-making establishment, who believe that communist terrorism's place has been taken up by revolutionary Islamist terrorism, masterminded by Iran.[7] While there is some truth to the notion that Islamism is the leading doctrinal ideology among terrorists today, that Iran supports such groups and that they do engage in limited tactical cooperation, the political dynamics of the Islamist terrorist groups are overwhelmingly nationalist and ethnic in scope.

In February 1993 the World Trade Center was bombed, demolishing the underground parking garage. More than one thousand people were injured, six were killed, and over $500 million in damage was done.[8] The perpetrators of the attack were a group of loosely related Islamic extremists living in the New York City area. The mastermind, Ramzi Yusif, was able to enter the United States by requesting political asylum. Yusif's and his coconspirators' capability to execute this terrorist attack was greatly enhanced by the open societal, technological, and economic forces which are shaping states and their societies.

Taking advantage of the civil liberties provided by the United States' open society, Yusif was allowed to enter and stay in the country while awaiting his asylum hearing. The other conspirators were able to enter and live in the United States by taking advantage of the fact that the "free movement" of people is a component of the country's open societal and economic system. The conspirators were able to associate freely together because of the protections guaranteed by the U.S. Constitution of their rights to assemble and to freedom of religious expression.

In addition, the technology needed to carry out the terrorist attack was readily available in the United States. The know-how to construct the fertilizer bomb was widely available in printed form and on the Internet, and the means to deliver the bomb was only as difficult as renting a van at a Ryder Truck rental office. Finally, the ability of some of the terrorists to leave the United States so quickly after the bombing was facilitated by the ease of today's international air travel.

The terrorist attack on the World Trade Center can be understood as an attack on the open societies, technologies, and economies that are spreading throughout the world. Ironically, these forces not only enhance the ability of terrorists to carry out their attacks, they also can be understood as part of the motivation for their actions. The operation of open societal, technological, and economic forces are eroding the very thing that people like Yusif want to protect, namely, distinctive ethnic, religious, or national identities based on the sovereign state.

ANTITERRORIST STRATEGY IN THE TWENTY-FIRST CENTURY

The way countries organize to fight terrorism has changed radically in the last several decades, particularly since the end of the Cold War, and is likely to change even more as we enter the next century. Before looking to the future, however, let us first review the components of terrorist policy in general and the evolution of counterterrorism policy to its present state.

The Components of Counterterrorism Policy

The components of counterterrorism policies are fairly standard throughout the world. They include public policy, diplomacy, law enforcement, public security, intelligence, and the use of force, including covert action. Public policy and diplomacy have to do with the political aspects of terrorism; law enforcement and public security have to do with the criminal aspects; intelligence has to do with the fact that terrorism is largely covert action and to combat it, governments must know who their foes are and when and where they plan to strike; and the use of force is proactive in contrast to the mainly reactive tactics of law enforcement and public security.

Traditionally, public policy is the responsibility of the political leadership; diplomacy, the responsibility of foreign ministries; law enforcement and public security, the responsibility of police and public forces; and intelligence and the use of force is the shared responsibility of intelligence agencies (intelligence collection and covert action) and the military (military and paramilitary operations and intelligence collection). Because terrorism is a multifaceted phenomenon, however, responsibility for combating it crosses over traditional bureaucratic boundaries. The military gets involved in diplomacy, diplomats get involved in covert action, and roles of law enforcement and intelligence agencies constantly overlap.

The first requirement in creating effective counterterrorism policy, therefore, is to realign institutional responsibilities. This is not always easy. Agencies that have jealously guarded their bureaucratic turf must share responsibilities with rival agencies and cooperate in ways they have never done before. Domestic intergovernmental bureaucratic rivalries are often an even greater handicap to effective counterterrorism policy making than difficulties in cooperating with other countries.

Problems in coordinating counterterrorism policy extend beyond bureaucratic politics. There is an old saying, "where you stand on an issue depends on where you sit." Each agency has a bureaucratic point of view as well as a bureaucratic stake in exercising policy. For politicians, diplomats, and civilian intelligence officers, terrorism is above all a political issue; for law enforcement and public security officials, it is primarily a criminal justice issue; and for military officers, terrorism is considered a type of low-intensity conflict at the opposite end of the spectrum from nuclear war. None of these perceptions is incorrect, but none of them alone is sufficient for a well-balanced policy. The only normative judgement in regard to these different perceptions is that, in the international arena, the political nature of terrorism predominates.

The Evolution of International Counterterrorism Policy

Terrorism has been around as long as recorded history. Before there were high-tech explosive devices, there were knives and poisons. In the eleventh to the thirteenth centuries, a tribe living between Syria and Persia made their livelihood from political violence, and their name—the Assassins—has stood for political murder ever since. In fact, *Assassin* is a Western deviation of the Arabic, *Hashashin,* the name given to them because they regularly imbibed hashish before doing their bloody business, an ironic reminder that drugs and terrorism have been linked for centuries.

The evolution of terrorism as a major international policy issue, however, occurred only in the last quarter century. Before that, it was generally viewed as ancillary to some other problem. For example, Middle East terrorism was generally viewed as a subset of the Arab-Israeli problem, IRA terrorism was viewed as a subset of the Northern Ireland problem, and so on. At the same time, the

Cold War created the impression in the West that the greatest threat of political violence came from communist insurgent groups supported by the Soviet Union intent on overthrowing anticommunist regimes. The perception of a terrorist threat distinct from an insurgent threat emerged in the late 1960s from the worldwide student antiwar protest movement in reaction to the Vietnam War. It spawned such terrorist organizations as the Bader-Meinhof Group in Germany, the Italian Red Brigades, and the Japanese Red Army. Following the humiliating Arab defeat in the 1967 Arab-Israeli War, radical Palestinian groups also began actively using terrorist tactics.

The United States was the first country actively to view terrorism as a generic problem. It is easy to see why. The United States during the Cold War was the favorite whipping boy of all left-wing dissident groups; and there were more potential overseas American targets than those from any other country—highly visible government and private business personnel and their families, as well as installations. Moreover, targeting Americans abroad and close to the terrorists' bases of operations was far less risky than attempting attacks in the United States. In addition, targeting American persons or installations was almost certain to generate more media coverage than non-American targets. Initially, most other countries tended to respond only to incidents in their own countries, treating them as domestic issues.

Ironically, the first major contemporary terrorist incident that was truly international in scope neither involved Americans nor was it the result of the Cold War. In September 1972, members of al-Fatah's Black September terrorist wing kidnapped Israeli athletes at the Munich Olympics. German security forces badly bungled rescue operations, and as the world looked on in horror the Israelis were killed. As a result of the incident, the major powers began to review their capabilities should such an attempt occur within their borders.

While international cooperation increased in intelligence sharing and security aspects of counterterrorism, there was still a gap in political cooperation. Many countries continued to view terrorism that did not involve their citizens, property, or territory as someone else's problem; and so long as terrorist organizations did not conduct operations against them, they would not be bothered residing within their borders. Those attitudes began to change in the 1980s when a number of spectacular attacks captured the world's attention, and it became apparent that without political cooperation, all countries would be at risk. By mid-1995, there were eleven major treaties and conventions against various kinds of terrorist acts, including such specific crimes as airline and maritime sabotage, hijacking, hostage-taking, security of fissionable materials, and protection of diplomats.[9] As a result, when the Cold War ended, there was probably more overall cooperation against international terrorism than against any other global issue.

Looking to the Future

The end of the Cold War created hopes among many for a "new world order" in which international tensions would be lowered and terrorism would fade away. Sober reflection would have indicated that this was not likely. Despite the broad appeal of communist doctrine among the politically disaffected during the Cold War, the root causes of terrorism were then and still are largely local. While the end of the Cold War did reduce global tensions, it also reduced the discipline of a bipolar world order facing nuclear holocaust and kept in check by mutually assured destruction.

The breakdown of bipolar discipline has enabled many age-old national and subnational ethnic and religious conflicts to reemerge. Terrorist organizations are much more fragmented, random and thus harder to track than they were in the Cold War years. The terrorist threat has moved away from externally financed, highly sophisticated terrorist groups to smaller, less sophisticated, and more transient groups. Global economic integration has also greatly facilitated the freedom of movement of persons, goods, and money, making the logistics of international terrorism vastly easier.

Relaxation of global tensions has led to a concurrent relaxation of safeguards against weapons of mass destruction falling into clandestine hands. Nuclear, chemical, and biological terrorism has never been highly likely. Not only are weapons relatively hard to manufacture, transport, and conceal, but all political organizations, even terrorist groups, need constituent support from a segment of the population. The threat or use of weapons of mass destruction would be almost certain to risk that support. Nevertheless, the risk of such an event taking place is so dreadful even to contemplate that doomsday terrorism must be taken seriously.

Finally, the end of the Cold War has ironically undermined the interest of sovereign states in becoming involved in combating terrorism on a global scale. The strategic threat of such attacks escalating into global confrontation has all but disappeared, at least for the time being. During the Cold War, terrorist campaigns were often seen as proxy wars between the superpowers. What happened in Cuba or Afghanistan or Vietnam thus took on global strategic dimensions. With the end of the Cold War, governments are increasingly asking how a terrorist campaign in some far away part of the world affects their vital interests. This has emboldened dissident organizations to adopt terrorist tactics by convincing them that no great power will consider itself any longer sufficiently threatened to justify intervention.

For all these reasons, the need to strengthen multilateral approaches to counterterrorism policies is greater than ever before. Just because terrorism is no longer a threat to trigger a global war does not mean it is no longer a major international threat to peace and stability. It is not only extremely destructive politically, economically, and socially wherever it is found, but because violence begets violence, international terrorism always has the potential to spread far beyond the initial geographical area in which it started.

CONCLUSIONS AND RECOMMENDATIONS

From this brief overview, we can reach several conclusions. First, perhaps the greatest change in the environment of terrorism since the Cold War has been the marked increase in the ability of people and materials to avoid surveillance in crossing international borders. This change has made international cooperation all the more vital to the success of counterterrorism efforts. Second, there has also been a marked decline in the national interest of states in combating terrorism now that it is no longer linked to East-West confrontation. In the absence of the discipline imposed by the Cold War, it is all too easy to refuse to acknowledge blatant acts of terrorism that do not directly affect a state and would be both politically and economically costly to oppose, particularly if a state supporting the terrorists applies economic sanctions.

Despite a lower commitment of many states to counterterrorism cooperation, however, the considerable degree of international cooperation against terrorism developed prior to the end of the Cold War is still in place. Any policy to increase international cooperation must build on this base. There are many avenues for doing this, nearly all of which involve creating an international consensus for not tolerating such acts no matter what the justification. Probably the most difficult but most important aspect of such a course would be no longer to tolerate even tacit support of friendly states for terrorist acts. A first step in creating such a consensus could be a concerted, multinational effort to depoliticize international terrorism and seek to treat it as a predominantly criminal justice issue, just as many countries treat domestic terrorism. The means to conduct terrorism are too cheap, too available, and too uncomplicated to eradicate it entirely, but by seeking to depoliticize it, perhaps terrorism can eventually be reduced to manageable proportions.

Notes

1. For two expositions of the theory that the Soviets were masterminding international terrorism during the Cold War, see Clare Sterling, *The Terror Network: The Secret War of International Terrorism* (New York: Holt, Rinehart & Winston, 1981) and Robert Goren, *The Soviet Union and Terrorism* (London: George Allen and Unwin, 1984).
2. Martha Crenshaw, "The Causes of Terrorism," *Comparative Politics* 13 (July 1981): 390.
3. This discussion of terrorist behavior draws from the "Understanding Terrorist Behavior," Chapter 2 in David E. Long, *The Anatomy of Terrorism* (New York: The Free Press, 1990), 15–27.

4. U.S. Department of State, *Patterns in Global Terrorism* (Washington, D.C.: Government Printing Office, April 1995), 10.

5. The lead agency for domestic terrorism in the United States is the Federal Bureau of Investigation (FBI), the premier federal law-enforcement agency, whereas for international terrorism, the lead agency is the Department of State.

6. For a more detailed discussion, see Long, *The Anatomy of Terrorism,* 4–13.

7. See (then Director of Central Intelligence) James Woolsey, "Iran Is the Most Active and Dangerous Sponsor of Terrorism," *Mideast Mirror* (April 22, 1993): 16–17. For a discussion of Iran's role in Islamist terrorism, see Geoffrey Kemp, *Forever Enemies? American Policy and the Islamic Republic of Iran* (Washington, D.C.: Carnegie Endowment for International Peace, 1994), 62–68.

8. Jim McGee, "N.Y. Bombing Motivation Still Unclear," *Washington Post,* April 5, 1993, A1.

9. U.S. Department of State, "Testimony to the House of Representatives Permanent Select Committee on Intelligence by Ambassador Philip C. Wilcox, Jr., Coordinator for Counterterrorism, Department of State," March 5, 1996, (mimeo), 8.

International Organized Crime

According to Brian Sullivan, organized crime "lacks ideology; has an organized hierarchy; has continuity over time; has willingness to threaten or use force; has restrictive membership; gains profits through criminal activity; provides illegal goods/services desired by segments of the general population; neutralizes some public officials and politicians by corruption or intimidation; seeks monopolies of specific goods or services; assigns specialized activities to gang members; has a code of secrecy; and carefully plans for long-term goals."[1]

The rise in global drug trafficking has increased the power and reach of international criminal organizations. The same open society, open market, and advancing technology developments that have fueled the business of legal multinational corporations like Coca Cola are also expanding the activities and the coffers of international criminal organizations. "The worldwide financial system now involves so many transactions that they cannot be monitored adequately. The establishment of a North American free trade area and the lowering of European customs and passport controls provides unintended opportunities for criminals. And, the weakening of state authority in former Communist countries and in so-called failing states has weakened their police agencies and judicial systems."[2]

Major international criminal organizations include the Wo Hop To Chinese Six Great Triads, the Columbian (and Mexican) Medellin and Cali cartels, the American and Sicilian mafia, the Japanese Boryokudan (Yakuza), the Russian mafiya, the Jamaican Posses, and the Kurdish/Turkish group "The Turks." These groups engage in a number of illegal activities, such as assassination, arms trafficking, counterfeiting of currency and legal documents, credit theft, fraud, money laundering, pirating of intellectual properties, production, transport and sale of narcotics, prostitution, slavery, smuggling illegal aliens, smuggling nuclear weapons fuel and components, terrorism, and other crimes. These groups operate with disregard for sovereign borders, and increasingly are joining forces in strategic alliances with each other and/or with government officials.[3]

Phil Williams notes that "these organizations violate national sovereignty, undermine democratic institutions even in states where these institutions are well established, threaten the process of democratization and privatization in states in transition."[4] For example, Director of the National Security Council Transnational Threats Office and National Coordinator for Infrastrucure Protection and Counterterrorism Richard Clarke has pointed out that "organized crime groups now possess such significant resources that they can almost buy and sell governments. Approximately 150 of the 185 United Nations members are vulnerable to one degree or another. . . . Transnational crime is an especially corrosive force against small governments, and it can undermine the transition to democracy in new and fragile governments . . . [such as] the former states of the Soviet Union, where democratic institutions and the rule of law are weak."[5] Russia is by no means alone, however;

attempts by the Italian government to reign in organized crime has led to attacks "by the Sicilian Mafia on the Italian state and the killing of judges, such as Giovanni Falcone."[6]

In response, the Clinton administration announced Presidential Decision Directive 42, specifying "U.S. Initiatives Against International Organized Crime." PDD 42 includes multilateral efforts: to increase information sharing and cooperation among governments and the United Nations; to stop money laundering and to strengthen international standards against money laundering; to stop international trade with front companies by increased multilateral cooperation, tracking, and intelligence sharing about such front organizations; to eliminate safe havens for criminals; to increase transparency of global financial transactions; to increase and regularize interagency cooperation and communication on transnational crime; to increase U.S. assistance and training for international anticrime efforts, including regional law enforcement and judicial training centers; and to negotiate and adopt an international declaration on organized crime, the Declaration on Crime and Public Security. The Declaration is intended to serve as "a symbol of collective determination to prevent any nation from becoming a haven" for transsovereign crime cartels, similar to the norm-setting function of the United Nations Declaration on Human Rights.[7] The UN's Crime Prevention and Criminal Justice Division and its regional institutes also work to develop agreements among states (concerning extradition of wanted criminals, seizing their assets, freezing bank accounts, retrieving stolen cars, etc.) and to provide assistance to strengthen law enforcement and judicial systems in weak states.[8]

Notes

1. Brian Sullivan, "International Organized Crime: A Growing Security Threat," *Strategic Forum*, Institute for National Strategic Studies, National Defense University, May 1996.
2. Ibid.
3. Phil Williams, "Transnational Criminal Organizations: Strategic Alliances," *Washington Quarterly* (Winter 1995): 57; Sullivan, "International Organized Crime: A Growing Security Threat."
4. Williams, "Transnational Criminal Organizations: Strategic Alliances," 57.
5. Richard Clarke, interview in *Trends in Organized Crime*, Spring 1996, 5.
6. Williams, "Transnational Criminal Organizations: Strategic Alliances," 57.
7. "Presidential Decision Directive 42: U.S. Initiatives Against International Organized Crime," White House Documents, Office of the Press Secretary, October 22, 1995.
8. Robert S. Gelbard, "The Threat of Transnational Organized Crime and Illicit Narcotics" (statement before the UN General Assembly, October 21, 1996), 2.

Strengthening Cooperation against Transsovereign Crime:

A New Security Imperative

Roy Godson and Phil Williams

INTRODUCTION

Transsovereign threats, by their very nature, demand responses that are novel in form, content, and forum.* Indeed, national strategies are inherently inadequate for responding to challenges that cross multiple borders and involve multiple jurisdictions. Such threats can take several forms, ranging from the spread of exotic diseases to environmental degradation and illegal migration flows. Among the most serious of these threats is the rise of transsovereign criminal enterprises. Organized crime, facilitated by political, economic, and cultural changes—including the globalization of trade (open economies), transportation, and financial systems and the rapidly evolving technologies of communications and information (open technologies)—has ceased to be a domestic or local problem. It has become transsovereign in scope.

Criminal enterprises, like their licit counterparts, have responded to global opportunities, crossing borders in search of lucrative targets. Transsovereign criminal organizations also use the capacity to cross borders as a means of eluding or circumventing law enforcement, exploiting lacunae in criminal justice systems. Although they exploit borders for defensive purposes, as far as their criminal enterprises are concerned they operate in what, for all intents and purposes, is a borderless world. Governments in contrast still operate, for the most part, in a bordered world, allowing antiquated notions of sovereignty—that remain symbolically appealing even though they have lost much of their substance—to inhibit efforts to combat transsovereign crime. Few governments are

---

*Selection Copyright © National Strategy Information Center, 1997.

able to cope effectively with organizations that can simply shift their activities to other locales to recover from losses or to evade pressure or scrutiny. Nor is this the only problem facing governments as they attempt to come to terms with a security challenge that, although corrosive and insidious rather than immediate and direct, has become pervasive. Governments are equipped and experienced in dealing with security threats from other governments. They are neither comfortable nor familiar with threats that are nonmilitary in character, that target society and the economy rather than the state per se, and that cannot be dealt with through traditional state-centric policy options. This is not to ignore or overlook the important initiatives already taken in the effort to combat transsovereign criminal organizations. But it is to argue that comprehensive strategies against transsovereign criminal organizations need to be based on a clear understanding of the kinds of threat they pose, a thorough assessment of their strengths and weaknesses, and a better sense than we currently have of those measures that have proved most effective against them.

Such strategies also need to encompass preventive measures, defensive or control measures, and steps aimed at mitigating costs where prevention and control have failed. They should also go beyond law enforcement and traditional national security responses and focus on creating partnerships with the private sector and on strengthening civil society. In addition, there might well be ideas and approaches that can be borrowed from other areas. While transsovereign organized crime poses a security threat and not a military threat, some approaches that are familiar in military strategy such as target hardening, centers of gravity, maneuver, surprise, layered defense, and the like could be applied in a social, political, and economic context that infuses them with both new meaning and a high level of effectiveness. Similarly, concepts and approaches can be borrowed equally well from the business world. After all, one of the main objectives of governments must be to put criminal organizations out of business. In this connection, efforts could be made to restrict the business opportunities for criminal organizations by disrupting existing patterns of supply and demand and imposing barriers against the creation of new markets. In addition, the kind of competitive intelligence that has become so pervasive in the business world could be employed in relation to criminal enterprises. Such an approach would highlight both strengths and weaknesses and opportunities and constraints. It would provide a basis for initiatives seeking to make the environment for these organizations far less congenial than is currently the case. Insofar as the rise of transsovereign criminal organizations can be understood in terms of opportunities, incentives and pressures, and resources, then constricting opportunities, removing pressures and incentives, and degrading resources would go some way toward halting or even reversing the momentum of growth and development currently enjoyed by criminals. Unless this is done, transsovereign organized crime could prove to be one of the major security threats of the twenty-first century. Without steps to dismantle and destroy criminal organizations, to disrupt their illicit markets, and to isolate and neutralize those who collude with them, whether in government or the private sector, their power and wealth—and their capacity to inflict political, social, and economic harm—can only increase.

The Transsovereign Threat

Organized crime is not what it was. The term itself is so evocative of the Prohibition era in the United States and Mario Puzo's *The Godfather* that it obscures the magnitude of what has become a critical challenge to democratic governance, to transition and modernization processes in many parts of the world, and to national and international security.

Threats can only be properly understood in the context of vulnerabilities, and in the post–Cold War world there are many vulnerabilities. Many states that, during the Cold War era, appeared militarily strong, politically and socially cohesive, and economically vibrant, now appear in a far different light. A world in which some states are experiencing a crisis of authority and legitimacy, while many others are undergoing a difficult, painful, and protracted transition toward liberal democracy and a free-market economy, is also a world in which transsovereign organized crime poses a serious challenge. There is a real danger that in some countries the new rulers will not be good democrats and legitimate businessmen, but a new breed of authoritarian criminals and illicit entrepreneurs— the result is simply the replacement of one form of authoritarianism by another. Moreover, to the extent that transitions yield "mafiocracies" rather than democracies, then hopes for what some observers have termed a "democratic peace" could all too easily fall by the wayside.

At the same time, it has become clear that globalization and interdependence have a dark underside. Developments that have made it possible to move goods (open economies), people (open societies) and money (open technologies) through the global economy—and have traditionally been regarded by international political economy specialists as positive and benign in their effects—have facilitated the movement of "dirty money" and contract killers as well as the transportation of drugs, arms, illegal aliens, and nuclear material. Just as borders no longer provide an impediment to licit business activities, they are no longer a barrier to illicit activities. The fact that these criminal enterprises are "sovereign-free" and rely predominantly on network structures only makes them all the more difficult to contain—especially for states that still conduct most of their activities through functional and geographic bureaucratic hierarchies.[1] Indeed, one of the problems for states is that they have become old-fashioned organizations: In effect, we are attempting to deal with a twenty-first century phenomenon, using structures, agencies, mechanisms, and instruments that are still rooted in eighteenth and nineteenth century concepts and organizational forms.

Typically, transsovereign criminal organizations have a home base where state authority is weak, corrupt, or collusive. Professional criminal enterprises cross borders in search of lucrative markets for their illicit products and in an attempt to minimize the risks they confront from law enforcement. They have become regional and even global problems. Italian criminal organizations, especially La Cosa Nostra and the 'Ndrangheta carry out sophisticated operations worldwide. Similarly, Chinese criminal enterprises and Colombian and Mexican drug cartels have developed extensive, sophisticated regional and sometimes global operations employing tens of thousands of people and dealing in billions of dollars worth of "business." Russian criminal organizations while less well-entrenched outside the territory of the former Soviet Union have also become transsovereign in scope, operating not only in Western Europe and the United States but also in Israel and the Caribbean. Nigerian groups are perhaps even more ubiquitous, operating in countries as diverse as Thailand, Brazil, Russia, and South Africa. In some respects, these groups vary considerably: Portfolios of criminal activities range from Colombian drug trafficking organizations which focus on a single product to Russian and Chinese criminal organizations with an extensive range of enterprises incorporating traditional criminal activities such as extortion and prostitution and more novel ventures such as the smuggling of illegal aliens or nuclear materials.

The implication of this, of course, is that the threat posed by transsovereign criminal organizations, even allowing for national and regional variations, is truly global in the sense that no state is immune. Historically, almost every society has had some form of localized criminal group, but they have seldom been a major threat to a state's survival or its ability to conduct the functions of government. This is changing. Increasingly, some criminal organizations are able to defy government authority, suborn it, partially supplant it, and generally create an environment hostile to legitimate governance and detrimental to the population's quality of life. When the situation deteriorates to a point at which criminal organizations can undermine a government's ability to govern, as in Italy, Russia, Colombia, and elsewhere, then the problem goes beyond a law-and-order issue and becomes a national and international security concern.

There are several possible explanations of the rise of organized crime to a powerful position in some states. In some cases, criminal organizations develop where the state is weak. Furthermore, to maintain a congenial environment in which and from which they can operate with a high degree of impunity, they try to perpetuate this weakness, using both corruption and violence. In other cases, criminal organizations develop where the state is strong but where there are too few checks and balances. Low levels of transparency encourage high levels of corruption. In such cases, the state might well "license" criminal organizations, allowing them to operate in carefully defined domains, while also exploiting them for its own purposes. If strong states sometimes adopt a permissive approach to criminal organizations, however, a loss of authority by state structures allows the criminal organizations to operate in a far less restricted manner—and sometimes even to challenge the dominance of the state apparatus. In extreme cases, symbiotic relationships between the state and the criminal organizations that were controlled ultimately by the state are replaced by symbiotic relationships in which the criminal organizations determine the terms of the relationship. Even when they are not weak, however, corrupt or collusive states can provide a congenial environment for criminal organizations. Although such states might have the capacity to act vigorously against criminal organizations—a capacity that weak states lack—they generally have neither the will nor the inclination to do so. Using states that are weak, corrupt, or collusive as their *home* bases, criminal organizations establish themselves in a variety of *host* states—where there are large markets for their illicit products, and lucrative targets for other illicit activities.

Yet other states are drawn in as *transshipment* states, with criminal organizations using corruption to ensure safe passage of their illicit commodities ranging from drugs to illegal aliens. Mexico in particular, situated between the drug-consuming United States and drug-producing Latin American countries as well as along some of the major alien trafficking routes, has had the integrity and security of its political and economic systems deeply affected by criminal activities that, initially at least, "merely" passed through its territory. Eventually, drug transshipment and linkages with Colombian drug trafficking groups contributed to the rise of indigenous and powerful Mexican drug trafficking organizations. In the past, some states viewed their role as transit countries as merely marginally detrimental or perhaps even slightly beneficial. Increasingly, though, this view is being replaced by a more circumspect understanding enlightened by experience.

Another category of states—especially those where emphasis is placed on bank secrecy—implicitly become *service* states for the criminal organizations. For these states, the benefits resulting from the inflow of bank deposits and the demand for financial services are still seen as outweighing the costs, although in the long run, the corrosion of institutional integrity could all too easily emerge as a major problem.

As criminal organizations have become transsovereign, they have also developed connections with one another. Claims that there is a global "pax mafiosa" are premature, to say the least. Nevertheless, it is clear that criminal organizations have begun to establish linkages or alliances with one another to improve their operational capabilities and to strengthen their ability to resist governmental control efforts. These linkages extend from one-of deals at the low end of the spectrum to full-blown strategic alliances in which the participants develop systematic and extensive patterns of cooperation and operate on the assumption that these will continue into the foreseeable future. Cooperation among criminal organizations preempts competition, makes use of complementary expertise and distribution channels, and ensures predictable supplier relationships.

Transsovereign criminal organizations also have become embedded in the licit world. They are symbiotically linked to government officials in an effort to protect their operations from law enforcement initiatives. Such linkages tend to be strongest in home states but also extend into host, transshipment, and service states, contributing to what has been termed "the global corruption epidemic."[2] Much corruption, of course, is self-generated by officials who place personal gain above the demands of public service. Stemming in part from the injection of capitalism into traditional patrimonial societies, corruption has pernicious consequences leading in some cases to a failure of governance, with corrosive effects on both political and economic life. Even when the more drastic consequences are avoided, corruption undermines fairness and impartiality in the enforcement of rules, encourages incompetence, and creates a pervasive malaise of state institutions. In addition, it has a distorting impact on the economy and can deter investment and stifle economic growth, consequences that are particularly debilitating in developing states and states in transition. As one commentator noted: "Corruption begets unsafe buildings, bridges, water, and air and the negligent, cynical government of inept officials. It undermines trust in government, breeds mutual distrust among citizens and investors, subverts the rule of law, and perverts the work ethic. Public office is seen as the road to riches, and productive enterprise appears risky in comparison."[3] If anything, corruption is even more dangerous and insidious when used as an instrument by transsovereign criminal organizations. In addition to the operational corruption that facilitates safe passage of illicit products, criminal organizations use systemic corruption to ensure the maintenance of a congenial low-risk environment in the home state and, on occasion, in critically important host, transshipment, and service states. Symbiotic relationships with political elites subordinate the purposes the state is intended to serve for the citizenry to the needs and demands of criminal organizations concerned with maximizing profit and minimizing risk.

Government and law enforcement officials, however, are not the only targets for transsovereign criminal enterprises. Banking personnel are sometimes recruited or co-opted in an effort to facilitate illicit financial activities such as money laundering. In addition, criminal organizations attempt to infiltrate and, in some cases, come to dominate licit industries such as construction and waste disposal. Both the potential for intimidation and violence and the easy access to liquid capital give them a capacity to drive out legitimate entrepreneurs, a process that can be particularly debilitating in developing states and states in transition. The activities of transsovereign criminal organizations also have adverse consequences for the development and functioning of legitimate businesses especially in states in transition. As Jonathan Winer has noted, criminal organizations use the profits derived from their activities "to purchase legitimate business. These in turn have a negative capital cost—criminals do not need to borrow—and can force out the competition through cut-rate pricing, until they control legitimate industries."[4] The second way in which criminal organizations impinge on licit business—through extortion—is equally if not more damaging. The need to pay protection money puts an added burden on businesses in the early stages of their development. Although firms in Russia find it preferable to pay what is, in essence, a form of criminal tax rather than the prohibitive level of government tax, criminals are more concerned with short-term benefits rather than long-term growth making it difficult for enterprises to invest their profits in future growth. In other words, extortion can be a serious and sustained impediment to dynamic, expanding, legitimate entrepreneurship.

Not surprisingly, therefore, the growth of these groups and their increasing capabilities in a world of states is a broad and direct challenge to governability, state sovereignty, and international security. The threat, however, lacks the highly visible, state-centric profile of a conventional military threat. Yet, this does not mean that organized crime is a marginal phenomenon. Like insurrectionists, members of transsovereign criminal organizations are largely indistinguishable from civilian populations and are able to mingle with or disappear into these populations. Their activities undermine the fibers of society—its economic and financial structure, its polity, and its physical security—but do so in a way that only becomes apparent when the process is well advanced and therefore more difficult to counter. Rather like some diseases in the early stages, a response is easy but detection is difficult; when detection becomes easier, the cure is much more difficult.

Further, the cure is likely to be increasingly elusive, as criminal organizations consolidate power and accumulate wealth. If legitimate entrepreneurs find it difficult to operate profitably in an environment in which criminal organizations are active, criminal enterprises are flourishing in a world of global business. Estimates of the profits made by criminal organizations, of the amount of money that is laundered, and of the size of illicit markets are inherently problematic. Even if they are little more than order of magnitude guesses, however, it is clear that the sums of money involved are huge. A recent study by the United Nations, for example, suggested that the total revenue accruing to the illicit drug industry is around 400 billion in U.S. dollars.[5] Drug money can have positive effects on the economies of producer countries, providing foreign exchange and economic multiplier benefits. But it can also make the tasks of macroeconomic management more difficult. The huge profits also provide opportunities for those involved to buy political influence. For the consumer countries, of course, the costs in terms of health, lost productivity, and increased crime and violence are difficult to measure, but are certainly very serious.

One area, where there are more precise estimates of the impact of criminal activities, is counterfeiting, which is believed to cost licit business somewhere in the region of $200 billion a year. More specifically, it has been suggested that U.S. automobile manufacturers and suppliers lose around $12 billion a year in revenue worldwide because of the sale of counterfeit parts, and that American job losses stemming from counterfeit goods run as high as 750,000.[6] Other areas where there are very obvious costs include ecocrimes that range from toxic-waste dumping to the smuggling of fauna and flora, which has now reached a level where it poses a real threat to biodiversity; trafficking in art and antiquities which is robbing states of their cultural heritage; and trafficking in arms which not only helps to fuel ethnic conflicts but also augments levels of violence in more stable societies.

Whatever the precise figures from these various activities, it is clear that both the turnover and the profits from illicit activities are extensive. It is also clear that many of the activities of transsovereign criminal organizations pose a threat to the fabric of societies. Drug trafficking, for example, is an inherently violent activity, whether the focus is on the opium fields of Burma and Afghanistan, the city of Medellin, or the streets of the inner cities in the United States. Violence is used by the organizations involved to protect turf and profits and to settle disputes. It is also used to eliminate or intimidate members of the government or the judiciary as well as investigative journalists. Not only do criminal organizations challenge the government monopoly of violence, but they also pose a threat at the individual level. If individual security is inversely related to the level of violence within society, the greater the violence—whether a result of civil strife, factionalism, or criminal activity—the less security is enjoyed by citizens. Furthermore, violence is often perpetrated on individuals by criminal organizations that traffic in women and children, treating them essentially as products and fundamentally depriving them of their human rights.

As well as posing significant threats to governments and to individuals, transsovereign criminal organizations also threaten the integrity of financial and commercial institutions at both the national and the international levels. While criminal organizations are more likely to exploit than attack financial systems, the threat is a subtle one, involving a gradual erosion of trust as banking officials are co-opted to launder money or perpetrate various kinds of fraud. Transsovereign criminal organizations also challenge efforts by governments to regulate the global political system and establish codes of conduct, principles of restraint and responsibility, and norms of behavior. Regimes to inhibit the proliferation of nuclear, chemical, and biological weapons, for example, are highly dependent upon cooperation among suppliers and the ability to isolate rogue states. Alliances of convenience between rogue states and criminal organizations willing and able to supply materials, components, or precursors of weapons of mass destruction could drive large holes through these regimes. For the criminals, using existing trafficking networks for product diversification is cheap, easy, and potentially quite lucrative.

The implication of all this is that organized crime poses a novel mix of direct and indirect threats to security and stability. Simply because the threat is very different from those that have traditionally dominated the security agenda does not mean that it can be ignored. Indeed, states, international organizations, and some private-sector groups have already moved at a variety of levels and in a variety of ways to combat transsovereign organized crime.

The Existing Response

It is clear even from this brief assessment of the threat posed by transsovereign criminal organizations that devising and implementing effective countermeasures has become a major security imperative. Moreover, because transsovereign organized crime has become ubiquitous and pervasive, countermeasures have to be global and regional as well as at the state level. Independent state responses will simply not suffice. The logic is simple: So long as transsovereign criminal organizations capitalize on global processes to structure their operations in ways which limit the effectiveness of initiatives by any single state, the response needs to be extensive in scope, multilateral in form, and to the extent possible, global in reach. Even several simultaneous but uncoordinated state responses can have only a limited impact on transsovereign criminal enterprises. An effective response requires, at the very least, the coordinated participation of a significant number of governments and the nongovernmental sector. As there is no global organization with the authority, the responsibility, and the capacity to develop comprehensive strategies to combat transsovereign organized crime, the optimum has to give way to the feasible.

In this connection, there has been a variety of initiatives based on cooperative approaches among states and some private-sector organizations. At best, this patchwork of international initiatives can be understood as a variable geometry approach in which different organizations and agencies pursue different but complementary approaches to the same objective and have a cumulatively positive impact. Yet, it can also be dismissed as a hodgepodge of separate but poorly coordinated programs and policies, some of which are valuable and others little more than symbolic. A critical assessment suggests that these initiatives create confusion about roles and responsibilities and uncertainty about which measures work most effectively. Even so, they are an indication that the international community has begun to recognize the seriousness of the challenge posed by transsovereign criminal organizations. Although no attempt can be made here to consider all these initiatives, a brief discussion of the more important ones can help to provide a fuller sense of both the strengths and weaknesses of the existing approach and to highlight the components that have to be put in place before a carefully crafted and fully coordinated strategy can be devised and implemented.

Perhaps the most venerable form of international cooperation against transsovereign crime is enshrined in Interpol. The organization is based in Lyon, France, with National Crime Bureaus (NCBs) in member states. Established in 1923, Interpol now operates in four official languages—Arabic, French, English, and Spanish. The aims of the organization, as enunciated in Article 2a of its Constitution, are "to ensure and promote the widest possible mutual assistance between criminal police authorities within the limits of laws existing in the different countries and in the spirit of the Universal Declaration of Human Rights." Interpol is a police organization and, as such, benefits from the professional trust police have in one another. At the same time, it suffers from several weaknesses among them an uncertain status stemming from its origins as a "policemen's club" rather than a formal intergovernmental organization. Its regular budget of about $30 million is hardly lavish for a global organization with 270 personnel.[7] There have also been some concerns that sensitive information is not always secure.

Nevertheless, Interpol clearly fulfils several important if modest functions, especially relating to the exchange of information. Interpol's system of notices covers requests for arrest of a suspect with a view to extradition (red notices); requests for information about a suspect; circulation of information about those who have committed or are likely to commit a crime; circulation of information about corpses, missing persons, and stolen property; and notification of criminals' methods of operation and places of refuge.[8] In recent years, this system has become much more useful as a result of a computerized communication system designed to link all 176 NCBs. The Interpol database, with 120,000 records containing fingerprints and photographs as well as biographical data on criminals—about 6,000 of whom are subjects of red notices—can be accessed by member countries through the Automated Search Facility (ASF). The capacity to circulate this information quickly and easily enhances the prospects for the capture of criminals seeking cross-border refuge from law enforcement. Interpol has extended its database capabilities to encompass stolen vehicles, increasing the prospects for identification and recovery even when these have been smuggled from one country to another. It has also organized a series of conferences dealing with various criminal activities. In addition, the creation of an Analytical Section has enhanced the quality of intelligence provided to member countries regarding crime trends and large-scale criminal activity. Interpol has also sought to strengthen its relationship with the United Nations and has extended its interests to cover environmental crimes, child pornography, and trafficking in women and children.

Interpol's automated search system and the communications network are important assets in the struggle against transsovereign organized crime.

Furthermore, efforts have been made to improve the services provided by and through the NCBs and to provide a round-the-clock "one-stop shop" for all international inquiries by law enforcement agencies. The state-level bureaus vary in effectiveness, however. In cases such as Great Britain, where the NCB is located within the International Division of the National Criminal Intelligence Service, the level of effectiveness and activity is reportedly quite high. In other cases, effectiveness and responsiveness are lower.

In spite of the modernization of Interpol's technological infrastructure and the development of a forward-looking strategy, its global membership and uncertain status have made it difficult for the organization to extend its level of information exchanges and go far beyond providing "useful if modest services." Consequently, some member states have begun to look for alternative institutions through which to develop international cooperation against transsovereign organized crime.

Partly because of the perceived inadequacies of Interpol and partly because of the momentum generated by European integration (which has had an inevitable spillover effect into law enforcement through the development of the third pillar dealing with justice and home affairs) the European Union decided to create its own agency for police cooperation. Largely an initiative of former German Chancellor Helmut Kohl, Europol, as it is known, is seen in many quarters as a promising effort to come to terms with transsovereign crime within the boundaries of an enlarged European Union. A European-wide program of information exchange is being developed, with a focus on illicit trafficking in drugs, radioactive materials, stolen vehicles, human beings, and illegal immigrants, as well as the criminal organizations and money laundering activities associated with such activities. In addition, Europol is beginning to provide criminal intelligence analysis and support for investigations to counter criminal activities involving two or more member states. It also has a remit to develop both training and expertise relevant to the struggle against transsovereign organized crime.

With a 1997 budget of $5.6 million Euro (plus $2.2 million Euro for the Europol Computer System) and about 119 personnel, Europol is still in the early stages of development. As such, it is still experiencing growing pains. One problem is the slow process of ratifying the convention on which it is based. Another stems from continued efforts by member states to protect state sovereignty and their desire to maintain exclusive control over national information. Relations with non-European police agencies and other international bodies is a third area of concern. In an effort to avoid duplication, cooperation might develop between Europol and Interpol, although there have already been a few cases of duplication. European cooperation might also come at the expense of continued Atlantic cooperation—something which remains essential given the extensiveness of many of the transsovereign criminal organizations discussed above. Criminal networks extend beyond the bounds not only of national law enforcement but also of regional law enforcement efforts.

This is not to suggest that regional initiatives are unimportant. The Caribbean Financial Action Task Force on Money Laundering, Organization of American States (OAS) efforts to combat corruption, and various initiatives to strengthen law enforcement cooperation in the Baltic region and in Southern Africa, all contribute to the overall effort to combat transsovereign organized crime. In addition to these regional initiatives, there are also measures designed to deal with particular kinds of transsovereign crime. The Convention on International Trade in Endangered Species (CITES), for example, prohibits trafficking in endangered species of wild fauna and flora. Similarly, the 1970 UNESCO Convention on the Means of Prohibiting and Preventing the Illicit Import, Export, and Transfer of Ownership of Cultural Property is intended to prevent illicit trafficking in art and antiquities.

Other relatively recent global initiatives should also be noted. The 1988 UN Convention on drug trafficking included a commitment for signatories to take action against money laundering. Subsequently, the UN's work in this area has been accompanied by the Financial Action Task Force (FATF). Set up by the Organization for Economic Cooperation and Development (OECD) in 1989, the FATF subsequently promulgated forty guidelines for the prevention and control of money laundering. FATF membership has subsequently extended beyond the initial member states and further initiatives have been taken to develop more stringent guidelines against laundering the proceeds of criminal activities. These are important early steps towards the development of a global anti-money laundering regime, but there is still far to go before an effective regime is in place. Although the FATF has made great progress in extending the number of states coming under its supervision and willing to develop anti-money laundering legislation, effective implementation remains patchy and sporadic. Moreover, tightening provisions against money laundering in some jurisdictions has led criminals to relocate such activities to offshore banking centers which still place a premium on secrecy and to states in transition and other jurisdictions in which there is no legislative base against money laundering.

This suggests that although regional and sectoral measures are important, in the final analysis they provide overly narrow—if very necessary—responses to what is a much broader phenomenon. A more holistic approach is clearly necessary. Such an approach is increasingly being adopted by the United Nations.

The need for the international community to respond more comprehensively and more energetically to transsovereign crime has been highlighted most obviously by the UN Crime Prevention and Criminal Justice Division (CPCJD). The origins of the division lie in the Fifth UN Congress on the Prevention of Crime and the Treatment of Offenders in 1975. Moreover, the division has a broad mandate and organized transsovereign crime is only one of many issues for which it is responsible. Nevertheless, during the late 1980s and 1990s increasing attention has been given to this problem. On the recommendation of the Eighth UN Congress in 1990, the General Assembly adopted

Model Treaties on Extradition and on Mutual Assistance in Criminal Matters. The most important single initiative, however, was the World Ministerial Conference held in Naples in November 1994. This conference led to the creation of both a Declaration of Principles and a Global Action Plan against organized transsovereign crime. The UN initiative crystallized recognition of the problem and gave added momentum in mobilizing the international community.

More specifically, the declaration and action plan emphasized international cooperation and placed on the agenda the possibility of a convention against organized crime. The urgent need to increase reliable knowledge about the nature, scope, and manifestations of the challenge posed by transsovereign criminal organizations, as well as about the capacity of criminal justice systems to respond effectively was also recognized. Assistance in both the legislative and regulatory areas as well as technical cooperation and the provision of technical assistance was deemed essential in order to increase and equalize the risks faced by transsovereign criminal organizations wherever they operate. The declaration and action plan not only embodied a broad-based agenda against transsovereign organized crime but also, in the words of the subsequent report of the Secretary-General, "demonstrated that the international community has reached agreement on a basic set of common objectives and on the fundamental elements of the modalities required to attain them."[9] This report also acknowledged, however, that "considerably more work is necessary . . . to operationalize this basic agreement by way of consistent and coordinated implementation."[10]

Part of the problem of implementation stems from the fact that the CPCJD is limited in resources and personnel. With a modest staff of around thirty-five and a budget of only about $4 million (U.S. dollars), the division is overextended. Moreover, like other international organizations it is dependent upon states for information and does not control the scope, pace, or even the extent to which the provisions of the action plan are implemented. Nevertheless, continued efforts have been made to collect and analyze information on the structure and dynamics of transsovereign organized crime and on the responses of states to this phenomenon. In addition, the division has begun to provide needs assessments and technical assistance for specific countries as part of its focus on ways to enhance state capacity to combat these organizations—something that is especially important for developing states and states in transition. For all the problems of implementation, therefore, the Naples Declaration and Action Plan remain important as the first systematic attempt to develop an integrated global program to combat transsovereign criminal organizations.

Another recent effort that seeks to develop a systematic global approach is that of the Group of Seven (G-7)/P-8 (the G-7 nations plus Russia). In 1995, the G-7 heads of state took an initiative to counter transsovereign organized crime with the creation of a group of experts charged with preparing recommendations for the annual G-7/P-8 summits. This group, known as the Senior

Expert Group on Transnational Organized Crime, followed the precedent of the FATF and developed a list of forty recommendations, most of which focused on practical and operational matters rather than more conceptual issues such as the definition of organized crime. Significantly, little attention was given to developing a strategic plan.

Drawing in part on the background papers for Naples, the recommendations underlined once again the importance of mutual legal assistance and extradition, arguing that cooperation was essential even in the absence of dual criminality. They also highlighted the need for a central authority within states to coordinate cooperation; techniques for mutual education (such as secondments and personnel exchanges); witness protection including reciprocal arrangements; the need to criminalize technological abuses and the smuggling of persons; the importance of removing safe havens (or sanctuaries) for criminals; better firearms regulations; and the development of international cooperation regarding electronic surveillance, undercover operations, and controlled deliveries. In addition, the group urged that states should consider adopting measures for asset forfeiture, and should adopt necessary regulatory and legislative measures to combat corruption. It also added to the debate about the merits of a single convention.

If there was little new in this, the group provided an inventory of instruments and practices of the P-8 member states. The conclusion was that although many practices of P-8 members overlapped or converged, dual criminality and extradition remained a problem as some states have criminalized membership in an organized crime group while others use the vaguer notion of criminal conspiracy. The overall implication, to reiterate something that the CPCJD has long argued, is the need for harmonization of national legislation.

The most significant aspect of the G-7/P-8's work in this area so far, however, lies in the fact that most of the world's major states have placed the fight against transsovereign organized crime firmly on their agendas, recognized the need for a vigorous response, and have developed a mechanism that could eventually assist in the formulation of strategies against transsovereign organized crime. There is a growing convergence on the threat and what needs to be done to counter it. There is some redundancy and duplication, but there is also a growing impetus from a variety of quarters to develop a more comprehensive approach.

INTERNATIONAL STRATEGIES

A single comprehensive and coherent strategy developed by a single guiding authority may be the ideal approach to combating organized crime. But such an ideal is unattainable. It is nevertheless important that unilateral, bilateral, multilateral, regional, and global efforts, governmental and nongovernmental, be complementary rather than contradictory, that they reflect similar overall priorities and guiding principles, and that they be directed toward feasible goals. Ideally, there should also be benchmarks for measuring progress in achieving these goals. Dictated in part by the need to meet these requirements, the strategies we are proposing stem from some simple but enormously important questions. What exactly are we dealing with? What should be the specific objectives of the international community in responding to the challenge? What are the major components of overall, well-integrated strategies? Who needs to be involved in the development and implementation of these strategies? What are the major obstacles and problems that have to be overcome for such a program to be effective?

In response to these questions it is clear that the basis for a more coherent approach is a continuing series of global and regional assessments. Developing coordinated strategies against transsovereign criminal organizations also requires specifying objectives and the means to pursue them. Among the major components of these strategies are efforts to mobilize the international community and the private sector. Intergovernmental cooperation is an integral feature of an effective response to transsovereign criminal organizations. It requires developing appropriate legal frameworks and methods for coordinating national efforts, using international law to bolster local activities, and providing mechanisms to share information that both anticipates and targets criminal activities. Cooperative relationships among police organizations in different countries, for example, are critical to sharing information and exchanging lessons learned regarding the most effective techniques and technologies. Government partnerships with various private-sector institutions are another approach to counter organized crime. Educational programs in schools and business, for example, can prevent or retard the growth of organized crime and corruption.

In addition to these measures, law enforcement and intelligence capabilities can be focused and strengthened and methods of disruption integrated into the strategy—albeit with appropriate legal safeguards. Moreover, judicial and civic institutions in some states can be supported in an effort to eliminate safe havens or sanctuaries for criminal organizations. Where this fails, a more punitive approach may have to be adopted in efforts to eliminate collusive relationships between a particular transsovereign criminal organization and members of the state apparatus. With these requirements in mind, this chapter enunciates an initial strategic design for comprehensive international responses to organized crime. This design will need to be revised and refined as part of a continuing learning process. Growing understanding of transsovereign criminal organizations and the dynamics of illicit markets will, over time, provide a basis for more effective strategy counteractions.

Comprehensive and Common Assessments

During the last several years, efforts have been made to highlight the challenge posed by transsovereign criminal organizations and to enhance understanding of the structures, operations, strategies and instruments of these organizations. Law enforcement agencies, at the state level and internationally, intergovernmental bodies such as the UN, and public policy analysts, have all begun to focus their attention on transsovereign criminal organizations. Research and analysis, however, has been fragmented rather than cumulative. Moreover, much more remains to be done in terms of the acquisition of information, and the development of a generally accepted base of knowledge. Carefully and sharply delineated threat assessment are required to facilitate prescription and to underpin policy. Elucidating the nature of the threat and its main characteristics and methods; analyzing how transsovereign criminal organizations work; developing the methodologies best suited for understanding the particularities of both substate and transsovereign criminal enterprises; and identifying the key vulnerabilities of criminal organizations that can be exploited by state and international law enforcement efforts are essential components of this effort.

Such assessments can be facilitated by the use of criminological and social science theories—concepts of globalization, theories of markets and migratory patterns, for example—to understand the overall scope of the transsovereign crime problem. Intelligence and law enforcement information can be analyzed to gain greater insight into and understanding of the specific activities engaged in by transsovereign criminal organizations, as well as the dynamics of the illicit markets in which they operate. Using such techniques and sources of information, an ongoing appraisal of transsovereign crime groups and their activities can be formed.

The assessment can also incorporate several approaches that have rarely been used by law enforcement. One would be a "SWOT" analysis that identifies the strengths and weakness of particular groups, as well as the opportunities and threats they face in their immediate environments. This should be done with a view to identifying the vulnerabilities not only of specific organizations but of transsovereign criminal organizations in general. Opportunities for action must be identified in this stage with analysts exploring potential avenues for effective policies designed to undermine the strengths of the organizations, exploit their weaknesses, minimize the market and other opportunities available to them, and maximize the threats. Discerning the vulnerabilities that criminal organizations have, due to their structure, their operations, or other factors, is a critical component of informing the policy-making process, making it possible to identify exploitable opportunities for policymakers to advance state interests vis-à-vis criminal organizations.

While it is important to bear in mind that different conglomerations of states will produce their own particular assessments, depending on specific state and regional circumstances, efforts should also be made to highlight both areas of consensus and areas of disagreement. While state and regional peculiarities and variations must be acknowledged, the use of a similar framework of analysis would facilitate a more fruitful dialogue among states and across regions. Indeed, wherever transsovereign criminal organizations are active, there are certain critical categories that need to be addressed:

⊙ **The home base** of any organization and the scope of its activities in one or more host states.

⊙ **The portfolio of activities** pursued by the organization and an assessment of the contribution in each area to the overall profitability of the criminal enterprise.

⊙ **The structure of the organization** and the extent to which it is hierarchical or based on a flatter, more fluid, network style of operation. It is important to note here that, although there is a tendency to equate hierarchy with organization and to treat networks more akin to disorganized crime, a network is, in fact, a very sophisticated organizational form—highly flexible and adaptable, rapid in responding to changed circumstances, whether the change is in threats or opportunities, and highly resilient. Even if networks are disrupted, they generally have sufficient redundancy that they are able to reconstitute themselves so long as some of the critical links remain intact.

⊙ **The major bonding mechanisms** that underpin the criminal enterprise, whether network or hierarchy. Bonding can be based on family, ethnic or tribal ties, or on shared experience in youth gangs or prison.[11] It is also a dynamic quality that can grow as the result of a series of criminal successes (or decline in the event that the criminal organization suffers a series of reverses), which encourage the members of the organization to develop a great deal of trust in one another's contributions to the criminal activities. In many cases, of course, criminal organizations attempt to create or perpetuate such bonding by developing a distinct ethos, evolving initiation rites, and imposing discipline and an identity on their members. Some criminal groups, in fact, have evolved from secret societies or frustrated ethnic and subcultural movements, and have developed elaborate rituals designed to maintain secrecy. These procedures help to instill loyalty and fear, thereby adding to the groups' security.

⊙ **The way the criminal organization** disburses its profits. Assessments of the global scale of money laundering are enormous, ranging from an annual figure of $200 billion at one end of the spectrum to over $1 trillion at the other. Yet very little is actually known about the ways in which criminal organizations use their proceeds. Some of the money is obviously spent in facilitating and protecting their illicit enterprises through bribery and corruption, or the purchase of high-tech equipment for intelligence and counterintelligence. Another portion of the proceeds is spent on personal acquisitions such as luxury homes and cars. Some is almost certainly reinvested in order to expand the criminal enterprise. Yet another part of the proceeds might simply be saved in locations that are designed to be beyond the reach of law enforcement. Finally, another part of the proceeds is likely to be laundered in such as way that it obscures both origin and ownership and is more easily invested in legitimate business. The precise breakdown of the money into these various categories is not something which has been fully discussed at least in the public domain.

⊙ **The major links** with other criminal organizations. As suggested above, important patterns of cooperation appear to be developing among various criminal organizations. Yet much more remains to be discovered about the nature of these linkages, why some are strategic and others tactical, the way they are created and maintained, their life cycle, and the distribution of benefits. This would provide the basis for strategies intended to dissipate trust among criminal organizations.

⊙ **The connections with the "upperworld."** Criminal organizations could not function effectively without collaborative relationships with the licit world. Efforts have to be made to identify points of vulnerability that criminal organizations typically exploit or that are exploited by political and economic elites. As part of this analysis, efforts should be made to identify patterns of defection by those members of the legitimate political and economic enterprises who are recruited by criminal organizations as well as ways in which the elites recruit professional criminals for their own purposes.

⊙ **The public relations strategies** of criminal organizations. In some instances, transsovereign criminal organizations attempt to mobilize support from among the legitimate population. This can be done through paternalism and apparently benevolent acts, and through efforts by leaders of criminal organizations to portray themselves as nationalistic entrepreneurs whose activities are beneficial to the society as a whole. Programs to eliminate slums in Colombia and provide food parcels during the Kobe earthquake in Japan are just two examples. A key question is whether or not this is typical. Are there similar initiatives taken by criminal organizations elsewhere? If so, how successful are these activities? Do they constrain the effectiveness of law enforcement to a significant degree?

⊙ **The ways in which** transsovereign criminal organizations penetrate the licit economy. Although organized crime traditionally has operated in the illicit economy, increasingly there is significant crossover into the licit economy.

This is not surprising as the legitimate economy provides the targets for extortion activities, the market for illicit products, and the financial infrastructure for laundering the proceeds of crime. The banking sector and industries such as construction and waste disposal have become favorite targets for criminal activity. Exploring this more fully would help to identify the vulnerabilities of the licit economy, something that is essential to the development of successful preventive strategies.

◎ **The measures undertaken** by transsovereign criminal organizations to manage the risks they confront from state authorities and rivals. While all business enterprises have to contend with risk as a normal part of their activities, criminal enterprises face a particularly distinct form of risk—from the efforts of law enforcement and their rivals to put them out of business. In reaction to this, the more sophisticated of these organizations develop a variety of risk prevention, risk control, and risk absorption strategies. Risk prevention, for example, can be achieved through widespread corruption that ensures the home base of the criminal organization remains a congenial environment. Risk control involves measures to defend against law enforcement and other criminal organizations—counterintelligence activities are an obvious component of this, as is the use of violence against those who are getting too close. Finally, risk absorption can be achieved through such measures as the transfer of assets from criminal leaders to their family members. In these circumstances, even if the leaders are arrested and their assets confiscated, the inroads into their wealth will be limited. Developing a greater understanding of these risk management measures is a prerequisite for neutralizing or even exploiting them.

◎ **The "cottage industry"** that has grown up to support organized crime. Transsovereign criminal organizations themselves depend to some extent on the provision of certain services and products such as false identity documents, safe houses, and legal assistance. It is essential to identify these support structures, structures that have become indispensable to the success of certain illicit activities such as alien smuggling or various kinds of fraud.

◎ **The dynamics of illicit markets.** While focusing on organizations is essential, such an emphasis needs to be supplemented by efforts to analyze market dynamics and trafficking patterns in products as diverse as drugs, nuclear materials, flora and fauna, clorofluorocarbons (CFCs), and art and antiquities. Both the demand and supply sides need to be examined, along with transaction flows and the nature of the participants whose activities complement those of criminal groups themselves. While some markets might be dominated by a few large organizations, more often than not the participants are much more varied, and include a mix of legitimate and semilegitimate entrepreneurs. The relationship between these entrepreneurs and criminal organizations needs to be explored.

⊙ **The extent to which** cultural factors impinge on the structure, operations, and activities of transsovereign criminal organizations. While most groups can be understood in terms of profit-maximizing and risk-reducing businesses, there are almost certainly distinctive cultural factors (such as *guanxi* in the Chinese case) that influence or facilitate criminal activities. Just as the impact of cultural factors on licit business activities has become a topic of research at many business schools, the relationship between culture and transsovereign criminal organizations needs to be examined much more carefully than seems to be have been done up to now.

⊙ **The major strengths** and weaknesses of each organization. Criminal intelligence analysis should amalgamate the kind of "net assessment" that sometimes has been used in military intelligence and military planning with the "SWOT" analysis discussed above that is often used in business and marketing. Both approaches would encourage a focus on the environment in which the criminal organization operates and an analysis of how the opportunities that are ripe for exploitation by criminal organizations can be reduced.

No list of this kind can be exhaustive. Nevertheless, these categories provide a set of "targets" that could be pursued through both open source intelligence and more clandestine sources. A lot is already known about certain criminal organizations and there are approaches to intelligence analysis—such as OASIS (the Organizational Attributes Strategic Intelligence System) used by the U.S. National Drug Intelligence Center—that are imaginative in both concept and design. These could usefully be extended from drug trafficking groups to other criminal organizations engaged in various kinds of activity. Good intelligence, however, is no guarantee of productive strategy. Intelligence has to be used effectively. In the case of transsovereign organized crime it also has to be widely (if sometimes selectively) shared in order to have maximum impact.

Information-Sharing Arrangements

Using this set of categories, or at least something very similar, it should be possible to provide a variety of assessments that can be shared. There are, of course, several dimensions of information-sharing and critical tradeoffs between access and security. The first tier of information-sharing—open sharing—would make analyses available to all interested and approved parties. The goal would be to inform policymakers in a variety of countries about the global crime problem and the activities of major criminal organizations. For some time, there has been a perception in the law enforcement community that international cooperation on countercrime matters has been frustrated by a lack of understanding on the part of a number of countries. Clearly, it is difficult for a country not affected by a particular type of crime or a particular transsovereign criminal organization to perceive the need for action in general and for its cooperation in particular. Yet, there is a growing recognition that no country is immune from becoming a home state, host state, or transshipment or service state for transsovereign criminal organizations. In these circumstances, shared information might well have increasing impact in countries that, in the past, were indifferent or oblivious to the challenge posed by transsovereign criminal organizations.

There will be sensitivities about this. For the most part, however, the information involved in first-tier sharing focuses on "strategic," or macrolevel issues rather than tactical, source-sensitive law enforcement information. Such a focus has some shortcomings, but provides a basis for a much more comprehensive and effective diagnosis of the overall challenge posed by transsovereign criminal organizations. Indeed, the exchange of governmental assessments at this level would enable global institutions such as the UN and regional bodies to form and disseminate their own comprehensive assessments of the transsovereign organized crime problem. And even if some of these macroassessments are leaked to the public or the criminals, the results are not likely to be disastrous. The benefits of sharing at this level are likely to outweigh the costs. Indeed, global assessments of the kind described here, general as they might be, would be useful for putting transsovereign criminal organizations and their activities in context—a group of OAS states cannot make strategy wisely while ignorant of criminal activity in Europe and Asia. Although not all states need to work together, they should be aware of the general trends elsewhere. In addition, such assessments could be filtered down to serve as an element of private-sector educational programs, corporate and business awareness efforts, and as an additional component of state planning.

A second modality of information-sharing would be the exchange of key secret information and/or intelligence about criminal organizations among governments and organizations on a consensual basis. Some states might have to be excluded from such information-sharing efforts as a result of internal corruption, criminal interests, or even governmental ineffectualness. There are precedents for sharing sensitive information internationally, including the exchanges which occurred in NATO's Nuclear Planning Group, the contributions of governmental assessments to the IAEA's action team investigating proliferation activities in Iraq, and the international sharing of intelligence on terrorism. Indeed, when the interests of states coincide and those interests can best be achieved multilaterally, sharing sensitive information is not a major obstacle. At the same time, some safeguards and restrictions would have to be built in. Because operational intelligence of this type might involve information regarding sources and methods, sharing secrets would undoubtedly take place among governments and organizations on a limited basis. States would share classified intelligence only with whom they saw fit, based on their comfort level with the disclosure of sensitive information. While selectivity could sometimes cause political problems, it is essential when a number of states suffer from systemic or institutionalized corruption. In fact, it is not always in the interests of opponents of criminal organizations to seek broad international cooperation when some states have been corrupted to the very highest levels. For example, it would have been nonsensical to bring Panama under the leadership of General Manuel Noriega into an international organization dedicated to fighting crime—Noriega's primary interests lay with criminal groups and activities, not in opposing them. To have included the Noriega regime would have compromised the integrity and operational security of an international body opposed to crime. A two-tier approach to the issue of information-sharing therefore is essential. Within this approach, exchanging classified information could help to enhance operational effectiveness against transsovereign criminal organizations and provide the basis for attempts to develop effective, well-coordinated international strategies. These strategies are the theme of the next section.

Devising Strategies against Transsovereign Organized Crime

Unlike transsovereign problems such as environmental degradation and the spread of infectious diseases, criminal organizations present a *strategic* threat to the international community, not just a policy problem. Transsovereign criminal organizations are engaged in significant *dynamic, adversarial* relationships with governments worldwide, co-opting, corrupting, or cooperating with some of these governments both to facilitate a continuation of their illicit activities and to help protect themselves against other governments which are more confrontational. Transsovereign criminal organizations adapt to their threat environment, restructuring and redirecting their operations along the path of least resistance, and developing new and sophisticated risk-management strategies. Consequently, static or one-of policy responses to criminal organizations are unlikely to have more than short-term impact. Given the capacity and inclination of criminal organizations to adjust to attacks against them, interested states must recognize that they are engaging a set of strategic adversaries and that they must therefore regularly assess and react to the actions of these adversaries. Assessing threat and readjusting strategy must be ongoing processes in which governments try to emulate the qualities of flexibility and adaptability displayed by transsovereign criminal organizations themselves—both in analysis and in response.

At the same time, governments need to ensure that there is accurate and timely assessment of new threats and appropriate recalibration of existing efforts to combat criminal groups and activities in light of these new threats. Anticipating emerging crime threats provides opportunities for both preventive and preemptive actions that can have maximum impact, by allowing government and law enforcement agencies to go beyond simple reactions. One innovation that might be effective in encouraging early recognition of emerging threats is to create small units within state intelligence and law enforcement agencies that are specifically charged with monitoring illicit markets and other activities of criminal organizations and highlighting anomalies or novel forms of behavior that could presage new trends. Such units should make it possible not only to react promptly and effectively to the activities of transsovereign criminal organizations but also to attempt to divine their future efforts and to act preemptively against them.

It is one thing to highlight the need for a coherent and effective international strategy against transsovereign organized crime; it is quite another to devise and implement this strategy. Part of the issue here is simply who should take the lead in developing such an international strategy. There is no single or simple answer to this question as many governments now recognize that organized crime is no longer simply a law enforcement concern, but rather a national security threat. Boris Yeltsin, Helmut Kohl, Ernesto Zedillo, and Bill Clinton, among others, have voiced strong concern about organized crime as a local, regional, and global problem. It is the United States, however, which has begun to take the most obvious leadership role in this area. President Clinton gave the organized crime threat an unprecedented prominence in his UN fiftieth anniversary speech of October 1995. At the same time he issued Presidential Decision Directive 42, declaring organized crime to be a threat to global security and mobilizing the entire U.S. government, rather than just law enforcement, in the fight to counter it.[12] This initiative included the use of economic instruments against transsovereign organized crime with the invocation of the International Emergency Economic Powers Act to freeze the assets of Colombian cartel front companies. Impressive as these initiatives are, however, some states sometimes balk at U.S. leadership on the grounds that it is often overly legalistic and heavy-handed.

It is likely, therefore, that leadership in developing and implementing an international strategy against transsovereign criminal organizations will take place on an ad hoc basis, both regionally and globally, as interested and willing states step forward to carry out the necessary diplomatic work. "Natural" groupings for states seeking to collaborate against crime already exist with the EU, the G-7/P-8, prominent among them. With a number of states affected by organized crime and willing to dedicate some resources to countering the problem, opportunities exist for developing a more ambitious program than any previous effort. International efforts, of course, will be most effective based on consensual arrangements. Yet leadership is important both to mobilize this consensus and to establish some priorities for the international community.

The Major Components of the Strategy

A strategy against transsovereign organized crime must do several things, but most important of all, should involve the pursuit of clear and unequivocal objectives. Unless there is agreement on what the international community is trying to achieve, the prospects for an effective, well-coordinated strategy are negligible. Unfortunately, law enforcement personnel often regard strategy with some disdain. As a result, many law enforcement efforts directed against transsovereign organized crime are largely reactive, and often go little further than arresting the key members. There is little sense of a larger purpose—rather like placing one's finger in the dike without considering the next step. In contrast, an overall strategy should have clearly enunciated objectives, as well as an explicit effort to relate ends to means. The objectives also have to be realistic. There is no prospect, for example, that transsovereign organized crime can be eliminated. Nevertheless, if reduction and containment are the objectives, the strategy should incorporate not only measures to deter organized criminal activities but also initiatives to defend societies against organized crime by reducing vulnerabilities and opportunities. Actions designed to "harden" societies and institutions, in both the public and private sectors, against infiltration by criminal organizations are essential. In addition, an overall strategy should encompass more aggressive measures to decapitate the leadership of criminal enterprises, undermine the integrity of their organizations, and strip them of their assets. Because the strategy is international, however, several other dimensions also have to be taken into account. These range from norm-setting to increasing and equalizing the risk faced by transsovereign criminal organizations irrespective of their home base.[13]

The other dimension of strategy that needs to be considered is time. While some measures are urgent, other initiatives are longer term. They will take several years to devise and implement effectively. This is neither surprising, nor daunting. Organized crime is not going to go away. Furthermore, strategies against organized crime have to be sustained over the long term. Successes against particular criminal organizations do not mean that these organizations are necessarily out of business. In some cases, when criminal organizations are under a great deal of pressure from law enforcement they simply adopt a low profile, almost hibernating, until the pressure is off and vigilance is relaxed. Then they gradually increase their activity level. In an environment where law enforcement has become more complacent, they can often make considerable inroads in infiltrating government and business before they once again become the target of vigorous and effective strategies.

It is also essential to effective strategy that governments think through the consequences of success in their efforts to combat transsovereign organized crime. Removing leaders of a particular criminal organization, for example, might serve simply to increase the rapidity of internal promotion, while destroying the organization might result only in its replacement by a rival group that is even more difficult to contend with. In some cases, success in one country can contribute to problems elsewhere as developments in Colombia and Mexico have shown only too well. Thinking through and anticipating alternative outcomes, therefore, is an integral part of any effective strategy designed to combat organized crime.

International Conventions and Establishing Norms

A regulatory approach to organized crime involves the creation of a policy framework that makes it both more difficult for criminal organizations to pursue their activities and easier for governments, either unilaterally or collectively, to take offensive actions against these organizations. Such an approach rests on states cooperating to achieve common interests. Little is to be gained from cajoling states into adopting regulatory regimes or policies that they have no intention or capability of enforcing. Therefore, one of the priorities in developing coordinated international responses is for states to identify common, actionable values that are threatened by transsovereign crime. Once these national values have been clarified and placed in the context of other states' values, the process of forming strategies and designing policies can move forward.

The major mechanisms for establishing these values and codifying and coordinating international responses include international conventions. Given the subject matter, the requirement that participating states consent to proposed international responses, and the need for international legal instruments to which national and international courts may have recourse, international conventions hold a promising place in the range of options available for coordinating policy internationally. In forming international conventions on criminal law and criminal activities, the problematic question of state sovereignty is sidestepped. Rather than weighing each international case individually and evaluating the merits of foreign claims against concerns of state sovereignty, accession to an international convention would signal a state's recognition that it is in its interest generally to cooperate with other states in this area. Moreover, international conventions would eliminate much of the ad hoc nature of current international efforts, promote rationalization of the system, and assure participating states of homologous treatment.

In devising a convention, efforts should also be made to engage in what (for lack of a better phrase) might be termed *anticipatory norm creation*—the establishment of international norms governing certain activities based on the assessment that organized crime *will* become a problem in this area, but enacted or emplaced *before* criminal organizations vigorously move in. For example, had the international community anticipated that transsovereign criminal organizations would begin to engage in large-scale alien smuggling five or ten years ago, it might have been possible to construct the outlines of a response (repatriation agreements, special maritime search agreements, immigration exclusion laws, etc.) before such a response was needed. This is not to argue that every facet of life should be regulated, as that would be as injurious to civil rights and quality of life as any threat from organized crime. In those instances where methods and techniques for anticipating organized crime indicate criminal opportunities, however, and where the cost of acting preemptively is relatively moderate, there might well be scope for action. In this connection, it is already clear that attention needs to be given to reducing criminal opportunities attendant on the increasing use of cyber-payments and electronic money. Criminals are adept at exploiting new technologies, and tendencies to dismiss this as a future problem can only lead to a situation in which government authorities and law enforcement agencies will play a game of catch-up.

In short, conventions against transsovereign organized crime would have important symbolic value, would help to legitimize state actions against criminal organizations, and would in some cases have a preemptive impact. They would also "provide a set of standards and expectations that the signatories would have an obligation to live up to" and "facilitate the exertion of peer pressure as a common effort of the international community in addressing the problem."[14] The signing of conventions would also provide opportunities for public education and for efforts by political leaders to mobilize those in the private sector whose support they need in order to be more effective.

Enhancing State Judicial and Legal Institutions

States with weak judicial and legal institutions are particularly vulnerable to transsovereign criminal organizations. Even where a state is sensitized to the threat posed by transsovereign organized crime, a lack of institutional effectiveness can preclude the formation and execution of a robust countercrime strategy. While the international community cannot (and probably should not) engage in building foreign institutions writ large, there are opportunities for education, training, and technical assistance to make a difference in key areas. Functional assistance is especially important when it contributes to the development of functional cooperation between police agencies or customs services in different nations, and the United States, Great Britain, and France take this subject seriously.

Beyond helping to develop organizations in some states, efforts may also be made to develop legal institutions. Some states, especially those in transition and those deeply affected by transsovereign criminal organizations, may need assistance in developing a regime of criminal law upon which their courts can operate more effectively. Russia's struggle to devise and institute a new criminal justice system is indicative of the magnitude of the challenge in this area. It is not only "underdeveloped" states that need advice and assistance, however. Industrialized states also need to recognize that some of their current laws, for example those regarding asset forfeiture for criminal activities, need to be reformed. Laws that require asset forfeiture directly related to a single predicate offense such as drug trafficking are not enough—neither is a system of "proportionality to social harm." Transsovereign criminal organizations adjust to such laws by separating their criminal activities from other assets potentially subject to forfeiture (for example, by making cashless drug transactions where payments are made completely separate from the transaction of narcotics). There needs to be a punitive element to forfeiture laws designed to deter criminal activities.

Harmonizing Regulatory and Legal Regimes across State Boundaries

Similarly, both developed and underdeveloped states must improve their oversight of international and national financial transactions and bring their regulations much more into line with one another. Such financial transactions offer not only opportunities for interdicting criminal activities, they also offer an avenue for law enforcement agencies to monitor, analyze, and plan against transsovereign criminal organizations. States with more sophisticated financial regulatory systems need to rationalize their systems across international boundaries to deprive criminals of the ability to skirt laws by moving funds in and out of certain countries according to their financial needs. Those states with less-developed regulatory systems, however, must be assisted in their efforts to bring their regulatory regimes up to the standards of the more developed states. Rationalization and improvement of regulatory regimes governing international finance are imperative to any strategy aimed at countering transsovereign organized crime that hopes to achieve reasonable success over time. Money is the root of most criminal enterprises. Gaining control over at least large portions of the ability of criminal organizations to move and use money as they please, therefore, is no luxury for the international community. It is an exigency.

State laws can also be brought more into line with one another. While standardization or harmonization is often held up as the ideal, a more immediate goal should be to achieve what might be termed greater *interoperability*. Many of the past problems in international law enforcement efforts have centered around differences in state legal systems and specific state laws. Although many of these differences were minor, the complications they caused were major.

Simply eliminating the complications and creating a situation in which the dual criminality that facilitates extradition is relatively common would be a step forward. In addition, achieving broad agreement among states in areas such as controlled deliveries would also enhance the capacity to attack criminal organizations. There are, in fact, several good examples of international agreements that have harmonized state criminal codes or created international criminal law regimes. The 1962 Benelux Treaty on Extradition and Mutual Assistance in Criminal Matters stands as an early and far-reaching example of this type of "deep" international cooperation. The Shengen Conventions, adopted by most EU members, represent significant achievements by European states to prevent and combat transsovereign crime while maintaining a concern for civil liberties. The Europol Convention, now under discussion, would go even further in harmonizing criminal law throughout Europe and bolstering international law enforcement within the European Union. More, however, clearly needs to be done. It is also critical that regional cooperation such as that within the European Union is not achieved in a way that precludes broader cooperation, such as that between Western Europe and the United States. There also needs to be a recognition that institutional change takes time and that even if the aim is the more modest one of interoperability rather than harmonization of national laws, this will take time.

Strengthening Law Enforcement

Even if legal systems are made more congruent with one another, this will not have maximum impact so long as state-level law enforcement capacities differ so markedly. An effective legal framework does not achieve much unless it is also accompanied by effective enforcement. Raising the overall effectiveness of law enforcement, therefore, should be another component of the international strategy being outlined here. As part of this effort, law enforcement officers from countries where expertise is limited and training is poor could be afforded more sophisticated police training by more developed countries. Should such efforts do no more than raise the morale of these police organizations, enable them to take advantage of global information systems, and train them in the use of important technologies, they would be an unqualified success. Of course, entire police forces cannot be trained by foreign specialists, but trainers may be trained. This is analogous to military officers going abroad to acquire more sophisticated military training and then returning to raise the standards of their parent organizations—and is the pattern being followed by at least some governments and international bodies such as the CPCJD and UN Drug Control Programme (UN DCP). The United States, France, and Britain have established training programs for foreign police from less developed areas and from countries in transition from totalitarian or authoritarian regimes to more democratic societies. In addition, other countries such as Germany have provided training and assistance to customs authorities in the Commonwealth of Independent States (CIS). These efforts are designed to acquaint foreign law enforcement officers and middle management from these regions with law enforcement investigative techniques, methodology, the rule of law, and standards of conduct in civil societies.

They also fulfill a very important function in that they help to create effective international law enforcement networks. The importance of this is difficult to overestimate as it often takes a network to defeat a network.[15] Because transsovereign criminal organizations are often network based, it is important to create parallel cross-border networks of law enforcement officers who also develop a relationship of trust with one another, and can exchange tactical and operational information with a high degree of confidence.

In addition to international or unilateral efforts to aid specific states, the international community will likely need to enhance and empower certain inter-governmental organizations, such as Interpol, to more effectively address organized crime in the contemporary era. As discussed above, Interpol has serious limitations but could well play an increasingly important role in coordinating relationships between Europol and non-EU members of Interpol. At the same time, it might be necessary to form a special organization comprising representatives of police and security services of various states to institutionalize expertise in dealing with organized crime internationally and to produce and distribute analyses of criminal operations for tactical use by national police organizations.

International enforcement mechanisms are necessary because criminal organizations have structured their operations so that in some cases only minor crimes, if any, are committed in any single national jurisdiction. As a whole, however, these activities may constitute crimes of massive proportions. In laundering money, for example, the process may be spread across a number of state jurisdictions and specific actions (such as the investment of cash into legitimate businesses, or the loss of cash at gambling establishments) may not in and of themselves constitute crimes. When these activities are considered in the context of the other activities transsovereign criminal organizations might be engaged in, however, at least two facts become apparent. First, crime in some cases must be considered not as a single act, but as participation in a process; and second, law enforcement along at the state level, bounded by state boundaries and limited outlooks and sources of information, is not competent to meet the challenge of transsovereign crime.

In this connection, a case can be made for the creation of an international criminal court. This could be an accompaniment to an international convention against transsovereign organized crime and would give teeth to the convention. Although states tend to resist the creation of an international criminal court as something which would trespass on state sovereignty, a clearer recognition that the activities of transsovereign criminal organizations are the real threat to sovereignty—and that relinquishing some of the formalities of sovereignty may be necessary to protect the underlying realities against further erosion. Details would obviously have to be worked out regarding precisely which criminal activities come under the jurisdiction of the court. Nevertheless, it can be argued that by giving the court broad authority to deal with the activities of transsovereign criminal organizations, considerable progress could be made in combating the problem. Though this is not yet an idea whose time has come, it is a natural concomitant to a truly international strategic response to transsovereign criminal organizations.

Removing or Isolating Safe Havens

In addition to general international initiatives, there is also scope for unilateral or multilateral policy actions as part of a robust international strategy to deal with transsovereign criminal organizations and ensure that they can no longer have a safe home base from which to operate with impunity. For example, interested states might provide security assistance—of a variety of forms—to imperiled governments on a bilateral basis. Destabilized states often fail to provide basic security for their own citizens. Colombia provides numerous examples of politicians, judges, and policemen who died fighting the drug cartels. The U.S., French, and other governments can play a role in helping to protect presidential candidates from shootings, judges from bombings, and off-duty police from kidnapping. Indeed, it was an American-trained group in Colombia, in collaboration with the United States, that defeated the Medellin Cartel in 1993–1994 and led to the capture of six of the nine Cali Cartel leaders in 1995, although drug trafficking, kidnappings, and murders continue to plague Colombia. In short, when the state is weak, assistance can help in providing the additional strength necessary to confront those criminal organizations using it as a safe haven from which to operate.

In some cases, of course, the problem is not so much weakness as collusion between criminal organizations and state authorities. Consequently, an international strategy for countering organized crime must incorporate both the will and the means to influence the behavior of states that wittingly contribute to organized criminal activity. In the most pronounced case to date—that of Panama under Noriega—the United States, after a period of negotiation and efforts to induce Noriega to leave office, resorted to the use of military force.

Clearly military force is not an attractive option, either for the state that carries it out or for the nation that suffers it. This is especially so when the "sanctuary" state for transsovereign criminal organizations is large and powerful. Although it is going to be near the bottom of an options list for any country, it should, nevertheless, remain on the list. There is a spectrum of available alternatives between large-scale military force and meaningless diplomatic demarches. Economic, political, intelligence-related, military, paramilitary, and other instruments have roles to play in this regard. Intelligence, for example, can be used to foil assassination attempts or to guide foreign police operations. Paramilitary forces can protect certain foreign persons. At the stage of strategy formation the specifics of how this variety of instruments might be used are not important;

what is important is to recognize the range of instruments available to states and to conceptualize new methods of applying them against an increasingly dangerous threat.

Employing Nontraditional Countercrime Methods

Simply pursuing traditional regulatory law enforcement strategies, although more intensively and efficiently than before, will not suffice to prevail over transsovereign criminal organizations. Disruption efforts are also necessary. The law enforcement approach in practice tends to attack a few persons in an organization and put them in jail; disruption activities directly target the organization and its ability to operate, irrespective of whether the criminals are formally brought to justice. In addition to the question of operational effectiveness, which is the primary rationale for disruption activities, there is also the issue of the cost of traditional legal approaches compared to potentially cheaper disruption activities. Indeed, in many cases, law enforcement efforts focus on criminal prosecutions, which can take years to develop, are difficult to carry out and may take additional time to bring to a close. Criminal organizations, however, are vulnerable to efforts designed to sow confusion and distrust. In this regard, various methods (such as the strategic penetration of criminal groups, the application of disinformation through narrow channels to undermine confidence and trust among criminal leaders, and the employment of double agents and sting operations for long-term disruption) might be intensified. Such an approach can be particularly useful in undermining strategic and tactical alliances among criminal organizations, since these alliances depend ultimately upon trust for their effectiveness. At the same time, this is a tricky subject. It goes beyond legal "due process." Consequently, disruption efforts must be used with care and with supervision and oversight from other parts of government than the agencies directly involved in the operations. With this proviso, however, this is an area that promises significant payoffs.

One of the main contributions sound intelligence can make is to assist in programs intended to disrupt criminal groups and their operations. Counterintelligence is also important. Just as governments try to infiltrate criminal organizations, so these organizations and their allies in government try to infiltrate and corrupt law enforcement in an effort to thwart or neutralize efforts to combat organized criminal activities. Criminals seek both information and protection. Consequently, protecting government assessments as well as maintaining the integrity of both intelligence and law enforcement services require measures to forestall or inhibit criminal penetration. This is particularly important in international collaborative efforts that involve participants of widely varying degrees of vulnerability to criminal penetration and influence.

Mobilizing and Incorporating the Nongovernmental Sector

Neither governmental nor intergovernmental efforts to combat organized crime can succeed fully without the participation of the private sector in the broadest sense of the term. Indeed, government action alone is neither feasible nor desirable in a civil society. Certainly it cannot "solve" the crime problem. Effective responses require the cooperation and creativity of the private sector, government–private sector partnerships, and community education programs in many parts of the world. Indeed, there are large roles for the private sector in protecting itself, educating the public to the threat, developing civic institutions and civil behavior in society, conducting research into the nature of the organized crime problem and means of dealing with it, and cooperating with government initiatives.

While few if any individual companies have the capability to take on organized crime alone, the opportunities for collective action in particular industries and for public-private partnerships are considerable. Where such partnerships are put into effect they allow the resources and ingenuity of the private sector to be used to prevent organized crime from making new inroads. The banking industry, for example, has begun to make preventive education a priority. The efforts of the OECD Financial Action Task Force are a good example of ways to develop this type of government-private sector cooperation as are some of the initiatives of the G-7/P-8. Governments can disseminate information to the private sector on the threat and how to deal with it, and the private sector can apprise governments of developing needs regarding organized crime and of changes in organized crime activities. Some measures have already been taken. Law enforcement agencies in some countries work with individual banks to sensitize them to the threat, as well as to investigate criminal activity. In addition, the security directors of many of the most sophisticated banks have created a professional association, the International Banking Security Association (IBSA), that meets regularly to exchange information and to consider preventative measures that can be taken without the involvement of government. Some member banks in the British Banking Association have produced first-rate audiovisual training material for their employees and for use in other countries. Similarly, the U.S. Overseas Advisory Council to the Department of State—representing American businessmen concerned about physical security and terrorism abroad—recently created a Transnational Crime Committee to address methods of improving private sector–government cooperation. In Britain, customs and the freight-forwarding industry have a memorandum of understanding in which customs promises to expedite movement of commerce in return for a commitment by the industry to provide information on suspicious activities. Such information can provide valuable and actionable intelligence and has led to some significant drug seizures. Morever, because this kind of scheme requires low investment and has potentially significant payoffs, it can easily be extended to other countries.

In addition to businesses, trade unions, and educational organizations, other groups can be mobilized for educational and preventive purposes. Preventative educational programs in primary and secondary schools throughout the world—what specialists refer to as "legal socialization"—might turn out to be an important ingredient in the overall global strategic mix. Already some regions have created civic education programs to counter crime and corruption. For example, in Palermo, Italy, 25,000 children annually participate in a multifaceted educational program that incorporates practical exercises, school projects, and classroom lectures. The goal is to change the cultural norms that allow the Mafia to flourish. These programs attack the clientilistic pattern of Sicilian life, in which corruption and the assistance of a Mafia boss (for example, to obtain a job, public housing, or a hospital bed) is accepted as a necessary part of everyday life. The Comitato dei Lenzuoli's "Nine Uncomfortable Guidelines for the Citizen Who Wants to Confront the Mafia" includes citizens learning to claim their rights from the state and not relying on the Mafia for assistance, and educating children about democracy and respect for law.[16] Other programs target what is perceived to be an "exaggerated individualism" that is at the heart of the Mafia culture. As part of this sense of individualism, defending one's turf is admired, and retaliation and vengeance are viewed as qualities that make a man. Civic education programs for children, in contrast, promote self-help and dispute resolution through activities that stress the concept of team play and peacemaking. Similar initiatives have been taken in Hong Kong, while the United States has long conducted educational efforts to combat drug abuse.

In addition, a new international nongovernmental organization, CIVITAS, based in Strasbourg, France, has been created to "strengthen effective education for informed and responsible citizenship in new and established democracies."[17] The members of CIVITAS recognize the need for civic education programs to challenge crime and corruption. Its statement of purpose notes that corruption, crime, and violence "all pose threats to the vitality of democracy."

While notable, most of these efforts are new and do not systematically address the entire school curriculum. One limitation of the Italian effort, for example, is that it is not well-integrated into the regular educational program. There are few, if any, programs that systematically teach a culture of lawfulness as a way of combating future organized crime and corruption. Consequently, there is a need to develop civic education programs that can be fully integrated into primary and secondary school curricula around the world and that draw upon the lessons learned from the current efforts.

Much as private companies and educational institutions can contribute to the success of a counter organized crime campaign, other types of nongovernmental organizations (NGOs) and civic organizations can also make significant contributions. NGOs often have access to or develop their own sources of information, and they are particularly adept at monitoring certain activities in the field. Human Rights Watch and Amnesty International, which monitor respect for human rights internationally exemplify the type of information-gathering and assessment role that NGOs might play. Examples related more directly to the activities of transsovereign criminal organizations include ECPAT (End Child Prostitution in Asian Tourism) which has succeeded in focusing attention on an extensive but long-neglected problem and which has had some success in pressing governments to impose criminal penalties on citizens who have sex with minors while overseas. Germany, Holland, and Australia have had several successful prosecutions involving such cases, though much more remains to be done in this area. When it becomes clear that abusing child prostitutes overseas can no longer be done with impunity, such efforts could have some effect on market demand. Another NGO making a contribution is Transparency International which monitors corruption and produces international rankings of states.

Greater transparency is also an area where there are opportunities for partnerships between governments and the media. Journalists in print and television, for example, should be encouraged to investigate and document transsovereign criminal organizations and their activities in an informed rather than sensationalist manner. They should receive not only government and law enforcement cooperation wherever possible, but also protection when necessary. While the press has an obvious adversarial role with government, particularly important in emerging democracies, it should also be regarded as a partner especially for those governments committed to rooting out corruption and combating transsovereign criminal organizations.

CONCLUDING OBSERVATIONS

Strategies are much easier to devise than they are to implement. Nevertheless, the strategy outlined above is intended to be both realistic and comprehensive. It rests on the belief that although the growing wealth of transsovereign criminal enterprises, their capacity to corrupt and co-opt governments, and the adaptability and resilience of their network structures make them extremely formidable adversaries, they are neither invulnerable nor invincible. Although organized crime is unlikely to be eliminated, there is much that can be done to combat it. Indeed, important initiatives have already been taken. Nevertheless, it is essential to bring a greater semblance of order to a situation that "is a rather untidy mix of global, regional, and bilateral arrangements, established without a great deal of thought given to the overall pattern."[18] Developing and synchronizing the approach outlined here would help to rectify this. Cooperation has grown up in incremental steps and without any overall design, but is now at a point where some planning and regularization would be productive. There has to be a clear and sustained commitment to dealing with what is obviously a long-term problem based on structural changes in global political, economic, and social relationships.

Political will is critical both in mobilizing support and resources against transsovereign criminal organizations and in ensuring that the resources are allocated more effectively. It is necessary, for example, to rearrange priorities in terms of the balance of effort in dealing with drug trafficking and with organized crime. As it stands, combating transsovereign organized crime is the poor stepsister of drug control in terms of overall resources devoted to the problem. An alternative approach would be to view the drug market as simply one of the illicit markets in which transsovereign criminal organizations are major players. In other words, the drug problem can be seen as a subset of the transsovereign organized crime threat. The other critical issue is to ensure that combating transsovereign criminal organizations remains high on the priority list of the major powers and is not relegated or sacrificed for the sake of political and economic convenience.

Even if there is a commitment by governments to a long-term strategy that is proactive, comprehensive, and involves extensive collaboration with the nongovernmental sector, there is no guarantee of success. But without such a strategy, failure in the struggle against transsovereign criminal organizations could well be inevitable.

Notes

1. See James Rosenau, *Turbulence in World Politics* (Princeton, N.J.: Princeton University Press, 1989).
2. See Robert S. Leiken, "The Global Corruption Epidemic," *Foreign Policy* (Winter 1996–97): 55–76.
3. Ibid., 70.
4. Jonathan M. Winer, "International Crime in the New Geopolitics: A Core Threat to Democracy," in *Crime and Law Enforcement in the Global Village*, ed. William F. McDonald (Cincinnati, Ohio: Anderson, 1997), 47.
5. *World Drug Report* (Oxford: Oxford University Press, 1997), 124.
6. These assessments are provided by the International Anticounterfeiting Coalition (IACC) on its Web site, <http://www.ari.net/iacc/economic.html>.
7. Details about Interpol can be found at its Web site, <http://193.123.144.141>. For a useful appraisal of its role see Paul Swallow, "Of Limited Operational Relevance: A European View of Interpol's Crime Fighting Role in the Twenty-First Century," *Transnational Organized Crime* 2 (Winter 1996): 103–126. This section also draws on Malcolm Anderson, "Interpol and the Developing System of International Police Cooperation" in McDonald, *Crime and Law Enforcement*, 89–102.
8. See Malcolm Anderson, "Interpol and the Developing System of Police Cooperation," 89–102.

9. See Phil Williams and Ernesto Savona, eds., *The United Nations and Transnational Organized Crime* (London: Cass, 1995), 174.
10. Ibid.
11. Francis J. Ianni, *Black Mafia* (New York: Simon & Schuster, 1974), 282–290.
12. The unclassified version of PDD 42 can be found in *Trends in Organized Crime* 1 (Spring 1996): 24–26.
13. This theme of increasing and equalizing risk is emphasized by Ernesto Savona.
14. See Williams and Savona, *The United Nations and Transnational Organized Crime,* 180.
15. This is an important theme in John Arquilla and Donald Ronfeldt, eds., *In Athena's Camp: Preparing for Conflict in the Information Age* (Santa Monica, Calif.: RAND, 1997).
16. Comitato dei Lenzuoli (the Committee of the Sheets) takes its name from a spontaneous expression of grief and rage following the murder of the magistrate Giovanni Falcone in May 1992. A family group hung slogan-painted sheets from their balconies. From this emerged a cohesive group that continues to promote educational materials to counter the mafia in Sicily such as the "Nine Uncomfortable Guidelines."
17. CIVITAS, an international nongovernmental organization, aims to strengthen effective education for information and responsible citizenship in new and established democracies. Civitas International, 8, rue des Ecrivains, Strasbourg 67000 France. E-mail: civitas96@aol.com.
18. This comment was made about police cooperation but has wider applicability. For the argument itself, see Malcolm Anderson, *Policing the World: Interpol and the Politics of International Police Cooperation* (Oxford: Clarendon Press, 1989), 33.

Refugee Flows

With the opening of markets and societies, and advances in transportation and communication technologies, movement of peoples across borders is easier than ever before (Figure 1). The rise in state collapses and internal violence has also caused refugee flows to increase sharply. But refugee flows not only stem from weak or collapsing states, they also contribute to the phenomenon. Refugees can overwhelm and drain the already fragile institutions and infrastructure of host states, increasing competition for scarce economic resources and jobs (this was the argument in Florida against the influx of Haitian and Cuban refugees). Refugees can destabilize delicate ethnic or political balances (as Palestinian refugees did in Jordan and Lebanon, and as Rwandan refugees have done in Burundi).

Refugee flows pose not just humanitarian concerns but security threats. Large migrations of refugees can destabilize neighboring states. With little to lose (having already lost their homes and roots), refugee populations can be ripe for the recruitment and training of warriors. For example, the Rwandan Patriotic Front (which took over Rwanda in 1994) was based, recruited, and trained in Rwandan Tutsi refugee camps in Uganda; in 1997 Rwandan Hutus from refugee camps in Zaire participated in the political violence that led to the end of the state of Zaire and the founding of the Republic of Congo. Refugee camps can become sites of violence, triggering reprisals from host countries (for example, the Israeli reaction to Palestinian refugee camps).

During the Cold War, refugee flows were used by the United States "to embarrass enemy nations and discredit their political systems ... to encourage 'brain drains' and the departure of much-needed skilled and professional workers, and to arm opposition groups. ... Of the 711,303 refugees admitted to the United States during the Reagan administration, 96 percent were from communist countries."[1] In the post–Cold War period, refugee movements are not encouraged by the US and Western states (to embarrass enemy regimes), but are discouraged in an attempt to contain the effects of state collapse and to protect allies from destabilizing refugee flows. Containing refugee flows is an uphill battle, as societal, economic, and technological developments make such flows easier than ever before. State collapse and internal violence create powerful push factors for refugee movements, and the widening gap in personal security and economic opportunities between developed and developing states creates magnetic pull factors. Allowing and encouraging refugee movements is increasingly a policy tool of choice for weak states. Nothing makes a more powerful state sit up and take notice of a weak state's problems than a politically inconvenient influx of refugees.

For these reasons the operations of the United Nations High Commissioner on Refugees (UNHCR) have undergone historic changes. During the Cold War, internally displaced persons in war zones were not aided by the UNHCR. By definition, a refugee could only be aided outside their country of origin, after taking flight. With

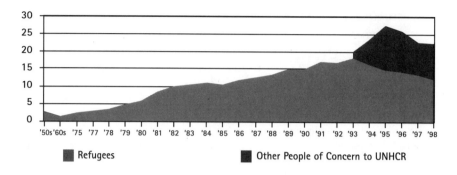

Figure 1

Refugees, 1975–1998 (in millions)

sovereignty under siege in the post–Cold War period, however, many states have pushed for allowing the UNHCR to take on a proactive (rather than reactive) stance toward refugees, serving an ever larger number of internally displaced persons in war zones, in an effort to contain the movement of refugees.[2]

Additionally, state militaries have been used to directly contain the flow of refugees, as when the Italian military contained the flow of Albanian refugees into Italy, or the U.S. military interdicted Haitians and Cubans at sea and settled them at Guantanamo naval base in Cuba. Strategic, more than humanitarian, concerns drive these activities. For example, in the "Operation Provide Comfort" mission to the Kurdish refugees in Northern Iraq, the United States sought to avert the destabilization of NATO ally Turkey that would be caused by a large influx of Kurdish refugees. Multilateral policies on refugees can be difficult to negotiate, however, because of disparities in resources available to states to deal with refugee problems, as well as to differing domestic attitudes toward refugee populations, and the conflicts that trigger refugee flows. Like many transsovereign problems, refugee issues tend to be dealt with on an ad hoc, case-by-case basis. NGO and IGO actors are thus crucial in responding to refugee problems, as states often either find it difficult to coordinate action, or turn away from the problem entirely.

Notes

1. Gil Loescher, *Beyond Charity* (London: Oxford University Press, 1993), 21.
2. Loescher, *Beyond Charity*; Hal Kane, *The Hour of Departure: Forces That Create Refugees and Migrants* (Washington, D.C.: Worldwatch Paper, 1995); UNHCR, *The State of the World's Refugees 1998* (New York: Oxford University Press, 1998).

Chapter Six

Leaving Home

The Flow of Refugees

Hal Kane

Refugees and migrants move in response to the pressures of world politics, the ebbs and flows of livelihoods lost and gained, the adequacy or poverty of resources at hand, and the wars and conflicts that result. Their travels tell the story of a changing world.

For many centuries, the story they told was of a world of inequality, a world where a few people controlled many others. Migrations from 1500 until the early nineteenth century, for example, were mostly of slaves. Some 14 million people were transported against their will, mainly to South America, the Caribbean, and the Arabian peninsula (and a much smaller number to North America). Voluntary movements of people were smaller, possibly only 2 to 3 million people during this entire time, until voluntary migration began to rise quickly in the beginning of the last century. Thus, for centuries the causes of migration centered on domination and economic ownership.[1]

During the Middle Ages, migration was rare. That lack of movement represents a history of economic isolation and political feudalism: peasant laborers worked near where they were born, and feudal systems from Europe through the Middle East, Asia, and parts of Africa kept people inside their lord's domain. Even earlier, as tribes swept down into Central Asia and Europe from the north and east, migration told an altogether different story. It was one of conquest by people who carried their civilizations along with them, and often battled or mixed with people they met on the way. At that time, migration was less of individuals than of whole communities.[2]

Those migrations formed history, creating an ethnic mix in Asia, Central Europe, and Africa; populating the Americas with foreigners; reducing overcrowding in Europe; and subjecting people to the tragedy of slavery. But nothing on that historical map prepares us for the sheer mass of people captured in the current picture of migration, when as many people can move in one year as previously moved in most centuries. And nothing in that history hints at the remarkable increase in the diversity of reasons why people now leave their homes and countries.

This is no aberration or temporary trend. Migration has become an ordinary activity: It occurs every day and in almost every part of the world. It has come to reflect the events of our time—the breakup of the Soviet Union, the desperation in Africa, widening income disparities around the world, and many other developments. More people became refugees in 1995 than left Spain—at their leisure—to colonize the Americas in the nineteenth century, one of the times of heaviest emigration. More people fled Afghanistan following the Soviet invasion of 1979 than left Germany during the last century, yet the Germans became one of the largest ethnic groups in the United States.[3]

Today's massive movements tell of countries where crime by organized clans or gangs or by individuals is replacing aggression by militaries, where internal conflict is replacing war with neighboring nations, where young people have to look for employment abroad, and where population growth and environmental degradation are making other stresses more acute. Many of these trends are accelerating. They will add to the pressures that make people leave.

Public debate has yet to address the broad question of why so many people are leaving home. Instead, policymakers continue to focus on the refugee crisis of the moment, on immigration quotas, and on which individuals to allow into their countries. A fundamental resolution of the issues of refugees and migrants will require us to look deeper and understand why the politics, economics, and security situation in today's world is causing so many people to move. That is the first step toward making people more secure in their homes.

THE DISPLACED

The world's refugee population has risen to 26 million people living outside their countries of origin. In 1989, the figure was 15 million. And as recently as the mid-1970s, only about 2.5 million people could claim refugee status—about the same number as in the 1950s and 1960s.[4]

But these numbers reflect the strict standard established by the 1951 UN Convention on Refugees, which remains in force today. This defines refugees solely in terms of persecution: any person who "owing to well-founded fear of being persecuted for reasons of race, religion, nationality, membership of a particular social group, or political opinion, is outside the country of his nationality and is unable to . . . return to it." That narrow definition is a remnant of the Cold War. Its purpose was largely to weaken the former Soviet Union and other states within its domain by granting asylum to people who fled from them.[5]

The official definition hardly begins to explain why people decide to leave home today. Many fall outside it because they did not flee persecution. Those who escape famine fail to qualify, even though they had no choice but to leave or perish. Those who fear that they are losing the means to feed their children do not qualify, even though that prospect may be as terrifying as the threat of violence. Those who are pushed out by natural disasters, such as the frequent floods in Bangladesh, are also excluded. Yet all these people can find themselves in the same conditions as official refugees.

Because these people fail to qualify as official refugees, they are not eligible for asylum in other countries. (In fact, many of them do not wish to enter other countries.) So they generally join the "internally displaced"—people forced from their homes but still in their home countries. Not counting people who leave their homes for economic reasons, the internally displaced number at least 27 million worldwide.[6]

Other people who fail to qualify as refugees do manage to cross a border into another country, but they do so illegally. The total number of illegal immigrants, both those who flee out of fear and those who seek better opportunities, is unknown but is probably at least 10 million.[7]

Some of the same pressures that force refugees out also lead other people to choose to leave; the difference is one of degree—the pressures are less urgent or severe for migrants than for refugees. Indeed, some migrants are people who had the foresight not to become refugees—they got out before it was too late in countries headed down a path toward war or economic chaos. Understanding these pressures provides insights into the situations of refugees and migrants alike.

Likewise, the reasons that some people move within their countries are often related to the reasons that others actually leave entirely, and internal migration is sometimes a first step to emigration. All these movements have at their bases the failure of societies to meet the basic needs and aspirations of their citizens.

Individuals who had moved in an attempt to improve their standard of living—migrants, not refugees—numbered about 100 million at the time of the 1985 censuses. That figure is quite rough, suffering from unreliable data from many countries, and it is also the most recent count available. Many of these individuals are simply pursuing better opportunities and could easily have remained at home. A similar group of people—those who move from rural areas to cities within their own countries—is far larger still. In China alone they number more than 100 million, and worldwide they outnumber all other kinds of migrants.[8]

All these people are a barometer of change. Their travels are symptomatic of underlying problems, from poverty to human rights abuses. Indeed, travel is one solution to the problems that migrants leave behind. From abroad they can send some of their wages home to their families or communities. They have access to education and entrepreneurial opportunities they would otherwise never have had. Migration itself is neither positive nor negative. It is simply a response to the workings of modern economies, transportation systems, and communications, to political pressures, and to individual drives.

Sometimes it is clearly bad: The fact that refugees flee in the night from the terror of persecution has no positive aspect. But others leave under bright circumstances—they move to somewhere they want to live and where they will contribute impressively to economies and cultures. Israel's innovative economy, for example, was built by Jewish immigrants and refugees who have a history of migration going back more than three millennia.

Of course, moving is not always the most desirable solution. Most people prefer to be able to improve their lives without the stress and disruption of leaving their homes or breaking up their families. They would like to have the personal security, economic well-being, and access to education, health care, and a healthy environment that would let them stay home. And many countries would like to avoid the "brain drain" of mass departure.

This human drama is still being written. Few countries have 100 million people. So imagine the novelty of a "floating" country, made up of more than 100 million souls, moving from countryside to city and from one town to another, as they are now in China. With that kind of motion, and with the economic change and population growth that have caused it, it is said that in southern China roads are being built so fast and in so many new directions that no maps are accurate. The same may be true of the way we think of demographics: So many people are on the move today, in so many different directions and for so many different reasons, that our old assumptions about demographic trends may be as out of date as the Chinese guidebooks that show rice fields where today there are small cities.[9]

Much of our thinking about migration comes from a handful of historical movements that have left a political mark on our thinking. The Exodus of the Old Testament followed a path of tribal conflict and persecution. The pilgrims of colonial America left religious persecution and oppressive government. In the twentieth century, Stalin shifted his subjects around the Soviet territories at will, Mao redistributed millions of Chinese, and the partition of India sent Hindus one way and Muslims the other.[10]

The overwhelming majority of migrants and refugees today come from developing countries, and many of them end up in other parts of the Third World. Some of the countries least able financially to cope with newcomers have been the most accepting of them. Pakistan and Iran, for example, have been temporary homes for millions of Afghan refugees for more than a decade. (Although, at roughly the same time that the United States decided to turn away Haitian boat people, Pakistan recently limited the entry of Afghan refugees, who are now congregating near the Pakistani border.) Many African countries have allowed in people fleeing famine and war. Straining under growing numbers of their own people, these countries are hardly in a position to be playing hosts to such influxes.[11]

The United States has been a longtime passionate defender of the principle of "first asylum," which says that people may not be returned against their will to a country where they may be endangered. Surprised by the magnitude of today's still-growing flows of refugees, however, the United States and some other governments are now backing away from this principle. In large part, this change stems from the difference between the people who fled the persecution envisioned in the 1951 UN definition and today's refugees, who more often flee war, social breakdown, and other problems. Western governments believed they had a vested interest in fighting the persecution they saw as a part of Communism in the former Soviet Union and China and of dictatorships in Southeast Asia and other places. (Some 96 percent of the refugees admitted to the United States during the Reagan administration were from communist countries.) Western policymakers feel less threatened by the social, economic, and political problems of today, no matter how severe those become.[12]

This leaves refugees in a difficult position. Their numbers have not dwindled after the Cold War, as many people had hoped. What has dwindled is the interest of foreign countries in absorbing them at the same time as more and more people have sought refuge from a diverse range of problems.

Once inside some of the wealthier western countries, newcomers have recently come up against growing levels of intolerance. In the United States, immigrants face a war of intolerance waged by people who seem to forget that, in an earlier generation, their relatives were newcomers too. Citizens' groups in California, Texas, and Washington, D.C., spend time and money lobbying to reduce quotas of newcomers, for example, as well as to lower government spending on those already here. In Germany, xenophobia has exploded repeatedly into anti-immigrant violence. Throughout Europe, anti-immigrant sentiment has become a plank in political platforms.[13]

But discrimination of this sort is generally based on ill-informed fears. Most studies in the United States indicate that immigrants have not taken jobs away from natives, and that their willingness to work for lower pay has had only a slight effect on wages overall. And immigrants rarely get credit for the positive economic effects that their incomes create. According to one comprehensive study, since 1970 immigrants in the United States paid a total of $70 billion in local, state, and federal taxes, generating $25 to $30 billion more in public revenue than they used in public services. In the words of Jeffrey Passel and Michael Fix of the Urban Institute, "that finding is sharply at odds with a number of seriously flawed studies done by groups advocating cuts in legal immigration or by governments seeking 'reimbursement' for their expenditures."[14]

It is true that the picture varies from place to place. In strong local economies, immigrants are most often found to increase economic opportunities; in weak ones, they have a small negative effect on economic opportunities for low-skilled workers. In such cases, local governments often lose revenue.

Sometimes state governments do also, but studies consistently find a net gain for the federal government and a net gain overall.[15]

THE HOUR OF DEPARTURE

When the nuclear reactor at Chernobyl exploded on April 26, 1986, an estimated 180 tons of radioactive dust were spread around the surrounding landscape. Because of the fallout, some 116,000 residents eventually left the "Zone of Estrangement," as the Ukrainians call it. Their reason for moving was unusually straightforward: one day a power plant blew up, and they had to leave. Chernobyl is a vivid symbol of the kinds of pressures that arise without warning.[16]

Natural disasters are another example of these pressures. Many Bangladeshis have left their country, one of the most densely populated on earth and a nation that suffers from frequent floods and natural disasters, in search of safety in India. Their migrations, which have touched off tensions between the two countries, are the result of people living on vulnerable floodplains and in squalid squatter settlements for lack of any place better. Acute land hunger has led people to move to places they know are risky. As the region's population grows, larger numbers of people will live on the lands most susceptible to floods, hurricanes, and other disasters. That means that in the future each natural disaster will send a larger group of people looking for sustenance in other places.[17]

Other migrants are also driven by a fairly simple rationale. Governments, for instance, may lure people away from their homes, or even force them out. China has practiced a form of "population transfer" as part of its strategy for quashing Tibetan nationalism. Chinese officials describe Tibet as a barren, inhospitable land. Nevertheless, areas that were populated entirely by Tibetans before 1950 are now majority Chinese. To accomplish that, the government doubles the pay and many rations of soldiers and settlers willing to go there. At 7.6 million, the Chinese now outnumber the 6.1 million Tibetans in their own homeland.[18]

The Chinese may have read Machiavelli. "Sending immigrants is the most effective way to colonize countries because it is less offensive than to send military expeditions and much less expensive," wrote the sixteenth-century Italian philosopher. The Dalai Lama catalogs similar moves in other parts of China: "Today, only 2 to 3 million Manchurians are left in Manchuria, where 75 million Chinese have settled. In Eastern Turkestan, which the Chinese now call Xinjiang, the Chinese population has grown from 200,000 in 1949 to 7 million, more than half of the total population of 13 million. In the wake of the Chinese colonization of Inner Mongolia, Chinese now outnumber the Mongols by 8.5 million to 2.5 million."[19]

Eviction is another strategy that has been used against minorities. Fearing Kurdish dissent, Saddam Hussein chased a million and a half Kurds out of Iraq and into neighboring Turkey during a three-week period in 1991. For the same reasons, he also forced Shiite Muslims from southern Iraq into Iran.[20]

Military invasion is a clear-cut cause for flight. In Afghanistan, for instance, the Soviet invasion coupled with internal fighting between rival Afghan forces provoked an outflow of people that peaked at 6 million. Before they began to return home in 1993, Afghan refugees far outnumbered those of any other nationality.[21]

Disease can also be a major factor in migration. In the former Czechoslovakia, for instance, pollution and industrial hazards have dramatically raised rates of heart disease, cancer, respiratory failures, and birth defects. The region is one of the few where these illness rates are so high that they have noticeably reduced life expectancy. Life spans in different parts of the former Czechoslovakia vary by as much as five years, with the shortest being in districts with the most disturbed environments. The highest illness rates are in the North Moravian, North Bohemian, West Bohemian, and Central Slovak regions. In these areas, divorce rates are also the highest, as are rates of crime and drug addiction—and they have frequent "inner emigration," as the government has called relocations of people from polluted regions to cleaner parts of the country.[22]

Overcrowding has caused people to move as well. From time to time during history, the size of a local community would surpass the carrying capacity of the land, outgrowing its farmland or water supply. Famous examples include the Mesopotamians and the Mayans. But today, overcrowding has become widespread, and plays a major role in the world's rural to urban migration. As they are divided among more and more heirs over the generations, for example, farms reach the point where they are no longer viable and some of the potential inheritors must look elsewhere for livelihoods. In Vietnam, overcrowding has caused whole communities to move. Few places are poorer than neighboring Cambodia, yet that country's open spaces and fish-filled rivers have proved irresistible for the inhabitants of overcrowded villages in Vietnam. Hundreds of thousands of them have moved to Cambodia over the years (though now many are fleeing an "ethnic cleansing" campaign by the Khmer Rouge guerrillas).[23]

Other people leave prejudice and head toward opportunity. One million Jews, for instance, left the former Soviet Union after the collapse of its communist government. About half of them have gone to Israel; the other half reside in the United States and other Western countries. More people left the former Soviet Union during the early 1990s than during the entire Cold War. If, as expected, future economic decline leads to even greater unemployment there, then still more people will leave. The loss of those emigrants, many of whom will be highly educated, could trigger additional decline. And in receiving countries, immigrants change political structures and demographic patterns.[24]

In other countries, some of the efforts to remedy poverty have caused people to migrate. Public works projects, for example, have a long history of prying people from their homes. Large dams flood residential areas; roads pass over land that once held buildings; shantytowns are cleared to make way for power stations. A World Bank study notes that public works projects now uproot more than 10 million "oustees" in the developing world every year. During the past decade, an estimated 80 to 90 million people have been resettled as a result of infrastructure programs specifically for dam construction and urban and transportation development. Other sectors have relocated millions more. As growing populations pursue economic growth in the future, they are likely to feel the need to build at an even faster rate than in the past, a trend well under way in parts of East Asia.[25]

The Indonesian government even has a development project with the sole designated purpose of population transfer. The goal is to reduce overcrowding. Between 1950 and 1974, the government resettled 664,000 people through its "transmigration" project, moving them off of Indonesia's main island of Java. With the World Bank adding its support and finances beginning in 1975, almost 3.5 million more people moved. The relocations took place despite warnings, which later proved accurate, that the soils on the islands of destination were poor and could not easily support so many people, and that the social costs of moving the people would be high.[26]

Environmental degradation is a common cause of flight. Millions of people have left lands where soils have become too eroded to support even subsistence agriculture. Their plights anticipate what could become the largest catalyst of migration ever: climate change. Ecologist Norman Myers has estimated that if global warming becomes a reality, rising sea levels and changes in weather patterns could turn 150 million people into refugees by the middle of next century, assuming a sea level rise of thirty centimeters by 2050. Disruption of agriculture and the flooding of settled areas would be the main causes of flight. Of course, uncertainty is an element in each part of that situation, from questions about climate change to the unknowns of social and economic results.[27]

Some of these pressures will escalate in the future. Overcrowding will increase as nearly 90 million people are added to world population every year. Pollution will become even more widespread as economic growth and industrialization arrive in parts of Southeast Asia that have lacked them. Water tables will continue to be drawn down far faster then they can replenish themselves in many countries; soils will continue to erode. And new people will react to these pressures in the future by leaving their homes.[28]

THE MOLOTOV COCKTAIL OF INSECURITY

Most displaced people are not on the move for any single, simple reason. They are forced out by a complex of pressures often exacerbated by underlying rapid population growth, ancient ethnic animosities, and resource scarcities. Unfortunately, accounts in the popular press have often reported singular causes for people suddenly leaving countries such as Rwanda or Georgia, creating an impression that the problems are more short-term or specific in nature.

Countries with stable populations and high levels of education and public health demonstrate a resilience against war and overt persecution, so refugee flows are rare. Many countries ravaged by high infant mortality, low literacy, eroding farmland, and hunger, on the other hand, have recently seen people leaving at record rates. Often these basic deficiencies are not the immediate cause for migration; instead, they set the stage for the despots, the politically motivated bigotry, and the extremist politics that eventually force people out.

The situation is analogous to the spread of a disease, since the causes of infection are often complex and obscure. Malnourished people, for instance, lose the resilience of their immune systems to fight disease. They rarely die of starvation, but starvation nevertheless underlies the illnesses that kill. Lack of proper sanitation increases the likelihood of a cholera epidemic, and serious mental stress sometimes predisposes people to colds and the flu. In such cases, the disease is only the final element in a series of deeper difficulties.

A frequent ingredient in the cocktail of insecurity is war, and since mid-century, warfare has spread. From fewer than ten wars at any one time during the 1950s, the number of major ongoing conflicts stood at thirty-four in 1993. According to one count, the average number of annual war deaths in the second half of this century is more than double that of the nineteenth century, and seven times greater than in the hundred years before that. More than 92 percent of all conflicts since World War II have occurred in developing countries.[29]

Lebanon offers a good example of how certain tensions underlie war. When the French established the state of Lebanon, they did so according to a demographic balance. At the time, half the population was Christian, mostly Maronite, and the other half was Muslim, with Sunni Muslims outnumbering Shiites. According to journalist Thomas Friedman, an unwritten but widely accepted "national pact" required that the Lebanese president be a Maronite, the prime minister be a Sunni Muslim, and the speaker of parliament, a Shiite. Parliament was to have a six-to-five ratio of Christians to Muslims.[30] By the 1970s, Christians were only a little more than a third of the population, while Muslims and Druse (a smaller Islamic sect) accounted for the remaining two-thirds. Shiites were the largest single community. When the new majority demanded a greater share of the power, the Maronites resisted and formed private armies to ensure the status quo. The Muslims and Druse established their own militias in response, and war eventually erupted. Although it was the militias that people fled from, behind the violence lay a changing demographic balance and the refusal to share power. More than a third of all Lebanese now live outside of Lebanon. The country is a place where differential population growth rates and a rigid political system converged to force people out.[31]

The most spectacular examples of the complex mix of reasons why people leave their homes are in Africa. The continent has the highest crude birth rate of any region and the highest infant mortality rate. Because of its population growth, its grain production per person is lower today than it was in 1950, despite the fact that grain yields have more than doubled. At 118 kilograms per person, annual grain production is only around half as much as would be needed, without imports, to keep people healthy. In some places, hunger alone has created refugee flows. But for most of Africa's refugees, hunger and overpopulation are not the sole causes of flight—they are two contributing factors.[32]

In Ethiopia, for instance, there is some famine even in years of good rain. The country made the news regularly in the 1970s and 1980s for its large flows of refugees seeking relief from a vicious circle of famine and civil war. At the end of 1993, nearly 230,000 Ethiopians lived outside the country, mostly in Sudan, and at least a half-million were internally displaced. At 57 million, Ethiopia's population has grown by 30 million within the last four decades. And the nation faces a colossal increase of 106 million during the next forty years, based on current growth rates. It is almost impossible to imagine how Ethiopia could possibly feed so many more people. It has some of the world's most severely eroded soils; much of its cropland is on steep slopes, and its tree cover stands at a mere 3 percent. Many in Ethiopia's next generation will probably have to choose between emigration and starvation.[33]

Just as desperate but perhaps more complex is the plight of Somalia. Clan warfare had forced some half-million Somalis out at the end of 1993, with another 700,000 internally displaced, and the conflict appears to be heating up again. A history of rapid population growth has hit that country hard, as its soils are heavily eroded and overgrazed and its forests are mostly gone, with defor-estation so severe that even fuelwood is scarce in many areas. One result was migration to cities, where tensions have flared. Demographic change and environmental degradation in Somalia have altered the traditional community and family structures and left people more vulnerable to the tyranny of warlords.[34]

In Kenya, which has the least cropland per person of any country in Africa and second least of any country in the world, a dispute rages that nevertheless may not involve land scarcity. Masai tribespeople have attacked Kikuyu farmers, chasing them off the land and converting it to a nomadic, pastoral economy. Yet many people believe that in Kenya's case, as in many countries, the source of conflict is political pressure from a leader who needs to manipulate ethnic tensions in order to retain power. In the future, though, with Kenya's population projected to double in twenty-one years, land scarcity will become progressively more acute and could easily join with political manipulation to exacerbate tensions.[35]

The implosion of Rwanda brought these issues to a new level of world attention. In the wake of the power struggle between Hutus and Tutsis, some 1.7 million Rwandans remained refugees at the beginning of September 1994. But despite the speed with which the crisis broke, it has its roots in long-term trends. The refugees fled hatred between two groups of people, as the mass media reported. But that hatred was based on Rwanda's colonial history, the inequities of its educational system, the ownership of its land, the control of its government, and other deep, long-standing tensions. Popular analysis of the disaster neglected to take most of those contributing stresses into account.[36]

War orphans and AIDS orphans, for example, played a role in the Rwandan tragedy. Like its neighbor Uganda, Rwanda was one of the countries hit first and hardest by AIDS. And years of internal warfare had already taken many casualties before the current tragedy. The generation of people twenty to forty years old—today's parents—bore a disproportionate number of the deaths from both causes. This resulted in a disruption of Rwandan family structure: large numbers of boys and young men lost their parents and had dim prospects for fulfilling lives. They were more readily recruited as soldiers as a result. Tina Malone, who organizes the relief effort for Catholic Relief Services, calls these children "cannon fodder—the stuff from which you can make a militia."[37]

Other demographic change is also behind some of the hatred. Rwanda is the most densely populated land in Africa. To feed itself, the country steadily expanded the amount of land in crop production until the mid-1980s, when virtually all arable land was in use. Today, the average farm size is less than half a hectare, and as land is subdivided among male heirs, plot size is dwindling. The practice of fallowing has virtually disappeared, manure is in short supply since many farms are too small to provide fodder for cattle, and yields have been declining. These are threatening trends to people with too little land to feed their children—the kind of situation that causes fear, jealousy, and hatred.[38]

These tensions were compounded by class friction between Hutus and Tutsis, who have been the enfranchised group. From colonial times, Tutsis have been better educated and richer. Of course, class resentment is sometimes a motive for slaughter. Indeed, a significant part of the fighting and killing that took place was poorer members of either group attacking richer members of the same group—social, political, and class struggle. *Tutsi* is not exactly the name of an ethnic group: historically it meant "people who own cattle." And *Hutu* meant "people who farm." Intermarriage between the groups is widespread, as it has been for years. When fighting stemmed from hatred between Hutus and Tutsis, it was largely a result of propaganda spread by disenfranchised factions who had more to gain from war than they had to lose.[39]

Malone explicitly connects some of these issues in her analysis of the Rwandan disaster. She suggests that the warfare was motivated in part by fears that family plots were too small and by poverty and past war. "People can easily turn around and blame misfortune on the fact that there's not enough land to go around," she says. "And then someone puts the idea into their heads about Hutus and Tutsis, and it starts." Had it not been for the land scarcity and demographic disruption and pressures, Rwandan society would have been more resilient. Yet those tensions will be even more powerful there in the future, with population size expected to double in thirty years.[40]

Similar forces are at work elsewhere in the world. In the new central Asian states, political leaders are trying to create national identities within borders that were arbitrarily carved out by Stalin. The republics of Tajikistan, Turkmenistan, Kazakhstan, Kyrgyzstan, and Uzbekistan have so little national cohesion that none of them demanded independence when the Soviet Union collapsed; they became independent by default. The lack of effective political structures has created a power vacuum. Widespread poverty and an abundance of weapons have exacerbated the insecurity that many people feel. In Tajikistan, the result has been fighting between rival clan, regional, and religious groups over political power. Civil war there produced a half-million refugees in 1992 and 1993, though most subsequently returned home.[41]

Farther west, the war between Armenia and Azerbaijan continues despite crippling shortages on both sides of electricity, wood, water, transportation, and food. Almost 1 million Azerbaijanis were displaced in 1993 alone. The main point of contention is the ethnic makeup of the country, which has an ethnic Armenian-majority enclave, Nagorno-Karabakh, within its borders. In Georgia, battles for succession by one region displaced a quarter-million people internally in 1993, and an additional 35,000 people left their homes following ethnic, religious, and territorial battles elsewhere in the country. With so many ethnic divisions in these countries, and with weak national identities and political structures, the involuntary movement of people in the region is likely to continue for some time.[42]

The nature of war itself is changing. Warfare in Burundi, Cambodia, Georgia, Rwanda, Somalia, Tajikistan, and many other places is taking place within states rather than between them. According to the United Nations, of the eighty-two armed conflicts in the world between 1989 and 1992, only three were between countries. The rest were the result of internal tensions, often occurring against a background of poverty, inequalities, and weak or rigid political systems. If this trend of internal war continues, it will send refugees fleeing from problems that were held in check in the past, many of them prevented by the dominating geopolitics of the Cold War.[43]

Journalist Robert Kaplan has taken notions of a new kind of war one step farther. He foresees a future in which crime becomes so prevalent that it replaces "traditional" war as the principal threat to stability, and becomes a major factor in migration. Kaplan describes hordes of young men who roam the squatter settlements of Third World cities as "loose molecules in a very unstable social fluid, a fluid that [is] clearly on the verge of igniting." Some of those young men become migrants themselves; others turn to crime, which includes the smuggling of people across borders. As the process develops, it can undermine state sovereignty, as by many accounts it is already doing in West Africa. No one trend accounts for the rising crime rates there; they are caused by many developments—by an infrastructure that allows the spread of diseases that leave children orphans, by unemployment, and by the disenfranchisement of particular classes or ethnic groups.[44]

In many parts of the world, people are on the move because borders are fragmenting, provinces are receiving autonomy, and states are collapsing. Eritrea has split off from Ethiopia; Yugoslavia has disintegrated; Czechoslovakia broke apart peacefully. Many people have left their homes to move into newly created states that they prefer, or to flee new states that they find unsafe. In the crowded countries of West Africa, state governments are said to control the borders only during the day. People flow freely across them at night. In the countries of the former Soviet Union, the process can be seen in an extreme form. In the past, the Soviet regime had relocated many peoples to regions far from their homelands. For instance, almost 25 million Russians live outside Russia, dispersed throughout the old Soviet republics. In Estonia, 30 percent of the population is Russian; in Latvia, the figure is 38 percent. Today, some of these expatriates will choose to return to the country of their ethnic origin; others will remain where they are.[45]

THE PUSH OF POVERTY, THE PULL OF WEALTH

The large gap in income between the rich and the poor of the world is at the root of some of the largest movements of all. Tens of millions of workers have moved from poorer countries to richer ones to take advantage of higher wages paid in stronger currencies. Some 900,000 Turks have relocated to Germany, Scandinavia, and other parts of Europe, for example. About 2.5 million Mexicans live in the United States. Some 400,000 South Asians and Middle Easterners were living in Kuwait before they fled war in 1991, and some 1.2 million foreign workers were in Saudi Arabia at the same time. Each of those migrations is a response to economic disparities between countries.[46]

Globally, the remittances of migrant workers—the money they earn abroad and then send home to their families and communities—are a vital economic resource. By the end of the 1980s, remittances amounted to more than $65 billion a year according to a World Bank study, second only to crude oil in their value to the world's economy, and larger than all official development assistance. Almost half these funds went to developing countries. Although that is vitally important, living abroad also poses problems: It often splits up families and communities, it can be difficult for migrant workers to adjust to their new surroundings, and it denies emigrant countries the labor and skills of those individuals. Yet without remittances, many families and communities would be in desperate circumstances.[47]

The flow of workers from poor countries to wealthier ones is likely to increase in the future. The world's labor force is projected to grow by about a billion people during the next two decades. Nine out of ten of these new workers will reside in the Third World, and few of these countries will be able to create sufficient jobs for them. Even the countries that reach their goals for economic growth are unlikely to have enough jobs for their young workers. From 1975 to 1990, world economic production grew 56 percent, but world employment rose only 28 percent. By 2000, world production is projected to have more than doubled since 1975, but employment is expected to be up by less than half. In Mexico, 1 million new jobs will have to be created every year to match the rate at which young people are entering the workforce; in Egypt, a half-million jobs a year will be needed.[48]

As young people reach working age, many will have little choice but to look for jobs abroad when there are too few at home. The countries of North Africa and the Middle East are already a major source of migrant labor, and the youthfulness of their populations virtually ensures that they will be in the future as well. More than 70 percent of Arabs have been born since 1970, for example. An even more dramatic scenario exists in Africa, where almost half the population has been born since 1980. The same is true of Cambodia, Guatemala, Laos, and Nicaragua, among many other countries. These areas are likely to be major sources of migrant workers in the future unless they receive considerable investment in job-creating industries.[49]

The disparity between rich and poor also makes people move for reasons other than the search for jobs. Poverty and the scarcities that go with it make people wish for better places to live. Exhausted supplies of firewood and timber for heating and cooking and building, depleted wells, overcrowded houses and schools, and a lack of electricity all plague the regions where the poorest people live. These scarcities often band together to form a cycle of inadequacy. Felled trees, for example, no longer anchor soil, which washes away and clogs rivers, and the disrupted flows of water cause further soil erosion. People are virtually pushed out of their homelands. Often they move to the nearest city, where they are attracted by the glitter and the hope of new lives.

In 1970, a quarter of the developing world's population lived in cities; by 2025, 57 percent will, if UN projections prove correct. In industrial countries, the urban population will have risen from 67 percent to 84 percent in that same time. One daring projection even found that about fifteen years from now the rural population of the Third World will begin to decrease—despite rapid overall population growth—while urban populations will keep growing. Much of the urban growth will come from children born in cities, but the size of the growth is also a testament to the combined pull of urban areas and the push of poverty on rural inhabitants.[50]

Once in a city, many of these migrants face squatter settlements with open sewers that run through the middle of the streets where children play; they live in cardboard or sheet metal shacks, where families crowd into one room; disease runs rampant. These cities then become international jumping-off points for migration by people trying to escape difficult living conditions. It is here that shady "travel agencies" take people's last savings in exchange for clandestine passages across state borders. For Chinese migrants, a highly specialized black market exists to move them to Eastern Europe, North America, Australia, and elsewhere.[51]

The world's already large disparities of income are rising, and that is showing up in the growth of cities. Despite the recent restoration of economic growth in Latin America, UN economists say that no progress is expected in reducing poverty, which is even likely to increase slightly by their calculations. And this takes place in a region whose countries already have some of the world's widest income disparities. Indeed, it is not entirely a coincidence that Latin America is by far the most urbanized region of the developing world. From 1950 to today, city dwellers have risen from 42 percent of the population there to almost three-quarters of the populatioin.[52]

For some years, China has been an example of some of the most equal distribution of income in the world. But now that is changing as incomes in its southern provinces and special economic zones soar while those in rural areas rise much more slowly. Moreover, the new income has led to inflation, as the rich and foreign importers buy more and more goods, bidding up the prices. The poor have suffered from these price increases without benefiting from the additional income in the country. And the Chinese government counts more than 100 million "surplus farm laborers," and says that every year another 15 million are added. The Chinese Academy of Social Sciences says that by 2010, half the population will live in cities, compared with 28 percent today and only 10 percent in the early 1980s. So even in formerly equitable China, widening disparities of wealth play a role in moving tens of millions of people from rural lands to cities and from one region to another.[53]

Meanwhile, in some regions almost no one is getting richer. The per capita income of most sub-Saharan African nations actually fell during the 1980s. After recent negotiations of the General Agreement on Tariffs and Trade (GATT) were completed, the *Wall Street Journal* reported that "even GATT's most energetic backers say that in one part of the world, the trade accord may do more harm than good: sub-Saharan Africa," the poorest geographic region. There, an estimated one-third of all college graduates have left the continent. That loss of talented people, due in large part to poverty and a lack of opportunities in Africa, will make it even more difficult for the continent to grow richer in the future and generate opportunities for its peoples.[54]

Increased international trade affects migration. It can take jobs to workers by letting them work in their home countries and then selling their goods to large foreign markets through export. It does, however, require investment in export industries before that can happen. Trade also can take workers to faraway jobs, such as the people who move to foreign countries that are doing better at trade, or those who work in the field offices of multinational corporations. Countries that follow an export-oriented path often experience unequal growth, in which small segments of their society who own capital and industries earn considerable income but the remainder benefit much less. The resulting inequitable distribution of income can itself contribute to migration.

As with many economic subjects, wide debate rages about whether trade is more often a cause or a mitigator of migration. Expressing a preference for taking jobs to workers rather than the other way around, an Irish politician allegedly once said, "All my life I've seen the lads leaving Ireland for the big smoke in London, Pittsburgh, Birmingham, and Chicago. It'd be better for Ireland if they stayed here and we imported the smoke."[55]

Economic events on one side of the world can pull people from their homes thousands of miles away. For example, changes on European or North American markets in the price of soybeans or coffee have led people to leave their homes in South America and Africa. In the late 1970s, coffee prices fell on markets around the world. In Brazil, a major coffee producer, farmers switched to different crops, especially soybeans. But coffee production is particularly labor-intensive, and soybean production, much less so. Unemployment rose, which led to a stream of migrants who moved into the frontier areas of uncut forests in the interior. (The massive migration was aided, to be sure, by one of the most unequal land distributions in the world, without which the numbers moving into the rain forest would have been far smaller.)[56]

Similarly with gold. In the late 1970s, gold prices rose sharply and gold mining in Brazil took off. Tens of thousands of landless workers left low-paying jobs in the coastal areas to move inland and prospect for the metal. They cleared virgin lands, opened large pits, and often forced out indigenous peoples, some of whom then had no choice but to migrate themselves.[57]

One attempt to lessen the push of poverty over the long term is the structural adjustment programs of the International Monetary Fund and World

Bank. Yet when Poland had its first experience with this economic shock therapy in 1990, inflation hit 240 percent and 1.3 million people lost their jobs. Tens of thousands abandoned the country. Other Eastern European countries have faced similar shocks. More often, though, it is cuts in social expenditures for government subsidies on food, education, health care, and home heating fuel, as well as changes in trade policies, exchange rates, and family incomes, that lead people to move.[58]

Research by the World Resources Institute on the effects of a structural adjustment program in the Philippines found that the program worsened short-term poverty in urban areas by cutting social expenditures. That led to an urban-to-rural migration to upland regions and coastal areas as people sought livelihoods from the fields, fisheries, and forests outside Manila and other cities, where they could no longer survive.[59]

An economic liberalization program in Sri Lanka beginning in the late 1970s cut social programs and increased emphasis on export industries, resulting in declining real wages, food insecurity for the lowest income group, deterioration of the social welfare system, and widening income disparities. The authors of one report argue that much of the movement of Sri Lankans to the Persian Gulf was a case of "survival migration" by those in the poorest strata of society, mostly women who went to work as domestic servants.[60]

This poses a dilemma, because the very adjustment programs that underlie unwanted emigration are needed to combat the high inflation and financial chaos that also can cause people to leave. Without adjustment, in some cases emigration will still occur, but for different reasons—because economies are completely out of control. The beginnings of a solution might come if the economists who plan adjustment programs took migration into account during their work by forecasting what movements of people could be expected. They could then at least consider the possibility of altering programs when emigration appears too severe.

DEFUSING THE PRESSURES

The problems that drive people to leave their homelands—war, persecution, famine, environmental and social disintegration—are often treated as inevitable "givens." Many people and governments feel powerless to do anything about them. But if we identify the failures and scarcities that underlie so many of these problems, perhaps we can find ways to build more stable societies. If we see in persecution, for example, the tensions wrought by inadequate livelihoods, farmland, or water, by lack of education and health care, by the fear that our children face a bleak future, then we can reduce the mistreatment by addressing those issues. Yet today's refugee policy consists of responding to crises as they happen rather than trying to prevent them.

Once refugees have fled their homes, no amount of money or assistance can fully restore their past lives. The fundamental solutions are those that will enable people to avoid flight in the first place. Indeed, even from a purely financial perspective, it is more efficient to head off refugee crises by spending money to make societies secure economically, socially, and militarily than to try to put them back together after a disruption. Preventing the emergencies that may come ten to twenty years down the road costs less, and must begin now.

In crises, of course, the international community will have to take expensive and drastic action. But even in such cases, the money and time invested yield a huge return. The troops dispatched to Somalia in 1992 and to Rwanda in 1994, for instance, were able to save hundreds of thousands of lives by getting food, protection, and medical help to vulnerable people. Rarely have government programs helped so many people in so short a time. Faced with growing numbers of refugees worldwide every year, it may be time to create a permanent emergency response unit out of the world's militaries, one that would get temporary shelter, medicine, food, and safety to refugee camps. The alternatives are to assign that task to the militaries of individual countries, as happened with the French and U.S. militaries on the border of Rwanda in 1994, or to leave the task to underfunded and understaffed voluntary organizations.

Yet governments are not jumping at the chance to turn their militaries to such tasks. According to one account in the *Washington Post*, for example, "Defense Department officials cringe at the notion of becoming a kind of super, musclebound Red Cross or Salvation Army." These operations sap time and attention of senior officials, cut into combat training exercises, tie up equipment and personnel, and take increasingly scarce defense dollars away from other operations. Used for humanitarian goals, however, militaries clearly can make a huge difference. In addition to saving many lives in Somalia and Rwanda, troops have recently protected tens of thousands of Kurds after the Gulf War, have gotten food to desperate Bosnians, and have given relief to victims of natural disasters in the United States and Bangladesh. These successes clearly contribute to security and to the protection of people—the basic reasons why we have militaries in the first place.[61]

Of course, military action can never be a substitute for more fundamental and long-term solutions. Efforts to help people remain in their homes and countries must reach across the entire spectrum, from prevention of emergencies to protection and relief during crises and rebuilding afterward. It is only through such a complete approach that the phenomenon of refugees—no longer an aberration, but an ordinary expression of the world of the 1990s—can be addressed. First, prevent crises. Second, protect victims. Third, try to restore as much as possible of their past lives. The first is preferable; the second and third cost heavily in human and financial terms.

But while crisis-driven expenditures are rising out of necessity, efforts to attack the underlying causes of flight are decreasing. Official development assistance from the world's twenty-five wealthiest countries fell by 8 percent in 1993. In 1994, the UN expected to spend at least $1 billion more on refugees and peacekeeping than on economic development. The budget of the UN Development Program is now not much larger than that of the UN High Commissioner for Refugees. It is ironic that emergency assistance is siphoning away the funds needed to prevent future emergencies.[62]

We do not have to and cannot achieve perfect stability. Many countries are able to absorb refugees and immigrants, and many countries need them to provide labor and to inject new vibrancy into societies. The goal should be to improve stability so that people who want to remain home can do so.

Some countries that are not sources of refugees today are likely to become so during the next few years. The UN recently voiced particularly strong concern about Angola, Iraq, Myanmar (formerly Burma), and Sudan. The collapse of Haiti did not come as a surprise to many observers. Zaire suffered from severe political and economic collapse for years before entering into war. Nigeria's elected government has been refused control by the military, and violent clashes have resulted, raising the possibility of a flight from that country.[63]

Efforts to head off crises and flows of refugees or emigrants from these countries will be more fruitful if they begin today rather than waiting for chaos, as happened in Haiti, Rwanda, Somalia, and elsewhere. In the words of J. Brian Atwood, head of the U.S. Agency for International Development, upon returning from a trip to Africa: "Just the other day we made a decision to contribute $35 million additional to handle this disaster [in Rwanda]. One wonders if we had had that $35 million in the previous two years whether we could have done something to avoid the killing."[64]

In this light, initiatives not normally considered relevant to refugees become central. Spending on sanitation, public health, and preventive medicine would reduce parental mortality, and intact families would give children a more secure future. Maintaining stable soils and waters for farming would defuse tensions over land and livelihoods. Investing in literacy can also have a profoundly stabilizing effect by helping people read about the actions of their governments and get more involved in solving the problems of their regions. Without such actions, the problems that people flee from will continue to return.

Many examples of attacking the underlying pressures exist. The International Conference on Population and Development in Cairo in September 1994 was one such effort. Its plan to keep world population below 9.8 billion people by 2050, and to do so by focusing on women and by spreading literacy, health care, and family planning technologies, directly attacks the underpinnings of some of the insecurities and wars that chase out refugees. Likewise, UNICEF's great successes recently at immunizing infants around the world is a significant contribution to stability. Tiny loans of a few dollars to poor villagers by the Grameen Bank in Bangladesh have brought success to people in the poorest class in one of the most densely populated countries on earth. These efforts should receive credit for their ability to enhance security.[65]

If topics like improved literacy seem far removed from the pressures that make people refugees, consider the fact that no democracy that has a relatively free press has ever suffered a major famine. If access by literate people to public debate seems too detached from warfare to be relevant, consider the fact that no two democracies have ever gone to war.[66]

Notes

1. Aaron Segal, *An Atlas of International Migration* (London: Hans Zell Publishers, 1993).
2. Ibid.; Colin McEvedy and Richard Jones, *Atlas of World Population History* (New York: Penguin, 1978).
3. U.S. Committee for Refugees (USCR), *World Refugee Survey 1994* (Washington, D.C.: 1994); Segal, *An Atlas of International Migration.*
4. Based on United Nations High Commissioner for Refugees (UNHCR), *The State of the World's Refugees 1993: The Challenge of Protection* (London: Penguin, 1993), on later updates, and on Worldwatch estimates based on press reports.
5. Gil Loescher, *Beyond Charity: International Cooperation and the Global Refugee Crisis* (Oxford: Oxford University Press, 1993).
6. USCR, *World Refugee Survey 1994.*
7. Worldwatch estimate based on Hania Zlotnik, UN Population Division, private communication, October 3, 1994; on Michael S. Teitelbaum, Sloan Foundation, private communication, October 3, 1993; and on Segal, *An Atlas of International Migration.*
8. Migrant figure is a Worldwatch estimate based on United Nations, "International Migration Stock, Trends in Total Migrant Stock" (electronic database), United Nations, New York, 1994; on Sharon Stanton Russell and Michael S. Teitelbaum, "International Migration and International Trade," *World Bank Discussion Paper 160* (Washington, D.C.: World Bank, 1992); on Teitelbaum, private communication; on Zlotnik, private communication; and on Segal, *An Atlas of International Migration*; Chinese migrants from World Bank, *China: Strategies for Reducing Poverty in the 1990s* (Washington, D.C.: World Bank, 1992).
9. Paul Theroux, "Going to See the Dragon," *Harpers* (October 1993).
10. William G. Rosenberg and Marilyn B. Young, *Transforming Russia and China: Revolutionary Struggle in the Twentieth Century* (New York: Oxford University Presss, 1982); Myron Weiner, "Rejected Peoples and Unwanted Migrants in South Asia," *Economic and Political Weekly* (August 21, 1993).
11. USCR, *World Refugee Survey 1994*; Morton Abramowitz, "Exodus: The World Refugee Crisis," *Foreign Policy* (Summer 1994).
12. Abramowitz, "Exodus"; refugees admitted to United States during Reagan years from Loescher, *Beyond Charity.*

13. Deborah Sontag, "Illegal Aliens Put Uneven Load on States, Study Says," *New York Times* (September 15, 1994); William Drozdiak, "Rolling Up a Worn-Out Welcome Mat," *Washington Post* (July 13, 1993).

14. Jeffrey S. Passel and Michael Fix, "Myths About Immigrants," *Foreign Policy* (Summer 1994).

15. Ibid.

16. Mike Edwards, "Chernobyl: Living with the Monster," *National Geographic* (August 1994).

17. *Bangladesh Flood Action Plan Newsletter* (National Audubon Society, New York), March 1993.

18. Department of Information and International Relations, Central Tibetan Administration of His Holiness the XIV Dalai Lama, "Tibet: Environment and Development Issues 1992," Dharamsala, India, 1992; International Campaign for Tibet, "The Long March: Chinese Settlers and Chinese Policies in Eastern Tibet, Results of a Fact-Finding Mission in Tibet," Dharamsala, India, September 1991.

19. Machiavelli quote from Christa Meindsma, quoted in "UN Recognizes Population Transfer As a Violation of Human Rights," *Tibet Press Watch* (December 1992); Dalai Lama quoted in "Dalai Lama: U.S. Must Help Stop Chinese Population Influx into Tibet," *Tibet Press Watch* (May 1993).

20. Iraqi exodus cited in Raymond Bonner, "Trail of Suffering As Rwandan Exodus Continues," *New York Times* (July 16, 1994).

21. USCR, *World Refugee Survey 1994.*

22. Josef Vavrousek, et al., Department of the Environment, State Commission for Science, Technology, and Investments, *The Environment in Czechoslovakia* (Prague: Institute of Technical, Economic, and Ecological Information, 1990).

23. Joseph A. Tainter, *The Collapse of Complex Societies* (Cambridge: Cambridge University Press, 1988); Victor Mallet, "Vietnamese Settlers in Cambodia Flee Attacks," *Financial Times* (March 31, 1993).

24. Robin Wright and Doyle McManus, *Flashpoints: Promise and Peril in a New World* (New York: Alfred A. Knopf, 1991).

25. World Bank Environment Department, *Resettlement and Development: The Bankwide Review of Projects Involving Involuntary Resettlement 1986–1993* (Washington, D.C.: 1994).

26. Bruce Rich, *Mortgaging the Earth* (Boston: Beacon Press, 1994).

27. Norman Myers, "Environmental Refugees in a Globally Warmed World," *Bioscience* (December 1993).

28. Population figures from U.S. Bureau of the Census, published in Francis Urban and Ray Nightingale, *World Population by Country and Region, 1950–90 and Projections to 2050* (Washington, D.C.: U.S. Department of Agriculture (USDA), Economic Research Service, 1993).

29. Number in 1950s from Ruth Leger Sivard, *World Military and Social Expenditures 1993* (Washington, D.C.: World Priorities, 1993); number of major wars in the 1990s from Birger Heldt, Peter Wallensteen, and Kjell-Ake Nordquist, "Major Armed Conflicts in 1991," in Stockholm International Peace Research Institute (SIPRI), *SIPRI Yearbook 1992: World Armaments and Disarmament* (New York: Oxford University Press, 1992), and from Peter Wallensteen and Karin Axell, "Major Armed Conflicts," in SIPRI, *SIPRI Yearbook 1994* (New York: Oxford University Press, 1994).

30. Thomas L. Friedman, *From Beirut to Jerusalem* (New York: Anchor Books, 1989).

31. Ibid.

32. Population Reference Bureau (PRB), *1994 World Population Data Sheet* (Washington, D.C.: 1994); USDA, "Production, Supply, and Demand View" (electronic database), Washington, D.C., November 1993.

33. USCR, *World Refugee Survey 1994*; Bureau of the Census, in *World Population by Country and Region*; USDA, "Production, Supply, and Demand View."

34. Bruce Byers, "Roots of Somalia's Crisis," *Christian Science Monitor,* December 24, 1992.

35. Kenyan cropland scarcity from United Nations, *Report on the World Social Situation 1993* (New York: 1993); Keith B. Richburg, "Kenya's Ethnic Conflict Drives Farmers Off Land," *Washington Post,* March 17, 1994; Leslie Crawford, "Suffering the Politics of Drought," *Financial Times,* March 17, 1994; Tribal Clashes Resettlement Volunteer Service, "Politically Motivated Tribal Clashes in Kenya," Nairobi, Kenya: undated; doubling time from PRB, *1994 World Population Data Sheet.*

36. Number of refugees from U.S. Agency for International Development, "Consolidated Rwanda Report, Update #10," August 30–September 8, 1994.

37. Tina Malone, Catholic Relief Services, Baltimore, Md., private communication, September 22, 1994.

38. Population density from PRB, *1994 World Population Data Sheet*; "Rwanda: A Case of Successful Adaptation," in World Bank, *Sub-Saharan Africa: From Crisis to Sustainable Growth* (Washington, D.C.: 1989); farm size from Centro Internacional de Agricultura Tropical, "Rwanda Civil War Disrupts Key African Food Program," *CIAT On-Line: News on Research Progress, Impact, and Achievement* (July 1994).

39. Benoit Bosquet, Africa Department, World Bank, Washington, D.C., private communication, July 19, 1994; Malone, private communication.

40. Malone, private communication; PRB, *1994 World Population Data Sheet.*

41. Gillian Tett, "Elegant Exorcism of Central Bogeymen," Review of *The Resurgence of Central Asia—Islam or Nationalism?, Financial Times,* July 28, 1994; Raymond Bonner, "Asian Republic Still Caught in Web of Communism," *New York Times,* October 13, 1993; number of Tajik refugees from USCR, *World Refugee Survey.*

42. "Refugees On Move In Azerbaijan War," *New York Times,* August 16, 1993; Mark A. Uhlig, "The Karabakh War," *World Policy Journal* (Winter 1993); USCR, *World Refugee Survey.*

43. Ian Steele, "Countries Prepare for War While People Die of Hunger, Disease," *Depth-news Asia* (June, 1994); United Nations Development Program (UNDP), *Human Development Report 1994* (New York: Oxford University Press, 1994).

44. Robert D. Kaplan, "The Coming Anarchy," *Atlantic Monthly* (February 1994).

45. Jaques Attali, "An Age of Yugoslavias," *Harpers Magazine* (January 1993, reprinted from *New Perspectives Quarterly,* Fall 1992).

46. Segal, *An Atlas of International Migration.*

47. Russell and Teitelbaum, "Internal Migration."

48. UNDP, *Human Development Report;* Emma Tucker, "Global Pressures are Getting Worse," *Financial Times* (January 31, 1994).

49. Kaplan, "The Coming Anarchy"; PRB, *1994 World Population Data Sheet.*

50. United Nations, *Prospects of World Urbanization 1988* (New York: 1989); Jane Pryer and Nigel Crook, *Cities of Hunger: Urban Malnutrition in Developing Countries* (Oxford: Oxfam, 1988).

51. Jorge E. Hardoy and David Satterthwaite, *Squatter Citizen* (London: Earthscan, 1989); Segal, *An Atlas*; Roberto Suro, "Chinese Smuggling Grows, Forcing U.S. Resentment,"

Washington Post (June 2, 1994); Ashley Dunn, "Golden Venture, Then a New Ordeal," *New York Times* (June 5, 1994).

52. "Latin American Speedup Leaves Poor Behind," *New York Times,* September 7, 1994; Thomas Kamm, "Epidemic of Slums Afflicts Latin America," *Wall Street Journal,* August 30, 1994; United Nations, *World Urbanization Prospects, The 1992 Revision* (New York: United Nations, 1993).

53. World Bank, *China*; Tony Walker, "China's Golden Era To Last Well Into Next Century," *Financial Times,* August 26, 1994; National Academy findings from "China's Next Revolution," *Financial Times,* August 26, 1994.

54. Helene Cooper, "Sub-Saharan Africa is Seen as Big Loser in GATT's New World Trade Accord," *Wall Street Journal,* August 15, 1994; brain drain from John Darnton, "'Lost Decade' Drains Africa's Vitality," *New York Times,* June 19, 1994.

55. "International Migration and Trade," *HRO Dissemination Notes: Human Resources Development and Operations Policy,* World Bank, Washington, D.C., June 20, 1994; Irish politician from Barbara K. Rodes and Rice Odell, compilers, *A Dictionary of Environmental Quotations* (New York: Simon & Schuster, 1992).

56. International Monetary Fund (IMF), *International Financial Statistics* (Washington, D.C.: various years); Ralph Hakkert and Franklin W. Goza, "The Demographic Consequences of Austerity in Latin America," in *Lost Promises: Debt, Austerity, and Development in Latin America,* ed. William L. Canak (Boulder, Colo.: Westview Press, 1989).

57. Ibid.

58. "Expert Group Meeting on Population Distribution and Migration," *Population Bulletin of the United Nations,* Nos. 34/35, 1993 (summary findings of the Expert Group Meeting held in Santa Cruz, Bolivia, January, 18–22 1993); Wright and McManus, *Flashpoints.*

59. Wilfredo Cruz and Robert Repetto, *The Environmental Effects of Stabilization and Structural Adjustment Programs: The Philippines Case* (Washington, D.C.: World Resources Institute, 1992); Hakkert and Goza, "The Demographic Consequences."

60. Sharon Stanton Russell, review of *Labour Migration to the Middle East: From Sri Lanka to the Gulf, Population and Development Review,* September 1993.

61. Bradley Graham, "Pentagon Officials Worry Aid Missions Will Sap Military Strength," *Washington Post,* July 29, 1994; Jane Perlez, "Aid Agencies Hope to Enlist Military Allies in the Future," *New York Times,* August 21, 1994.

62. Wealthiest-country development assistance from Organization for Economic Cooperation and Development, "Sharp Changes in the Structure of Financial Flows to Developing Countries and Countries in Transition," press release, Paris, June 20, 1994; UN development and peacekeeping spending from Erskine Childers with Brian Urquhart, "Renewing the United Nations System," *Development Dialogue* (Dag Hammarskjöld Foundation/Ford Foundation), 1994:1; UNHCR budget from Heather Courtney, public information officer, UNHCR, Washington, D.C., private communication, October 4, 1994; UNDP budget from Ad de Rad, UNDP, New York, private communication, October 19, 1994.

63. Ian Steele, "Peacekeeping Gives UN Serious Money Troubles," *Depthnews Asia,* June 1994; UNDP, *Human Development Report*; Oscar-Jean N'Galamulume, "Arms Embargo, Food Aid Could Stay Zaire's Crisis," *Christian Science Monitor* (March 16, 1994).

64. Jennifer Parmelee, "U.S. Aims to Head Off Threat of an African Famine," *Washington Post,* May 31, 1994.

65. UN General Assembly, "Draft Programme of Action of the International Conference on Population and Development," New York, September 19, 1994; UNICEF and World Health Organization, New York and Geneva, private communications, February 17, 1994; Andreas Fuglesang and Dale Chandler, *Participation As Process: What We Can Learn from Grameen Bank, Bangladesh* (Dhaka, Bangladesh: Grameen Bank, 1988).

66. Amartya Sen, "The Economics of Life and Death," *Scientific American* (May 1993); Harald Muller, director, Frankfurt Peace Research Institute, private communication, February 1991.

The Spread of Disease

Although open society, technology, and economy forces have contributed to great advances in public health in this century, natural selection and adaptation have created more dangerous and drug-resistant strains of infectious diseases, which open societies, economies, and technologies then help spread. "Microbes have appeared that can grow on a bar of soap, swim unabashed in bleach, and ignore doses of penicillin logarithmically larger than those effective in 1950. In the microbial soup, then, is a vast, constantly changing lending library of genetic material that offers humanity's minute predators myriad ways to outmaneuver the drug arsenal."[1]

Malaria, once thought to be conquered, now infects some 110 million and kills 1 to 2 million people per year, because a new strain of the disease has "grown resistant to chloroquine, the 'golden bullet' that once prevented the disease. The development of drugs to take its place are years away."[2] As James Hughes, director of the National Center for Infectious Diseases at the Centers for Disease Control and Prevention in Atlanta describes the process of developing new drugs to combat new, more virulent strains, "The pipeline is dry. We really have a global crisis."[3]

Before 1991, cholera was virtually eliminated from the Americas. By July of 1991, there were over a quarter million new cases of infection and over 2,600 dead.[4] This is due in part to the increase in polluted water. Over 25 percent of the world does not have access to safe drinking water.[5]

Tuberculosis (TB) is another infectious disease, once thought to be under control, that has developed a more virulent strain which "is resistant to every available drug, and kills half its victims." New York City alone has spent more than $1 billion battling TB, yet there were 3,000 TB cases in the city in 1994.[6]

The worldwide AIDS epidemic is another example. According to the 1998 World Health Organization's Report on HIV/AIDS, over 30.6 million people are currently infected with HIV/AIDS; over 1.1 million of those cases are children. Over 16,000 people a day are infected with HIV/AIDS.[7]

> Most HIV-infected people live in urban areas, and 70 percent are in the prime productive ages of 20–40 years. . . . [Over 6 percent] are children. In the United States, AIDS is now the prime cause of death for men aged 25–44, and the fourth most important for women in that age group. The cumulative direct and indirect costs of HIV and AIDS in the 1980s have been conservatively estimated at $240 billion. . . . Future projections are alarming. By 2000, the number of HIV-infected people is expected to rise to between 30 and 40 million—13 million of them women. By that time, the epidemic would have left more than 9 million African children as orphans. The geographical distribution of HIV and AIDS is changing. In the mid-1980s, the epidemic was well-established in North America and Africa, but by 2000, most of the new infections will be in Asia. . . .

> The global cost—direct and indirect—of HIV and AIDS by 2000 could be as high as $500 billion a year—equivalent to more than 2 percent of global GDP.[8]

In 1991, the World Health Organization estimated that 9 to 11 million people were infected with HIV, with the majority of cases in the United States, followed by Brazil.[9] Despite greater public awareness, information, and prevention efforts concerning AIDS, by 1998 the HIV-infected population had grown to over 31 million people with HIV/AIDS. The rate of infection among U.S. citizens is no longer increasing as rapidly, but in India 3 million are infected with HIV, giving India a dubious "number one" distinction. The vast majority of HIV infections now occur in developing states which may be least equipped to check the spread of the disease; two-thirds are in sub-Saharan Africa. No state is immune, however. Open societies, economies, and technologies ensure that previously isolated states such as Russia, China, and Vietnam are now experiencing increased rates of infection.[10]

The costs of combating the disease, along with the decreased productivity of the workforce infected, are taking their toll on fragile state institutions. As Dr. Michael H. Merson, director of the World Health Organization's (WHO) Global Program on AIDS put it, "The AIDS pandemic has become a major factor to be reckoned with in the world economy. The deaths of as many as one-fifth of young and middle-aged adults over a short period of time will lead to social turmoil, economic disruption, and even political destabilization in many countries."[11]

While the major causes of death in developing countries are infectious and parasitic diseases, which kill about 17 million people annually, the developed countries are not immune. Open societies, open economies, and open technologies create greater opportunities for infectious diseases to spread.

> Geographic sequestration was crucial in all postwar health planning, but diseases can no longer be expected to remain in their country of origin . . . in 1996, when some half a billion passengers will board airline flights. Everyday, one million people cross an international border. One million a week travel between the industrial and developing worlds. And as people move, unwanted microbial hitchhikers tag along. In the nineteenth century most diseases and infections that travelers carried manifested themselves during the long sea voyages that were the primary means of covering great distances. Recognizing the symptoms, the authorities at ports of entry could quarantine contagious individuals or take other action. In the age of jet travel, however, a person incubating a disease such as Ebola can board a plane, travel 12,000 miles, pass unnoticed through customs and immigration, take a domestic carrier to a remote destination, and still not develop symptoms for several days, infecting many other people before his condition is noticeable.[12]

Thus, while open society, open economy, and open technology forces can help contribute resources to combat the spread of infectious disease, these dynamics also create an infrastructure that allows and encourages diseases to spread.

Notes

1. Laurie Garrett, "The Return of Infectious Disease," *Foreign Affairs* (January/February 1996): 68.
2. Foreign Policy Association, "AIDS Pandemic: Global scourge, U.S. challenge," *Great Decisions 1992,* 74.
3. Garrett, "The Return of Infectious Disease," 68.
4. Foreign Policy Association, "AIDS Pandemic: Global scourge, US challenge," 74.
5. UNDP, *Human Development Report 1994,* 28.
6. Garrett, "The Return of Infectious Disease," 76.
7. United Nations World Health Organization, "Global HIV/AIDS and STD Surveillance Report," June 1998.
8. UNDP, *Human Development Report 1994,* 28.
9. Foreign Policy Association, "AIDS Pandemic: Global scourge, US challenge," 70.
10. Dr. Peter Piot, quoted at the 11th international AIDS meeting in Vancouver, British Columbia, Canada, by Lawrence K. Altman, "India Quickly Leads in H.I.V. Cases, AIDS Meeting Hears," *New York Times,* July 8, 1996, A3.
11. Foreign Policy Association, "AIDS Pandemic: Global scourge, US challenge," 69.
12. Garrett, "The Return of Infectious Disease," 68.

Ecological Interdependence and the Spread of Infectious Disease

Dennis Pirages and Paul Runci

Viruses, bacteria, and various kinds of plants and animals have never respected national borders. They have traveled across frontiers with the winds, waters, explorers, merchants, and mercenaries. Most of the time these crossings have been quite innocent, but occasionally whole societies or ecosystems have been reshaped by them. Now there is growing concern over the impact of increasing globalization on the potential development and spread of new and resurgent diseases across increasingly porous borders.

Over the course of history, populations of human beings have been involved in struggles with various kinds of other species as well as potentially pathogenic microorganisms. Only during the last century has technological innovation given Homo sapiens a clear, but perhaps temporary, competitive edge in this struggle. There is now growing evidence that various kinds of destructive microorganisms are making a comeback in an increasingly interdependent and urbanized global system. And various plant and animal species, being accidentally introduced to new environments through expanded trade and more rapid transportation, are exacting a heavy economic toll in many countries. The changes associated with increasingly open societies, open economies, and dependence on new technologies—growing economic integration, the gradual disappearance of national borders, more rapid movement of people and goods among regions, weakening of the authority of the state, and changing patterns of human settlements and behavior—are combining to make the resurgence of pathogenic microorganisms, as well as the worldwide spread of various kinds of other potentially destructive species, an important threat to future human security and well-being.[1]

The processes associated with globalization have been quietly under way for quite some time. Their feeble origins can be detected in the period soon after a scattering of the world's human populations in a period referred to as the great human diasporas. The first modern humans lived about one hundred thousand years ago and inhabited areas in Eastern Africa and/or the Middle East. From there a series of expansions and migrations moved outward until most of the habitable world had been at least loosely settled between ten or fifteen thousand years ago.[2] Since then, there has been a slow but accelerating reintegration of these previously scattered and mostly isolated human populations into larger units as the barriers among them gradually disappeared. The Roman Empire, the Mongol empires, and European colonialism are all examples of the ways that previously isolated human populations have been concentrated into much larger administrative units. This long-term and sporadic reintegration process is now culminating in the creation of a very large global village with many different neighborhoods. But each step in this reintegration of human populations has had significant ecological, political, and socioeconomic consequences, not the least of which has been the insecurity associated with the rapid spread of disease.

INTEGRATION AND DISEASE IN HISTORY

Homo sapiens is one species among millions now sharing the global ecosystem. Like most other species, Homo sapiens live in and identify with basic units called populations. Populations of any species can be defined as "dynamic systems of interacting individuals . . . that are potentially capable of interbreeding with each other."[3] Thus, the boundaries of human populations could theoretically be located by mapping subtle genetic differences resulting from generations of interbreeding. But it is easier to identify population boundaries through related marked gaps in communication efficiency. These communication gaps and inefficiencies both help to maintain and are maintained by so-called ethnic differences that are reflected in different language, behavior, values, and beliefs.[4]

Throughout much of human history, the boundaries of human populations, their political administrative units, and the local ecosystems in which they have been embedded have overlapped. The early great outward dispersals of the Earth's human populations resulted in a world inhabited by thousands of geographically isolated human populations that were administered as clans, tribes, and kingdoms. These populations coevolved with other species and microorganisms within the constraints of shared local ecosystems. It was only with the evolution of larger administrative units, such as empires, that the large-scale mingling of previously isolated human populations and the microorganisms that they carried, began to take place.

Technological innovations in transportation and warfare spurred conquests that eventually culminated in larger and more powerful political units. But the integration of previously small and isolated populations of human beings into empires and cities exacted a tragic toll of deaths from warfare and disease. Thus, William McNeill has observed that the Roman Empire was repeatedly wracked by the scourge of strange diseases. There were at least eleven microbial disasters in republican times. A major epidemic struck the densely packed city of Rome in 65 C.E., but that paled in comparison with a more widespread epidemic that began to sweep the Roman Empire in 165 C.E. Mortality as a result of this latter plague was heavy: one-quarter to one-third of those exposed to the disease died.[5]

In more recent history, the integration of growing European populations into a nascent global community has had similar disease ramifications. By the year 1350 the various populations (states) of the Western European region had become large and dense enough to press against the carrying capacity of relevant ecosystems and even up against each other. Such pressures led to local European famines which were reported in most years between 1290 and 1350 C.E.[6] At the same time contacts and commerce among populations was increasing, even spreading out to lengthy trade routes between Western Europe and China. The intensification of caravan traffic across Asia and contact among those previously isolated populations reached a high point under the Mongol empires. At the height of Mongol power, the empires embraced nearly all of China and Russia as well as Central Asia, Iran, and Iraq.[7]

During this period of European population increase, urban growth, and expanded commerce, significant numbers of people, including messengers, merchants, and mercenaries, were moving among previously isolated human populations. And this increased contact resulted in the spread of new diseases to Europe from the Orient, the most infamous being *Pasteurella pestis,* also known as the black death. The arrival of the black death in Europe in 1346 began a lengthy pruning process by which successive waves of disease trimmed the region's population by nearly 40 percent, with the highest mortality rates being in the urban areas.[8]

Contact among previously separated populations took another great leap forward during the age of European exploration and colonization. The ships of Christopher Columbus, which arrived in the Caribbean in 1492, were the first of a wave of European vessels that eventually brought the Europeans into contact with numerous indigenous American Indian populations. Not only did this contact eventually result in the absorption of this territory into Spanish, Portuguese, British, and French empires, but the microorganisms accompanying the conquerors wiped out a significant portion of the indigenous peoples.

The military history of the period is replete with tales of miraculous conquests of huge numbers of Indians by mere handfuls of European troops. But in reality there were few bonafide miracles. Epidemics, particularly smallpox, unwittingly launched by the invaders, killed approximately two-thirds of the indigenous populations, leaving them in disarray and unable to muster a decent defense of their territories. As William McNeill has put it, "From the Amerindian point of view, stunned acquiescence to Spanish superiority was the only possible response. . . . Native authority structures crumbled; the old gods seemed to have abdicated. The situation was ripe for the mass conversions recorded so proudly by Christian missionaries."[9] The spread of smallpox was followed by measles and eventually by typhus, with diseases from Africa such as malaria and yellow fever transplanted in the tropics. By the time that these transplanted diseases had run their course, it is estimated that only one in twenty of the indigenous populations in the affected areas survived.[10] Indeed, as the European colonial networks expanded to embrace much of the world, an exchange of diseases among the conquerors and the conquered took a tremendous toll on all sides.

More recently, another spurt of disease accompanied the large-scale global movement of troops during World War I. While the eyes of the world were focused on the military casualties associated with the hostilities, a deadly influenza epidemic originating in the state of Kansas in 1918 spread quickly around the world along with the troops. By the time the casualties began to taper off, this unexpected spin-off from the war resulted in the greatest epidemic in world history. Estimates are that somewhere between 20 and 30 million people died, many times the number of battlefield casualties.[11]

An Evolutionary Perspective

Since World War II there has been a tremendous acceleration in the pace of globalization and urbanization. The historical record makes it clear that such periods of growing interactions among previously separated populations are often punctuated by serious outbreaks of disease. The period since World War II has already witnessed the spread of exotic and lethal diseases in tropical areas of the world, several deadly worldwide influenza epidemics, and a slow-moving AIDS epidemic that now has become global in scope. There is a heightened fear that more frequent international travel, growing resistance to antibiotics, and changing human behavior and settlement patterns is leading to outbreaks of new forms of deadly disease and a resurgence of others.[12] In spite of the development of a broad spectrum of antibiotics and new medical technologies, the world remains a biologically dangerous place. "At the root of the resurgence of old infectious diseases is an evolutionary paradox: The more vigorously we have assailed the world of microorganisms, the more varied the repertoire of bacterial and viral strains thrown up against us."[13]

The key to comprehending why there are so many new challenges to human microsecurity is to understand the nature and evolution of ecological interdependence. Populations of Homo sapiens have coevolved with other species and a variety of microorganisms within the ever-changing constraints of physical environments. Ecological interdependence refers to the maintenance and growth of a delicate network of relationships among these organisms and between them and the sustaining physical environments. Rapid changes in any of these relationships can rebound to the detriment of human beings, other creatures, microorganisms, or even the ecosystem itself. Thus, a mutation in a pathogenic microorganism, a rapid increase in populations of voracious pests, or even a change in rainfall can destabilize an ecosystem with unfortunate results for all creatures that share it.

For most of human history the units within which this coevolution has been occurring have been local and isolated ecosystems. Because of the mutual adaptation processes involved, localized bouts of pestilence or nonfatal outbreaks of disease have been common. But as previously isolated populations are now being forced together by the pressures of globalization, there are increasingly complex and unforeseen consequences. The world is now beginning to experience ecological interdependence on a much larger scale; the complicated network of interdependence among human populations and between them and other species and various microorganisms now has moved to the global level.

Large-scale outbreaks of disease, called epidemics or pandemics, occur when something happens to disturb the evolutionary equilibrium that has been maintained locally between human beings and disease organisms. Stable populations of human beings in isolation from other people and ecosystems for long periods of time are likely to develop fairly stable equilibriums with local pests and microorganisms. The human immune system, which helps to fight off disease, is the product of generations of interactions between people and disease organisms. Natural selection processes, which help to shape human immune systems, represent learning by bitter experience. People with naive immune systems often succumb to deadly diseases and don't live to reproduce, while more resistant survivors of disease episodes are likely to give birth to children having some degree of immunity to serious diseases.

Epidemics develop when biologically or socioculturally naive human populations come in contact with new pathogens. Obviously, people who move into new environments are at substantial biological risk of contracting new illnesses. This is why businessmen or scholars attending international conferences often come down with influenza or similar illnesses upon return, or why people who move from one coast of the United States to the other are frequently ill during their first year of residence. But people or animals moving into new environments can similarly bring pathogens with them. Thus, *Rattus Rattus,* traveling with merchants along trade routes, brought disease-bearing fleas with them in their fur to Europe from Asia, introducing the black plague to the region in the fourteenth century. But social and cultural practices can also accelerate the spread of disease. For example, among certain African tribes marrying and supporting a widow becomes the responsibility of the dead husband's brother. Since many African males are now dying of AIDS, this custom can accelerate the spread of the virus from widows of AIDS victims to the dead man's family.[14]

Problems can also arise when changes (mutations) take place in microorganisms, sometimes making them more lethal to human beings. For various reasons, including environmental changes, exposure to chemicals or radiation, or interactions with other microorganisms, destructive mutations can occur, thus potentially confronting the human organism with novel challenges.

Pathogens can also be liberated by people from previously nonpopulated geographic locations, or they can move from animals to people. Population growth in tropical areas of the world is leading people to clear land at the edges of rain forests, liberating various kinds of microorganisms from their previous isolation and animal hosts. Thus, AIDS, Ebola, Marburg, and yellow fever viruses were probably first found in monkeys; Rift Valley fever in cattle, sheep, and mosquitoes; and Hantaan virus in rodents. "These pathogens probably lurked relatively undisturbed in their animal hosts in the tropics, jumping to humans only on rare occasions. They had little opportunity to adapt to humans, who usually were 'dead end' host species, because the viruses would fizzle out once they swept through a small population at the edge of the forest."[15] But these and other viruses can make successful leaps from animals to denser human populations, thus putting deadly new diseases in motion. In late 1997 and early 1998, for example, viruses were making leaps from monkeys to humans in Congo (Monkeypox) and from chickens to humans in Hong Kong (influenza H5N1).[16]

In a parallel process, larger species, which are often called pests, can wreak havoc when they jump from their home ecosystems to naive ecosystems that have had no contact with them. Historically, plants and animals native to Europe had both positive and negative impacts as they moved around the world with colonists.[17] But in the contemporary world it is often the unintended movement of plants and animals, largely as a result of expanded trade, that can have a devastating impact. In the United States, species ranging from the blue water hyacinths of South America that now clog Florida's waterways to the Africanized honey bee, an aggressive stinger brought to Brazil in 1959 to improve honey production which then moved north, have both nuisance and severe negative economic and environmental impacts.[18]

In summary, history's major epidemics that have transformed the nature of societies have occurred when human immune systems have encountered pathogenic microorganisms with which they have had little experience on a large scale. When the black death arrived in Europe from the Orient, nearly half of the population was wiped out in many areas, thus leading to major sociopolitical transformations. Similarly, the "conquest" of the Americas was aided and abetted by new European and African microbes transplanted into naive human environments. And this is why there is great concern at present about the erosion of sovereignty, disappearance of borders, failures of states, and the rapid integration of local human populations into the emerging global village. The rapid movement of people, produce, animals and microorganisms around the world has given rise to concern about the resurgence of old diseases, the emergence of new ones, and economic and environmental damage from traveling plants and animals.

ECOLOGICAL INTERDEPENDENCE: SOME EVIDENCE

In the face of the challenges engendered by rapidly growing ecological interdependence, weakened and impoverished governments are often slow to react. The current political attitude toward nonhuman immigrants remains much the same as it was in the 1870s, when Spencer Fullerton Baird of the U.S. Fish Commission attempted to improve upon nature by bringing a new tasty species of Eurasian carp into the United States. His venture was a great economic success and the fish became the culinary craze of the nation. But ever since then the carp have been reproducing prolifically in U.S. waters, destroying natural habitats and crowding out native fish. The legacy of these attempts to make nature more productive through the introduction of new species lingers on in U.S. regulations. There is rigorous screening to catch potentially dangerous agricultural pests, but much less attention is paid to imported species that don't directly threaten to ravage crops. For example, individual states can import exotic fish species from other countries or regions without even consulting their neighbors.[19]

Until very recently, the potential spread of infectious diseases was similarly treated. The development and large-scale deployment of antibiotics and other pharmaceuticals has fostered complacency in the face of growing global disease challenges. In 1969, for example, the U.S. surgeon general declared that infectious diseases had been conquered and that the time had come to focus on chronic diseases like cancer and heart disease.[20] But things are now changing rapidly and in 1996 the World Health Organization (WHO) recently emphasized that infectious diseases are still the world's leading cause of death.[21] The technological optimism of an earlier era is beginning to fade in the face of seemingly incurable HIV/AIDS virus and the resurgence of several diseases in antibiotic-resistant form. About one-tenth of the new cases of tuberculosis (TB) worldwide are now resistant to at least one of the drugs commonly used to treat the disease.[22]

There is now ample evidence of the impact of growing ecological interdependence and the large scope of infectious disease, but overall changes in the personal and economic impact of various diseases and migrant organisms are difficult to quantify for several reasons. First, it isn't necessary for people to die from an infectious disease for it to have an enormous impact on their quality of life. Various painful and debilitating diseases can disable large numbers of people for considerable periods of time without actually making them into statistics. Second, infectious disease statistics are often deliberately manipulated downward by some countries as a matter of national pride or economics. People don't frequent countries that admit to being hosts for plagues. Finally, there are few reliable historical data to use as a baseline for assessing the extent to which disease has increased or decreased in many areas of the world, particularly in the most poverty-stricken countries when diseases are likely to be most prevalent.

It is clear that in the United States there recently have been several unexpected bouts with pathogenic microorganisms including lethal outbreaks of cryptosporidium in Milwaukee and hanta virus in the Four Corners area of the Southwest. There have also recently been several widespread cases of food poisoning, a major influenza epidemic, an outbreak of antibiotic-resistant intestinal disease in New York, periodic attacks of "flesh-eating" bacteria and repeated incidences of intestinal disorders associated with eating imported fruit.

In other parts of the world the situation is much more serious. More than 500 million people are now stricken with tropical diseases. Approximately 400 million people suffer from malaria, 200 million from schistosomiasis, and 100 million from lymphatic filariasis.[23] The spread of AIDS across national borders has created a crisis situation in many areas of the world. It is estimated that by the year 2005 there will be 47.4 million cumulative HIV infections worldwide, with 20.7 million cumulative HIV infections in Africa and 19.1 million in Asia. This is projected to result in 16.8 million cumulative AIDS deaths.[24] Estimates indicate that by the year 2000 fully one-fifth of the population of South Africa will be HIV positive.[25] In Latin America more than a million people have been struck with a resurgence of cholera in recent years and several thousand have died. And malaria is now active in 103 countries and is a serious threat to half of the world's population. About 300 million people become infected with the parasite each year and from 1 to 2 million die.[26]

Fifty years ago many of these diseases surely afflicted human beings. But it is unclear how much globalization and urbanization have affected the geographic scope and prevalence of these diseases because there is only anecdotal evidence for comparison. What is clear is that these diseases now move much more rapidly along with the large flow of travelers in the contemporary world. There is thus growing worry about a potential worldwide spread of killer viruses. A recent outbreak of pneumonic plague, which can be spread through the air, killed hundreds of people in India and disrupted air travel in the region. Airports as far away as Kennedy in New York City were screening dozens of flights daily for potential carriers. And an outbreak of a deadly chicken or bird flu in Hong Kong caused a major drop-off in tourism and resulted in the execution of 1.5 million chickens and other birds in an attempt to stop the spread of the virus.[27]

Although the many exotic species of flora and fauna that now also travel around the world rarely kill people, they often do extensive damage to the recipient economies. There is no dependable data on the worldwide economic impact of such biological hitchhikers, but it is considerable. In the United States it is estimated that more than four thousand exotic species of flora and fauna have been naturalized (able to survive without human help) over the past century. Just seventy-nine of those species cost the nation an estimated $97 billion between 1906 and 1991 in damage to agriculture, ecosystems, industry, and health. Most of the species brought into the United States unintentionally have been the inadvertent by-products of commerce, tourism, or travel.[28]

Many new species make their way into the United States and other countries associated with other imported commodities. Agricultural products, nursery stock, cut flowers, and timber often harbor insects, plant diseases, and snails, while bulk commodities like gravel, sand, or wool often contain hidden seeds. Ballast water on commercial ships, taken on to provide stability at sea and often dumped when ships load at different ports, is also a major transport medium spreading nonindigenous species around the world. Since 1980, at least eight new species—including the harmful zebra mussel in the Great Lakes and associated waterways—have entered the United States in this manner.[29]

ECOLOGICAL SECURITY: CONTEMPORARY CHALLENGES

The ongoing globalization process represents a growing challenge to human health and ecological stability. Facilitated by innovations in transportation, information, and telecommunications technologies, and by a worldwide current of economic liberalization, the geographical boundaries of the world are becoming much more permeable. Although ecological interdependence has been growing at a more gradual pace for some time, it is only recently that a confluence of change drivers—rapid technological innovation and the broad, worldwide diffusion of liberal ideology—has created a historically unique climate that has accelerated change processes.[30]

Throughout history, trade and interactions between distant populations have been associated with the spread of disease, and this remains a threat in the contemporary world. As globalization proceeds in tandem with human disturbances of remote ecosystems where many pathogens reside, the likelihood of new outbreaks grows. Pathogens which have previously been restricted to isolated geographic locations became capable of spreading rapidly and with relative ease to other areas as the world's transportation networks and economic interdependence increases.[31]

There are now two obvious ways that diseases are being spread more rapidly and widely: increased commerce and contact among people and the integration of world food markets. More frequent contacts are now occurring among human populations across political boundaries that once served as relatively impermeable barriers. Spatial separation in general has become a far less significant hindrance to human interaction as technological advances in telecommunications, transportation, and computers have accelerated and expanded the possibilities for transnational flows of information, money, goods, and people. In 1996, for example, world trade was valued at approximately $5.2 trillion, up from $2 trillion less than a decade earlier—an expansion of over 250 percent.[32]

Professional journals and the press now carry accounts of public health incidents related to globalization with alarming regularity, as pathogens old and new move worldwide amid the rising volumes of trade and travel. In recent years, for example, the number of people traveling internationally by plane jumped from only 2 million per year in 1950 to 280 million per year in 1990. This figure is expected to reach 600 million annually by the year 2000.[33] Commercial jets have been implicated in the transmission of TB among airline passengers and the reintroduction of dengue fever to the United States through cargo containing hitchhiking Asian mosquitoes.[34]

In the face of the accelerating pace of contemporary globalization, governments around the world are in many respects ill-equipped to respond to the emerging health risks associated with travel and trade, inadequate food safety, and ecosystemic changes. A major irony of globalization is that, at a time when the spectrum and level of ecological risks are growing as never before, the abilities of government to respond appropriately may be increasingly limited.[35]

A second set of health risk factors emerges from the growth and deeper integration of the world food market. Like other economic sectors, agriculture and food production have become increasingly global in the 1990s. Since the 1980s, food imports to the United States have doubled, and over 30 percent of the fruits and vegetables the nation consumes now originate in other countries.[36] The growing cross-border traffic in food and agricultural products increases the risks to human health by creating more opportunities for pathogens to migrate from their native environments in food shipments and cause disease outbreaks among biologically naive populations in other countries.

U.S. public health officials now report a sharp increase in the number of disease outbreaks linked to imported food, particularly to produce. The list of outbreaks in the 1990s implicating imported foods is lengthy, including, for example, raspberries from Guatemala; strawberries, scallions and cantaloupes from Mexico; coconut milk from Thailand; and canned mushrooms from China. Imported food-borne microbes and parasites, such as cyclospora, hepatitis, and salmonella, have resulted in several thousand illnesses and deaths in the United States alone over the past five years. The Centers for Disease Control and Prevention (CDC) estimate that cyclospora, a rare parasite linked to produce in Guatemala, by itself accounted for over 2,300 cases of food poisoning in the United States last year.[37]

But food safety concerns are not limited to products originating in less-industrialized countries. Radish sprouts grown in Oregon, for example, are thought to have caused an outbreak of food poisoning in Japan. And the South Korean agricultural ministry recently claimed it found a dangerous strain of Escherichia coli (E. coli) bacteria in a shipment of frozen beef from a large U.S. meatpacking firm.[38] The ongoing "mad cow" disease crisis in the United Kingdom further illustrates how unsound agricultural practices in industrial countries can result in potentially serious risks to human health. Even within the United States, serious health effects from high-technology food production have recently been experienced. In the Chesapeake Bay area, for example, foul agricultural runoff from poultry megafarms has been implicated in the emergence of large plumes of pfisteria bacteria in several rivers, which damaged many of the region's fisheries and in several cases of human illness as well.

Part of the emerging food safety problem is associated with trade liberalization. While tariff and trade barriers in the agricultural sector have been reduced and transportation technologies have enabled more rapid movement of food products from farm to market, health and food safety standards and practices in many exporting countries remain poor. Thus, the risk of exposure to food-borne disease is rising, as more countries pursue export-oriented agricultural production under various global and regional free-trade regimes.[39]

The increasing global traffic in food products is now straining the world's food safety monitoring systems. For example, as one official from the Food and Drug Administration recently noted, the United States designed its system of standards, monitoring, and inspection one hundred years ago for an agrarian economy that was largely domestic. That system cannot cope with the demands of a global marketplace, particularly in an era of declining government budgets and restricted state intervention. Moreover, the tension between food safety and free trade grows more acute when it becomes a matter of international economic diplomacy. This occurs, for instance, when more stringent food safety standards in importing countries are attacked as nontariff trade barriers. Such conflicts highlight the challenges that increased economic interdependence poses to state sovereignty. Trade disagreements, for instance, are increasingly likely to be settled by the dispute resolution bodies of free-trade regimes like the World Trade Organization or the North American Free Trade Agreement, rather than by the actions of national governments. Consequently, the limitations that trading regimes place on state sovereignty conceivably make it more difficult for countries to deal effectively with growing risks to public health.

MIGRATION, URBANIZATION, AND DISEASE

While there is currently much greater contact among the various neighborhoods of the nascent global village, the neighborhoods themselves are becoming more densely packed and prone to the spread of disease. People are migrating much more freely among and within countries, often carrying harmful viruses and bacteria with them. The United Nations has estimated that by the year 2015 there will be thirty-three urban areas of 8 million inhabitants or more (known as "megacities"), twenty-seven of which will be in less-industrialized nations. While urban growth might not seem to present a problem in itself, the fact that the most rapid growth is occurring in the cities of the politically unstable less-industrialized world raises additional health concerns, given the limited resources, health infrastructures, and formal institutional arrangements available to governments in rapidly urbanizing countries.[40] Since greater human population densities mean more frequent interaction, urbanization creates the conditions necessary for the potential rapid spread of infectious disease. Just as the densely populated city of ancient Rome was prone to rapidly spreading epidemics, the rise of megacities in impoverished countries presents future challenges to public health.

Several forces are driving this unhealthy urbanization trend. Environmental decay in rural areas of poorer countries is a major contributor to the growing rural-urban migration. Degradation of the agricultural resource base is driven by a complex interplay of population pressures, desertification, deforestation, droughts, and salination of soils due to irrigation. These problems have contributed directly to increases in the number of migrating rural poor in many regions of Africa, Asia, and Latin America, and have led to agricultural productivity declines, particularly in marginal areas. Compounding matters, throughout the developing world, population growth rates in rural areas are particularly high and numbers often exceed the sustaining capabilities of local ecosystems. The lure of urban areas, where industry and related economic opportunities are perceived to be growing, becomes almost irresistible to many in the countryside for whom living conditions have grown increasingly difficult. Thus, the migration of marginalized rural residents to urban centers is propelled by a complex set of ecological and economic "push" and "pull" factors.[41]

The prevalence of unemployment, poverty, pollution from municipal and industrial wastes, poor nutrition, and an inadequate public health infrastructure (particularly sanitation and sewers) in urban areas, however, means that the urban poor of these growing megacities in less industrialized countries frequently encounter and carry a host of "first" and "third" world maladies. They experience the problems characteristic of poverty (for example, deaths form infectious disease and higher infant mortality rates) and those characteristic of wealth (higher rates of death form heart disease, neoplasms, and accidents). Nonetheless, many migrants in the developing world still regard themselves as better off in cities than in the countryside, where economic circumstances are often worse due to resource depletion, lack of jobs, and high population growth rates.[42]

This urbanization trend is now especially troubling for human health because of the rising incidence of infectious waterborne diseases (such as cholera, typhoid, hepatitis A and E) and vector-borne diseases like malaria that thrive around stagnant water, particularly in cities of the less industrialized world. The ever-increasing numbers and densities of the urban poor also help to create conditions for the occurrence of epidemic outbreaks as well as for the persistence of endemic infectious disease.

Health threats associated with megacities are not limited to the less industrialized world. Recent viral and bacterial challenges in New York illustrate the emerging threats that infectious diseases pose to urban populations, even in the industrialized world. New York has witnessed a rebirth of TB in the 1990s, facilitated by the convergence of at least three key trends: the spread of HIV, the economic recession of the late 1980s, and budgetary reductions in public health programs. In the early 1970s, when TB appeared to be under control, programs in the United States aimed at detecting and controlling the disease were downsized and phased out. But HIV began its spread into segments of the urban population in the 1980s, creating ideal hosts through which TB could make a comeback. Unchallenged by the usual defenses of a healthy human immune system, TB found hospitable breeding grounds in the systems of AIDS victims. When the economic recession of the late 1980s hit, it left poorer, TB-infected AIDS victims in New York and elsewhere unable to gain access to adequate medical care. As a result, many of the urban poor with active TB cases didn't complete the necessary six-month regimen of antibiotics, thereby enabling surviving bacteria to become drug resistant.[43] Not surprisingly, the number of TB cases in the United States has increased by 20 percent over the past decade. Worldwide, TB cases have increased by over 30 percent, and the disease has accounted for some 36 million deaths since 1990.[44]

Thus, the growth of megacities in all countries affects ecological interdependence in many ways and creates conditions for the spread of infectious disease. Megacities, with their extremely dense populations, facilitate epidemic outbreaks and the endemic presence of infectious disease. The ecological balance is tipped further in favor of disease-causing pathogens by virtue of the unsanitary conditions in the poorly developed health infrastructure found in poorer parts of major cities all over the world. Finally, just as in the time of the Roman

Empire, the more intense intermingling of different peoples, through rural-urban migration and through international travel among large cities, continues to make large-scale urbanization a most serious challenge to public health.

POLICY RESPONSES TO EMERGING HEALTH RISKS

These emerging health threats are symptomatic of many of the new challenges raised by increasing globalization, and they require comprehensive, sustained policy responses at both the national and international levels. Surveillance, reporting, and international response capability should be key elements to these programs. Surveillance and reporting could rely on new telecommunications technology and a network of clinics, hospitals, and laboratories that could serve as listening posts in the United States and around the world. Each should have a staff with epidemiological expertise to recognize unusual cases and patterns of diseases incidence. Ideally, each of these facilities would be linked to a more centralized agency capable of providing information, scientific support, and of mobilizing effective intervention when necessary. In this way, each associated clinic and laboratory would function as a node in a worldwide surveillance web.

A network of this sort need not be built entirely from scratch. For example, the WHO has recently established a global surveillance network, called WHONET, linking microbiology labs around the world to a central database aimed at detecting and preventing the spread of drug-resistant strains of microbes. Similarly, a group of scientists in the United States has set up a Program to Monitor Emerging Diseases (ProMED), a global electronic mail network that facilitates reporting on and discussion of disease outbreaks around the world. Since ProMED was initiated in 1993, the program has rapidly grown into a worldwide unofficial disease reporting system with over ten thousand subscribers in 120 countries.[45]

The existing surveillance network, however, has significant limitations. For example, communications and medical capabilities are inadequate in many tropical countries where new diseases are most likely to emerge. Even in the United States, for that matter, reporting to the CDC is haphazard, and, due to insufficient funding, the public health infrastructure in some states has deteriorated to the extent that detection of diseases cannot be assured.[46]

Moreover, it is of little use to report on disease outbreaks if adequate national or transnational response capabilities do not exist. In the absence of such capabilities, local doctors, scientists, and public health officials have little reason to participate in reporting networks. The CDC does deploy teams of epidemiologists to various parts of the world to assist communities where outbreaks occur, but sufficient international response demands a more centralized agency with access to state-of-the-art facilities, world-class staff, sufficient funding, and a political mandate to take the lead in responding to the threat of emerging or reemerging diseases. The WHO would appear to be the logical choice, given its established role as the coordinator of international health programs. Yet, on further examination, WHO lacks all of the necessary elements—authority, mandate, funding, staff, and facilities—sufficient for the task at hand.[47]

This lack of a robust global program for the surveillance of and response to emerging disease threats highlights important political dilemmas that are characteristic of global ecopolitics. For example, the current U.S. disposition to reduce its international commitments, minimize involvement in international organizations, and cut foreign aid flies in the face of a growing need for leadership and assistance to deal with the spin-offs of globalization, such as the need for worldwide disease monitoring and prevention. Moreover, while the largest global health risks frequently originate in poor countries and failing states, those least capable of managing them, countries with the resources necessary to address such problems often lack the political will to use them in the absence of an imminent crisis. From the perspective of U.S. policymakers, for example, there is little apparent political gain, and much potential damage, associated with sponsoring the creation of new international programs designed to combat threats that are not perceived to be serious by the American public.

There are additional dilemmas involved in attempting to curtail the global risks of infectious disease. For instance, surveillance is intrusive and there is a reluctance on the part of some governments to report on disease outbreaks for fear of serious international political and economic fallout. Thus, when India experienced its outbreak of pneumonic plague in 1996, the government at first failed to report the incident to the international medical community, anticipating de facto quarantines and declines in trade and tourism. The Indian government's reticence is understandable in the light of the costs and benefits it must have considered. Similarly, the outbreak of bird flu in Hong Kong not only resulted in economic damage from a loss of tourism, but also damaged the political fortunes of the new governmental regime. If reporting is perceived as unlikely to muster assistance in combating disease outbreaks, and highly likely to result in economic losses of various sorts, then there is no advantage to reporting.

Finally, the status of the international policy responses to the emerging threats from infectious disease is indicative of some of the broader political dynamics incumbent in the process of globalization. In an increasingly integrated, interdependent, and technologically advanced world, the role of the sovereign state is becoming more ambiguous. The diffusion of communications and information technologies, for example has empowered the scientific and medical communities and facilitated more effective global surveillance of infectious disease in the absence of any major government initiatives. The ProMED network demonstrates the extent to which technology can place real power in the hands of nongovernmental groups, enabling them to act swiftly to bridge gaps in existing government programs.

In effect, technology has enhanced the ability of nonstate actors to assume authority in areas where governments fail to provide leadership. The technologically augmented power of international professional networks might, on the one hand, be viewed as enhancing the authority and legitimacy of government by helping to fill vacuums in government functions. But on the other hand, this power might as easily be viewed as further reducing governmental authority by expropriating some of the traditional responsibilities of government in the public health arena.

Thus, the nascent responses to emerging disease threats, like the threats themselves, raise questions about the future of state sovereignty in an increasingly global system. The current lack of a comprehensive response to the challenges of emerging and resurging diseases at both the national and international levels reflects two trends. First, it illustrates the continued weakening of the state and its withdrawal from some of its historic oversight and regulatory roles. This reflects the impact of the "privatization" of key public functions, growing budgetary constraints, and other limitations that have made private or market-based approaches appear more seductive. And, of course, it demonstrates the extent to which technology is enabling citizens or groups to act directly on matters of concern to them, circumventing government involvement and limitations.

Contemporary globalization, the intensification of trends that have been at play in the international system for several centuries, thus increases challenges to state sovereignty and capabilities. The threats from new and reemerging infectious diseases, many of which have played a major role in shaping societies throughout human history, continue to exert their influence on human populations and governance at the beginning of the third millennium in spite of humanity's best efforts to eliminate them. The complex interactions of technological advances and the growing levels of interdependence among nations are giving rise to new pathways for the transmission of disease as well as to new weapons in the war against them. In the long run, one of the casualties of these dynamics may be the vitality of the state system that initially set the forces of globalization in motion.

Notes

1. See Dennis Pirages, "Microsecurity: Disease Organisms and Human Well-Being," *Washington Quarterly* (Autumn 1995).
2. Luigi Cavalli-Sforza and Francesco Cavalli-Sforza, *The Great Human Diasporas* (Reading, Mass.: Addison-Wesley, 1995), 157–159.
3. Kenneth Watt, *Principles of Environmental Science* (New York: McGraw-Hill, 1973), 1.

4. Karl Deutsch, *Nationalism and Social Communication* (Cambridge, Mass.: MIT Press, 1964), 100.
5. William McNeill, *Plagues and Peoples* (Garden City, N.Y.: Anchor Press, 1976), 115–117.
6. Henry Hobhouse, *Forces of Change: An Unorthodox View of History* (New York: Arcade Publishing, 1990), 11.
7. See McNeill, *Plagues and People,* chap. 4.
8. Hobhouse, *Forces of Change,* 11–23.
9. McNeill, *Plagues and People,* 208.
10. Ibid., 215, and references cited therein.
11. See Alfred Crosby, *America's Forgotten Pandemic: The Influenza Epidemic of 1918* (Cambridge: Cambridge University Press, 1990).
12. See Laurie Garrett, *The Coming Plague: Newly Emerging Diseases in a World Out of Balance* (New York: Farrar, Straus, and Giroux, 1994); Stephen S. Morse, ed., *Emerging Viruses* (New York: Oxford University Press, 1993).
13. Marc Lappe, *Evolutionary Medicine: Rethinking the Origins of Disease* (San Francisco: Sierra Club Books, 1994), 8.
14. See Stephen Buckley, "Wife Inheritance Spurs AIDS Rise in Kenya," *Washington Post,* November 8, 1997.
15. Ann Gibbons, "Where Are 'New' Diseases Born?" *Science* (August 6, 1993): 680.
16. See Keith B. Richburg, "Hong Kong Faulted on Handling of 'Bird Flu' Crisis," *Washington Post,* January 4, 1998; Diane Brady and Peter Stein, "Hong Kong's Tourism Trade Gets the Chills as Airline Travelers Come to Fear Avian Flu," *Wall Street Journal,* December 23, 1997; John Cohen, "Is an Old Virus Up to New Tricks," *Science* (July 18, 1997).
17. See Alfred W. Crosby, *Ecological Imperialism: The Biological Expansion of Europe, 900–1900* (Cambridge: Cambridge University Press, 1986).
18. See Elizabeth Culotta, "Biological Immigrants under Fire," *Science* (December 6, 1991).
19. Ibid., 1444.
20. Cited in David P. Fidler, "Return of the Fourth Horseman: Emerging Infectious Diseases and International Law," *Minnesota Law Review* (April 1997): 773.
21. World Health Organization, *The World Health Report 1995* (Geneva: World Health Organization, 1995).
22. David Brown, "1 in 10 TB Cases Worldwide Resist Common Treatment, Survey Shows," *Washington Post,* October 23, 1997.
23. World Health Organization, *The World Health Report 1995,* table I.
24. This is the medium variant in projections made in John Bongaarts, "Global Trends in AIDS Mortality," *Population and Development Review* (March 1996): 32.
25. Lynne Duke, "Opening of S. Africa Brings Rapid Advance of AIDS," *Washington Post,* July 23, 1995.
26. Philip J. Hilts, "Effort to Fight Malaria Seems to Have Failed," *New York Times* (October 9, 1991); Bob Drogin, "Deadly Malaria Returns with a Vengeance," *Washington Post,* November 10, 1992; Eliot Marshall, "Malaria Parasite Gaining Ground against Science," *Science* (October 11, 1991).
27. See David Brown, "World Responds Swiftly to Track 'Bird Flu' Spread," *Washington Post,* January 11, 1998.
28. See U.S. Congress, Office of Technology Assessment, *Harmful Non-Indigenous Species in the United States* (Washington, D.C.: U.S. Government Printing Office, September 1993), 92, 69.
29. See "Zebra Mussel Invasion Threatens U.S. Waters," *Science* (September 21, 1990); Biological Immigrants under Fire," *Science* (August 21, 1992).

30. See James N. Rosenau, "The Complexities and Contradictions of Globalization," *Current History* (November 1997): 360–364.
31. See Stephen S. Morse, "Regulating Viral Traffic," *Issues in Science and Technology* (Fall 1990): 81–82.
32. "Delivering the Goods," *Economist* (November 15, 1997): 85.
33. Figures are from Laurie Garrett, *The Coming Plague,* 571.
34. See, for example, Ellen Ruppel Shell, "Resurgence of a Deadly Disease," *Atlantic Monthly* (August 1997); Thomas A. Kenyon, et al., "Transmission of a Multidrug-Resistant Mycobacterium Tuberculosis During a Long Airplane Flight," *New England Journal of Medicine* 334 (1996); "E. coli Is Found in Shipment of IBP Frozen Beef to Korea," *Wall Street Journal,* September 29, 1997; Jeff Gerth and Tim Weiner, "U.S. Food Safety System Swamped by Booming Global Imports," *New York Times,* September 29, 1997; Rachel Nowak, "WHO Calls for Action Against TB," *Science* (March 24, 1995).
35. For a discussion of the effects of globalization on state sovereignty, see Susan Strange, *The Retreat of the State* (Cambridge: Cambridge University Press, 1996), chap. 1; also see Ken Conca, "Rethinking the Ecology-Sovereignty Debate," *Millennium* 23 (1994): 701–711.
36. Gerth and Weiner, "U.S. Food-Safety System Swamped."
37. Ibid.
38. "E. coli Is Found in Shipment of IBP Frozen Beef to Korea," *Wall Street Journal.*
39. Gerth and Weiner, "U.S. Food-Safety System Swamped."
40. United Nations Centre for Human Settlements, *An Urbanizing World: Global Report on Human Settlements 1996* (New York: Oxford University Press, 1996), 6.
41. World Commission on Environment and Development, *Our Common Future* (Oxford: Oxford University Press, 1987), 95–102.
42. World Bank, *Urban Policy and Economic Development: An Agenda for the 1990s* (Washington, D.C.: World Bank, 1991), 51; Mike Parnwell, *Population Movements in the Third World* (London: Routledge, 1993), 18–24.
43. Clark Merrill and Dennis Pirages, "Ecological Security: Micro-Threats to Human Well-Being," *Futures Research Quarterly* (Spring 1997): 49–50; Richard M. Krause, "The Origin of Plagues: Old and New," *Science* (August 21, 1992): 1074.
44. Anne E. Platt, "Why Don't We Stop Tuberculosis?," *WorldWatch* (July/August 1994): 32; Lappe, *Evolutionary Medicine,* 102–107.
45. Stephen S. Morse, "Too Close for Our Own Good," *Washington Post,* November 30, 1997.
46. See Merrill and Pirages, "Ecological Security," 59–60.
47. See Robert Hunt Sprinkle, *Profession of Conscience: The Making and Meaning of Life-Sciences Liberalism* (Princeton, N.J.: Princeton University Press, 1994), 146–155.

Editor's Preface to Chapter Eight

Environmental Degradation

Environmental problems are clearly transsovereign in nature: They do not respect state borders and they are not very responsive to unilateral state action. In Canada, for example, stricter internal restrictions on sulfur dioxide emissions were unable to protect Canadian lakes and forests from acid rain damage; the majority of acid rain falling in Canada comes from pollution emitted in the United States. Some 48,000 Canadian lakes are acidic, but the Canadian government acting alone cannot get at the heart of the problem.[1]

Unfortunately, movement toward economic and technological advancement in this century has too often proceeded with little regard for the environmental consequences. In 1955, carbon dioxide emissions from fossil fuel consumption and cement manufacturing totaled 7.5 billion metric tons. Carbon dioxide emissions since then have been steadily rising; 1991 emissions were more than triple the 1955 levels, at 22.7 billion metric tons released.[2] Despite an international treaty signed in Rio de Janeiro in 1992 designed to reduce carbon dioxide emissions and pollution from other greenhouse gases, the United States (and many other industrialized states) have released more greenhouse gases every year since. Not surprisingly, greenhouse gases collecting in the upper atmosphere have been steadily rising. The World Energy Council estimates that carbon dioxide emissions rose 12 percent from 1990 to 1995.[3] The concentration of carbon dioxide in the atmosphere increased 25 percent over the last three decades.[4] Evidence of global warming increased during the same time period, with a one meter rise in the sea level that erodes coast lands and threatens coastal nations such as Bangladesh.[5]

Air pollution has consequences. Respiratory and asthma problems increase as air quality decreases. Los Angeles produces 3,400 tons of air pollutants each year; Mexico City produces 5,000 tons of air pollutants annually. Poor air quality warnings in both these cities are now more common than bad weather warnings. Air pollution in Bangkok is now so severe that over 40 percent of the city's traffic police reportedly suffer from respiratory problems.[6]

More significantly, pollutants attack the ozone layer, which protects us from ultraviolet radiation, a leading cause of skin cancer. From 1979 to 1989 the ozone layer over Antarctica was reduced by 50 percent, causing a "continent-size hole in the ozone layer."[7] Ozone layers over North America reached record low levels in 1993. Incidents of melanoma in the US, the most dangerous form of skin cancer, increased by 80 percent between 1982 and 1989.[8]

Deforestation also contributes to ozone depletion and the greenhouse effect, but economic development and growing population levels has led to depletion of 55 percent of the world's temperate rainforests. Overall, 8 to 10 million acres of forest are cut or burned down annually.[9] Since rainforests contain 50 to 90 percent of the world's species,[10] biologists estimate that destruction of rainforests destroys species at a rate one to ten thousand times faster than the natural rate of extinction.[11] By the year 2000, 20 percent of the species now living may have vanished.[12] Deforestation also contributes to soil erosion and desertification. "In sub-Saharan Africa alone in the past fifty years, 65 million hectares of productive land turned to desert."[13]

The demise of the Soviet Union and the opening of societies has led to a greater understanding of the environmental costs of the Cold War. Safety took a back seat to security concerns in the nuclear race between the superpowers during the Cold War. Resulting accidents were covered up by state authorities, until the 1986 accident at the Chernobyl nuclear power plant exposed more people to nuclear radiation than the Hiroshima and Nagasaki atomic bombs.[14] The opening of these societies revealed severe environmental damage throughout the former Soviet Union and Warsaw Pact countries, with related high rates of leukemia, lead poisoning, mental retardation, birth defects, and respiratory problems.[15] In the United States, General Accounting Office (GAO) and Department of Energy estimates place the cost of cleaning up and managing U.S. nuclear weapons production and sites at $375 billion. Military bases are among the most polluted areas in the United States, further complicating attempts to close bases and turn them over for other uses in the aftermath of the Cold War. Rather than base closings being a source of a "peace dividend," high environmental cleanup costs of military bases will drain the U.S. treasury for years to come.[16]

Environmental degradation and scarcity can lead to violent conflicts which undermine state institutions, as occurred in Chiapas, Mexico, and Rwanda.[17] The legitimacy of state institutions may be directly undermined by environmental problems, as the Chernobyl disaster undermined the Soviet state.[18] Further, environmental problems can combine with other transsovereign problems to reinforce negative feedback loops. Environmental degradation and scarcity can cause violence and refugee flows. For example, in Haiti and Rwanda, deforestation and population growth radically decreased productive farmland per capita, further diminishing economic opportunities and increasing violence among societal groups and refugee flows.[19] The flow of refugees can cause further environmental damage and the spread of disease. In July 1994, lacking proper hygienic facilities, the Rwandan refugees polluted local water supplies, and spread cholera; countries downwater from the lake region as far away as Egypt feared contamination of their water supply from the cholera outbreak. States with economies and institutions weakened by environmental problems, disease, and refugee flows (such as Haiti), may be more vulnerable to drug smuggling and international criminal organizations. Unfortunately, transsovereign challenges tend to be mutually reinforcing, and together can have a more devastating effect on sovereignty than any of the issues might present alone.

Notes

1. UNDP, *Human Development Report 1994,* 36; Dr. Vicki Golich, "United States–Canadian Negotiations for Acid Rain Controls," Washington, D.C.: Georgetown University, 1995, Case Program.
2. World Resources Institute, *World Resources 1994–95,* 366.

3. John H. Cushman Jr., "U.N. Agencies Say Warming Poses Threat to Public Health," *New York Times,* July 8, 1996, A2.

4. Jessica Tuchman Mathews, "The Environment and International Security," in *World Security: Challenges for a New Century,* eds. Michael Klare and Daniel Thomas (New York: St. Martin's Press, 1994), 281.

5. UNDP, *Human Development Report 1994,* 36.

6. Ibid., 29.

7. Mathews, "The Environment and International Security," 281.

8. UNDP, *Human Development Report 1994,* 36.

9. Ibid., 29.

10. Ibid., 36.

11. Mathews, "The Environment and International Security," 277.

12. Ibid.

13. UNDP, *Human Development Report 1994,* 29.

14. Jessica Tuchman Mathews, "The Lessons of Chernobyl," *Washington Post,* April 1996.

15. Public Television, "Risk Assessment: Environmental Damage in the Former Soviet Bloc," 1993.

16. U.S. Department of Energy (DOE) Office of Environmental Management, "Estimating the Cold War Mortgage: Executive Summary Report," March 1995; DOE, Office of Defense Programs, "The Stockpile Stewardship and Management Program: Maintaining Confidence in the Safety and Reliability of the Enduring U.S. Nuclear Weapon Stockpile," May 1995; DOE Office of Environmental Management, "Closing the Circle on the Splitting of the Atom: The Environmental Legacy of Nuclear Weapons production in the United States and What the Department of Energy Is Doing about It," January 1995.

17. Thomas Homer-Dixon, "Environmental Scarcity and Violent Conflict: The Case of Chiapas, Mexico," and "Environmental Scarcity and Violent Conflict: The Case of Rwanda," University College, University of Toronto, 1995.

18. Mathews, "The Lessons of Chernobyl."

19. Hal Kane, "The Hour of Departure: Forces that Create Refugees and Migrants" (Washington, D.C.: The Worldwatch Institute, July 1995).

Globalizing the Environment

David A. Wirth

As the United States and the world prepare to move into the twenty-first century, the interdependence implicit in the increasingly popular term "globalization"[1] is ever more apparent. In a very real sense, one can now say both that the environment is global and that environmental policy is caught up in the process of globalization. The process of globalization has revealed deeply rooted linkages between environmental quality and other public policy agendas once thought to be distinct. These interrelationships were recently exposed in a highly visible manner when environmental objections contributed to the demise of President Clinton's request to Congress to authorize "fast track" negotiating authority for trade agreements, rendering him the first President since the procedure was initiated in the mid-1970s from whom that power has been withheld. The recent flare-up over fast track was not an isolated juncture, but an example of a much more pervasive phenomenon. In the more mundane, day-to-day conditions under which environmental policy is normally crafted, implemented, and enforced, the interpenetration of environment and other public policy agendas is, if anything, even more evident.

These connections often manifest themselves under a rubric of "environment and . . ." some other subject matter area. Thus, the collapse of fast track is readily identifiable as a component of a larger debate on environment and trade. Similarly, there are ongoing dialogues over the relationship between environment and development and environment and security. Each of these three subject matter couplings has acquired a fairly well-defined shape, along with a following of scholars, government officials, and advocates who specialize in these often difficult-to-penetrate, interdisciplinary inquiries.

One common attribute of the "environment and . . ." subject matter pairings is the splicing of two apparently divergent public policies, both of which are nonetheless intended to promote human welfare. On this level, it is pointless or even counterproductive to employ the kinds of good-versus-evil metaphors often associated with mission-oriented public policy agendas in areas such as the environment. After all, trade, development, and security also provide social benefits and often employ their own palette of symbolism.

While the "environment and . . ." formulation is perhaps helpful in identifying the essential "interconnectedness" between environment and other public policy agendas, that approach also has limitations. For one, this phraseology unfortunately tends to encourage a view of the phenomenon of globalization based on an array of horizontal, bipolar relationships. If environmental policy can be scrutinized in this mix-and-match fashion, there would appear to be no reason why other social welfare demands could not also be treated in this manner. So, for example, one might imagine juxtaposing trade and development, security and trade, or security and development—each of which, incidentally, has been attempted with some degree of analytical rigor. For another, these pairings facilitate an approach that attempts to reconcile conflicts or tradeoffs between apparently competing policy goals. There is a considerable risk that this focus on the "bilateral" overlap between previously established categories of public policy subject matter will obscure a better approach that synthesizes these disparate elements at a higher level of conceptual generality.

A different, but related theme concerns the question whether globalization is good or bad for the environment. Each of the "environment and . . ." modes of analysis tracks this motif, inquiring into the beneficial or harmful effects, for instance, of trade or of development on environmental quality. In this author's view, such questions are, in a deeply fundamental sense, unanswerable. One can criticize as an oxymoron George Will's invocation of the "exhilaratingly unknowable"[2] future catalyzed by the North American Free Trade Agreement (NAFTA), but there is little in the way of meaningful policy responses that would halt or even slow trends toward greater global interdependence. Thanks to such innovations as widespread access to the Internet and other modern communications technologies (open technology), globalization is proceeding apace, with or without fast track, continued development assistance provided by the U.S. Agency for International Development, or the expansion of NATO, to name only a few of the pertinent recent public policy junctures.

The terms and directions of such trends, however, do appear to be amenable to a certain degree of molding or shaping. The better interpretation of the fast track failure is not that the U.S. public has rejected the benefits of international trade (open economy), but that the electorate (open society) is dissatisfied with the rules governing that trade. While it is extraordinarily difficult or impossible to predict whether globalization as such is good or bad for the environment, the policy choices that guide the process can arguably be crafted so as to ameliorate adverse environmental impacts or to encourage beneficial ones. The terms being established today that govern relationships among such entities as governments, corporations, international organizations, and individuals in a globalized world are likely to have impacts, environmental and otherwise, indefinitely into the future.

THE ENVIRONMENT AND . . .

In addressing the implications of increased global interdependence, this chapter first selectively surveys three of the areas in which environment has been linked with other social policy issues: (1) development; (2) trade; and (3) security. Drawing on insights from each of these issue areas, the chapter then attempts to draw some admittedly tentative conclusions about how the fundamental structural dynamics of the globalization phenomenon might be channeled for the benefit of the environment.

Development

Although the necessary responses may be frustratingly complex, the interface between environmental and development policies is probably the easiest of the "environment and . . ." areas to grasp from a conceptual point of view. Anyone who has ever witnessed suburban sprawl firsthand knows intuitively that misguided or inadequate development policies can despoil the environment. Although technically speaking the environment-and-development dialectic applies to any country, concern about the nexus between the two areas has been greatest in the developing world. One substantive reason revolves around the desire to conserve fragile ecosystems such as tropical forests, wetlands, and grassland savannahs. In countries that are often heavily dependent on the resource base, poorly advised development strategies can have a devastating impact on the lives and livelihoods of the human population, particularly those at the margins of subsistence.

The role of donor-financed assistance has substantially heightened attention to the role of environmental quality in economic development. The United States provides development assistance to developing countries directly, on a bilateral basis, through the U.S. Agency for International Development. The United States is also a member of multilateral financial institutions which, in one manner or another, are engaged in related operations: the International Bank for Reconstruction and Development (IBRD), the International Development Association (IDA), and the International Finance Corporation (IFC)—collectively, the "World Bank group"; regional development banks, including the Inter-American Development Bank (IDB), the African Development Bank (AfDB), the Asian Development Bank (AsDB), and the European Bank for Reconstruction and Development (EBRD); the International Monetary Fund (IMF); and the United Nations Development Program (UNDP). These bilateral and multilateral institutions can significantly affect both development strategies and the environment. World Bank loans can finance massive interventions in the natural environment, such as large dams and irrigation systems, of a scale that would be difficult to imagine domestically. Significantly, the donor-financed nature of these interventions creates a situation in which donor country governments and the public in donor and recipient countries alike can influence development-related investments in recipient countries.[3]

The most significant international policy-making event on the environment-and-development issue was the UN Conference on Environment and Development (UNCED), dubbed the "Earth Summit," held in the summer of 1992 in Rio de Janeiro. This meeting firmly introduced the concept of "sustainable development" into the policy lexicon. Although there is no consensus definition of the term, the following has gained broad acceptance:

> Sustainable development is development that meets the needs of the present without compromising the ability of future generations to meet their own needs. It contains within it two key concepts:
>
> ⊙ the concept of 'needs,' in particular the essential needs of the world's poor, to which overriding priority should be given; and
>
> ⊙ the idea of limitations imposed by the state of technology and social organization on the environment's ability to meet present and future needs.[4]

The term *sustainable development* has now been used in such a wide variety of contexts by so many different people with such divergent agendas that its core meaning has been seriously attenuated, if, indeed, it ever was clear. In at least one interpretation, the concept implies tradeoffs between development imperatives on the one hand and environmental integrity on the other. This characterization is at least arguably consistent with the tone of the Rio meeting and the content of its principal official statements.[5]

While the World Bank was created and began operations soon after World War II with a development-oriented mission, a more recent policy trend has been to target donor-financed development assistance specifically for environmentally beneficial purposes. The best example is probably the Global Environment Facility (GEF), established to provide financial support for environmentally beneficial activities and, in particular, to serve as the interim financial institution under two major multilateral conventions adopted as part of the UNCED process, on climate change[6] and biodiversity,[7] respectively. The facility was established on a pilot basis in 1991[8] and restructured and replenished in 1994 with $2 billion.[9] The GEF operates under the tripartite direction of the World Bank, the UNDP, and the United Nations Environment Program (UNEP). Notwithstanding its expressly stated mission of "provid[ing] grants and concessional funding to recipients for projects and programs that protect the global environment and promote sustainable economic growth,"[10] the GEF has nevertheless come under considerable environmental criticism because of its governance structure and project design.[11]

Trade

Although the linkage between policies on environment and trade has been extensively examined, the deeper significance of the interface between these two social welfare goals has been elusive. Trade rules, such as those of the newly created World Trade Organization (WTO), the successor to the General Agreement on Tariffs and Trade (GATT) adopted in 1947, consist of primarily "negative" obligations in which states promise to refrain from taking actions, such as imposing certain tariffs, that could impede market access. Trade negotiations, whether multilateral, regional, or bilateral, usually take the form of reciprocal promises to reduce or eliminate barriers to market access that would be unlikely to be implemented unilaterally in the absence of such a bargained-for exchange; many recent trade agreements consequently have the character of generic solutions to specific trade problems, such as standards for imported food products. The efficacy of the trade regime can be accounted for to a large extent by the simplicity of its central free-market message: less governmental intervention almost by definition promotes liberalized trade. To a large extent, this situation also describes "open markets," as that term is used elsewhere in this book, with somewhat greater precision as purposefully deregulated markets—perhaps the most readily comprehended component of the phenomenon of globalization.

By contrast, international obligations with respect to the environment, and many other social policy areas such as labor, anticipate and require the implementation of affirmative governmental actions intended to address particular problems. In a microcosm, this explains the recent clash between trade and environment. One regime is designed to facilitate the implementation of affirmative governmental measures, and the other is intended to ensure their absence. To a proponent of free trade, environmental regulations are potential barriers to trade; to an environmentalist, the rules of the international trade regime may constrain governmental policy responses, such as prescriptive regulatory requirements, to address environmental and public health risks. As on the domestic level, the "cognitive dissonance," if not outright conflict, between deregulation and the implementation of affirmative public policy goals is clearly evident.

The shape of the environment-and-trade dialogue has now settled into a number of well-defined problems. From the environmental side, concerns arise over the vulnerability of environmental regulations to trade-based challenges; the potential for triggering a "downward spiral" in the rigor of environmental regulation through multilaterally established, least-common-denominator harmonized standards responsive more to trade considerations than to public health or the environment; the appropriateness from an institutional point of view of organizations such as the WTO for consideration of environmental matters; and the possibility that even multilateral environmental agreements might face trade-based constraints. From the trade point of view, there are commensurate worries over the abuse of environmental measures for protectionist purposes; the deployment of unilateral trade-based actions to address international environmental challenges; and the consideration of trade measures in multilateral instruments or by multilateral bodies dealing with environmental hazards. While the ways in which some or all of these contentious issues are resolved may have significant impacts on public policy, the general approach has been one of delicate delineation of the appropriate sphere for each regime, implying a counterproductive kind of zero-sum set of tradeoffs between the two. Because it does not address terms of trade or affect the regime of trade-based rules, the so-called environmental "side agreement" to NAFTA[12] is of little utility in suggesting an appropriate model for international trade.

An alternative approach might avoid asking the question, either explicitly or implicitly, whether international trade is consistent with environmental protection or vice versa. Instead, one might consider the role of both international trade and environmental protection as embedded in the larger public policy goal of encouraging sustainable development. While, as discussed above, the content of the term may be vague, it is clear that the phrase is plainly intended as an overarching construct that encompasses international trade and environmental protection,[13] as well as other compartmentalized public policy goals such as development assistance and national security. From this point of view, one might well ask whether certain environmental protection measures are so inappropriately burdensome that they unreasonably interfere with the capacity of present generations to meet their own needs. This is one way of interpreting the nontariff barrier problem discussed above. Similarly, one might identify the notion of "sustainable trade" as trade that facilitates the efforts of present generations to satisfy their needs while preserving the capacity of future generations to meet their own needs. Without further elaboration, the concept of "sustainable trade" thus defined is probably not capable of precise application as a legal test. It does, however, accommodate the relatively elementary notion that some types of trade can encourage sustainability, while other kinds of trade might undermine that goal.

Security

As the Cold War drew to a close, an area of research emerged linking environmental integrity and national security. Population pressures, resource degradation, the effects of global warming and stratospheric ozone depletion, nuclear safety concerns, competition over natural resources, and other environmental stresses, so the argument goes, can lead to armed conflict.[14] At an intuitive level, it is reasonably obvious that in some cases environmental stresses might somewhat exacerbate the risk of armed conflict. However, demands for greater rigor in demonstrating this cause-and-effect relationship have produced a lively, if occasionally strident, debate.[15] But even if environmental deterioration contributes significantly to the risk of war, a proposition about which there is by no means a consensus, what does that mean in concrete, operational terms? Should the United States rank its foreign policy initiatives on the environment, or should international organizations choose among competing candidates for multilateral diplomacy based on the potential for armed conflict? Such a test might even produce a skewed set of priorities, especially in such geographic regions as North America where the likelihood of war is small. Or in the unusual situation in which competition over resources is plausibly related to armed attacks,[16] does that of itself suggest that the underlying environmental risks are that much more pressing by comparison with competing public policy concerns? Maybe so, but these are still difficult questions that have not received satisfactory answers as a matter of principle.

Fortunately, there is little or no need as an analytical matter to establish definitively this cause-and-effect relationship before realizing the security benefits of international environmental diplomacy and multilateral cooperation in solving environmental problems. Antecedents addressing environment in a security context can be found at least fifteen years before the end of the Cold War, most notably in the context of the Conference on Security and Cooperation in Europe (CSCE), popularly known as the "Helsinki process."[17] Within the CSCE and its successor, the Organization for Security and Cooperation in Europe (OSCE), environment has been a so-called "economic dimension" or "Basket II" topic, along with economics, science, and technology.[18]

While some of the recent literature has made stark assertions about the causes of armed conflict that are difficult to verify empirically, that debate has indeed been helpful in broadening the concept of security to encompass not just military defense capabilities, but social, economic, and political stability more generally. In this view, environmental integrity is one of a number of attributes that contribute to stability and hence long-term national security. Environmental degradation, by contrast, is a destabilizing factor that tends to undermine national, regional, and even global security. In effect, the concept of military security is replaced by stability, of which environmental integrity is one, but not the only, indicator.[19]

This view is very much consistent with the mission of the OSCE, which fosters a comprehensive approach to security, including arms control, preventive diplomacy, confidence- and security-building measures, human rights, election monitoring, and economic security. The OSCE emphasizes conflict prevention and avoidance, peaceful settlement of disputes, and the creation of a cooperative system of security. Consequently, the OSCE's work in the "human dimension" has sounded such themes as respect for human rights, the rights of national minorities, election monitoring, the development of civil societies, and democracy- and institution-building, as well as the importance of the rule of law and peaceful settlement of disputes more generally.[20] This point of view, which would treat environmental diplomacy as a mechanism for reducing risks to stability and preventing armed conflict, is surely a preferable way of thinking about the environment-and-security nexus.

GLOBALIZATION AND THE ENVIRONMENT

Although perhaps tempting, an approach that seeks to demonstrate a cause-and-effect relationship between globalization and environmental effects, either beneficial or negative, is unlikely to serve as a helpful analytical tool. For one, the universe of possible directions in which civil society might develop, markets and economies might be opened to trade and foreign investment, and new technologies might be disseminated in the post–Cold War era is extraordinarily broad. It is consequently impossible to speak of "globalization" as a unitary phenomenon with a precisely defined outcome. Simplistic syllogisms such as the following have been proposed to deal with the phenomenon of globalization: Deregulated markets promote trade, trade generates wealth, and wealthier countries have more resources to deploy for realizing environmental protection and other public welfare goals. Mainstream economists are increasingly realizing the limitations of such oversimplified models that, except as applied to certain simple cases such as environmentally harmful subsidies, are essentially articles of faith.[21]

Further, causal relationships between broad-gauge social policies and trends on the one hand and environmental effects on the other are exceedingly difficult or impossible to establish with any degree of rigor. As noted above, much of the environment-and-security dialectic revolves around precisely this question. Similarly, the suitability of an environmental impact statement (EIS) required by a major environmental statute[22] was contested during the policy discussion over NAFTA. Serious questions were raised as to whether the EIS methodology, customarily employed to assess the likely environmental effects of specific infrastructure projects such as a dam or a highway, could be applied to trade rules that operate at a high level of policy generality.[23] The executive branch declined to prepare an EIS for the implementing legislation for NAFTA, instead substituting an environmental study of generic bilateral problems.[24] Likewise, the amenability of World Bank lending in the form of sector loans—which may support governmental activities in an entire sector like energy and which do not necessarily finance specific infrastructure projects—and policy-based adjustment lending—which targets macroeconomic variables like exchange rates, government deficits, and subsidies with the goal of fundamental economic reform—to analysis from an environmental perspective has been the subject of considerable disagreement.[25]

At the same time it is indisputable that the governments, private-sector business and industrial interests, and civil society generally are in a state of profound transition. Despite perhaps limited capacity to predict the environmental effects of global trends, it is difficult to deny that there may or will be environmental repercussions, for better or worse.

To be sure, there are some stories of at least partial success in overcoming collective action problems at the international level. In December 1997 at Kyoto, Japan, over 150 countries concluded an agreement on global warming.[26]

The new pact calls for participating countries to reduce greenhouse gas emissions that contribute to the warming of the earth. The prediction of global warming and its potential negative consequences is now widely accepted by the scientific community. However, there is no such consensus on how to reach the goal of greenhouse gas reduction among the countries of the world. The impediments to joint action are great, and unanimity of purpose breaks down when it comes to deciding what percentage of greenhouse gases should be cut, which countries should do it, how they should do it, and when these cuts should be made.

Developing states, like China or India, believe that those developed, wealthy countries that produce and have historically produced most of the greenhouse gases, such as the United States, should take the first steps in controlling them. Some developing countries prefer to assume substantive obligations to reduce emissions only after they have reached the levels of economic development and living standards that the developed countries now enjoy. The United States and other developed states believe that it is unwise to grant the developing countries an emissions control "holiday" until some future date, because they will be major producers of greenhouse gases very soon. Just as concerns of equity expose deep-seated cleavages, so, too, the all-pervasive nature of the problem—associated as it is with the very essence of industrial society—strains the capacity of the international community to respond. The new agreement, moreover, is unlikely to make more than a preliminary dent in the looming problem of greenhouse warming.

Under such circumstances, what meaningful observations can nonetheless be made? First, environmental policy requires a new awareness that environmental problems are embedded in a much larger global setting and cannot be treated in isolation. Even such metalevel connections as between environment on the one hand and development, trade, or security on the other have largely outlived their usefulness. Once liberating because of their inherent need for interdisciplinary analysis and communication between professional communities characterized by divergent policy cultures, even these relatively new categories have now become confining. In place of a bipolar, linear spectrum, environmental policy now requires treatment at a higher level of conceptual generality by reference to such overarching principles as sustainability.

With the end of the Cold War, the essential "interconnectedness" of such issues as environment, development, trade, and security is more readily apparent. This vision of a global order is not necessarily new. Rather, the bilateral arms race artificially obscured more fundamental dynamics in the international order. The Marshall Plan has long been understood as an express recognition of the tight causal relationship between security interests in the United States and political stability and social well-being in Western Europe. Less obviously, even at the end of World War II, open markets and liberalized trade were understood to facilitate political stability and regional and global security.[27] A more recent example is the linkage between human rights and security in context of the Helsinki process.

As suggested by each of these examples, the efficacy of addressing problems of environmental quality in a globalized world will very likely turn on the vigor of multilateral institutions. Unfortunately, at a time of consolidation of such institutions as the WTO on other social policy fronts, the trend in environmental management at the international level appears to be one of compartmentalization and fragmentation. The mission of only one international organization, the UN Environment Program (UNEP), is exclusively environmental. In the past few years, UNEP has been subject to serious criticism from a number of governments and other constituencies for a lack of focus and efficacy in its work.[28] Even under the best of circumstances, UNEP's mandate is limited. Numerous other international organizations established for a variety of other purposes consequently have also played significant roles on international environmental challenges: the International Maritime Organization (IMO), under whose auspices a number of marine pollution agreements have been negotiated; the Economic Commission for Europe (ECE), which has been the vehicle for negotiating a number of important agreements on traditional air pollution questions; the Organization for Economic Cooperation and Development (OECD), which in the past has been a principal forum for discussing transboundary pollution and is now working on the environment-and-trade nexus; and the UN Food and Agriculture Organization (FAO), which has played a major role in work on pesticides at the international level. The negotiation of the UN Climate Change convention adopted in 1992 was entrusted to another, new body, the Intergovernmental Negotiating Committee (INC). Several influential observers have made serious proposals advocating the creation of a new international organization with greater powers in the environmental field,[29] but so far those suggestions have not translated into policy action and the institutional impediments are significant.

What a multilateral institution does is as important as what it is. Although perhaps not particularly exciting as a concept, "multilateral coherence" among international institutions is essential to realizing environmental quality goals in a globalized world. In recent years, the World Bank and other multilateral and bilateral aid donors have increasingly emphasized environment as a component of development assistance, sometimes termed *green conditionality*. To that extent, the environment-and-development nexus has been at least partially internalized by such multilateral institutions as the World Bank. The actual policy impact, however, may be minimal. Although the Bank's (IBRD and IDA combined) annual lending to governments of approximately $20 billion may appear to generate considerable policy leverage, rules governing trade flows among private parties are likely to be far more powerful agents of change in encouraging improvements in environmental quality than direct lending will ever be.

But while development assistance is increasingly tied to environmental performance, market access is not. Indeed, the WTO regime of trade rules may very well send conflicting messages. For example, a recipient country government may violate a loan covenant, a commitment analogous in legal effect to the breach of a treaty,[30] by allowing the manufacture of a product under conditions that degrade the environment. At the same time, the WTO regime of rules may compel an importing country, such as the United States, to provide market access for that product. Refusing market access, notwithstanding the violation of the World Bank loan covenant, could itself amount to a violation of U.S. international obligations under the WTO regime. Such a situation, quite appropriately described as "incoherent," creates a conflicting array of incentives in an area where a much higher degree of congruence in international policies is plainly necessary.

Concrete examples demonstrate a major lack of coordination among multilateral policies with respect to environment. A festering trade dispute between the United States and the European Union (EU) over hormone-treated beef, a dispute representative of the larger policy exchange over the relationship between environment and trade policy, is the subject of two recent reports of WTO dispute settlement panels and the WTO's appellate body.[31] The EU prohibits the use of six growth hormones in the breeding of cattle, proscribes the sale of beef treated with those hormones, and bans the importation of such meat. The United States, where those hormones are permitted, has strongly objected to the ban as a nontariff barrier to trade unsupported by scientific evidence. A WTO agreement adopted in 1994,[32] which was motivated in large measure by this dispute and which is designed to prevent the abuse of food-safety measures as nontariff barriers to trade, establishes new science-based disciplines for food-safety measures. The panels and the appellate body in the two beef hormone disputes found that the EU measures were inconsistent with this agreement. In reaching this conclusion, the panels and the appellate body expressly rejected the application of the "precautionary principle," codified at UNCED in a document adopted by more than one hundred heads of state, which asserts the need for policy action in cases of scientific uncertainty.[33]

A similar development falls neatly within the environment-and-security paradigm. The Group of Seven (G-7) industrialized countries at their annual summit in Munich in 1992 established a Nuclear Safety Account (NSA), to be administered by the EBRD.[34] The NSA, a multilateral mechanism to which ECU 257.2 million has since been pledged, was intended to support operational safety and technical improvements to Soviet-designed nuclear power plants and the improvement of regulatory regimes in countries in which such reactors are located, as well as ensuring long-term safety by supplying funds to support the replacement or upgrading of existing plants. In November 1996, the Ukraine signed an agreement with the G-7 and the EU supporting a comprehensive program totaling more than $2.3 billion in U.S. dollars for the closure by the year

2000 of the Chernobyl nuclear power plant, including support for power sector restructuring, an energy investment program, and nuclear safety and decommissioning.[35] As of this writing, however, the requisite amounts have yet to be pledged to the NSA.[36] The modern-day analogy with the Marshall Plan is all too clear, and the failure of political will by comparison with the earlier effort by the United States to rebuild Western Europe after World War II is stark indeed.

More generally, there is a broad conceptual connection between the environment-as-security debate and the environment-and-development dialectic. While poorly designed or ill-advised development projects financed by overseas sources—whether bilateral, multilateral, or private—can have destabilizing effects, under appropriate circumstances foreign assistance can also ameliorate the risk of conflict. Traditional security institutions—whether national, bilateral, or multilateral—are unlikely to be either well-positioned or effective for addressing the social welfare issues of poverty, population pressure, resource degradation, and inequitable income distribution that destabilize many national and regional settings, especially in the Third World. Moreover, foreign aid by its very nature is consensual,[37] an essential attribute not ordinarily found in traditional security debates involving external interventions, where the exogenous exercise of suasion or armed force are more frequent tools. Notwithstanding the element of consent required of foreign governments, external inputs in the form of development assistance have often been ineffective or counterproductive for lack of popular support. For this reason, a consensus is emerging, catalyzed by specific examples of environmental debacles financed by the World Bank and other international financial and development assistance institutions, concerning the need for democratization of the development process to assure both efficacy and accountability.[38] This new understanding, a lesson from more than a decade of experience, would apply equally well to assuring the effectiveness from a security point of view of foreign assistance deployed for that purpose.

Just as power has ebbed from national governments to international institutions such as the World Bank and the WTO by virtue of the need for supranational cooperation on issues such as environment, development, trade, and security, there has been a commensurate pressure for decentralization and democratization in the internal affairs of states. That these trends are related to environmental policy was apparent during the peaceful revolutions in Eastern Europe, in which environmental demands from the populace played a key role. In 1989, the CSCE sponsored a Meeting on the Protection of the Environment in Sofia, Bulgaria, the first convocation under the auspices of the Helsinki process exclusively devoted to environment. The Sofia meeting, which became a lightning rod for radical political upheavals in the host country, itself conspicuously reinforced the close nexus between environmental activism on the one hand and demands for democracy and political change on the other. In the words of a member of the only nongovernmental delegation present, the environmental activism surrounding the CSCE Sofia meeting, during which the Bulgarian government harassed and beat environmental demonstrators, was "plainly political" in its motivation.[39] The Romanian government blocked the adoption of the final document from this conference[40] expressly because of its language on the need for popular participation in establishing environmental policies.[41] Some have asserted that the 1986 Chernobyl accident played a key role in the breakup of the former Soviet Union. Similar concepts of ensuring that power resides at the local level are familiar in the principle of "subsidiarity" in the EU.[42]

Principles of subsidiarity, local control, and democratic accountability (open societies) directly to the public provide a counterweight to the globalizing trends of deregulated markets (open economies) and expanding communications technologies (open technologies). As with other currents in the globalizing world, the environmental impacts of this phenomenon are difficult to quantify. Nevertheless, as a general matter, broad-gauge popular demands for environmental quality can exert a powerful influence on the direction of public policy.[43] A general level of concern among the electorate is a desirable, and perhaps necessary, precondition for crafting effective governmental strategies with respect to the environment. But even though the revolutions in Eastern Europe provide empirical evidence that environmental activism can trigger political change, the proposition that democratic principles of accountability foster environmental quality is harder to establish.

It is now well known that, while the Soviet government authored some of the strictest environmental standards in the world on paper, as a practical matter it also ravaged the environment in that country.[44] Part of the explanation of this phenomenon may lie in the lack of responsiveness of a centrally planned economy,[45] but the USSR was also a totalitarian political system. It is apparent that an unaccountable political system felt little or no need to inform the public as to the state of the environment, to consult with its citizenry, or to act in a manner consistent with the public's expectations. After the breakup of the Soviet Union, Russia was faced with discontinuities in social, political, and economic policies. Institutions such as the EBRD have stepped in to facilitate the opening of Russia, the Eastern European countries, and the former Soviet republics to foreign investment and international trade.

It is considerably less apparent that a commensurate expenditure of effort and resources is being devoted to institution-building to ensure a sense of equilibrium among potentially competing public policy goals, such as environment, foreign investment, development, and trade. While this disparity is painfully obvious in the country whose territorial extent is the greatest on the face of the planet, the same observation quite likely applies everywhere. The price of a "democracy gap" or a "democracy lag" may well turn out to be paid at least in part in terms of environmental quality, not just overseas, but here at home as well.

Notes

1. The term *globalization,* although in wide use, appears to elude precise definition. While the term encompasses the concept of doing business in a global marketplace, in practice the word is often used to describe a much broader spectrum of social, cultural, political, and even economic trends. Perhaps because of the definitional difficulty, many elaborations of the term are phrased in descriptive terms. For example, see, Organisation for Economic Co-operation and Development, *Economic Globalisation and the Environment* 19 (1997) ("Globalisation can be thought of as a process in which economic markets, technologies, and communication patterns gradually exhibit more 'global' characteristics, and less 'national' or 'local' ones."); C. Ford Runge, "Globalization and Sustainability: The Machine in the Global Garden," Center For International Food and Agricultural Policy Working Paper WP97-4 (September 1997) (" 'Globalization' nearly always describes international economic competition and its impact on 'connectedness', specifically, the increasing transboundary flow of goods, services, bads and disservices, including not only materiel, but information, environmental pollution, and people.")

2. George F. Will, "Judicial Exhibitionism," *Washington Post,* July 8, 1993, A17.

3. For criticisms of the activities of international financial institutions from an environmental perspective, see, Patricia Adams, *Odious Debts: Loose Lending, Corruption, and the Third World's Environmental Legacy* (1991); *International Institute for Environment and Development, Banking on the Biosphere?* (1978); Raymond F. Mikesell and Larry Williams, *International Banks and the Environment: From Growth to Sustainability: An Unfinished Agenda* (1992); Bruce Rich, *Mortgaging the Earth: The World Bank, Environmental Impoverishment, and the Crisis of Development* (1994); Pat Aufderheide and Bruce Rich, "Environmental Reform and the Multilateral Banks," *World Policy Journal* 5 (1988): 301; John Horberry, "The Accountability of Development Assistance Agencies: The Case of Environmental Policy," *Ecology L Q* 12 (1985): 817; Zygmunt J. Plater, "Multilateral Development Banks, Environmental Diseconomies, and International Reform Pressures on the Lending Process," 17 *Denv. J. Int'l L. & Pol'y* 17 (1988): 121, revised and reprinted in *B.C. Third World L.J.* 9 (1989): 169; Bruce Rich, "The Multilateral Development Banks, Environmental Policy, and the United States," *Ecology LQ.* 12 (1985): 681; Rich, "The Emperor's New Clothes: The World Bank and Environmental Reform," *World Policy Journal* 7 (1990): 305; David A. Wirth, "The World Bank and the Environment," *Env't* (December 1986): 33.

4. *World Commission on Environment and Development, Our Common Future* (1987). Constituted by the UN General Assembly in 1983, the World Commission was composed of twenty-one eminent personages appointed in their personal capacities, was chaired by Gro Harlem Brundtland, prime minister of Norway, and was charged with "propos[ing] long-term environmental strategies for achieving sustainable development to the year 2000 and beyond," G.A. Res. 161 sec. 8(a), 38 U.N. GAOR Supp. (No. 47) at 131, U.N. Doc. A/38/47 (1984). Despite the World Commission's effort, there still appears to be no consensus definition for the term *sustainable development.* Cf. Rio Declaration on Environment and Development, June 14, 1992, Principle 4, U.N. Doc. A/CONF.151/5/Rev. 1 (1992), reprinted in 31 *I.L.M.* 876 (1992) ("In order to achieve sustainable development, environmental protection shall constitute an integral part of the development process and cannot be considered in isolation from it.") This passage has been described as "the closest the Rio Declaration comes to a definition of "sustainable development." Jeffrey D. Kovar, "A Short Guide to the Rio Declaration," *Col. J. Int'l Envtl. L. & Pol'y* 119, 127

(1993). However, this passage imposes less demanding constraints on development that is sustainable, both in terms of meeting the needs of current and future generations and in conserving environmental integrity, than the World Commission's definition.

5. See, David A. Wirth, "The Rio Declaration on Environment and Development: Two Steps Forward and One Back, or Vice Versa?," *Ga. L. Rev.* 29 (1994): 599.

6. "United Nations Framework Convention on Climate Change," May 9, 1992, reprinted in *I.L.M.* 31 (1992): 851.

7. "Convention on Biological Diversity," May 22, 1992, reprinted in *I.L.M.* 31 (1992): 822.

8. "World Bank, Documents Concerning the Establishment the Global Environment Facility," reprinted in *I.L.M.* 1735 (1991).

9. "Instrument Establishing the Global Environment Facility," reprinted in *I.L.M.* 33 (1994): 1283. See generally Andrew Jordan, "Paying the Incremental Costs of Global Environmental Protection: The Evolving Role of GEF," *Env't* (July–August, 1994): 12.

10. *Introduction to the Global Environment Facility,* <http://www.worldbank.org/html/gef/intro/gefintro.htm>.

11. See Ian A. Bowles & Glenn Prickett, *Reframing the Green Window: An Analysis of the GEF Pilot Phase Approach to Biodiversity and Global Warming and Recommendations for the Operational Phase* (Conservation International & Natural Resources Defense Council 1994); David Reed, ed., *The Global Environment Facility: Sharing Responsibility for the Biosphere* (World Wide Fund for Nature International, 1993); *The World Bank's Greenwash: Touting Environmentalism While Trashing the Planet* (Greenpeace International, 1992); David Reed, "The Global Environment Facility and Non-Governmental Organizations," *Am. U.J. Int'l L. & Pol'y* 191 (1993).

12. "North American Agreement on Environmental Cooperation, September 8–14, 1993, U.S.-Canada-Mexico," reprinted in *I.L.M.* 32 (1993): 1482.

13. For example, the WTO constitutional instrument refers to "optimal use of the world's resources in accordance with the objective of sustainable development." "Agreement Establishing the World Trade Organization," preamble para. 1, *I.L.M.* 33 (1994): 15.

14. See Norman Myers, *Ultimate Security: The Environmental Basis of Political Stability* (1993); Lester Brown, *Redefining Security* (Worldwatch Paper No. 14, 1977); Jessica Tuchman Mathews, "Redefining Security," *Foreign Aff.* (Spring 1989): 162; Thomas Homer-Dixon, "On the Threshold: Environmental Changes as Causes of Acute Conflict," *Int'l Security* 16 (Fall 1991): 76, reprinted in *Conflict After the Cold War: Arguments on the Causes of War and Peace* 425 (Richard Betts ed. 1994); Ted Robert Gurr, "On the Political Consequences of Scarcity and Economic Decline," *Int'l Studies Q.* 29 (1985): 51; Arthur Westing, "An Expanded Concept of International Security," in *Global Resources and International Conflict: Environmental Factors in Strategic Policy and Action* 85 (Arthur H. Westing ed. 1986); Richard H. Ullman, "Redefining Security," *Int'l Security* 8 (1983): 129; Gareth Porter, "Environmental Security as a National Security Issue," *Current History* 94 (May 1995): 21; Norman Myers, "Environment and Security," *For. Pol'y* (Spring 1989): 23. See also Sherri Wasserman Goodman, Deputy Under Secretary of Defense (Environmental Security), *The Environment and National Security,* address at National Defense University (Aug. 8, 1996) ("it is clear that environmental degradation and scarcity and related conditions (such as increased population growth, urbanization, and migration, and the spread of infectious diseases) may contribute significantly to instability around the world"), reprinted in <http://denix/cecer.army.mil/denix/Public/ES-Programs/Speeches/speech-22.html#tabe>; Warren Christopher, *American Diplomacy and the Global Environmental Challenges of the 21st Century,* address at Stanford

University (Apr. 9, 1996)("The second element of our strategy—the regional element—is to confront pollution and the scarcity of resources in key areas where they dramatically increase tensions within and among nations."), reprinted in id. See generally <http://chs.ida.org/s05/biblio/oldbiblio.html> (NATO CCMS pilot project bibliography).

15. See Marc A. Levy, "Is the Environment a National Security Issue?," *International Security* (Fall 1995): 35, 36 ("the indirect, political threat from environmental degradation . . . is . . . the weakest substantive threat to U.S. security"); Daniel Deudney, "The Case Against Linking Environmental Degradation and National Security," *Millennium* 19 (1990): 461.

16. See generally Joyce Starr, "Water Wars," *Foreign Policy* (Spring 1991): 17; Peter H. Gleick, "Water and Conflict: Fresh Water Resources and International Security," *International Security* 18 (1993): 79.

17. See "Final Act of the Conference on Security and Cooperation in Europe" ("Helsinki Final Act"), Aug. 1, 1975, reprinted in *I.L.M.* 14 (1975): 1292.

18. The Conference on Security and Cooperation in Europe (CSCE) was established in the early 1970s to serve as a multilateral forum for dialogue and negotiation between Eastern and Western European states, including the United States, Canada, and the Soviet Union. The 1990 summit-level meeting in Paris, the first since the Helsinki meeting in 1975, formally recognized the end of the Cold War, identified the CSCE as a crucial institution in the subsequent historic developments in Europe, and commenced a greater institutionalization of the CSCE process. See "Charter of Paris for a New Europe," Nov. 21, 1990, reprinted in *I.L.M.* 30 (1991): 193. In recognition of the increasing institutional and structural development of the institution, its name was changed at the 1994 Budapest Summit to the Organization for Security and Cooperation in Europe (OSCE). See "Budapest Summit Declaration: Towards a Genuine Partnership in a New Era," December 6, 1994, reprinted in *I.L.M.* 34 (1995): 767. Today, the OSCE has fifty-five participating states, including the United States, Canada, all the countries of Europe, and all the former Soviet republics from Europe through Central Asia. See generally Alexis Heraclides, *Helsinki-II and its Aftermath: The Making of the CSCE Into an International Organization* (1993); Vojtech Mastny, *The Helsinki Process and the Reintegration of Europe 1986–1991: Analysis and Documentation* (1992); *The CSCE and the Turbulent New Europe* (Louis B. Sohn ed. 1993); *The Conference on Security and Co-operation in Europe: Analysis and Basic Documents 1972–1993* (Arie Bloed ed., 2d ed. 1993); *From Helsinki to Vienna: Basic Documents of the Helsinki Process* (Arie Bloed ed. 1990); *From Helsinki to Madrid: Conference on Security and Co-operation in Europe 1973–1983* (Adam Daniel Rotfield ed. 1986?); Jeffrey S. Palmer, "The New European Order: Restructuring the Security Regime Under the Conference on Security and Cooperation in Europe," *Temple Int'l & Comp. L.Q.* 5 (1991): 51; Gregory F. Treverton, "Elements of a New European Security Order," *J. Int'l Aff.* 45 (1991): 91.

19. The natural response is that equating security and stability so attenuates the former concept as to render it near meaningless. Levy, "Is the Environment a National Security Issue?", 43–44 ("It is possible to imagine such constructions of security, but they would take the discussion so far from the mainstream as to forswear any hope of linking environmental issues to the conventional security agenda.")

20. See *The Human Dimension of the Helsinki Process: The Vienna Follow-Up Meeting and Its Aftermath* (A. Bloed and P. van Dijk ed. 1991); William Korey, *The Promises We Keep: Human Rights, the Helsinki Process, and American Foreign Policy* (1993); Thomas Buergenthal, "The CSCE Rights System," *Geo. Wash. J. Int'l L. & Econ.* 25 (1991): 333.

21. C. Ford Runge, with François Ortalo-Magné and Philip Vande Kamp, *Freer Trade, Protected Environment: Balancing Trade Liberalization and Environmental Interests* 95 (New York: Council on Foreign Relations Press, 1994) ("trade rules alone are inadequate to the task [of raising environmental standards in developing countries]: environmental rules are also required"). Kenneth Arrow, Bert Bolin, Robert Costanza, Partha Dasgupta, Carl Folke, C.S. Holling, Bengt- Owe Jansson, Simon Levin, Karl-Göran Mäler, Charles Perrings & David Pimentel, "Economic Growth, Carrying Capacity, and the Environment," *Science* 268 (1995): 520.

22. "National Environmental Policy Act (NEPA)," 42 U.S.C. §§ 4321–4370.

23. See, Will, "Judicial Exhibitionism," ("What kind of mind believes it is possible to anticipate and quantify the 'impact' on the entire 'human environment' of an agreement establishing the world's largest free trade zone, encompassing 360 million people and substantially enlarging trade with America's third largest trading partner, Mexico?").

24. "The NAFTA: Report on Environmental Issues" (1993). The Clinton administration released the final version of this document to the public a scant four days before the House of Representatives voted on the NAFTA implementing legislation. In litigation asserting the need for an EIS, the executive branch did not argue that this document or its precursors met the statutory requirements. See *Public Citizen v. Office of the United States Trade Representative,* 822 F. Supp. 21, 27–29 (D.D.C. 1993), rev'd, 5 F.3d 549 (D.C. Cir. 1993), cert. denied, 510 U.S. 1041 (1994) (enumerating potential adverse environmental effects in concluding that plaintiffs have standing to sue). *Public Citizen v. Office of the United States Trade Representative,* 970 F.2d 916 (D.C. Cir. 1992) (no EIS required to accompany negotiation of NAFTA).

25. Such activities have nonetheless been successfully analyzed in case studies. See Wilfrido Cruz and Robert Repetto, *The Environmental Effects of Stabilization and Structural Adjustment Programs: The Philippines Case* (World Resources Institute 1992); *Structural Adjustment and the Environment* (David Reed ed., 1992) (case studies of Côte d'Ivoire, Mexico, and Thailand).

26. Kyoto Protocol to the UN Framework Convention on Climate Change, December 10, 1997, 37 I.L.M. 32 (1998).

27. See G. John Ikenberry, "The Myth of Post–Cold War Chaos," *Foreign Affairs* (May–June 1996): 79 ("Security and stability in the West were seen as intrinsically tied to an array of institutions—the United Nations and its agencies and the General Agreement on Tariffs and Trade (GATT) only some among many—that bound the democracies together, constrained conflict, and facilitated political community. . . . The postwar liberal democratic order was designed to solve the internal problems of Western industrial capitalism. It was not intended to fight Soviet communism, nor was it simply a plan to get American business back on its feet after the war by opening up the world to trade and investment. It was a strategy to build Western solidarity through economic openness and joint political governance.")

28. See Leyla Boulton, "UN Environment Chief Under Pressure Not to Seek New Term," *Financial Times* (July 29, 1996): 16.

29. See Runge, *Freer Trade* (advocating new World Environmental Organization); Daniel C. Esty, *Greening the GATT: Trade, Environment, and the Future* (Washington, D.C.: Institute for International Economics, 1994) (advocating new Global Environmental Organization).

30. See Lester Nurick, "Certain Aspects of the Law and Practice of the International Bank for Reconstruction and Development," in *The Effectiveness of International Decisions 100,* 127 (1971) (statement by World Bank Deputy General Counsel).

31. "United States–EC Measures Concerning Meat and Meat Products" (Hormones), WTO Doc. No. WT/DS26/R/USA (Aug. 18, 1997), reprinted at <www.wto.org/wto/dispute/distab.htm>; "Canada–EC Measures Concerning Meat and Meat Products" (Hormones), WTO Doc. No. WT/DS48/R/CAN (Aug. 18, 1997), reprinted at id.; European Communities–Measures Concerning Meat and Meat Products, WTO Doc. No. WT/DS26/AB/R & WT/DS48/AB/R. World Trade Organization Appellate Body, January 16, 1998, reprinted at *id.*

32. "Agreement on the Application of Sanitary and Phytosanitary Measures," Uruguay Round Final Act, reprinted in *I.L.M.* 33 (1994): 1143.

33. See "United States–EC Measures Concerning Meat and Meat Products" (Hormones), 146–147. See generally Wirth, "The Rio Declaration," 634–37 (discussing treatment of precautionary approaches at UNCED).

34. "Munich Economic Summit Declaration," July 7, 1992, paras. 42–49 (statement of Group of Seven major industrialized nations in Munich), reprinted in *Weekly Comp.* Pres. Doc. 1222 (1992).

35. "Memorandum of Understanding Between the Government of Ukraine and the Governments of the G-7 Countries and the Commission of the European Communities on the Closure of the Chernobyl Nuclear Power Plant," November 1996 (? undated) (available on Web site at <www.ebrd.com>).

36. See "EBRD/Chernobyl: Plea for More Money," Europe Information Service, June 27, 1998 (quoting acting President of EBRD as stating that unless more funds can be identified to finance repairs to Chernobyl sarcophagus, the consequences will be "too horrible to imagine") (available in Lexis, News library, Curnws file); and Leyla Boulton and Simon Holberton, "West's Policies on Eastern Nuclear Plants 'Misguided,' " *Financial Times* (February 10, 1997): 2 (quoting consultant as saying that "governments have not been prepared to invest the sums required to achieve their goals").

37. See David A. Wirth, "The United States and the World Bank: Constructive Reformer or Fly in the Functional Ointment," *Michigan Journal of International Law* 15 (1994): 687, 700 (review of Bartram S. Brown, *The United States and the Politicization of the World Bank: Issues of International Law and Policy,* 1992).

38. Ibid.; David A. Wirth, "Partnership Advocacy in World Bank Environmental Reform," in *The Struggle for Accountability,* eds. Jonathan Fox and L. David Brown (in press).

39. Author's personal communication with Liz Hopkins, IUCN/The World Conservation Union (Dec. 9, 1997). See generally *Environmental Problems in Eastern Europe* (F.W. Carter and David Turnock ed. 1996).

40. "Sofia Meeting on the Protection of the Environment: Recommendations," November 3, 1989, reprinted in *Envtl. Pol'y & L.* 20 (1990): 107.

41. Ibid., 85 (describing subsequent Romanian support for document).

42. See "Treaty on European Union," February 7, 1992, art. G, para. 5, reprinted in *I.L.M.* 31 (1992): 253 (adding new article 3b to "Treaty of Rome," providing that "[i]n areas which do not fall within its exclusive competence, the Community shall take action, in accordance with the principle of subsidiarity, only if and in so far as the objectives of the proposed action cannot be sufficiently achieved by the member states and can therefore, by reason of the scale or effects of the proposed action, be better achieved by the Community").

43. See Lynton Keith Caldwell, Lynton R. Hayes, and Isabel M. MacWhirter, *Citizens and the Environment: Case Studies in Popular Action* (1976); "United States Environmental Protection Agency, Science Advisory Board, Unfinished Business: A Comparative

Assessment of Environmental Problems," (1987); Zygmunt J. B. Plater, Robert H. Abrams, and William Goldfarb, *Environmental Law and Policy: Nature, Law, and Society* 22–23 (1992); John H. Adams, *Responsible Militancy—The Anatomy of a Public Interest Law Firm*, Rec. Ass'n B. City N.Y., Nov. 1974, at 1, 2.

44. See Murray Feshbach and Albert Friendly, Jr., *Ecocide in the U.S.S.R.* (New York: Basic Books, 1992); Murray Feshbach, *Ecological Disaster: Cleaning Up the Hidden Legacy of the Soviet Regime* (New York: Twentieth Century Fund Press, 1995).

45. See Ikenberry, "The Myth of Post–Cold War Chaos."

Editor's Preface to Chapter Nine

Intergovernmental Organizations

During the Cold War, intergovernmental organizations (IGOs) were often hamstrung by East-West divisions, which tended to neuter the effectiveness of many IGOs, or at least kept them from reaching their full potential. With the end of the Cold War there has been a resurgence of interest in and expectations of IGOs. IGOs are increasingly called upon to solve transsovereign problems that no individual state can effectively tackle alone. However, because they are made up of state members, IGOs are in the difficult position of trying to manage transsovereign problems from within the logic and limitations of sovereign states.

The number of IGOs has increased dramatically this century, especially since the end of the Cold War (Table 1). This is not surprising, since the rise in open technologies, societies, and markets makes it both easier and more necessary for IGOs to organize to manage problems of mutual concern. Among just traditional IGOs, the number has grown 5,000 percent from 37 in 1909 to 1,850 in 1997; the bulk of that growth occurred since the 1980s.

Many of these IGOs fall under the umbrella of the United Nations system, but other bodies come into existence as a result of treaty commitments or regional organizations, such as the Organization of American States (OAS). For example, ratification of the North American Free Trade Agreement (and its supplemental side agreements) by the United States, Canada, Mexico, and Chile has created new IGOs charged with monitoring and adjudicating disputes that arise as states comply with the treaty. The Labor Commission is charged with resolving labor disputes that arise as NAFTA is implemented, and tries to ensure enforcement of labor laws; the Commission for Environmental Cooperation resolves environmental disputes.[1]

IGOs are scrambling to adapt with the changing times, both to be more relevant and efficient in responding to transsovereign problems and to reinvent their structures now that they are no longer bound by Cold War rivalries. For example, in 1948 following the Nuremberg and Tokyo trials after World War II, the UN General Assembly first recognized the need for a permanent International Criminal Court (ICC) to hear charges of war crimes, crimes against humanity, genocide, and other grave human rights abuses. But an ICC was never created during the Cold War, and has only recently begun evolving in the aftermath of the horrific war crimes witnessed in the 1990s in Rwanda and Bosnia. On July 17, 1998, 120 nations voted in favor of a statute to establish a permanent ICC in the Hague, the Netherlands.[2] Although the treaty will not enter into force until sixty states have ratified the statute (and so far the United States is in opposition), the agreement to create an ICC for hearing war crimes was hailed as "a giant step forward" by UN Secretary-General Kofi Annan.[3]

The creation of the ICC directly responds to the problem of failed or weak states. When state courts are either nonexistent or unable or unwilling to hear war crimes

Table 1

The Growth of Intergovernmental Organizations

IGOs	1909	1951	1960	1968	1976	1978	1983
Traditional	37	123	154	229	252	289	1,465
Special	––	––	––	––	––	––	1,084
Total	37	123	154	229	252	289	2,549

IGOs	1985	1987	1989	1991	1993	1995	1997
Traditional	1,632	1,649	1,711	1,794	1,736	1,763	1,850
Special	1,914	2,248	2,357	2,771	3,367	3,905	4,265
Total	3,546	3,897	4,068	4,565	5,103	5,668	6,115

Data from the *Yearbook of International Organizations, Vol. 1, 1997/98,* Union of International Associations (ed.), Brussels, Belgium: K. G. Saur Verlag, Munichen. Appendix 4.

or similarly grave cases, the ICC will provide an international court capable of properly dealing with such crimes.[4] Currently, tribunals are created on an ad hoc basis each time atrocities occur (as has been the case with the Bosnian and Rwandan War Crimes Tribunals). These tribunals face the difficulty of starting from scratch each time in a highly volatile and politicized environment, trying to develop institutions, prove their credibility, and garner resources without the benefit of any track record. Rather than reinventing the wheel whenever atrocious war crimes occurred, the ICC would create a ready-made body that would consume far fewer resources than continually recreating and duplicating institutional structures and would focus resources as the court built a reputation for fair and professional adjudication.

Similarly, intergovernmental financial institutions like the World Bank and the International Monetary Fund were not created with the interdependence of state financial markets in mind. When forty-four states met in July 1944 in the small New Hampshire resort town of Bretton Woods to devise new postwar international economic institutions, their attentions were focused on the problems of large-scale economic reconstruction and recovery necessary after World War II's end, and the need to promote free trade and economic development. The founders of the Bretton Woods system could never have anticipated the day when states would no longer have sole control over monetary policy, or when currencies could change hands and capital be transferred over borders with a keystroke using e-mail. In the aftermath of the Asian financial crisis, and with the troubles of Russia's liberalizing economy in mind (as well as those of other former communist states), many states are clamoring for a fundamental revision of economic IGOs—a Bretton Woods II. Some argue that the free market dynamics which are stabilizing for trade flows can foster speculation and destabilization of currencies, while others argue that the free movement of capital is good or at least inevitable given changes in transportation, communication, and the interpenetration of world financial markets.[5] Some rethinking of economic IGOs already has begun, with the founding of the World Trade Organization in 1993 to adjudicate trade disputes among member states. Open economies, open societies, and open technologies have forced the restructuring of IGOs in the economic sphere.

Other IGOs are undergoing changes as well. Under the supervision of American Joseph E. Connor, UN undersecretary-general for management, the United Nations has instituted a number of reforms to make the organization more efficient and less bureaucratic. Nearly 1,000 jobs have been eliminated from the UN Secretariat, which has adopted a zero-growth budget. An Office of Internal Oversight was established in 1994 to eliminate waste, fraud, and mismanagement and to promote more effective and efficient operations. Nevertheless, despite reorganization within the UN system to make it more efficient, the United States still has not payed its $1.6 billion debt to the United Nations.

Financial constraints on UN organizations are significant. These IGOs rely on the contributions of states to function, but states contribute far less to IGOs than they allocate for their own government operations. For example, "The United Nations and its agencies, funds, and programmes—mainly UNICEF, UNDP, UNFPA, WFP, and WHO—have $4.8 billion a year to spend on economic and social development, to assist countries in such areas as health care, sanitation, agriculture, and food distribution. This is the equivalent of 81 cents per human being. In 1996 the world's governments spent about $797 billion in military expenditures—the equivalent of $135 per human being."[6] The UN headquarters in New York City employs fewer than 4,700 workers. In contrast, the government in the Swedish capital of Stockholm employs 60,000 workers. McDonald's Corporation employs three times more people than the approximately 52, 280 people who work in all the various UN organizations combined (such as UNICEF) around the world. The United States' $298 million share of the UN's regular budget for 1998 equals approximately $1.11 per American for UN services for an entire year,[7] less than half the price of a Big Mac and less than the cost of cable TV for one day.[8] The budget for the UN's core functions is a billion dollars less than the annual budget of Tokyo's fire department, about 4 percent of the annual budget of New York City, and $3.7 billion dollars less than the State of New York's university system.[9] IGOs routinely have large problems placed at their doorsteps without the concomitant resources to attack the job.

Thus, while states are increasingly "contracting out" problems for IGOs to solve, IGOs can only be as effective as states allow them to be. Funding and jurisdiction issues are largely determined by states, who often do not "put their money where their mouths are" as far as the work of international organizations is concerned.

Notes

1. Mary E. Lovely, "Thinking Locally, Acting Globally: Congressman Jim Walsh and the NAFTA Vote" (Washington, D.C.: Georgetown University, 1994), Pew Case Studies in International Affairs, 15.
2. The United States, however, voted against the Statute of the Court, fearing that the ICC would be used for politically motivated prosecutions of American troops deployed across the globe. Senator Jesse Helms (R-N.C.), chairman of the Senate Foreign Relations Committee, "declared war on the ICC for not giving '100 percent protection' from

prosecution to American GIs." Ruth Wedgwood, "Fiddling in Rome: America and the International Criminal Court," *Foreign Affairs* (November/December 1998): 21.

3. "Setting the Record Straight: The International Criminal Court," United Nations Department of Public Information, October 1998.

4. Ibid.

5. Jagdish Bhagwati, "The Capital Myth: The Difference between Trade in Widgets and Dollars," *Foreign Affairs* (May/June 1998): 7–12; Shailendra J. Anjaria, "The Capital Truth: What Works for Commodities Should Work for Cash," *Foreign Affairs* (November/December 1998): 142–143.

6. "Setting the Record Straight: Facts About the United Nations."

7. Ibid.

8. McDonald's Corporation, Union Station, Washington, D.C., October 1998; District Cablevision, October 1998.

9. "Setting the Record Straight: Facts About the United Nations."

Intergovernmental Organizations

Ursula C. Tafe

INTRODUCTION

Intergovernmental organizations (IGOs) are associations of states created to advance common goals and whose activities extend beyond national boundaries.[1] IGOs are based on the principle of *sovereign equality:* each state is the legal equal of all others. Membership in and withdrawal from IGOs is voluntary, although many IGOs have provisions for suspending the institutional privileges of member states who violate rules of the organizations.[2] IGOs vary in both size (number of member states) and scope, depending upon the principles and purposes stated in their charters, and the specific interests being advanced by the participating governments. Membership in IGOs can be limited or open to all the independent states of the international community. While IGOs are based on the principle of sovereignty (including nonintervention in the internal affairs of states) IGOs were also created to deal with the problems of sovereignty, problems which states cannot deal with well alone. Thus, IGOs are in an ironic position. They are based on sovereignty, yet they are charged with going beyond sovereignty to gain multilateral cooperation in critical international issues.

IGOs have been actors in international relations throughout most of the twentieth century, though they are relatively new actors. The League of Nations, created in the aftermath of World War I (1920), was the first organization which aspired to true universality. Other, more limited, regional institutions had been created during the late nineteenth century but were of little real influence. It was not until the founding of the United Nations, during the waning days of World War II (1945), that IGOs became widely accepted by states as legitimate instruments for advancing national interests. Governments realized that there were issues which could be addressed and managed more effectively and efficiently through IGOs than through multiple unilateral or bilateral initiatives. IGOs provided a much needed single location for the representatives of states to discuss issues of mutual interest. They also provided a permanent infrastructure which could continuously work on issues of importance to the governments of member states.

During the Cold War, though, many IGOs were unable to fulfill the roles envisaged for them at their creation due to the superpower conflict between the United States and Soviet Union. This was especially true of the UN. With the end of the Cold War and the emergence of a "new world order," however, IGOs have enjoyed a renaissance of sorts, having been rediscovered as institutions through which critical issues facing the international community can be addressed and managed. In 1992, then UN Secretary-General Boutros Boutros-Ghali wrote:

> a conviction has grown, among nations large and small, that an opportunity has been regained to achieve the great objectives of the Charter–a United Nations capable of maintaining international peace and security, of securing justice and human rights and of promoting . . . social progress and better standards of life in larger freedom. This opportunity must not be squandered. The Organization must never again be crippled as it was in the era that has now passed.[3]

This chapter will explore, among other issues, the question of how well the UN and other IGOs have been able to live up to these expectations in the post–Cold War era. Have IGOs, those created during the Cold War as well as the post–Cold War periods, been able to achieve their objectives? How have the new transsovereign problems of the post–Cold War era been addressed by IGOs? What are the prospects for the effective management of international affairs by IGOs in the twenty-first century?

THE COLD WAR ERA: A WORLD DIVIDED

Historical Background

In the aftermath of World War II it became clear to state leaders that institutions were needed to provide governments with mechanisms for alleviating international conflict and promoting the conditions necessary for ensuring that world war would not occur again in the twentieth century. To this end, the victors of World War II established the United Nations. The architects of the UN were determined, as stated in the preamble to the organization's charter, "to save succeeding generations from the scourge of war." Chapter one of the UN charter sets forth the central purposes of the organization:

> (1) To maintain international peace and security . . . ; (2) To develop friendly relations among nations based on respect for the principle of equal rights and self-determination of peoples . . . ; (3) To achieve international cooperation in solving international problems of an economic, social, cultural, or humanitarian character . . . ; (4) To be a center for harmonizing the actions of nations in the attainment of these common ends.

To fulfill these purposes an extensive network of IGOs was established, commonly known as the "UN system." Political organizations within this system cover a broad range of institutions, including the International Labor Organization (ILO), World Health Organization (WHO), Universal Postal Union (UPU), and the UN Educational, Scientific, and Cultural Organization (UNESCO), to name only a few. The role of these organizations is to improve the physical lives of peoples around the world through better health care, education, and agricultural resources, as well as to establish international standards in areas such as postal service, aviation, the environment, and workers' rights. Economic institutions created in the aftermath of World War II as part of the UN system include the World Bank,[4] the International Monetary Fund (IMF), and the General Agreement of Tariffs and Trade (GATT). These organizations are responsible for maintaining a stable international financial system, providing investment funds to less-developed countries (LDCs) to help facilitate their economic growth, and regulating nondiscriminatory world trade.

Military activities are less developed in the UN system than are those of a political or economic nature. In 1945, a Military Staff Committee was planned as part of the UN's Security Council structure. This committee was to consist of the chiefs of staff of the five permanent members of the Security Council (United States, Great Britain, France, China, and the Soviet Union) and was to be responsible "for the strategic direction of any armed forces placed at the disposal of the Security Council."[5] Because the East-West conflict was often played out within the Security Council during the Cold War, this military staff never materialized. The UN did eventually establish a peacekeeping function, but each mission is created on an ad hoc basis and is subject to the veto power of any of the permanent members of the Security Council.

The post–World War II era saw the creation of IGOs outside the UN systems as well. Several military alliance and collective security organizations were created, including the Inter-American Treaty of Reciprocal Assistance (Rio Treaty, 1947), the North Atlantic Treaty Organization (NATO, 1949), the Western European Union (WEU, 1954), and the Warsaw Treaty Organization (Warsaw Pact, 1955). IGOs with multipurpose mandates created in this era include the League of Arab States (Arab League, 1945), the Organization of American States (OAS, 1948),[6] the Council of Europe (1949), and the Nordic Council (1952). The coordination and expansion of economic activities were addressed through such organizations as the European Coal and Steel Community (ECSC, 1952), the European Economic Community (EEC, 1958), and the Council for Mutual Economic Assistance (COMECON, 1949), established by the Soviet Union to coordinate the economic activities within her Eastern European "satellites." In addition, these years saw the emergence of a variety of regional financial institutions, including the Inter-American Development Bank (IDB, 1959) and the European Investment Bank (EIB, 1958).

This partial listing of IGOs established in the decade and a half following World War II illustrates two key factors. First, the number of IGOs increased dramatically in the post-war era, indicating a strong belief on the part of the members of the international community that multilateral action was important for promoting national interests. Second, the organizations founded during this period were a reflection of the Cold War conflict, or bipolar international political system. That is, the IGOs of this period were divided, in both membership and purpose, between the communist East and the capitalist/democratic West. Universal cooperation was achieved in many important areas, including nuclear nonproliferation, control of atomic materials, and humanitarian assistance, but these activities were facilitated primarily within the UN system. Few other IGOs functioned across ideological lines during this period.

The ensuing fifteen years, 1960 to 1975, challenged both the composition and character of many IGOs. These were the final years of European colonialism when dozens of new, independent and sovereign states were created by decolonization processes, especially in Africa. One of the first acts taken by these new states was to apply for membership in the UN and other IGOs. The increase in UN membership shown in Table 9-1 illustrates the dramatic effect of decolonization on the organization.

As was the case for the founders of the UN system and other post–World War II IGOs, new states recognized the importance of membership in such institutions for participating in international relations. The utility of IGOs during these years is seen not only in this "clamor for membership," but in their steadily increasing numbers.[7] Influential multipurpose and political IGOs formed during the 1960s and 1970s include the Organization for African Unity (OAU, 1963), the Association of Southeast Asian Nations (ASEAN, 1967), and the Conference on Security and Cooperation in Europe (CSCE, 1975).[8] Economic institutions also emerged, including the Organization of Petroleum Exporting Countries (OPEC, 1960), the Asian Development Bank (1966), the African Development Bank (1964), the Economic Community of West African States (1975), and the Caribbean Community (CARICOM, 1973).

The participation in IGOs by so many new Third World members affected not only the composition of these organizations, but the kinds of interests the member states chose to advance. In general, the less-developed member states redirected the focus of many IGOs, especially multipurpose organizations,

Table 9-1

UN Membership: 1945–1975

1945	1955	1965	1975
51	76	118	143

Source: *Basic Facts About the United Nations* (United Nations Publications, 1995): 307–308.

away from the management of the economic and security interests affecting the more developed member states, which had dominated the organizations' activities in the immediate post–World War II period, toward establishing programs for improving the economic and social conditions in LDCs. This shift in focus created an often deep division between the more advanced industrial member states of the northern hemisphere and the less-developed Third World member states found primarily in the southern hemisphere. This north-south divide complicated the work of IGOs, which were already struggling with the restrictions placed on their activities by the East-West conflict.

THE ROLE OF IGOs: 1945–1989

During the Cold War era the activities of IGOs fell primarily within four categories: peace and security, social and economic development, human rights, and humanitarian assistance. Cooperative multilateral initiatives undertaken by the international community were responsible for such achievements as the eradication of smallpox and other deadly and debilitating diseases; overseeing the modernization and expansion of agricultural production; establishing internationally accepted criteria for the humane treatment of the world's citizens by their governments; and providing food, shelter, and medicine to people left homeless or displaced by war and natural disaster. Perhaps the most important achievement of the extended system of IGOs established during this period was something that *didn't* happen: a third world war.

Peace and Security Issues

While it is true that no military conflict erupted during the Cold War era on a scale equal to either of the century's world wars, conflict was present throughout this period. Although IGOs were limited in their ability to prevent conflicts, they were often utilized when parties to a conflict were ready to resolve their differences and required assistance to establish and implement a peace process. It was for this purpose that peacekeeping activities were created by the UN in 1956.[9]

During the Cold War, UN peacekeepers were sent into areas of conflict once a cease-fire had been established by the combatants. Peacekeepers were deployed as a "buffer" between the two sides and were responsible for monitoring the cease-fire while the parties negotiated a permanent peace. This has become known as "first generation" peacekeeping. During the Cold War era, some fifteen operations of this nature were undertaken by the UN. A few, including those in Cyprus (UNFICYP, 1964) and Lebanon (UNIFIL, 1978), have been in existence for decades. The presence of UN peacekeepers over such long periods certainly indicates an inability on the part of the organization to facilitate a final peace between the parties in conflict. But, on the positive side, having peacekeepers on the ground has helped to prevent these conflicts from escalating once again into full-scale wars.

UN peacekeeping missions are authorized and deployed under provisions found in Chapter VII of the organization's charter. These provisions authorize the Security Council, the body with "primary responsibility" over issues of international peace and security, to "determine the existence of any threat to the peace . . . or act of aggression." Once such a determination is made, the Security Council may "decide what measures shall be taken [to] maintain or restore international peace and security."[10] Only twice in the UN's history (Korea, 1950 and the Persian Gulf, 1991) did the Security Council authorize military intervention beyond that of peacekeeping. This was due primarily to the divisions between the United States and Soviet Union. As permanent members of the Security Council, each has veto authority over all military activities undertaken by the organization.[11] The UN and other IGOs were unable to intervene in many conflicts across the globe because these were often superpower "proxy wars," conflicts to which the United States and Soviet Union were not direct parties but were the political and military supporters of the combatants. When the UN did become involved in such conflicts it was usually after the two superpowers had agreed to disengage and were open to assistance.

First generation peacekeeping missions were restricted not only by Cold War politics, but by the protection of the sovereign rights of member states and the conditions imposed on intervention guaranteed by the UN charter. Peacekeepers could not be dispatched by the UN unless their presence was requested by the parties to the conflict. Neither the UN nor any other IGO had the legal authority to intervene in the internal affairs of a member state unless invited to do so by the sovereign governmental authority involved.

In addition to collective-security efforts, such as peacekeeping, IGOs facilitated the establishment of various international regimes[12] dedicated to disarmament, nuclear nonproliferation and other issues related to preventing the "scourge of war." One of the most successful of these efforts was the Treaty on the Non-Proliferation of Nuclear Weapons, or Non-Proliferation Treaty (NPT). Entered into force in 1970, this treaty requires states possessing nuclear weapons to refrain from their use and proliferation, and obliges nonnuclear states to refrain from obtaining nuclear weapons. All states are allowed under the NPT to pursue the peaceful application of nuclear energy. The NPT is entered into freely by nuclear and nonnuclear states alike. Although skepticism was high during the first years after the treaty's ratification, the number of nuclear states remained relatively constant throughout the Cold War era.

As previously noted, military alliances created during the Cold War were of a clearly adversarial nature. The two primary alliances, NATO and the Warsaw Pact, divided not only Europe but the entire world. These and other alliances were of a distinct nature from most other nonmilitary IGOs. Membership was restricted, and the organizations were not based on the principle of sovereign equality. The United States was the acknowledged leader of NATO, while the Soviet Union dominated the Warsaw Pact nations. Although this alliance system was inherently confrontational and the source of many "near-misses" during the Cold War, they did achieve their fundamental goal of preventing another European war.

Social and Economic Development Issues

The majority of the work done by IGOs is in the area of social and economic development. Social and economic development issues integrate the array of IGOs found within the UN system. The UN Economic and Social Council (ECOSOC) is the central organizing body for economic development issues in the UN system, coordinating activities with regional economic commissions (for Europe, Latin America and the Caribbean, Asia, and Africa), the World Bank, as well as other agencies. The GATT and IMF, although more independent than other IGOs, are also part of the vast UN system dedicated to improving economic and social conditions around the world. Although the needs of the world's citizens often seem to outpace the ability of IGOs to meet them, economic and social development initiatives have contributed greatly to improving both the quality of life and living standards of millions of people over the past half century.

While IGOs were successful in improving social and economic conditions across the globe during these years, they were often constrained by two forces: the Cold War and north-south divide. The allocation of resources and the kinds of projects these resources would support were subject to both of these forces. Economic and social development may seem like benign endeavors, but within the context of the Cold War, which pitted two political systems with distinct philosophies regarding the "correct" path toward progress against each other, very few issues escaped bipolar lenses. The north-south divide was most apparent when it came to issues of development. Although it cannot be denied that economic gains were recorded throughout the developing world, in relative terms the developed nations of the north continued to get richer. And while north-south issues continue to be reflected in the work of IGOs in the post–Cold War world, they have been supplanted and in some ways ameliorated by the end of communism and the expansion of capitalist economies worldwide.

Human Rights Issues

The advancement of universal human rights standards is one of the major accomplishments of IGOs during the Cold War era. The atrocities committed during the Holocaust exposed what one author calls "the moral flaw of international sovereignty," that which results when "the state itself poses the primary threat to the well-being of its citizens [and] these citizens have nowhere to turn for recourse or protection."[13] Providing mechanisms of external recourse and protection was at the heart of the creation of the UN and other IGOs in the immediate postwar years.

The protection of internationally recognized human rights by IGOs can be seen as a modern limitation on state sovereignty. States that violate the human rights of their citizens are subject not only to the moral condemnation of the international community, but to its punishment. International human rights have been codified in such documents as the United Nations Declaration of Human Rights (1948), The American Convention of Human Rights (1948), and the European Convention on Human Rights (1950). More specific political, social, and economic rights have also been recognized through subsequent international conventions and treaties.[14] Human rights courts were established at regional levels to hear cases against states charged with human rights violations. But, as is the case with many international judicial bodies, the judgments of these courts have limited or no enforcement powers. That is, judgments against states cannot be carried out without the acquiescence of the violating governments.

Nonetheless, the area of human rights was one in which pressure by the international community and its IGOs often produced compliance during the Cold War, and in the long term helped to change human rights conditions in countries around the world.[15] Many authoritarian regimes which originally signed international human rights documents with little intent of abiding by the details, found themselves forced to adhere to their international legal obligations as opposition to their regimes grew during the 1970s and 1980s. Human rights commitments made decades earlier, often as mere palliatives to the international community, proved to have more influence and longevity than many of the signatories. In the post–Cold War world the promotion of human rights continues to be an important activity of IGOs.

Humanitarian Issues

During the Cold War, humanitarian issues addressed by IGOs fell mainly in the areas of refugee assistance and disaster relief. In the early post–World War II era, this assistance concentrated on those people left displaced by the war in Europe. To facilitate this effort, the UN General Assembly created the Office of the United Nations High Commissioner for Refugees (UNHCR, 1951). The Council of Europe Social Development Fund was also established during this period, in 1956, to finance projects aimed at helping refugees and victims of natural disasters. These and similar IGOs provided clothes, shelter, and other necessities to millions of needy people throughout the Cold War years, in addition to facilitating their repatriation or resettlement. During the 1980s, assistance was also extended to thousands of people fleeing communist states and seeking asylum across Western Europe.

Although the UNHCR has a "nonpolitical" mandate, the superpower rivalry of the Cold War often limited the authorization of humanitarian missions to areas and peoples in need. This was especially true in regard to needs created by superpower proxy wars. Humanitarian assistance was also restricted by the governments of member states. Like most IGO activities, humanitarian aid could not be delivered to refugees or victims of disasters without the approval of the governments with authority over the people and territories involved.

With the end of the Cold War, cooperation between the United States and Russia[16] has eased the tensions which inhibited many humanitarian missions in the past. More importantly, the post–Cold War era has seen the willingness of the international community to authorize humanitarian relief missions in situations where approval has *not* been obtained from the relevant sovereign governments. An important reason for these changes is undoubtedly the fact that the number of people in need of assistance has grown dramatically in the post–Cold War era. In 1982, there were almost 8 million refugees throughout the world. In 1992, this number had increased to more than 16 million.[17] By January 1996, the UNHCR estimated that there were over 23 million "populations of concern" across the globe.[18] The reasons for these increases will be explained more fully in the following section.

COLD WAR CONSTRAINTS ON IGOs: 1945–1989

The Cold War international political environment constrained IGOs from fully attaining their objectives. In his 1989 report, then UN Secretary-General Javier Pérez de Cuéllar discussed the impact of the Cold War on the organization: "To put it mildly, it left the United Nations in a waiting position—waiting until common sense and the dynamics of the world situation would induce a return to the way of handling international affairs outlined in its charter."[19] The end of the Cold War, he wrote the following year, "wears both the aspect of hope and the countenance of dangerous unrestraint."[20] The Secretary-General's words have rung quite true, not only for the UN but for many IGOs.

IGOs were forced to function during the Cold War era within the parameters set by the superpower conflict which dominated the instruments of international relations for over forty years.

IGOs were also restricted in what they could accomplish by the lack of *enforcement mechanisms* available to them. Because each of the member states within IGOs is sovereign, with ultimate authority over its territory, people, and resources and legally equal internationally to other states, these organizations had little or no authority to force states to comply with their basic principles or follow through on specific initiatives. UN Secretary-General Pérez de Cuéllar addressed this problem in 1982. "There is a tendency in the United Nations," he wrote, "for governments to act as though the passage of a resolution absolved them from further responsibility for the subject in question. Nothing could be further from the intention of the Charter . . . the best resolution in the world will have little practical effect unless governments of the member states follow it up with the appropriate support and action."[21]

The intention of the charter, though, is distinct from its provisions. Except for the collective-security enforcement mechanisms found in Chapter VII, few options are available to the UN to enforce its decisions. This may seem strange given the fact that it is the member states themselves who set the organization's agenda. It must be remembered, though, that sovereign states wrote the charters of the UN and other IGOs. States were not intent on creating supranational organizations, those with authority which supersedes that of states, but institutions that would facilitate cooperation and provide assistance when this was in the self-interest of the member states. If the burden of fulfilling particular obligations was deemed too great, individual member states could choose not to do so. Other members might publicly or privately attempt to persuade the reluctant member state(s), but they could do little else. In the post–Cold War era, IGO member states have attempted to address the problem of enforcement, with mixed results.

A third restriction on the activities of IGOs during the Cold War era merits examination here. Due to the sovereign equality of all member states, IGOs are prohibited from intervening in the internal affairs of states. According to the UN charter, except in cases related to Chapter VII enforcement measures, "Nothing contained in the present charter shall authorize the United Nations to intervene in matters which are essentially within the domestic jurisdiction of any state or shall require the members to submit such matters to settlement."[22] Other IGOs have similar requirements. The OAS charter, for example, states that the organization "has no powers other than those expressly conferred upon it by this charter, none of whose provisions authorizes it to intervene in matters that are within the internal jurisdiction of the member states."[23] Respect for the sovereignty and territorial integrity of states are the "foundation-stones" of the work of IGOs.[24]

The principle of nonintervention is a necessary evil for the work of IGOs. Member states certainly accept the forfeiture of a measure of sovereignty when joining IGOs. That is, states realize that every action taken by IGOs will not exactly reflect their preferred goals, but states calculate that these organizations will more often than not produce results which are in their self-interest. And if an IGO acts contrary to the self-interest of a member state, the state may refuse to comply with little threat of retribution, or the state may withdraw from the organization completely. Few states, though, ever take such an extreme measure to show their displeasure with an IGO.

Adhering to the principle of nonintervention does inhibit the effectiveness of IGOs, but it also protects states from having their political, social, or economic systems infringed upon by more powerful members of the international community. Due to their sovereign equality, all member states within IGOs are guaranteed some measure of protection against unprovoked or unsolicited interference in their domestic activities. With the end of the Cold War, this near-impenetrable commitment to nonintervention has been weakened to some extent, but it remains the fundamental principle undergirding all IGOs.

THE POST–COLD WAR ERA: A WORLD IN TRANSITION

The period of transition from one international political system and another is turbulent. It is a time when all is in flux as states recover from the confusion associated with the demise of one system and create the conditions necessary for the stability which, hopefully, will accompany the new one. The post–Cold War era is unique from other transition periods in that "the end of the Cold War has not to date resulted in the sort of official documentation by the winning coalition that marked the end of previous hegemonic conflicts."[25] The Soviet Union and its allies certainly "lost" the Cold War, but the Western victors have not been empowered to unilaterally construct a "new world order." The absence of such authority has made the post–Cold War era one of incremental change, adapting the institutions of the previous era to the needs of the present.

For intergovernmental organizations, the transition from the Cold War to post–Cold War era has been one of both continuity and change. Continuity is most pronounced in the fact that IGOs created during the Cold War are being utilized to address and manage the problems of the post–Cold War world. New IGOs have been created, but IGOs established during the Cold War period are being given the primary responsibility for handling new problems. These new responsibilities are being undertaken in addition to the traditional roles IGOs continue to perform in the areas of peace and security, social and economic development, human rights, and humanitarian assistance.

Continuity is seen as well in the fact that IGOs are still based on the fundamental principles of sovereign equality and nonintervention. However, some IGOs have amended their charters to increase the organizations' ability to respond to crises which would have been considered within the exclusive domestic jurisdiction of states during the Cold War, particularly in the areas of humanitarian intervention and the support of democratization processes. These changes have been made in an effort to increase the ability of the international community to enforce the basic principles and purposes of IGOs, as well as their specific resolutions and mandates. The ability to expand, however narrowly, IGO mechanisms to intervene into the internal affairs of member states was made possible by the increased international cooperation which accompanied the end of the Cold War and the belief on the part of member states that IGOs could play a more constructive role in the emerging post–Cold War era if provided with more effective enforcement powers.

The post–Cold War era has also been a time of change for IGOs. In 1989, the international community consisted of 169 sovereign states; by 1996, that number had increased to 192 states. The vast majority of these new states emerged from the dissolution of the Soviet Union and in the eastern block. Other independent states emerged from the final vestiges of European colonialism. As had been the case in the 1960s and 1970s, the increase in independent governments across the globe was accompanied by a concomitant increase in both the number of IGOs and the size of the membership in existing organizations. In 1989, there were approximately 93 intergovernmental organizations, compared with 101 in 1996.[26] Table 9-2 shows the rapid increase in the number of UN member states in the immediate post–Cold War years. A similar increase in membership occurred throughout the UN system (Table 9-2).

The increase in both the size and number of IGOs is a reflection of the fact that in the post–Cold War era IGOs have taken on a more central role in facilitating multilateral cooperation than during the Cold War. One measure of this increased cooperation is seen in the sharp increase in the number of UN Security Council meetings and resolutions between the final years of the Cold War and the first years of the post–Cold War era (Table 9-3).

With this more central role have come opportunities and challenges. Opportunities arise from the absence of ideological and political divisions which restricted the work of IGOs during the Cold War period. These divisions have been replaced by a near universal acceptance by governments of the merits of democratic political systems and free-market/capitalist economies. The globalization of democracy and capitalism unleashed the forces that are the central theme of this book: open societies, open markets, and open technologies. IGOs have been given the opportunity in the post–Cold War era to help their member states reap collective benefits from these forces. But, IGOs have also been called upon to assist the international community in managing the transsovereign problems

Table 9-2					
UN Membership: 1985–1999					
1985	**1990**	**1991**	**1992**	**1993**	**1994–1999**
158	160	167	179	184	185

Source: *Basic Facts About the United Nations* (United Nations Publications, 1995): 307–308.

Table 9-3							
Security Council Formal Meetings: 1988–1995							
1988	1989	1990	1991	1992	1993	1994	1995
55	69	70	115	133	171	165	135

Security Council Resolutions: 1987–1995			
1987	1991	1993	1995
15	53	78	63

Source: Boutros Boutros-Ghali, "Supplement to An Agenda for Peace" in *An Agenda for Peace,* second edition (New York: United Nations Department of Public Information), 8, and Boutros-Ghali, *The Fiftieth Anniversary Annual Report on the Work of the Organization, 1996* (New York: United Nations Department of Public Information), 14.

which are the negative consequences of these same forces. Providing such assistance is the central challenge for IGOs in the post–Cold War era.

There is a great irony to the work of IGOs in the post–Cold War era: These organizations are at the forefront of both *promoting* the forces of open societies, open markets, and open technologies, and *protecting* the international community against the transsovereign problems that are often the product of these very same forces. Open societies are promoted by IGOs primarily through efforts to support democratization processes and protect human rights in member states. Open markets are promoted through the expansion of free-market economies and practices across the globe. Most of the IGOs created since the end of the Cold War have been economic in nature, organizations whose central function is to coordinate the free flow of goods, services, and people across borders. IGOs help to promote open technologies in the post–Cold War world by providing the forums for states to negotiate economic and security treaties which facilitate the transfer of advanced technology, thus narrowing the divide between developed and less-developed states.

Protecting the international community against the transsovereign problems that arise from the forces of open societies, open markets, and open technologies is proving to be a great challenge for IGOs. This is so because there is less consensus among member states regarding how best to address the problems of drug trafficking, international criminal activity, nuclear smuggling, increased refugee flows, and "saving" failed states. Although these transsovereign problems affect all the members of the international community to some extent, consensus solutions are difficult to achieve because they affect states differently, and the means for addressing these problems are unevenly dispersed. In addition, because these problems are often the byproduct of the "positive" work IGOs do in promoting democracy, free markets, and technology transfer, member states are often caught in a catch-22 situation: how to protect the international community against the destructive consequences of transsovereign problems while continuing to advance the goals of open societies, open markets, and open technologies.

Where there is consensus among states is in their understanding that transsovereign problems defy unilateral or bilateral solutions. Because transsovereign problems ultimately affect all members of the international community and threaten the stability of the post–Cold War "new world order," states realize that they cannot "go it alone," and that solutions can only be found, implemented, and enforced through multilateral initiatives. This is why IGOs have become a focal point for addressing transsovereign problems. In essence, IGOs are being asked to find solutions to problems which states cannot manage on their own.

The ability of IGOs to find effective solutions to transsovereign problems is challenged not only by the complex nature of these problems, but by the lack of resources and political will provided to IGOs by their member states. One of the most difficult challenges facing IGOs in the post–Cold War era is the disparity between the number of problems they are being asked to address and the resources member states are providing to solve them. The consequences of this disparity will be discussed at length at the end of this chapter.

Failed States

One of the distinguishing features of the post–Cold War international political system is the "disturbing new phenomenon,"[27] of failed states. Failed states are those which are "utterly incapable of sustaining [themselves] as [members] of the international community."[28] Endowed with sovereignty and independence, failed states are nonetheless unable to function without assistance from other members of the international community. Examples of failed states include Somalia, Haiti, and Rwanda. During the Cold War, such states were often supported by the superpowers, affording them a "safety net" against the failings of their own political and economic systems. In the post–Cold War era, no such safety net exists because the United States and Russia have withdrawn much of their financial support to these states. In addition to failed states, the post–Cold War era has seen an increase in the number of weak states, whose political systems have difficulty meeting the challenges of governing. In weak states, the institutions of governance, which would provide their political systems with stability and the capabilities necessary to meet the concerns of domestic and international forces, are not yet fully established or consolidated. The new states created from the dissolution of the former Soviet Union are examples.

The failure of a state has both domestic and international consequences. Within failed states the absence of functioning institutions, as well as ongoing military conflict, can lead to the internal migration of the citizenry. Such migrations can result in the presence of hundreds of thousands of "displaced" persons within failed states. This occurred in Somalia, Rwanda, and Bosnia. The

UNHCR estimates that as of January 1, 1997, there were over 4.9 million internally displaced people throughout the world,[29] most of whom were displaced due to the failure of states. Other domestic consequences of a state failing include a lack of housing, food, safe water supplies, and medical attention.

The international community is affected by the failure of states because associated problems tend to spread.[30] Lawlessness, refugee flows, human rights abuses, and the spread of infectious disease are all potential threats to the neighbors of failed or weak states. It is for this reason that IGOs have intervened with failed states to protect member states against threats to international peace and security.

IGOs have been on the front lines of efforts to "save" failed states and strengthen weak states. The activities of IGOs have been undertaken by two means: as a response to requests from the states involved, and through direct intervention. Requests for assistance are often made when the parties to a conflict decide to negotiate a settlement. In these circumstances IGOs are asked to participate in the peace process, and subsequently to assist the parties in implementing the peace settlement. IGOs have participated in this capacity in such countries as Angola (UN), El Salvador (OAS, UN), Cambodia (UN), Nicaragua (UN, OAS), Haiti (UN, OAS), and Bosnia (UN, NATO, OSCE). In each of these cases, IGOs have been partners in the peace process and empowered by the governments and other actors involved to play a role in rebuilding a stable political system in their countries. Such efforts by the UN have been called "second generation"[31] peacekeeping missions, or "peace-building" missions.[32]

The extent of IGO activity in regard to peace-building within weak or failed states was most dramatic in the case of Cambodia. The UN was authorized by the sovereign leaders of Cambodia to control the administrative functions of the government for over a year in preparation for holding elections, after which time the winners of the election would take the reins of governance. The UN mission in Cambodia (UNTAC), which cost over $3 billion, was the most extensive and most expensive ever undertaken by the organization. Although the elections in May 1993 were deemed "free and fair" by the international community, with almost 90 percent of eligible voters participating, the ensuing peace was less than enduring. In July 1997, the Cambodian government was toppled by a swift and bloody coup. Other missions undertaken by IGOs at the request of involved member states have also had questionable results, including those in Angola and Haiti. There have been success stories, in Nicaragua and El Salvador for example, so the overall results of such missions are definitely mixed. But, as is the case with much of the work done by IGOs, it is the failures that receive the most attention within the international community and affect the future of similar missions.

The second form of intervention to "save" failed states is rare, but of great significance to the conduct of international relations in the post–Cold War era. In a few cases the international community, through the UN Security Council, has authorized intervention into the internal affairs of a member state by invoking its Chapter VII mandate. That is, in the post–Cold War era, some internal conflicts have been recognized as "threats to international peace and security." The threat is often identified in terms of humanitarian concerns about the probability of the existing conflict spreading across national boundaries. The first such intervention took place in 1992 in Somalia. In this case, the UN Security Council deployed a military force for the purpose of providing humanitarian relief to starving Somalis. This action "established a precedent in the history of the United Nations: it decided for the first time to intervene militarily for *strictly* humanitarian purposes."[33] This precedent served to legitimize future interventions by the UN and other IGOs in the former Yugoslavia and Rwanda.

Although the number of crises where such intervention has taken place is small, the impact of this change in the concept of threat to international peace and security is dramatic. In the post–Cold War world, the international community has determined that the dangers posed to it by failed states are serious enough to infringe upon the privileges of "sovereign equality" of IGO member states, and warrant loosening the principle of nonintervention. Conditions must be extreme for such intervention to take place, but this is a new conception about the role of IGOs in the post–Cold War era and fundamentally alters the relationship between IGOs and its member states.

In the cases where IGOs have intervened into the internal affairs of a member state as a response to a threat to international peace and security, the results have not been promising. Failed states do not have the capabilities to resist such intervention, but IGOs do confront great challenges to their presence once intervention has taken place. Because failed states lack infrastructure of all kinds—political, economic, and physical—there are few means available to IGOs for organizing the activities necessary for rebuilding the state and reestablishing order and stability. IGOs often confront hostility from the citizens and forces within the states, as was the case in Somalia. Without support from such domestic actors, IGOs are hard-pressed to achieve their goals. Short of reestablishing some form of trusteeship,[34] IGOs will have little success "saving" failed states if those who still hold the levers of power within the states refuse to cooperate and can continue their conflict once IGOs have intervened.

Due to the lack of success IGOs have had in saving failed states, the international community may now be moving toward a policy of "containing" failed and weak states. The costs of intervention, in terms of human and financial resources as well as the loss of prestige to IGOs from their inability to produce better results, has made IGO member states reluctant to initiate additional missions, and inclined to cut short existing ones. The international community seems to be more interested in preventing the spread of conflict to neighboring countries than in solving crises within failed states. Whether IGOs become more concerned with containing conflicts within states or continue to try to save failed states and strengthen weak ones will be determined by their member states.

What appears certain, however, is that the international community will continue to engage in finding solutions to threats posed by the internal crises of states.

The intervention of the international community into the internal affairs of states is likely to continue because in the post–Cold War era conflict is present far more often within states than among them. "From 1989 to 1996 there have been ninety-six armed conflicts, of which only five have been between states."[35] Although interstate conflict is not absent in the post–Cold War world, it is internal conflict that poses the greatest threat to international peace and security. The recognition of this threat by IGOs can be seen in the fact that between 1988 and 1996, the UN Security Council authorized twenty-nine peacekeeping missions, the majority of which were second-generation missions deployed to end conflicts within member states. This number represents over two-thirds of the total peacekeeping missions deployed by the UN since its founding, in 1945.[36]

PROMOTION OF OPEN SOCIETIES, OPEN MARKETS, AND OPEN TECHNOLOGIES

Open Societies

The primary means that IGOs use to promote open societies is to support democratization processes and human rights in their member states. The efforts of IGOs to support democratization processes are extensive and include electoral observation, civic education, and the consolidation of democratic institutions. The IGOs with primary responsibility in this area are multipurpose IGOs such as the UN, OAS, and the Council of Europe. Other IGOs, including those with military and economic mandates, are also involved in promoting democracy.[37] In the post-Cold War era, all IGOs have either expanded existing mechanisms for supporting democratization processes or have established new programs in response to the dramatic increase in the number of democracies within their memberships. This increase in the number of IGO member states with democratic governments is a reflection of the "third wave" of democratization that has occurred across the globe over the past twenty-five years.[38] In 1974, there were only 39 formal democracies, or less than 28 percent of all countries; in 1995, this number had increased to 117 democracies, which represented over 61 percent of the 191 states in the international community.[39] IGO activities in the area of promoting open societies is a response to this fundamental change in the composition of the members of the international community.

Since the end of the Cold War, the observation of electoral processes by IGOs has become almost commonplace.[40] This activity, though, is relatively new to most IGOs, and its rapid expansion has resulted in questions concerning its long-term utility. Two IGOs, the UN and OAS, have long histories in observing elections, but the observation of the Nicaraguan elections in 1990 was a turning point for both organizations, and the role of electoral observation in general. As participants in the Central American peace process, the UN and OAS were asked to organize elections in Nicaragua. For the UN, this was the first time that the organization was observing the elections of a member state. For the OAS, these elections would be the first to receive an official delegation of the Secretary-General. Each organization would be called upon to verify the "free and fair" nature of the entire electoral process, including the voting results.[41] The process in Nicaragua was an undisputed success which encouraged the members of the UN and OAS to expand the IGOs' role in legitimizing or delegitimizing the results of elections in member states. Other IGOs, including the Council of Europe and the OSCE, also began performing electoral assistance and observation missions.[42]

The extent of IGO commitment to providing electoral assistance to their member states is seen in the fact that many IGOs have created offices within their organizations to coordinate such efforts. In 1992, the UN established the Electoral Assistance Division, housed within the organization's Department of Peacekeeping Operations. The location of this division is significant in that it reveals the UN's commitment to electoral assistance as part of its broader mandate to maintain international peace and security. In the OAS, electoral assistance activities are conducted out of the Unit for the Promotion of Democracy, created in 1990. The OAS's promotion of civic education and democratic consolidation are also coordinated within this department. As part of its overriding concern for "democratic security," the Council of Europe assists new democracies in Eastern Europe through the European Charter of Local Self-Government; this assistance includes electoral observation. The OSCE has entered the field of electoral assistance through its Office for Democratic Institutions and Human Rights, created in 1990. The OSCE's "biggest operational challenge" in this field is presently underway as the organization supervises the very complicated electoral process in Bosnia.

As previously discussed, multipurpose IGOs have been promoting human rights throughout the post–World War II period. Since the end of the Cold War, human rights have assumed an even more central role in the work of IGOs. Open societies and democracy cannot be sustained without the adherence by governments to the human rights standards guaranteed to their citizens by international law. To promote such standards throughout their member states, IGOs have created specific centers within their organizations to coordinate human rights activities. In 1990, the OSCE created the Office for Democratic Institutions and Human Rights. In 1993, the UN established a High Commissioner for Human Rights to be responsible for that organization's human rights activities, and the Council of Europe called for the creation of a single European Court of Human Rights.

Perhaps the most significant undertaking in the area of promoting and protecting international human rights in the post–Cold War era was the creation by the UN of the International Criminal Tribunals for the Former Yugoslavia and Rwanda to investigate crimes against humanity, including genocide, committed by the combatants in these two bloody conflicts. These tribunals, authorized by the UN Security Council in 1993 and 1994 respectively, are responsible for bringing those who committed war crimes to justice. Although the success of these tribunals to date is debatable, their existence indicates the commitment of the international community to upholding human rights standards in the post–Cold War era. There has also been serious discussion since the end of the Cold War about creating a permanent international war crimes court which would investigate the conduct of combatants in the conflicts across the globe on an ongoing basis.

IGOs support civic education and the consolidation of democratic institutions in order to strengthen and deepen the roots of democracy in newly democratic states. IGOs provide citizens with information regarding their role, and their rights, in electoral processes in states where democratic elections are new and thus citizens are not familiar with their role in the process. IGOs also educate elected officials through seminars which bring political leaders and administrators together to discuss the practical, day-to-day workings of democratic governance. IGOs do not write the laws of newly democratic states, but they do provide access to expertise that can assist these states in their democratization processes. IGOs which conduct such consolidation efforts include the UN, OAS, the Council of Europe, and OSCE.

Open Markets

The pursuit of global free markets has been both a unifying and divisive force in the post–Cold War era. States with new free-market systems are eager to develop their economies, receive assistance from the advanced capitalist economies, and join international organizations which promote free-market initiatives. The extent of this desire is seen in the fact that most of the new IGOs created in the post–Cold War era are dedicated to economic issues, especially the integration of free-market economies. Examples of such IGOs include the Southern Cone Common Market (Mercosur), the European Bank for Reconstruction and Development (EBRD), and the Central European Initiative (CEI).

The most universal organization created in the post–Cold War to advance free-market goals is the 131-member WTO.[43] The WTO replaced the GATT in January 1995 as the international community's foremost institution for facilitating the free flow of goods across the globe by limiting trade barriers such as state-imposed tariffs. What differentiates the WTO from its predecessor is the fact that the GATT was a treaty, not an organization, which dealt mainly with the trade of goods between its signatories. The WTO, however, is an organization that regulates trade in goods, services and intellectual property. The addition of the latter two areas is significant in light of the fact that these commodities are more difficult to regulate and are sources of conflict between advanced and less-advanced economies. And, unlike the GATT, the WTO has enforcement mechanisms at its disposal to use against states that violate the rules and regulations of the organization. Enforcement mechanisms include the right to levy financial penalties against countries which violate WTO rules. Although critics of the WTO believe that the organization's enforcement mechanisms are too weak, the fact that such mechanisms have been created at all illustrates the commitment of member states to promoting open markets.

The creation of the WTO is a reaction to the expansion of free-market economies across the globe, but the promotion of open markets by IGOs is most prominent at the regional level. That is, in the post–Cold War era numerous IGOs have been created, or reconstituted, to advance the integration and regulation of neighboring economic systems. During the Cold War many such "economic communities" were tried at the regional level but only one, the European Union (EU), had any measure of success. In the post–Cold War era, though, the proliferation of such IGOs is seen in every region of the world. In the Americas alone there are several IGOs of this nature, including Mercosur, the Andean Pact, CARICOM, and the North American Free Trade Agreement (NAFTA).[44] In addition, OAS member states are working to create a hemisphere-wide Free Trade Area of the Americas (FTAA) by 2005. Similar ideas are under consideration in Europe, Asia, and Africa, although few have yet to reach fruition.

Open Technologies

The promotion of open technologies by IGOs is intricately related to the areas of open markets, as well as issues of international peace and security. It is through these two arenas that most technology transfers occur between states. Technology is transferred through open markets by the free flow of goods, services, and people, and through the provisions established in individual free-trade agreements and the treaties creating economic communities. In the area of international peace and security, open technology is facilitated through conventions, which oblige states to reveal the presence of specific weapons systems or components, and to share information regarding the means toward safeguarding, dismantling, or upgrading specific military matériel.

Multipurpose IGOs promote open technology through their programs to advance open markets and their role as the focal point for the establishment of multilateral arms control treaties and other weapons-related agreements. The expansion of open markets has already been discussed in some length in this chapter, so this section will focus primarily on the impact of the post–Cold War era on the expansion of arms control agreements.

Two of the most significant international treaties dealing with controlling the proliferation of weapons of mass destruction in the post–Cold War era are the NPT and the Chemical Weapons Convention (CWC). Both of these documents were achieved after extensive and delicate negotiations among the vast majority of states within the international community, and under UN auspices. Other multilateral security conventions have been established at the regional level, particularly in Europe, but these documents represent the most comprehensive view of the post–Cold War advances by the whole of the international community in the area of international peace and security.

The NPT treaty was extended indefinitely in 1995 when 174 UN member states signed the revised treaty. With so many signatories, the NPT "extends the scope of formal international regulation over the single most consequential assertion of national power—the deployment of nuclear weapons."[45]

With ratification by sixty-five member states in 1996, the CWC entered into force in April 1997. This convention prohibits the development, production, stockpiling, and transfer of chemical weapons. This treaty mandates that "all chemical weapons and related production facilities have to be completely eliminated or converted to peaceful purposes within ten years of the entry into force of the convention, under international supervision."[46] The success of this treaty is evident in the fact that only three months after taking effect more than a half-dozen states admitted possessing chemical weapons or the ability to produce them. Before the CWC went into effect, only the United States and Russia had publicly admitted to having such weapons.[47]

PROTECTION OF OPEN SOCIETIES, OPEN MARKETS, AND OPEN TECHNOLOGIES

Open Societies

The promotion of open societies has led to fundamental changes in the mandates of many IGOs. In the OAS, for example, fundamental changes have been made to the organization's charter to allow for diplomatic intervention. The OAS Secretary-General is authorized by the charter to "bring to the attention of the General Assembly or the Permanent Council any matter which in his opinion might threaten the peace and security of the hemisphere or the development of the member states."[48] In 1991, the OAS approved additional measures to secure democracy in the region with the Santiago Commitment to Democracy and the Renewal of the Inter-American System, and Resolution 1080. In the Santiago Commitment, the nations of the Americas articulated their support for democracy in the region and recognized democracy as "indispensable . . . for the stability, peace and development of the region."

Resolution 1080 approved measures to give the OAS enforcement power in its commitment to democracy. This resolution empowered the Secretary General to call an immediate meeting of the Permanent Council in the event there is a "sudden or irregular interruption of democratic political institutional process or of the legitimate exercise of power by the democratically elected government in any of the organization's member states." In addition, the OAS member states approved changes in the organization's charter, The Protocol of Washington, in 1992 that would suspend the rights of a member state "whose democratically constituted government has been overthrown by force." Although not yet entered into force, this amendment to the OAS charter would give the organization enforcement powers well beyond any available during the Cold War.

The Council of Europe restructured its focus in the post–Cold War toward the conception of democracy as a security issue. The Council of Europe has developed the concept of "democratic security" to define its purpose, as outlined in the organization's 1993 Vienna Declaration. The council's main role in the post–Cold War era "is to strengthen democracy, human rights, and the rule of law throughout its member states." At the Vienna summit, the member states "recognized how important it was for security and stability in Europe that all its countries should accept the principles of democracy, human rights and the rule of law."[49]

Similar organizational changes have been implemented in the OSCE and other IGOs. The changes in the UN, however, have been primarily rhetorical and functional. That is, although the UN has spoken out strongly in support of democracy since the end of the Cold War, and has expanded its activities to include those which advance democratization processes and human rights, the charter of the organization has not been amended by the member states to include specific advocacy of democracy or mechanisms for preventing democratic reversals. There are practical reasons for this, not the least of which is the fact that amending the UN charter is a very complicated process, with 185 opinions in need of consultation. In addition, the universality of the UN means that there are a significant number of nondemocratic member states in the organization. Amending the UN charter to specifically advance democracy could pose a serious challenge to the viability of the organization which is now open to all "peace-loving nations."

Open Markets

One of the difficulties IGOs have in promoting open markets among their member states is the economic divisions that still exist between more- and less-advanced market economies. The most successful economic communities, NAFTA and the EU, have very limited memberships. As of this writing, NAFTA consists of three member states (United States, Canada, and Mexico), and the EU's fifteen member states constitute the most advanced economies within Europe.[50] Less-advanced economies within Europe and the Americas have expressed the desire to join these IGOs, but have so far been denied. Although many of the new free-market economies of Eastern Europe and the Americas have been given assurances that their membership is under consideration and while some states have been given special status as potential member states, the governments of these states are frustrated with the lack of progress and a sense of betrayal is growing among them. This is especially true in Eastern Europe where the governments of the former communist states believe that membership in the EU is a necessary condition not only for advancing their economic growth but for guaranteeing their security. The connection between economic growth and security is not only present in Europe, it is a connection articulated throughout the international community, and particularly through IGOs.

Open markets have been perceived by IGOs as part of the peace and security issue. The connection between free markets, democracy, and international peace and security has been highly emphasized in IGO documents. Economic assistance by the IMF and World Bank to developing economies is now being judged not only by economic criteria but political as well; "each organization is issuing formal guidelines warning that financial assistance will be denied unless corrupt politicians and officials are reined in."[51] These IGOs are making the presence of "good governance" a necessary factor for receiving assistance. This is a fundamental change from the Cold War era.

The issues of international peace and security are intimately connected to those of open markets in the post–Cold War era. One of the most disturbing consequences of the pursuit of open markets is the destructive activities it helps to facilitate. Such forces include drug trafficking, nuclear smuggling, and other international criminal activity. As borders are opened for the free flow of goods, services, and people, they are also opened to the free flow of illegal activities. This is an example of the catch-22 for IGOs: States want to restrict the activities of illegal actors, but not the expansion of economic activity. Efforts have been taken to control the transsovereign illegal activities, but the most effective means of control will most likely be in strengthening the governing capacities of new democracies. State corruption facilitates illegal activities. IGOs can help end state corruption by continuing to support democratization efforts and efforts to strengthen market forces so that more people share the benefits of economic transformation.

Two of the transsovereign problems most influenced by the expansion of open markets are drug trafficking and international criminal activity, problems which are themselves intimately related. Each feeds off the other. Often, organizations which participate in one activity will be involved in the other. The most important relationship between these two transsovereign problems is their combined negative effect on the peace and stability of governments. Drug trafficking and international criminal organizations threaten the political stability and economic viability of many governments, especially young democracies. Drug trafficking and other criminal activities "[eat] away at the fabric of societies until democratic institutions needed to sustain democracy collapse."[52] Such dangers threaten new democracies across the globe. IGOs have created multiple mechanisms to help protect their member states against these threats. At the Miami Summit of the Americas in 1994, the OAS member states agreed to "join the battle against the consumption, production, trafficking and distribution of illegal drugs." This agreement was possible due to the recognized "pernicious effects of organized crime and illegal narcotics" on the social, political, and economic spheres of their countries, and the hemisphere as a whole.[53] To this end, the OAS implemented an Anti-Drug Strategy in the Hemisphere in 1996. The new strategy, according to the member states, "represents a fresh commitment to international cooperation to combat the drug problem, based on the principle of shared responsibility and the need for a policy that balances preventive and law enforcement measures."[54] The plan focuses on issues of legal development, supply reduction, demand reduction, and information coordination.

The UN has played a role in trying to curb the trafficking in illicit drugs for over thirty years since the creation of the International Narcotics Control Board in 1968. To meet the expanded needs of the post–Cold War era, the United Nations International Drug Control Program (UNDCP) was established in 1990 and "serves the worldwide [center] of expertise and information on drug abuse control."[55] To show the organization's dedication to fighting drug trafficking, the UN General Assembly called a special session in 1990 to proclaim a Decade against Drug Abuse (1991–2000). At this session, the General Assembly asserted "the conviction of member states that action against drug abuse and illicit trafficking should be accorded higher priority by the international community."[56]

The high priority placed on combating the drug trade by the international community is not questioned, but the approaches IGOs take often end up causing conflict among member states. Conflict most often arises between producer and consumer states. Producer states are predominantly those with less-advanced economies and political institutions, while consumer states are made up predominantly of advanced industrial societies with more stable political institutions. Producer states tend to stress the need for investment in alternative economic opportunities for development, while governments in consumer states approach the problem of drug trafficking from a law enforcement perspective. The need for alternative means of economic development in producer countries is critical because drug trafficking activities produce profits of up to $300 billion per year,[57] and other international criminal activities are estimated to produce profits of $1 trillion.[58] The differing priorities between advanced and less-advanced states within the international community makes establishing effective strategies to combat drug trafficking and other forms of international criminal activity complicated and at times confrontational. IGO efforts are stymied by the sovereignty dilemma: They are created to deal with the problems of sovereignty, yet they must answer to their constituent member states.

Open Technologies

The division between less- and more-advanced economies is played out in the area of open technologies. More-advanced states want to limit the free flow of technologies to protect their economic advantage and to limit the use of this technology by illegal criminal elements, especially in the area of technologies that have nuclear and military applications. Less-developed states, though, want to have access to many technologies so that their economic development may advance more quickly and to ensure that their development is not perpetually behind that of other economies. LDCs believe that they cannot make the kind of economic advances necessary if they are not allowed to have access to vital technologies.

One of the most protected areas of technology transfer is related to nuclear materials and especially components that can be used to construct nuclear weapons. The threat of nuclear weapons is not new to the post–Cold War era. However, in the post–Cold War world, the nuclear threat is not posed by the superpowers, but by terrorist organizations and even lone individuals.[59]

IGOs are involved in protecting states against nuclear smuggling primarily through the International Atomic Energy Agency (IAEA). All of the 174 signatories of the NPT subject themselves to safeguards maintained by the IAEA, including the inspection of their nuclear facilities. By maintaining a constant accounting of nuclear materials and preventing the dissemination of technology that could be used for the purpose of constructing a nuclear weapon, the IAEA plays a central role in protecting states against nuclear smuggling. The evidence of attempts to smuggle nuclear materials is evidence, unfortunately, of the limits of IAEA preventive measures.

POST–COLD WAR CONSTRAINTS ON IGOs

Financial Imbalances

This overview of IGO activities during the post–Cold War era provides only a sketch of the full spectrum of issues in which these institutions are involved. Although we noted throughout this chapter that IGOs often do not accomplish all of their many mandates, what should perhaps be emphasized more often is how much they do achieve. As mentioned previously, IGOs are being asked to address and manage some of the most difficult problems facing the international community. The magnitude of these problems is, unfortunately, disproportionate to the resources allocated to IGOs by their member states to alleviate them.

Table 9-4 offers information about the annual budgets of five of the IGOs discussed in this chapter. Together, these organizations were allocated less than $2 billion in 1996 to fulfill the mandates discussed in this chapter, as well as all other functions. The entire UN system, consisting of all the IGOs listed in Table 9-5, received just $18 billion the same year.

Although these figures certainly represent a substantial investment, the financial resources of IGOs are relatively insignificant when compared to the tasks they are expected to tackle and to the resources available to other, less complex organizations. For example, the 1996 operational budget of the UN, $1.3 billion, is equal to less than 5 percent of the budget of New York City. In addition, the number of people working in the entire UN system, less than 54,00, is just one-third the number of worldwide employees of McDonalds.[60]

Much of the difficulty IGOs face in fulfilling their mandates is due to the conflict that arises among member states. Although states are often in agreement when it comes to identifying the broad goals they wish to pursue, and are aware of the universal problems facing the international community, achieving consensus on the particular means for reaching these goals and finding workable solutions to these problems is difficult. The interests of individual states are not always easily reconciled or compatible. The UN Secretary-General Kofi Annan has compared running the UN to "running an organization with a board of directors of 185 members."[61] Efficiency and effectiveness are not easy to achieve, and perhaps should not be expected to be achieved, under such circumstances.

The imbalance between IGOs' resources and mandates is further strained in the post–Cold War era by the fact that as IGO mandates are being expanded to include transsovereign and other problems, financial and personnel resources are remaining relatively constant, and in the case of the UN are actually diminishing. The decrease in resources available to the UN is a result primarily of the withholding of funds by one of the organization's founders, the United States.

Table 9-4

Annual Budgets of Selected IGOs

Council of Europe	OAS	OSCE	United Nations	WTO
$235 million	$84.3 million	30.6 million*	$1.3 billion	$193 million

*Figure represents 1995 data.

Table 9-5

Membership of the UN and Specialized Agencies: 1986–1996*

	1986	1989	1992	1996
UN	159	159	179	185
FAO	159	158	161	175
GATT/WTO	90	96	104	128
IAEA	112	113	114	124
IBRD	149	151	172	180
ICAO	156	161	171	184
IDA	133	137	146	159
IFAD	139	143	147	160
IFC	127	133	148	170
ILO	150	150	157	174
IMF	149	151	173	181
IMO	127	133	137	154
ITU	160	167	167	187
UNESCO	158	158	171	185
UNIDO	137	152	158	169
UPU	168	169	176	189
WHO	166	166	179	190
WIPO	112	122	127	158
WMO	159	160	160	184

*Data compiled from *Political Handbook of the World: 1986, 1989, 1992, 1997,* Arthur Banks, et al., eds. (Binghamton, NY: CSA Publications, 1986–1997).

As a result of domestic political concerns, the United States began withholding its UN dues in the 1980s. By 1996, the U.S. government is estimated to owe the UN in excess of $1 billion.[62] In all, arrears by all the member states of the UN total almost $3 billion.[63]

In addition to this level of financial delinquency by the United States and forty-two other UN member states, demands are being made for the UN to operate with a no-growth budget. This consideration is being made at a time when the mandates being placed on the organization are increasing. The financial crisis at the UN has reduced the willingness of member states to commit to new activities, particularly in the area of peacekeeping, and threatens the viability of the organization to fulfill many of its other obligations. Without a stable and sufficient financial base, the UN will be hard pressed to meet the challenges of the post–Cold War world. Considering the extreme financial limitations of the UN in the 1990s, it is a credit to the organization that it has been able to undertake so many of the efforts discussed in this chapter.

Political Imbalances

A new division may be forming between states within IGOs. This division is not based on ideology, as was the case during the Cold War, although there are still states that do not adhere to the dominant democratic/free-market values of the post–Cold War era. This new division is between new and advanced democracies. As discussed throughout this chapter, much of the work of IGOs in the post–Cold War years has been dedicated to assisting new democracies in developing their political and economic systems. But, many of the new democracies do not feel that they are advancing as quickly as they could if they received more assistance and more opportunities. At the same time, the more-advanced democracies are not ready to provide the level of resources and opportunities necessary for satisfying these demands.

The emerging divisions between more- and less-advanced democracies are most pronounced in the areas associated with protecting the forces of open societies, open markets, and open technologies. The measures taken by IGOs to protect open societies, which include much more stringent regulation of democratic processes within member states, have been seen by some states as infringements on the independence of their political development. Many of the measures taken to protect open markets are considered as infringements as well. This is especially true of measures that restrict the access of new free-market democracies to technologies or markets which they believe will allow their economies to grow more rapidly. This restriction to markets is felt most keenly by new democracies in the slow pace of expansion of two of the most prosperous free-market trade communities, the EU and NAFTA. In the area of protecting open technologies, the divisions between more- and less-advanced democracies result from perceived imbalances in access to technologies which would provide new democracies with higher levels of economic and military security.

The end of the Cold War ideological divisions was heralded as the beginning of an era of cooperation among states in the international community. The truth of this is evident in the expansion of issues that IGOs have been called upon to manage, and the level of agreement their member states have reached in adopting mechanisms to address these issues. The work of IGOs will only be frustrated if the cooperation of their member states is constrained by divisions between more- and less-advanced democracies. Perfect harmony of interests is not possible, neither is it expected in an international community composed of almost two hundred sovereign states, but the memory of the effect on IGOs of a clear and conflict-ridden division among states should cause member states to pause before intensifying any divisions which may be emerging in the post–Cold War era.

PROSPECTS FOR THE FUTURE

Intergovernmental organizations are vital actors in the post–Cold War international political system. The promotion and protection of open societies, open markets, and open technologies cannot be conducted without them. The transsovereign problems, which pose the primary threat to the international community in the post–Cold War era are, by definition, issues that cannot be addressed and managed through unilateral initiatives by individual states. But, in order for IGOs to help states effectively and efficiently manage the challenges of the post–Cold War there must be a convergence between the *expectations* placed on IGOs, the *resources* allocated by member states to fulfill these expectations, and the *political will* of member states to follow through on IGO initiatives. The convergence of these three factors cannot guarantee the success of the international community in its efforts to combat the transsovereign problems addressed throughout this chapter, but without such convergence the prospects for success are limited.

Notes

1. Robert L. Bledsoe and Boleslaw A. Boczak, *The International Law Dictionary* (Santa Barbara, Calif.: ABC:CLIO, 1987): 75–76. *Encyclopedia of Public International Law* 5 (New York: North-Holland, 1982), 120. IGOs are often referred to as *international organizations*. To avoid the confusion that can arise from the distinction between universal, regional, or subregional organizations, this chapter uses the term *intergovernmental organization* which incorporates all institutions whose members are sovereign states.
2. Examples of states that have seen their membership privileges suspended include Cuba which has been suspended from the OAS since 1963 due to its "interventionist activities throughout Latin America, and Iraq, whose UN privileges have been restricted since its invasion of Kuwait in 1991.
3. Boutros Boutros-Ghali, *An Agenda for Peace*, 2nd ed. (New York: United Nations Department of Public Information, 1995), 39.
4. The World Bank's official name is the "International Bank for Reconstruction and Development" (IBRD).
5. UN Charter, chapter VII, article 47.
6. Although the OAS was established in 1948, its antecedents go back to the late nineteenth century to the First International Conference of American States of 1889–90. This long history of inter-American cooperation has given the OAS its status as the oldest IGO in existence.
7. A. Leroy Bennett, *International Organizations: Principles and Issues*, 4th ed. (Englewood Cliffs, N.J.: Prentice Hall, 1988), 437.

8. Not technically an IGO because the Helsinki Act of 1975 was not a treaty, the CSCE functioned as an informal structure with strong influence until 1990, when the organization's principles were institutionalized, culminating in its official change in 1994 to the Organization for Security and Cooperation in Europe (OSCE).

9. Some historians have dated peacekeeping as far back as 1948, with the establishment of the UN Truce Supervision Organization (UNTSO) to supervise Arab-Israeli truces. See Steven R. Ratner, *The New UN Peacekeeping* (New York: St. Martin's Press, 1996), 9–10.

10. UN Charter, chapter VII, article 39.

11. Between 1945 and 1990, the veto power of the permanent members of the Security Council was exercised 279 times. See Boutros-Ghali, *An Agenda for Peace*, 43.

12. International regimes are defined as "principles, norms, rules, and decision-making procedures around which actor expectations converge in a given issue area." International regimes are distinct from IGOs in that regimes are less formal and less institutionalized. See Stephen D. Krasner, "Structural Causes and Regime Consequences: Regimes As Intervening Variables," in *International Regimes*, ed. Stephen D. Krasner (Ithaca: Cornell University Press, 1983), 1.

13. Kathryn Sikkink, "Human Rights, Principled Issue-Networks, and Sovereignty in Latin America," *International Organization* 47:3 (Summer 1993): 413.

14. Examples of international treaties concerning additional rights include *The American Declaration of the Rights and Duties of Man* (1948), *The International Covenant of Civil and Political Rights* (1966), and the *Helsinki Final Act* (1975).

15. The case of South Africa illustrates the impact, however long-term, of consistent international pressure to end human rights abuses within a state. To put pressure on the South African regime to end its apartheid political system, which restricted the majority black population to second-class citizenship, in 1974 the UN General Assembly excluded the South African delegation from participation by not accepting the credentials of the delegation. This act was followed by a Security Council resolution in 1977 imposing sanctions against the sale of arms and related material to South Africa. These and other acts taken by IGOs and individual governments helped to end apartheid and led to the country's first multiracial elections in 1994.

16. Russia has taken the seat and responsibilities of the Soviet Union at the UN and other IGOs since the latter's dissolution in 1991.

17. Data tabulated by Myron Weiner, "Bad Neighbors, Bad Neighborhoods: An Inquiry into the Causes of Refugee Flows," *International Security* 21 (Summer 1996), 12.

18. The term *populations of concern,* is new in the post–Cold War era. UNHCR now has responsibility not only for refugees and returnees, but for internally displaced persons and those in "refugee-like" situations. See UNHCR web site, <www.unhcr.ch>, June 1997.

19. Javier Pérez de Cuéllar, *Anarchy or Order: Annual Reports, 1982–1991* (New York: United Nations Department of Public Information, 1991), 212.

20. Pérez de Cuéllar, 263.

21. Pérez de Cuéllar, 11.

22. UN Charter, chapter I, article 2/7.

23. OAS Charter, chapter 1, article 1.

24. Boutros-Ghali, *An Agenda for Peace*, 44.

25. J. Samuel Barkin and Bruce Cronin, "The State and Nation: Changing Norms and Rules of Sovereignty in International Relations," *International Organization* 48 (Winter 1994): 126.

26. Data tabulated from *Political Handbook of the World: 1989, 1997.*

27. Gerald B. Helman and Steven Ratner, "Saving Failed States," *Foreign Policy* 89 (Winter 1992–93): 3.

28. Ibid.

29. *UNHCR and Refugees: Basic facts,* <www.unhcr.ch>, June 1997.

30. See Helman and Ratner, "Saving Failed States," 3.

31. Second-generation peacekeeping missions are "UN operations, authorized by political organs of the Secretary-General, responsible for overseeing or executing the political solution of an interstate or internal conflict, with the consent of the parties." See Steven R. Ratner, *The New UN Peacekeeping: Building Peace in Lands of Conflict after the Cold War* (New York: St. Martin's Press, 1996), 17.

32. Peace-building is defined as "comprehensive efforts to identify and support structures which will tend to consolidate peace and advance a sense of confidence and well-being among people." See Boutros-Ghali, *An Agenda for Peace,* 61–62.

33. Boutros Boutros-Ghali, *Report on the Work of the Organization, September 1993* (New York: United Nations Department of Public Information, 1993), 148 (italics added).

34. Chapter XIII of the UN Charter established a Trusteeship Council which was composed of those states which had control over "non-self-governing" territories. The purpose of the Trusteeship Council was to facilitate the peaceful transfer of independence to the territories under its care. As of 1997, there are no more territories within the jurisdiction of this Council. Some scholars and practitioners have suggested that a new form of trusteeship be established to give the UN more authority over the activities necessary to "save" failed states. These suggestions have received little international support.

35. Steven R. David, "Internal War: Causes and Cures," *World Politics* 49 (July 1997): 553.

36. *Setting the Record Straight: Facts about the United Nations* (United Nations Department of Public Information, November, 1996), 4.

37. Such IGOs include NATO, OSCE, the IMF and World Bank.

38. Samuel P. Huntington, *The Third Wave: Democratization in the Late Twentieth Century* (Norman: University of Oklahoma Press, 1991).

39. Data from Freedom House, *Freedom in the World: The Annual Survey of Political Rights and Civil Liberties, 1990–91, 1991–92, 1993–94, 1994–95* (New York: Freedom House, 1991 and years following); and *Freedom Review* 27 (January–February 1996), as reproduced in Larry Diamond, "Is the Third Wave Over?" *Journal of Democracy* 7 (July, 1996): 26.

40. Election observation, simply defined, involves the sending of impartial representatives of IGOs, at the request of host governments, to observe their electoral processes. The defining moment of this practice occurs during the day(s) of the elections when international observers are present at polling stations and other critical locations to verify the voting conditions were "free and fair."

41. Various understandings of "free and fair" elections exist. At a minimum, the concept implies that the losers accept the results as fair, and that the process was free of substantial and significant "irregularities." See Robert Pastor, "The Making of a Free Election," *Journal of Democracy* 1 (Summer 1990): 14.

42. Many NGOs (nongovernmental organizations) also participate as electoral observers in new and consolidating democracies.

43. WTO membership as of April 1997.

44. NAFTA is similar to GATT in that it is not an institutionalized IGO, but an agreement among state signatories. NAFTA is discussed here due to the fact that its effect on economic integration is similar to more formal IGOs.

45. John D. Steinbruner, "Unrealized Promise, Avoidable Trouble," *Brookings Review* (Fall 1995): 8.

46. Anil Wadhwa, "Convention Set to Go," *UN Chronicle* 33, (1996): 20.

47. Barbara Crossette, "Countries Admit Use of Poisons in Weapons," *New York Times*, August 17, 1997: 4.

48. OAS charter, chapter XVII, article 15, entered into force 1988.

49. Council of Europe Web site, <www.neon.coe> "About the Council of Europe," July 7, 1997.

50. The current members of the EC [EU] are Austria, Belgium, Denmark, Finland, France, Germany, Great Britain, Greece, Ireland, Italy, Luxembourg, Netherlands, Portugal, Spain, and Sweden.

51. Harry Dunphy, "IMF, World Bank Link Aid to 'Good Governance.' " *Washington Times*, August 21, 1997: A15.

52. Peter A. Penfold, "The European Connection," *Hemisphere* 7: 44.

53. "Summit of the Americas: Declaration of Principles," <www.sice.oas.org> July 28, 1997.

54. Organization of American States, *Annual Report of the Organization, 1996–1997* (Washington, D.C.: OAS Office of Public Information, 1996).

55. *Basic Fact About the United Nations* (New York: UN Department of Public Information, 1995), 180–81.

56. Ibid., 182.

57. R. James Woosley, "Global Organized Crime: Threats to US. and International Security," in *Global Organized Crime: The New Empire of Evil*, eds. Linnea P. Raine and Frank J. Cilluffo (Washington, D.C.: Center for Strategic and International Studies, 1994): 134–144.

58. L. Raine and F. Cilluffo, "Executive Summary," in *Global Organized Crime: The New Empire of Evil*, ix.

59. Craig R. Whitney, "Smuggling of Radioactive Material Said to Double in a Year," *New York Times*, February 18, 1995: 2.

60. UN, "Setting the Record Straight," 1.

61. Interview with Kofi Annan, "Talk of the Nation," National Public Radio, July 17, 1997.

62. There is a discrepancy between the U.S. Congress and the UN over the exact amount owed to the organization by the United States. The UN calculates the total at $1.3 billion, while Congress asserts that the government's arrears are just over $800 million.

63. This figure reflects arrears to the UN regular budget as well as obligations to peace-keeping and other activities.

Nonstate Actors

While nongovernmental organizations (NGOs) and multinational corporations (MNCs) have been around for some time, their number, size, budgets, range of activities, power, and level of international recognition have drastically increased in recent years, to the point where some commentators suggest "we are in the midst of a global 'associational revolution.' "[1] For example, the International Committee of the Red Cross (ICRC) was founded in 1863 as a humanitarian relief organization and sanctioned with special status in international law in 1951 by the Geneva Conventions. But the ICRC has now grown to more than 6,300 employees and a budget of over $608 million.[2] This does not include the personnel and budgets of the associated state Red Cross and Red Crescent societies. Thus, the largest NGOs, such as CARE, Catholic Relief Services, and World Vision, and MNCs such as Microsoft, Coca Cola, or McDonalds, often have more highly trained personnel and greater budgets and resources than many sovereign states.[3]

The rise in number and importance of NGOs is driven by the rise in state failures,[4] and the rise in transsovereign problems which states have trouble addressing unilaterally. As states fail, NGOs increasingly step in to alleviate the symptoms of state failure, such as refugee flows, disease, and human rights violations. The rise in number and importance of MNCs and NGOs is also facilitated by the rise in open societies, open economies, and open technologies, which increasingly allow businesses and organizations to follow no flag.

As states find it more difficult and less effective to "go it alone" in formulating and implementing policy concerning transsovereign issues, increased multilateral action becomes necessary to deal with problems that move beyond sovereignty. Better coordination of policy across state and bureaucratic boundaries helps "to spread the risk, share the burden, and increase the impact of common efforts."[5] NGOs and sometimes even MNCs are well placed to help facilitate multilateral activities. NGOs and MNCs have been involved in negotiating international treaties containing global warming and restricting chemical weapons. MNCs have been key critics of state corruption which distorts business practices, and their cooperation is crucial in efforts to make the money flow transparent in international criminal activities.

However, coordinating action among a wide variety of very eclectic organizations with different agendas, cultures, and operating procedures is difficult. As Andrew S. Natsios, director of World Vision and former director of the U.S. Office of Foreign Disaster Assistance, observes, "Many of the institutional players really don't like or trust one another."[6] The abilities of nonstate actors to work well with states in combating transsovereign problems has so far been inhibited by poor communication and coordination among the varying groups. Government foreign policy organizations too often deal with NGOs and MNCs in an ad hoc, nonsystematic manner.

Notes

1. Lester M. Salomon, "The Rise of the Nonprofit Sector," *Foreign Affairs* (July/August 1994): 109–122.
2. As of 1993.
3. Andrew S. Natsios, "The International Humanitarian Response System," *Parameters* (Spring 1995): 68–81.
4. Salamon, "The Rise of the Nonprofit Sector," 115.
5. President Bill Clinton, "The UN at 50: A Pledge of Support by the White House," *New York Times,* October 23, 1995, A8; Alison Mitchell, "U.S. Freezes Assets of Cartel in New Effort against Drugs, *New York Times,* October 23, 1995, A11.
6. Natsios, "The International Humanitarian Response System," 79.

Private-Sector Transsovereign Actors — MNCs and NGOs

Maryann K. Cusimano,
Mark Hensman,
and Leslie Rodrigues

Multinational corporations (MNCs) and nongovernmental organizations (NGOs) are two sides of the same coin, the for-profit and nonprofit sides of private-sector transsovereign organizations. Both types of organizations are thriving, increasing in number, size, personnel, resources, budgets, profile, and political clout. Open economies, open technologies, and open societies facilitate the growth and activities of NGOs and MNCs. These nonstate actors also actively work to promote open societies, open economies, and open technologies. Additionally, the rise in transsovereign problems, which states cannot solve unilaterally, has contributed to the rise in nonstate actors, who grapple with issues that states have not been successful in solving. In some circumstances, however, NGOs and MNCs may inadvertently weaken fragile states, thus continuing the cycle of some transsovereign problems.

MNCs and NGOs in some cases eclipse the power of states. For example, the yearly sales of General Motors exceeds the GNP of economically advanced states such as Norway, Finland, Portugal, Greece, Israel, Thailand, Saudi Arabia, South Africa, Venezuela, and Ireland. General Motors, Ford Motor, Exxon, Royal Dutch/Shell, Toyota, Hitachi, IBM, General Electric, Daimler-Benz, Mobil, Nissan Motor, Samsung, Philip Morris, IRI, and Siemens all earn more per year than New Zealand (hardly an underdeveloped economy).[1]

Not only do some NGOs and MNCs commandeer more resources than many states, but the activities of these organizations are increasingly impinging upon functions which previously were jealously guarded by states. Not only have health, education, welfare, and development functions been carried out by nonstate actors, but MNCs and NGOs are now also active in law enforcement and police training, economic and environmental policy making, land use, and even arms control.

THE RISE OF NGOs

NGOs are increasing in number, resources, reach, and influence. As former UN Secretary-General Boutros Boutros-Ghali explains it,

> Until recently, the notion that the chief executive of the United Nations would have taken this issue (NGOs) seriously might have caused astonishment. The United Nations was considered to be a forum for sovereign states alone. Within the space of a few short years, however, this attitude has changed. Nongovernmental organizations are now considered full participants in international life.[2]

Nongovernmental organizations form a diverse and eclectic category, including church groups, trade and professional associations, labor unions, civic groups, service providers, advocacy and lobbying groups, membership organizations, and foundations. NGOs range from small, grassroots, local groups run on shoestring budgets to huge international organizations with deep pockets, from single-issue outfits to umbrella organizations, and include the Boy Scouts, Quaker Relief Services, Teamsters International, Save the Children, Amnesty International, the Carter Center, the Soros Foundation, the Ancient Order of Hibernians, and the Puerto Rican Conservation Trust.

Because NGOs incorporate such a wide range of functions, issues, and organizational structures, developing a comprehensive definition of NGOs is almost impossible. Thus, NGOs are an odd category, defined negatively by what they are not, rather than by any attempted positive statement of what they are. First, the name indicates that NGOs are *not governments,* but even this fundamental distinction can be a bit misleading. NGOs may be supported by governments, directed by governments, receive resources from governments or offer resources to governments, and may only involve themselves in certain areas or issues with the permission of government. But NGOs are a broad and eclectic group, so these statements do not apply to all groups. Some never accept government aid. A strong tradition of autonomy prevented the Red Cross[3] from accepting U.S. military airlift capabilities to transport food into Somalia during the famine in 1992; after the Bush administration had publicly announced the airlift, they learned that the Red Cross could not allow their food to fly into Somalia in military-marked planes. Other NGOS, such as CARE, Catholic Relief Services, World Vision, and the Adventist Development and Relief Agency, derive significant portions of their budgets and resources from the relief and development aid of government agencies. This is because states often prefer to contract out development assistance to NGOs, whom they presume have less bureaucracy, are more efficient and accountable, and have greater knowledge and networks with local populations than governments.

Because they are not in the public (governmental) sector, NGOs are thought to be private-sector organizations, but they are assumed to be public interest groups. Again, this can vary widely, depending on the focus of the particular organization and the interpretations of the reader. Do the International Association of Model Plane Builders or the Mennonite Church serve the public interest? Many in the United States refer to NGOs as PVOs, private volunteer organizations, but the term "volunteer" is generally misleading, as most international NGOs have paid, permanent, full-time, professional staffs.

Finally, NGOs are generally nonprofit groups, but again, this can be misleading. Many NGOs, such as community development banks, do turn a profit, but rather than giving that profit to a board of trustees, stockholders, or investors, any resources generated are reinvested in the community. Profit is not the organization's primary goal, but rather a means to achieving the NGO's primary goal, such as stabilizing communities by developing homes and businesses in poor areas where banks will not lend their money. Nevertheless, the nonprofit criterion is central to the definition of NGOs.

With such a flexible definition—mostly nongovernment, private sector but public interest, sometimes volunteer, for the most part nonprofit—it is no wonder that counts of NGOs vary widely, although it is conceded that the number of NGOs is on the rise. Former UN Secretary-General Boutros-Ghali estimates there are large numbers of NGOs, both internal and international. "In France, 54,000 new associations have been established since 1987. In Italy, 40 percent of all associations have been set up within the last fifteen years. This phenomenon is also occurring in developing countries. Within a short space of time, 10,000 NGOs have been established in Bangladesh, 21,000 in the Philippines, and 27,000 in Chile."[4]

The Union of International Associations tracks NGOs and IGOs (see Table 10-1). They list 15,965 "traditional type," international NGOs in 1997, such as universal membership organizations and internationally oriented national organizations. They count 24,341 "special" NGOs, such as religious orders, national organizations, recently reported bodies not yet confirmed, or suspected inactive organizations. Thus, in 1997 they reported a total of 40,306 international NGOs,[5] but other authors put the total much higher.

NGOs, Open Societies, Open Technologies, and Open Economies

Open societies, open technologies, and open economies make it easier to form NGOs, so it should come as no surprise that we are witnessing an explosion of NGOs worldwide at precisely the time when liberalizing trends are spreading. Boutros Boutros-Ghali notes that

> Nongovernmental organizations are a basic form of popular participation and representation in the present-day world. Their participation in international organizations is, in a way, proof of this. It is therefore not surprising

Table 10-1

Worldwide NGO Growth

	1909	1951	1960	1968	1976	1978	1983
Traditional NGOs	176	832	1,268	2,577	5,155	8,347	11,523
Special NGOs	––	––	––	741	1,067	1,174	5,507
Total	176	832	1,268	3,318	6,222	9,521	17,030
	1985	**1987**	**1989**	**1991**	**1993**	**1995**	**1997**
Traditional NGOs	13,768	14,943	14,333	16,113	12,759	14,274	15,965
Special NGOs	6,866	8,305	5,730	7,522	16,142	21,780	24,341
Total	20,634	23,248	20,063	23,635	28,901	36,054	40,306

Data from the *Yearbook of International Organizations, Vol. 1, 1997/98,* Union of International Associations, ed. (Brussels, Belgium: K. G. Saur Verlag, Munichen) Appendix 4.

that in a short time we have witnessed the emergence of so many new NGOs, which continue to increase in number on every continent. . . . In Eastern Europe since the fall of communism, nongovernmental organizations have been playing an increasingly important role in people's lives. This development is inseparable from the aspiration for freedom that in various forms is today shaking international society.[6]

The spread of democracy lowers the barriers to forming NGOs. Some of the hallmarks of democracy are freedom of expression and freedom of association. Under nondemocratic government forms, the formation of citizen interest groups independent of the state are often illegal; because they are autonomous from the state, states look upon such private organizations suspiciously, fearing they may form a base of opposition to the government. Just organizing people in states with closed political systems, like China, North Korea, or Iraq, can be a dangerous proposition, risking imprisonment, torture, and death.

Sometimes, NGOs helped to bring about the fall of nondemocratic regimes. Lester Salomon, a scholar who researches the nonprofit sector, notes that, "under Pope John Paul II Catholic churches in Warsaw, Gdansk, Krakow, and elsewhere in Eastern Europe provided a crucial neutral meeting ground and source of moral support for those agitating for change in the latter 1980s. The Lutheran Church played a comparable role in East Germany."[7]

Certainly, the democratization process encourages the creation and spread of NGOs, as part of the effort to build civil society. A Hungarian activist, Andras Biro, describes his efforts, "For the first time in forty years we are reclaiming responsibility for our lives."[8]

Open technologies also greatly assist the formation and maintenance of NGOs. Any group with a personal computer can maintain a database and mailing list, circulate a newsletter, or e-mail information to members. Phones and faxes also lower the time and resource barriers to organizing a group. Small and inexpensive video cameras allow private citizens to more easily provide evidence of government abuses, and the Internet allows such evidence to be widely disbursed, quickly and cheaply. Decentralization of phone and communication companies has made it more difficult for governments to control access to or to censor use of the Internet. "The invention or widespread dissemination of the computer, fiberoptic cable, fax, television, and satellites opened even the world's most remote areas to the expanded communications links required for mass organization and concerted action."[9] NGOs can now more readily identify members, solicit funds, and communicate their goals and activities. NGOs existed long before personal computers were widely and inexpensively available, but technological changes have facilitated an explosion in NGOs.

The rise in NGOs is also facilitated by open economies. Economic liberalization allows money to freely follow NGOs across borders, and allows NGOs to contribute capital to foreign development projects. Additionally, capitalism encourages the growth of the private sector, of which NGOs are a part. Free-market economies tend to emphasize grassroots, private-sector responses to societal problems, rather than top-down, state-sponsored solutions. NGOs thus fit with the entrepreneurial norms of capitalist societies.

Not only do NGOs benefit from open societies, open technologies, and open economies; they also promote these trends. NGOs have been instrumental in pressing for open societies, and advocating for human rights and democratization. During and after World War II, NGOs kept the issue of human rights on the international agenda, when state representatives meeting to construct the postwar international organization (what became the UN) tried to exclude or water down concern for human rights. States were skeptical about including human rights in the UN charter. They feared a loss of sovereignty over internal treatment of their citizens if the topic were broached in the UN charter. But NGOs such as the American Jewish Committee, the American Bar Association, the National Association for the Advancement of Colored People, and the League of Women Voters reminded states that the failure to protect individual and minority rights after World War I contributed to the conflict and genocide of World War II. Sustained lobbying by NGOs ensured that respect for human rights became one of the four purposes of the United Nations, set forth in the UN Charter, and that the charter called for the creation of a UN Commission on Human Rights. NGOs provided expert advice, research, and helped to draft language and lobby for the adoption of the 1948 Universal Declaration of Human Rights, and other subsequent human rights treaties.[10]

NGOs often are created as the locus of resistance to nondemocratic regimes. One dramatic example was the NGOs which emerged in opposition to the military dictatorships in Argentina and Chile in the 1970s and 1980s. Citizens who criticized or were seen as a threat to these regimes, and many who were in the wrong place at the wrong time, became the "disappeared"; they were kidnapped, imprisoned, tortured, and killed. In a final insult, the children of the disappeared were sold to childless military couples. "One torturer estimated that about sixty babies passed through [his clandestine detention center], and that all but two—whose heads were smashed against the wall in efforts to get their mothers to talk— were sold."[11]

> Children were tortured in front of their parents, and parents in front of their children. Some prisoners were kept in rooms no longer or wider than a single bed. And the torture continued for days, weeks, months, even years, until the victim was released or, more often, killed. The sadistic brutality did not always even end with the death of the victim. "One woman was sent the hands of her daughter in a shoe box." The body of another woman "was dumped in her parents' yard, naked but showing no outward signs of torture. Later the director of the funeral home called to inform her parents that the girl's vagina had been sewn up. Inside he had found a rat."[12]

In a heroic response to such brutality, a small group of middle-aged mothers of disappeared children organized in 1977. Calling themselves the "Mothers of the Plaza de Mayo," at first they numbered only fourteen. Frustrated in their attempts to locate their children, they began a silent vigil every Thursday afternoon in the main square of Buenos Aires, in front of the president's residence and seat of government. Although the women were subject to harassment and attack (some of them even disappeared themselves), they continued their efforts to draw attention to the atrocities of the military government. They were followed by the "Grandmothers of the Plaza de Mayo," who attempted to trace and recover the trafficked children and babies. Quickly, the numbers of these groups swelled across Latin America, and they soon became the NGO Federation of Families of Disappeared Persons and Political Prisoners (FEDEFAM).

Joined by groups such as the International Commission of Jurists, the Service for Peace and Justice, the Committee of Cooperation for Peace, and the Catholic and Lutheran Churches in Chile, these NGOs fought the military dictatorships and their brutality, at great personal risk to themselves. When the dictatorships eventually fell, these groups helped to build democracies, to strengthen the legal protections for human rights, and to reunite political prisoners with their families.[13]

NGOs promote open societies in a number of ways. They expose abuses of regimes, tracking facts and disseminating information, and mobilizing public opinion to try to end the abuses and improve conditions. They communicate with national and international decisionmakers, dispensing information and advocating for legal changes. They are direct service providers, offering education, advocacy, and legal-aid services. They teach citizens what their rights are and "how to act upon them."[14]

As discussed earlier, the rise in NGOs has been due in no small part to the advent of new technologies that make organizing easier. However, NGOs have not just been the neutral recipients of open technologies; they actively work to expand the reach of open technologies, especially to less-developed countries. Democracy and human rights NGOs support the spread of communications technologies that make regimes more transparent, and make it easier to transmit news of abuses to the outside world.

NGOs have been at the forefront of the movement toward sustainable development, which incorporates environmentally sensitive technologies to encourage more appropriate development patterns. Environmental NGOs press for the adoption of cleaner, greener technologies, such as water and air filtration systems for industries which emit fewer toxic pollutants into the environment. Public health NGOs disseminate health technologies, such as filtration systems for drinking water, X-ray and diagnostic equipment, as part of their disease eradication programs. Development NGOs disseminate technologies for agriculture, irrigation, water systems, and electrification.

Typically, international NGOs work with local counterparts. In this way, regardless of the issue focus, NGOs spread computer, phone, and fax technologies, just as part of the standard operating procedures for doing business. Some NGOs target open technologies as their focal issue. The nonprofit Association for Progressive Communications, for example, "provides 50,000 NGOs in 133 countries access to the tens of millions of Internet users for the price of a local call."[15]

NGOs vary in their receptiveness to open markets, however. Some, such as trade and professional associations, are in the forefront of lobbying efforts to expand free-market arrangements such as NAFTA, the North American Free Trade Agreement. Other NGOs in the development, environment, and human rights arenas are often skeptical of open markets. Concerned that open markets may come at a cost to labor, health, and the environment, they push for enforceable international standards on worker safety, labor issues, environmental conditions, and public health.

NGOs and States

NGOs may work with states to aid existing states. The Carter Center, the Soros Foundation, and the Center for Democracy are all involved in aiding the former communist states of Eastern Europe and the former Soviet Union with their democratic and market transitions. NGOs have been quite active in aiding South Africa's transition from apartheid.

Donor states often prefer to funnel development aid through NGOs, rather than giving it directly to recipient foreign governments that may be neither efficient nor accountable in their use of the funds. In states undergoing transitions, new institutions may be weak and lack proven track records. Donor governments may not be confident that development dollars given directly to unproven institutions will actually be spent on development projects. In an effort to get more efficient, "leaner, meaner" relief and development projects, donor governments increasingly turn over their aid budgets to NGOs. For example, from 1975 to 1985 U.S. government assistance funds channeled through NGOs increased more than tenfold.[16]

Governments believe that aid funneled through NGOs is more politically acceptable than direct government-to-government assistance. They also believe that NGOs can better reach the grassroots level, that NGO efforts are more efficient because they involve less bureaucratic red tape and overhead, and that working with NGOs helps to develop the private sector. Many believe that having NGOs serve as contractors for government relief and development activities is a win-win situation: the government "has found an efficient, less costly means of carrying out its legislative mandate, while the [NGO]s have discovered a relatively dependable source of money, available in large sums."[17]

There may be a downside to the close relationship between donor governments and NGOs, however. NGOs risk losing the perception of their autonomy and independence from government actors, if they rely too heavily on government sources for funding. And their reputation for integrity and autonomy is an important tool in NGOs' legitimacy and effectiveness. One NGO executive director described the question of accepting funding from the U.S. Agency for International Development as the dilemma of not wanting "to look like the tool or the fool of the United States government."[18]

NGOs are also concerned about the potential for conflict of interest between the goals of the nonprofit and the political goals of the government donor. NGOs are concerned about becoming dependent on government donors for resources, and potentially neglecting their traditional bases of support. They do not want to change their focus to fit more closely with government priorities in order to attract state funding. The "strings" that may come attached to accepting government funds (such as the "buy American" requirement that goes along with U.S. aid dollars) may detract from their program principles (such as, whenever possible, buy locally to help the local economy). And NGOs fear that the reporting and accounting procedures required of government contractors may make them more bureaucratic and entangle them in red tape (the very characteristics states were trying to avoid in funneling aid through NGOs in the first place).

When recipient state governments are cut out of the aid loop, animosity may develop between state institutions and NGOs. In Haiti, for example,

Critics argued that, while these approaches might provide more rapid and more accountable project implementation in the short run, they strained the government of Haiti's already scarce human resources by removing qualified people from the government bureaucracy, and that it failed to contribute to the institutional capacity of government to carry out long-term development projects . . . while most people would agree that the [NGO] should not be the long-term provider, this strategy may mean that no government or private institution will be ready to take over.[19]

As citizens turn to NGOs as service providers, the state is further undermined, which can perpetuate a feedback loop. NGOs may become involved to attend to problems which states are not addressing; in so doing, NGOs may further undermine the capacity and legitimacy of states, which can exacerbate transsovereign problems rather than fight them.

As an increasing number of states collapse, this is becoming a larger issue. Many NGOs do not wait for a state invitation before entering a country to provide services. This is especially true in countries such as Somalia, Rwanda, or the former Yugoslavia, where there was no working state government. If NGOs fulfill the functions of states where there are no functioning sovereignties, how do sovereign states get rebuilt? Many NGOs are not concerned with the question. Individuals in need, not states, are their priorities. They regard sovereignty not only as a right to nonintervention (negative or de juris sovereignty), but also as a responsibility to provide some benefit to citizens (positive or de facto sovereignty). If states are unable or unwilling to fulfill their responsibilities toward individuals in need, NGOs are tempted to step in.

The NGO Doctors Without Borders (Medecins Sans Frontieres) developed specifically out of the creed that they would provide medical assistance where needed, regardless of whether government actors existed or welcomed them.[20] Save the Children developed out of the efforts of a British woman, Eglantyne Jebb, to provide aid to the children victimized by World War I, regardless of whether they were the citizens of a winning or losing state in the conflict.[21] Similarly, Amnesty International began in 1961 with the efforts of a London lawyer, Peter Benenson, to win the release of some Portuguese political prisoners. His campaign soon developed into a worldwide watchdog and advocacy organization for human rights. Amnesty International is fundamentally concerned with protecting the human rights of individuals and groups; they are less concerned with the effect their activities may have on state capacities. Faith-based NGOs likewise are concerned with higher principles. The Jewish, Catholic, and Lutheran religions existed before the advent of the modern nation-state, and they likely will be around long after its demise. While not necessarily antagonistic to states, faith-based NGOs feel they answer to a higher authority than the state.

Understandably, then, NGO-state relations are often adversarial. In Central America in the 1970s and 1980s, NGOs were targeted by the state, particularly four types of NGOs—human rights, training, humanitarian, and organizations representing those uprooted by the violence and civil wars.

> Physical attacks on NGOs started in the 1970s. . . . Governments responded violently to the growth of peasant groups in El Salvador, and to the expanding Guatemalan cooperative movement. Self-help farmers organizations were also systematically destroyed. In the 1980s uprooted populations were methodically subjected to harassment, army abuses, disappearances, and assassinations. . . . Governments have tried to destroy human rights NGOs since their creation. They have endured because of personal courage, the mix of financial, technical, and political support received from international NGOs, and survival strategies crafted to suit local conditions. For example, the Catholic Justice and Peace Commission and El Salvador's Tutela Legal operated under the umbrella of church protection. . . . Most survived because of strong international links and small, low budget, decentralized administrative operations; some . . . perished. NGOs documenting and researching issues related to uprooted populations were also intimidated because of their infringement into policy areas considered the armed forces' preserve.[22]

Adversarial NGO-state relations are not limited to Central America. Human rights NGOs such as Human Rights Watch and Amnesty International are not welcome in China. Environmental groups, such as the Environmental Defense Fund, Greenpeace, the Sierra Club, the World Wildlife Fund, and the Natural Resources Defense Council, opposed the U.S. position in environmental summits in Kyoto, Japan, and Rio de Janeiro, Brazil. One sign of the adversarial relationship between states and NGOs is the establishment of NGOs by governments, "in order to infiltrate and gather information on the NGO community. These 'government NGOs' are of particular concern in the field of human rights."[23]

NGOs and State Functions

NGOs are increasingly taking up functions that were once performed by states. Feeding, public health, development, and education functions have been largely abdicated to NGOs in many regions where states are weak or collapsing, such as sub-Saharan Africa. In Nigeria, public education has generally disappeared under the military regime. The only education taking place in the country is provided by faith-based NGOs such as the Jesuit Mission Bureau. In abdicating educational functions to NGOs, states lose out on the opportunities to proselytize and socialize their youth in the viewpoints of the state.

But even strong states are allowing NGOs to perform functions previously undertaken by states only.

> Nongovernmental organizations play an increasingly prominent role in international environmental institutions, participating in many activities— negotiation, monitoring, and implementation—traditionally reserved to states. . . . For better or worse NGOs are now a regular part of the cooperative process. Within limits, they address delegations as a state would. They participate actively in the corridor diplomacy which is so central to negotiations, receive documents, present proposals, and are consulted by and lobby delegations. These changes are all relatively new. . . .[24]

For example, at the Earth Summit in Rio de Janeiro in 1992, "NGOs set the original goal of negotiating an agreement to control greenhouse gases long before governments were ready to do so, proposed most of its structure and content, and lobbied and mobilized public pressure to force through a pact that virtually no one else thought possible when the talks began."[25] NGOs provide policy research and development, monitor state commitments, report on negotiations, lobby participants, and facilitate negotiations. NGOs even have legal standing in most of the major environmental treaties negotiated in the last decade.[26] At the Rio Summit, "more members of NGOs served on government delegations than ever before, and they penetrated deeply into official decision-making. They were allowed to attend the small working group meetings where the real decisions in international negotiations are made . . . *Eco,* an NGO-published daily newspaper, was [the] negotiators' best source of information on the progress of the official talks and became the forum where governments tested ideas for breaking deadlocks."[27]

Certainly, negotiating international treaties is a function usually reserved for states. Determining land and resource use policy is also intricately bound up with statehood. NGO activities in these realms are significant changes. But perhaps even more telling, is the increasing role of NGOs in the police and arms control arenas. Besides exclusive control over territory, sovereignty is also commonly defined as being the authority with the exclusive, legitimate monopoly on the use of force. Thus, NGO activities in the arms control, police, and law enforcement realms exemplify a significant shift in state functions.

The Anti-Personal Landmine Treaty (APL), signed in Ottawa on December 4, 1997, was not only a disarmament agreement that was achieved in record time, but also an example of unprecedented activism by NGOs. The campaign to ban APLs was born out of the dissatisfaction of humanitarian organizations who had to deal with the continuing casualties caused by long-ended wars. "No other issue has mobilized such a diverse coalition of states and NGOs in such a short timeframe. In 1994, not a single country promoted the idea of banning landmines; by October 1995, 14 countries favored it. A year later at the Ottawa Conference, 50 countries pledged their support for a global ban; and in December 1997, 122 nations agreed to ban landmines. The treaty and momentum were the result of tremendous campaign efforts taken by NGOs. Such a treaty would not have been created if it was not for the aggressive measures adopted by the NGOs."

NGOs and Transsovereign Problems

NGOs often arise to deal with transsovereign problems that states are not adept in handling. Boutros Boutros-Ghali believes the rise of NGOs is attributable in part to the rise of transsovereign issues, which do not fit the old state-to-state rubric, focused on political and military relations. As he puts it,

> Today we are well aware that the international community must address a human community that is transnational in every way. For a long time, the international order was regarded as political and firmly established. Now we must learn to accept and to deal with a world that is both social and mobile. The movement of people, information, capital, and ideas is as important today as the control of territory was yesterday. We therefore must build a framework that takes into account not only political issues, but economic behavior and social and cultural aspirations as well.[28]

As discussed earlier, NGOs are increasingly active in combating environmental degradation. Environmental problems are indifferent to state borders, and the information and technical expertise needed to make environmental policy often exceeds the capacity of states. NGOs thus provide valuable services on environmental issues, since they can track environmental problems and effects on resources across borders, presenting the wider perspective needed to write treaties, and create and monitor regimes.

NGOs are actively working to resolve other transsovereign problems, too. The efforts of NGOs have been critical in fighting AIDS, especially because states have often been slow to react to this health crisis.

> Efforts to prevent or halt the spread of AIDS encroach upon the private and personal spheres that are normally beyond the purview of states. AIDS is a fatal infection that spreads through behavior considered private or even taboo, such as premarital sexual relationships, extramarital sex, commercial sex, sex between men, and needle sharing when injecting drugs. Though present, these practices are seldom openly acknowledged in any society. Some governments even choose to deny them altogether.[29]

To treat the disease, AIDS service organizations have sprung up all over the globe. In concert with advocacy and activist groups such as Act-Up and the Gay Men's Health Crisis in the United States, human rights organizations such as Rights and Humanity, and medical associations such as the Canadian AIDS

Society, NGOs have put the AIDS problem on the international agenda. Since AIDS cases are growing fastest in the regions of the world where government control is weakest (70 percent of AIDS cases are estimated to be in Africa), NGOs are often the major, and sometimes the only, player seriously working to fight, diagnose, and treat the disease.[30]

NGO activities have also been pivotal in responding to the transsovereign problem of refugee flows. The International Red Cross was created in part to help the refugees of nineteenth century wars; Save the Children was founded to attend to refugees after World War I. In April of 1994, a half million Rwandans were brutally massacred (primarily of the Tutsi group). Tutsis were identified, hunted, herded, and killed en masse in stadiums, churches, homes, in hiding, or while fleeing, shot by machine guns and hacked by machetes. Another 1.7 million fled as refugees. The refugees faced violence, hunger, and lethal outbreaks of cholera in the refugee camps, which were hastily erected on volcanic rock, with no drainage or safe water supplies. Despite the genocide and the largest human exodus in a twenty-four hour period in history, state governments and the UN stayed out of Rwanda. NGOs went in where states feared to tread, to respond to the plight of the refugees. NGOs, such as the International Rescue Commission, and Refugees International, eventually shamed and goaded outside governments and the UN into some limited and late action, but NGOs provided the bulk of the relief response.

NGOs work hard to combat transsovereign problems. But because NGOs also promote open society, open technology, and open economy forces, and because they may undercut the authority of states, NGOs may unintentionally create circumstances which allow transsovereign problems to flourish.

THE RISE OF MNCs

Like NGOs, MNCs are a diverse and eclectic group. They range from corporations like Exxon or Shell Oil which extract raw materials and natural resources, to manufacturers like Coca Cola or the Walt Disney Corporation or Microsoft which produce consumer goods, to companies like Bankers Trust or Citicorp which offer services such as banking, investment, insurance, and consulting. Many MNCs are hybrids of these functions, like IBM (International Business Machines) which sells computer and business products as well as providing consulting services.

MNCs are not simply companies which engage in foreign trade or market their products abroad. MNCs engage in foreign direct investment (FDI) and carry out production in foreign countries. MNCs engage in FDI because local firms have a "home court advantage." They are more knowledgeable about local business practices and consumer tastes, and it is generally less costly for local firms to do business in their home markets than for foreign firms. So foreign firms "hook up" with local firms to gain the best of both worlds. They can bring the advantages of the parent company (such as novel or superior products, marketing techniques, or improved production processes) to bear in a foreign market, while tapping into local knowledge via investment into a "host" company. FDI may take many forms: buyouts of a foreign subsidiary, joint ventures, licensing agreements, or strategic alliances.

Like NGOs, MNCs come in a variety of organizational shapes and sizes. Some allow greater autonomy of "host" subsidiaries; others insist on a high degree of "parent" company control.[31]

> Firms are considered to be more multinational if (1) they have many foreign affiliates or subsidiaries in foreign countries; (2) they operate in a wide variety of countries around the globe; (3) the proportion of assets, revenues, or profits accounted for by overseas operations relative to total assets, revenues, or profits is high; (4) their employees, stockholders, owners, and managers are from many different countries; (5) their overseas operations are much more ambitious than just sales offices, including a full range of manufacturing and research and development activities. . . . MNCs are firms that have sent abroad a package of capital, technology, managerial talent, and marketing skills to carry out production in foreign countries.[32]

In some senses, MNCs are nothing new. Foreign investment, banking, resource extraction, trade, and production were part of imperial expansion and colonial trade by the Romans, Venetians, Genoese, English (British East India Company) and the Dutch (Hudson Bay Company). "By the early 1890s, large U.S. manufacturing firms—like Singer Sewing Machines (the first large multinational corporation), American Bell, General Electric, and Standard Oil, to mention but a few—had large investments abroad."[33]

What is new is the number, size, power, predominance, and extent of MNCs? "The number of [MNCs] in the world's fourteen richest countries has more than tripled in the past twenty-five years, from 7,000 in 1969, to 24,000. . . . The world now boasts a total of 37,000 [MNCs]."[34]

In 1992, the sales of each of the top ten MNCs were more than the gross domestic product (GDP) of at least one hundred states. The 1992 sales of the largest MNC, General Motors, were more than all but the richest twenty-one states. "During the early 1990s . . . at least 37,000 multinational parent firms controlled over 206,000 foreign affiliates. Even the formerly communist countries are now promoting inflows of FDI. The result is that globally oriented MNCs of various nationalities are increasingly influential players in the world economy."[35]

States and MNCs

Sometimes, states are criticized for doing the bidding of MNCs. For example, in 1954, a CIA-assisted coup deposed the democratically elected government of Jacobo Arbenz Guzman in Guatemala and installed a military dictatorship. The Arbenz government had instituted land reforms that the U.S.-based United Fruit Company opposed. The U.S. government acted on behalf of United Fruit Company, and out of Cold War concerns in Latin America (even though the Arbenz government was neither communist nor allied with the Soviets).

Often the relationships between states and MNCs are cozy. States court the business, employment, and foreign direct investment opportunities that MNCs bring. Governments may move to dilute internal regulatory requirements on MNCs to attract their business, as Panama did in instituting the Colon Free Trade zone to attract foreign business.

In turn, MNCs seek cordial relations with host governments to smooth business interactions and decrease the cost of doing business. MNCs may be reluctant to criticize state behavior, as when the Disney Corporation opted not to distribute films and products in China which might be interpreted as critical of the Chinese government and its human rights record. Poor relations between the state and MNCs can cut into corporate profits.

MNC and state interests have often been intertwined in the free-trade and free-market economic agreements reached in the 1990s such as NAFTA, the EU, and the GATT agreements including the establishment of the World Trade Organization (WTO). Governments want to attract FDI to their states, and to increase employment opportunities and state revenues. MNCs likewise want to reduce nontariff barriers to trade and investment which add to the cost and complexity of doing global business. State and MNC interests were aligned when President Clinton intervened to stop the free-fall of the Mexican peso in 1995 with U.S. loan guarantees. The U.S. government did not want to see the destabilization of a key ally, and MNCs did not want to lose investments in Mexico due to a Mexican financial crisis. Although the U.S. government made money on the interchange (the Mexican government paid back the loan early and with interest), many criticized the government for doing the bidding of MNCs, questioning why the U.S. taxpayer should be responsible for bailing out the bad investments of MNCs and investors.

State and MNC interests were also joined when the U.S. government voted to continue to offer China most-favored-nation trading status after the massacre and imprisonment of Chinese dissidents protesting for democracy and political reforms in Tiananmen Square. The U.S. government wanted to maintain good relations with the Chinese government due to China's influence in key Asian security issues, such as the conflicts in Cambodia and Korea. But the state and

MNCs were also interested in protecting the $6 billion in U.S. exports and $13 billion U.S. imports from China, and the $300 million U.S. corporations had invested in China.[36]

MNCs and state interests are not always correlated, however. States often want to restrict the sale of sensitive technologies that can have military applications, whereas MNCs may be against trade restrictions of dual-use technologies. The German, British, and U.S. governments fought the Persian Gulf War against an Iraqi army which German, British, and U.S. firms had supplied with the chemical ingredients to make weapons. In 1987, while the United States, Japan, and Norway were officially allied to fight the Cold War against the Soviet Union, the (Japanese) Toshiba and (Norwegian) Kongsberg MNCs violated export restrictions and sold technologies to the USSR to help them build quieter and less detectable nuclear submarines (of the type depicted in the Tom Clancy novel and film *The Hunt for Red October*).

MNCs, Open Economies, Open Technologies, and Open Societies

MNCs require FDI and foreign trade for their businesses; barriers to FDI and trade increase the costs and obstacles to their businesses. Not surprisingly, then, MNCs are at the forefront of lobbying to increase free-market economic systems and reduce barriers to FDI and trade. Whether through regional trading blocks such as NAFTA or the EU, or more multilateral free-trade agreements like GATT and the WTO, MNCs seek to decrease tariff and nontariff barriers to trade and investment, as well as to decrease state control or state subsidies of key industries, and instead to open up economic behavior to market forces. In the democratizing states of the former communist block, Latin America, and South Africa, MNCs are pressing for protections of private property and the free movement of goods and capital in their newly liberalized economies.

MNCs also promote the spread of technology in a number of ways. First, they do this by example. Successful integration of transportation, communication, and production technologies not only makes MNCs profitable but it makes them possible; without advanced technologies such far-flung business enterprises would be neither possible nor profitable. By hooking up with local host subsidiaries, MNCs spread their successful uses of technology to new industries and areas. Local companies not affiliated with MNCs also adapt new technologies to keep pace with competitors and to mimic the behavior of successful business operations.

Second, MNCs often spread open technologies because it is their business to do so. Many MNCs are high-tech companies that seek new markets in which to produce and sell their products. From video cameras to home computers, global sales of technology products is good business.

Third, MNCs press governments to ease restrictions on the sale and use of technology products, because fewer restrictions lessen the costs and obstacles to their businesses. Fewer restrictions also increase the potential for MNC profits by opening new markets for sales of technology products.

The relationship between MNCs and open societies, however, is contested. In states such as China, Indonesia, and even Mexico, MNCs have pursued a capitalist economic agenda without pushing hard for democratic political reforms. In corporatist societies (like Chile and Argentina in the 1970s), authoritarian regimes ally with and co-opt business elites, protecting business interests while repressing democratic rights and principles. Order is central for the stable, efficient, and profitable conduct of commerce. Political upheavals, even those associated with democratization, create costs and uncertainties for the investment, production, and trade of MNCs. Do MNCs favor repressive regimes as a way of ensuring a stable, orderly, and favorable business environment? The behavior of ITT in Chile (discussed later in this chapter) and the United Fruit Company in Guatemala would seem to give credence to this theory.

A 1991 study analyzed MNC cash flows to developing states from 1975 to 1986 to determine whether MNCs are more or less likely to invest in repressive states with abusive human rights records. The study concluded that "MNCs in general [forgo] locating larger amounts of [foreign investment] in those [developing states] that consistently implement fewer human rights reforms . . . it does not appear that MNCs view a lack of human rights reforms and the high use of repression in [developing states] as acceptable."[37] There are a number of reasons MNCs may not favor repressive regimes. Arbitrary exercise of police powers and military brutality affect MNC executives, workers, and citizens alike. Repressive regimes may rule by force rather than law, but respect for law (and particularly for property rights) is crucial for successful business transactions. Without the rule of law, business transactions become uncertain and potentially more costly.

Even if MNCs do not prefer to invest in states with repressive regimes, MNCs still do invest in states with poor human rights records, and in the quest for cheap labor and cheaper production costs, MNCs may commit human rights abuses themselves. For example, Nike has been criticized for its labor policies in its athletic shoe and clothing factories in Southeast Asia. Workers are not allowed to leave their posts to eat or even to go to the bathroom; they may be fired for such offenses. Women workers are subject to sexual harassment. Although Nike contends that no one is forcing workers to take these jobs, and that any wage is better than none, "a worker making Nike running shoes in Jakarta, Indonesia, for example, makes $2.28 a day. . . . The wage paid in Indonesia is not sufficient to live on. The Indonesian government admits that an individual needs no less than $4 a day to pay for basic human needs in an urban area such as Jakarta."[38]

MNCs counter that they generally obey the laws and standard business practices of their host countries. But host countries often lower wage and safety rules in an effort to attract MNCs. MNCs then often fight legislative attempts to raise wages, working conditions, and worker safety standards. Sometimes MNCs preempt state efforts to improve worker conditions by threatening to move elsewhere. MNCs often contend that abuses are due to poor local management rather than parent company directives. Critics counter that if parent companies share in the profits generated by foreign subsidiaries, they must also share in responsibility for the practices which help create the profits.

The impact of MNCs on human rights can cut both ways, however. Sometimes the very presence of a multinational corporation can place an international media spotlight on local worker conditions, creating a "race to the top."[39] Concerned with protecting their image, companies will pressure local governments to improve workers' conditions. An MNC's instinct to protect its reputation, and thereby its bottomline, can have the beneficial side effect of exporting a concern for human rights. Thus, while MNCs fully promote open economies and open technologies, their record of promoting open societies (including respect for human rights) is contested and mixed.

MNCs and State Functions

It is perhaps not surprising that with the spread of free-market economic systems, MNCs are increasingly important players in determining economic policy. Multinational banks can practically dictate states' economic policies, by forcing states to accept austerity measures and structural adjustment policies to qualify for foreign loans. As the debt crisis intensified in the 1980s (described later in this chapter), multinational banks gained leverage over states. States were forced to adopt economic policies focusing on spending restraint, reduced social, health, and educational spending and subsidies, higher taxes, increasing exports, tightening monetary policy, limiting wages, and devaluing local currencies. These policies were not popular with domestic populations, but state governments had little choice—their economies could not survive without the investments, loans, and credibility ratings of MNCs and international lending agencies.

MNC influence is not restricted to economic and monetary policy, however. As states seek to attract FDI and the jobs promised by MNCs, corporations have a powerful voice in determining state land-use and environmental policies. Some states curb, do away with, or restrict enforcement of their environmental laws in order to attract international businesses. For example, in creating the Colon Free Trade zone, the government of Panama significantly restricted environmental laws in the zone to create a higher potential for profits for MNCs, who would not have to spend as much money obeying pollution, waste emission, and dumping laws. By catering to MNCs' cost concerns regarding environmental policy, Panama hoped to attract MNCs. Even in the United States, MNCs often have a pivotal role in creating land-use and environmental policy. In the 104th Congress, MNCs had unrestricted access to Republican legislators in closed-door sessions, to rewrite U.S. environmental policy legislation such as the Clean Air Act, the Endangered Species Act, logging policy in old-growth forests, and mining and oil extraction policy.

More surprising, though, is the role MNCs are playing in other functions traditionally reserved for states, such as arms control negotiations, and police and law enforcement. For example, in 1978 when the negotiation process for the Chemical Weapons Convention (CWC) began, few government officials had more than superficial knowledge of the chemical industry. Therefore, officials from the United States Arms Control and Disarmament Agency (ACDA) requested input and assistance in the negotiation process from the chemical industry. Recognizing the importance and impact of the chemical weapons ban for their industry, the chemical manufacturers adopted a policy of cooperation and assistance to the U.S. government. An industry group, the Chemical Manufacturers Association (CMA), assisted the government in developing procedures for on-site inspections and participated in special sessions of the Conference on Disarmament. What resulted was an unprecedented industry-government relationship giving government officials and the diplomatic core access to technical expertise critical to forging an effective treaty. For industry, opposition to the treaty would have not only resulted in negative publicity, but it would also have risked the creation of a treaty that was technically unsound and detrimental to industry interests.

MNCs and Transsovereign Problems

MNCs are involved in trying to stem some transsovereign problems. For example, a key component of the Clinton administration's plan to combat drug trafficking and other international criminal activities involves the cooperation of legitimate international businesses to help identify and weed out front companies used to conceal illicit profits, and to increase the transparency of global financial transactions.

In other cases, however, MNCs can add to transsovereign problems, as when they are the source of environmental abuses. For example, on the night of December 2–3, 1984, Union Carbide Chemical Corporation was responsible for the worst industrial accident in history. Forty-one tons of poisonous gas were released from its plant in Bhopal, India, killing 10,000 people and inflicting permanent disabilities on 50,000 people.[40]

As people ran with their families, they saw their children falling beside them, and often had to choose which ones they would carry on their shoulders and save. This image comes up again and again in the dreams of the survivors: in the stampede, the sight of a hundred people walking over the body of their child. Iftekhar Begum went out on the morning after the gas to help bury the Muslim dead. There were so many that she could not see the ground—she had to stand on the corpses to wash them.[41]

After the accident, Union Carbide worked to see that the case was heard by a more lenient judge in India rather than face a stricter U.S. judicial system. After years of legal battles, the MNC agreed to pay survivors generally $2,857 for each death (although a few received as much as $4,286). Ninety percent of the personal injury cases received a settlement of $714. These are the gross figures; subtract the bribes, legal fees, and administration costs survivors had to pay to stake their claim, and most survivors actually netted much less. These settlements are very low even by Indian standards. The standard compensation offered by Indian Railways for accidental death is $5,714, and $3,429 for disability, which is disbursed quickly and with minimal additional fees.[42]

Union Carbide is not alone in its poor environmental record. Hundreds of factories, or maquiladoras, have sprung up along the U.S.-Mexican border to take advantage of the cheaper labor supply in Mexico and the free-trade provisions of NAFTA. Many MNCs are attracted by less stringent Mexican environmental regulations and laxer enforcement of existing environmental laws, which translate into cheaper short-term operating costs for plants. Matamoros, Mexico, across the border from Brownsville, Texas, has suffered the environmental and public health effects of the maquiladoras. Congressman Richard Gephardt described the situation, "In Matamoros, some of America's biggest corporations dump toxic waste directly into the water supply—water that turns the colors of the rainbow. When I stood outside the homes of families living near Mexican factories owned by U.S. chemical corporations, the emissions made my skin burn."

The pollution is visible to the naked eye—orange and purple slime pours out of discharge pipes and flows down open canals, eventually discharging into a sensitive coastal lagoon south of Matamoros on the Gulf of Mexico. One can often see dead animals in these ditches. Children, oblivious to the contamination, play at the edge of the murky water. When the Matamoros city dump is on fire, as it often is, the billowing black smoke can be seen from the north side of the river in nearby Brownsville.[43]

Across the border in Brownsville, health care workers have documented "a sky-rocketing rate of birth defects, particularly in the number of babies born with undeveloped brains, a condition known as anencephaly. Researchers have found that anencephaly rates in Brownsville are over three times the U.S. national average . . . [and] that environmental toxins which are emitted by many of the maquiladoras operating in Matamoros may indeed be one possible cause of this tragedy."[44]

A U.S. Government Accounting Office (GAO) report notes that about half of the maquiladoras in Mexico may generate toxic waste, and that environmental testing done shows high levels of toxic contaminants associated with hazardous waste. Hazardous waste generated by U.S.-owned maquiladoras is supposed to be returned to the United States, but "Mexican and U.S. environmental officials acknowledged that they cannot account for most of the waste." Illegal dumping is common, and Mexican environmental enforcement, as well as the Border Environmental Cooperation Commission (BECC) and the North American Commission on Environmental Cooperation (CEC) set up by NAFTA, have not been able to muster the resources or quick response to stop the polluters.[45]

Even MNCs that have spotless environmental records may indirectly contribute to transsovereign problems. MNCs help to create the infrastructure which makes international crime, drug trafficking, nuclear smuggling, refugee smuggling, terrorism, and other transsovereign problems possible. Illicit actors adopt the same business techniques and advanced technologies that successful and legal MNCs use. Drug profits are invested, moved internationally, and hidden in the volume of legal international financial transactions. The ease of FDIs, Ecash, financial privacy laws, and international legal protections of private property are all tools MNCs have worked hard to establish. MNCs built the international financial networks and structures that are now used by both legal and illegal actors, thus facilitating transsovereign problems.

MNCs VERSUS NGOs?

Sometimes MNCs and NGOs work toward the same goals. Both are interested in stemming international crime and increasing security in developing countries, for example. Crime and corruption put workers of NGOs and MNCs alike in danger abroad, and so MNCs, NGOs, and intergovernmental organizations (IGOs) are increasingly communicating and working together to try to solve the related crises of the state which can lead to dangerous and unstable conditions in developing countries.[46] NGOs work on a variety of issues such as education, development, and establishing civil society and criminal justice codes and courts to stop the roots of criminal behavior. The Center for Democracy works to help establish democratic systems of law and police enforcement, while Food for the Poor works to establish microenterprises to provide legal business opportunities as an alternative to crime. MNCs work on economic advancement, professionalization, and capitalization to help states and individuals acquire the resources and tools to maintain law and order. AT&T lays the phone lines that law enforcement officers use; Microsoft installs the computers while Price-Waterhouse serves as a consultant to governments establishing democratic law and police systems. From very diverse angles, nonstate actors work on similar goals of reducing criminal violence and increasing civic order in developing states.

In Eastern Europe, MNCs and NGOs often work together to help former communist states in their transitions to become market-oriented, democratic states. The Carter Center works to promote ethnic tolerance and civic institutions in several former communist states, while Coca Cola is interested in legal reforms in Eastern Europe and Russia which protect private property, contracts, and foreign investments, and generally promote the rule of law which facilitates a stable business climate.

In other instances, however, NGOs and MNCs may work at cross-purposes. In the environmental summit on global warming at Kyoto, Japan in December 1997, for example, the most powerful MNCs representing oil and car manufacturers worked to defeat stringent new environmental standards that might decrease carbon emissions (and thereby cut into the sales of existing fuels or cars). They lobbied for nonbinding, flexible "targets" to aim toward returning to 1990 levels of greenhouse gas emissions by 2020. But 1990 was hardly a healthy benchmark; that year, levels of greenhouse gas emissions were large enough to create a "continent-size hole in the ozone layer,"[47] contributing to an 80 percent increase in the incidents of melanoma in the United States, between 1982 and 1989.[48] In contrast, leading environmental and health NGOs lobbied for stricter standards to decrease greenhouse gases, global warming, and the environmental and health problems they cause, including deeper, binding restrictions on carbon emissions which would take effect sooner. Stricter standards were defeated at the Kyoto meetings.

Likewise in the NAFTA negotiations, many MNCs, such as General Motors, General Electric, AT&T, IBM, Citicorp, Nike, and Johnson & Johnson, pushed for the agreement. Decreased regulations governing cross-border trade and investments would decrease the costs and increase the profits of their North American operations. At the same time, NGOs representing environmental and labor interests, such as the Sierra Club, Greenpeace USA, Friends of the Earth, Public Citizen, Citizen Action, and the AFL-CIO Labor Unions, lobbied to either derail NAFTA or strengthen its provisions toward environmental protection and worker safety and wages. This tangle produced something of a draw: MNCs won passage of NAFTA, but NGOs won side agreements to provide opportunities to address labor and environmental abuses.

Sometimes MNCs are guilty of abuses to which NGOs draw international attention and decry. In the early 1970s, International Telephone and Telegraph

(ITT) supported the overthrow of the democratically elected, socialist Chilean leader Salvador Allende, who opposed their business interests. ITT offered the CIA money to undertake right-wing, anti-Allende, subversive activities in Chile. The CIA later carried out such activities and the Chilean military overthrew Allende, ushering in years of human rights abuses by Chilean dictator Augusto Pinochet. It has never been proven whether the CIA took ITT's money, but ITT certainly favored the right-wing overthrow of Allende. NGOs such as Americas Watch and Amnesty International, however, actively worked to expose the outside role in overturning the Chilean government, and the subsequent human rights abuses which occurred under military rule in Chile.

MNCs whose properties were nationalized when Fidel Castro came to power in Cuba support the U.S. economic embargo of Cuba. NGOs such as Catholic Relief Services oppose the embargo of Cuba because they believe the sanctions do not punish the regime but instead disproportionately hurt the most vulnerable members of society, especially children.

THE STATE CONTRACTS OUT: NGOs, MNCs, AND DEBT-FOR-NATURE SWAPS

An example of MNCs and NGOs entering into activities previously performed by states is the increasing number of debt-for-nature swaps. Debt-for-nature swaps entail creative and complicated agreements in which corporations (often MNCs like Citibank, Bankers Trust, IBM, and Honeywell International) seek to sell off some of the riskier or less profitable debts of developing states which they hold, and NGOs (such as Conservation International, the World Wildlife Fund and the Nature Conservancy) agree to buy these developing states' loans in return for the developing states' agreement to turn over critical environmental territories for conservation.

In the 1970s, first world investors were looking for expanded investment opportunities for the glut of profits produced by the oil crisis. At the same time, developing states were looking for outside investors to finance development projects in their countries. The banks and MNCs often overextended loans to shaky foreign development projects. Developing states likewise accepted too many loans requiring repayment in foreign currency. Both groups overestimated the pace and effectiveness of development projects and the profits these projects would bring in; therefore, both groups thought that developing countries could "handle" a debt burden (based on rosy projections of future earnings and continued low-interest loan rates) that later turned out to be crushing to developing economies.

In the 1980s the bubble burst. Interest rates rose sharply on the (flexible rate) loans, greatly increasing the costs to developing states of servicing their debts. States were trapped in an underdevelopment feedback loop: They were hard pressed to earn enough hard currency from their foreign exports to even pay the interest on their loans, let alone to ever pay back the principal. By focusing their attention on paying back loans, they were not channeling money back into their own economies for development. By emphasizing export industries (to earn foreign currencies for debt repayment), they were not able to focus attention on increasing the size and strength of the domestic market, a key target of economic development. With the short-term emphasis on loan repayment, development strategies were pursued with disastrous long-term impacts on the environment. Yet, developing states did not want to default on their loans and hurt their present and future opportunities to attract foreign investors.

The banks and MNCs were likewise stuck: They did not want to forgive or too generously refinance the loans. They feared not only losing the loan principal and the profit they had expected back in interest from developing states, but they also feared losing their reputation and credibility with investors by admitting that these loans were bad, thereby severely compromising the strength of their own financial institutions.

Into this picture came NGOs trying to convince developing states to take better care of environmentally threatened territories under their control. States had a penchant for quick and dirty development in these areas, in the quest for hard currencies with which to repay the interest on their loans. For example, "Between 1950 and 1983, 38 percent of Central America's . . . forests disappeared."[49] Each year "an area the size of Austria is deforested."[50] Latin American rain forests were slashed and burned to increase farming acres for export crops (which yielded hard currencies to pay back foreign loans). Thus, for many states, debt repayment often superceded environmental conservation efforts.

By purchasing some of a developing country's debt, NGOs were directly removing some of the state's incentive for developing environmentally sensitive lands. Less debt lessens the pressure to pursue quick and dirty development plans. Additionally, NGOs would only purchase this debt if states agreed to specific environmental protection provisions. Often these entailed the state's agreement not to develop specific tracts of environmentally sensitive land, and to turn over management of these lands to a private party. Because NGOs were purchasing present debt in return for promises of future environmentally sound behavior by states, third parties (often local NGOs or citizens' groups) were brought in to monitor agreements and keep states accountable for their future environmental records regarding the specifics of the debt-for-nature swap agreements. States gave up some control over territory in return for debt relief.

The first debt-for-nature agreement was signed in 1987 among the Bolivian government, Conservation International, and Citicorp. Less than a million dollars in Bolivian debt forgiveness was traded for the enlargement and long-term management of the Beni Biosphere Reserve, which contained many endangered species. Since then dozens of debt-for-nature swaps have been carried out in Ecuador, Costa Rica, the Philippines, Madagascar, Zambia, Poland, the Dominican Republic, Mexico, and Ghana. Participating NGOs include Conservation International, World Wildlife Fund, Nature Conservancy, Fundacion de Parque Nationales, Puerto Rican Conservation Trust, Rainforest Alliance, Monteverde Conservation League, and the Debt for Development Coalition. MNCs include Citicorp, Citibank, Bankers Trust, Salomon Brothers, American Express, IBM, and Honeywell International.[51]

Advocates of debt-for-nature swaps argue that these are win-win agreements. Developing countries win debt relief, and thereby face less pressure to focus on export-oriented, environmentally destructive, economic development strategies. MNCs get rid of some of their questionable investments in developing states without losing their reputations among investors. NGOs purchase environmental protection of endangered areas, monitored by credible local groups. All parties win international goodwill.

Critics argue that these agreements are a new form of imperialism over postcolonial societies. Colonialism used to be carried out by foreign, conquering armies. This form of neocolonialism, it is argued, is now carried out by armies of foreign bankers and environmentalists. Foreigners, be they international NGOs, MNCs, or foreign governments (some debt-for-nature swaps have been conducted where the holder of the loan was not a bank but a foreign government), are still controlling the territory and interfering with the sovereignty of developing states.

Regardless of one's esteem toward debt-for-nature swaps, they do reveal important changes in sovereignty. Richard Rosecrance argues that a new form of sovereignty is emerging, the virtual state, in which territory is becoming passé. He notes that the Westphalian sovereign state was born into the mercantilist economic system, in which the control of territory was important for economic production. Raw materials, labor, and capital were fixed, not fluid. Therefore, whoever had more (and more lucrative) territory had more wealth and power. Today, however, the economy has changed; in an information- and service-based economy, economic productivity no longer depends on territorial size. "In economies where capital, labor, and information are mobile and have risen to predominance, no land fetish remains. The virtual state—a state that has downsized its territorially based production capability—is the logical consequence of this emancipation from the land . . . land becomes less valuable than technology, knowledge, and direct investment."[52]

Debt-for-nature swaps would seem to give direct substantiation to Rosecrance's theory. When faced with a direct choice between control over potentially lucrative, undeveloped, resource-rich land, or economic growth based on attractiveness to foreign direct investment and moving away from export-based economic strategies, states choose modern economies over land. Maintaining foreign direct investment is more important to states than maintaining absolute control over land-use strategies.

The lesson of debt-for-nature swaps is not that states are obsolete. States are an integral player in reaching these agreements; swaps cannot be forced upon recalcitrant states. However, states are not entirely free or autonomous actors in the process, either. They face tremendous pressure from their debts and from powerful outside actors (MNCs, the IMF, the World Bank). They are thus willing to do almost anything to right their swamped financial boats, even give up some of the most traditional base of sovereignty, control over land. Rarely have debt-for-nature swaps ever included the state's directly deeding away territory. Rather, they generally entail the state agreeing to limit land use in specific territories or to turn over some specific aspects of environmental policy to outside actors (local and international NGOs) for their monitoring and implementation.

The state is not going away; rather the state is increasingly contracting out. As states downsize and decentralize in response to the pressures of open societies, open markets, and open technologies,[53] nonstate actors such as MNCs and NGOs are picking up some functions that used to be part and parcel of sovereignty.

Notes

1. Charles Kegley and Eugene Wittkopf, *World Politics: Trend and Transformation* (New York, N.Y.: St. Martin's Press, 1997), 194.
2. Boutros Boutros-Ghali, "Forward," in *NGOs, the UN, and Global Governance*, eds. Thomas G. Weiss and Leon Gordenker (Boulder, Colo.: Lynne Rienner Publishers, 1996), 7–8.
3. Technically speaking, the International Committee of the Red Cross (ICRC) is not an NGO. It is an international organization with a mandate assigned to it by international law in the Geneva Convention and subsequent protocols. However, unlike most other IGOs, it is not composed of states as members, and it is not part of the UN system. Instead, it is made up of the national Red Cross and Red Crescent societies, which are NGOs. Thus, the ICRC most resembles a hybrid NGO-IGO. See Andrew Natsios, "NGOs and the UN System in Complex Humanitarian Emergencies," in Weiss and Gordenker, *NGOs, the UN, and Global Governance*, 73–74.
4. Boutros-Ghali, "Forward," 7–8.
5. Union of International Associations, ed., *Yearbook of International Organizations 1997/98* (Brussels, Belgium: K. G. Saur Verlag, Munchen, 1997), 1762–1763.
6. Boutros-Ghali, "Forward," 7–8.
7. Lester Salomon, "The Rise of the Nonprofit Sector," *Foreign Affairs* 73 (July/August 1994): 113.
8. Andras Biro as quoted in Salomon, "The Rise of the Nonprofit Sector," 112.
9. Salomon, "The Rise of the Nonprofit Sector," 117.
10. Felice D. Gaer, "Human Rights, Nongovernmental Organizations, and the UN," 52–53.
11. Jack Donnelly, *International Human Rights*, 2nd ed. (Boulder, Colo.: Westview Press, 1998), 43; John Simpson and Jana Bennett, *The Disappeared: Voices from a Secret War* (London: Robson Books, 1985), 110.

12. Donnelly, *International Human Rights*, 39; Simpson and Bennett, *The Disappeared*, 225.
13. Donnelly, *International Human Rights*, 44–45.
14. Gaer, "Human Rights, Nongovernmental Organizations, and the UN," 57–58.
15. Jessica Tuchman Mathews, "Power Shift: The Age of Nonstate Actors," *Foreign Affairs* 76 (January/February 1997): 54.
16. Charles Downs, "Negotiating Development Assistance: USAID and the Choice between Public and Private Implementation in Haiti," *Pew Case Studies in International Affairs* (Washington, D.C.: Georgetown University, Institute for the Study of Diplomacy, 1994), 4.
17. Ibid., 7.
18. Ibid., 8.
19. Ibid., 4–5.
20. Medicins Sans Frontieres, *Life, Death, and Aid: The Medicins Sans Frontieres Report on World Crisis Intervention* (New York: Routledge, 1993).
21. Angela Penrose and John Seaman, "The Save the Children Fund and Nutrition for Refugees," in *The Conscience of the World: The Influence of Nongovernmental Organisations in the UN System*, ed. Peter Willetts (Washington, D.C.: Brookings Institution, 1996), 241–248.
22. Peter Sollis, "The State, Nongovernmental Organisations, and the UN," in *The Conscience of the World: The Influence of Nongovernmental Organisations in the UN System*, 194–195.
23. Willets, *The Conscience of the World: The Influence of Nongovernmental Organisations in the UN System*, 6.
24. Kal Raustiala, "States, NGOs, and International Environmental Institutions," *International Studies Quarterly*, 41 (December 1997): 719–724.
25. Mathews, "Power Shift: The Age of Nonstate Actors," 55.
26. Raustiala, "States, NGOs, and International Environmental Institutions," 726–731.
27. Mathews, "Power Shift: The Age of Nonstate Actors," 55.
28. Boutros-Ghali, "Forward," 7–8.
29. Christer Jonsson and Peter Soderholm, "IGO-NGO Relations and HIV/AIDS," in *NGOs, the UN, and Global Governance*, 122–123.
30. Ibid., 122–129.
31. Joan E. Spiro and Jeffrey A. Hart, *The Politics of International Economic Relations* (New York: St. Martin's Press, 1997), 98–103.
32. Ibid., 96, 98.
33. Ibid., 97.
34. *The Economist*, July 30, 1994, 57, as reprinted in James Lee Ray, *Global Problems* (New York: Houghton Mifflin, 1998), 465.
35. Spiro and Hart, *The Politics of International Economic Relations*, 97–98.
36. U.S. General Accounting Office, *International Trade: U.S. Government Policy Issues Affecting U.S. Business Activities in China* (Washington, D.C.: May 4, 1994), 21–23.
37. Bret L. Billet, "Safeguarding or International Morality? The Behavior of Multinational Corporations in Less Developed Countries, 1975–86," *International Interactions* 17 (1991): 171, 184, as quoted in James Lee Ray, *Global Problems* (New York: Houghton Mifflin, 1998), 476.
38. Bruce Stokes, "Globalization: Workplace Winners and Losers," in *Great Decisions 1997*, ed. Nancy Hoepli (New York: Foreign Policy Association, 1997), 80.
39. Deborah L. Spar, "The Spotlight and the Bottom Line: How Multinationals Export Human Rights," *Foreign Affairs* 77 (March/April 1998): 7–12.

40. Ward Morehouse and M. Arun Subramaniam, *The Bhopal Tragedy: A Report for the Citizens Commission on Bhopal* (New York: The Council on International and Public Affairs, 1986); William Board, *The Bhopal Tragedy: Language, Logic, and Politics in the Production of a Hazard* (Boulder, Colo.: Westview Press, 1989); Paul Shrivastava, *Bhopal: Anatomy of a Crisis* (Cambridge, Mass.: Ballinger Publishing Company, 1987).

41. Suketu Mehta, "Bhopal Lives," *Village Voice* (December 3, 1996): 51.

42. Ibid., 55.

43. Mary E. Kelly, "Free Trade and the Politics of Toxic Waste," *Multinational Monitor* (October 1993): 13.

44. Ibid., 16.

45. Andrew Wheat, "Troubled NAFTA Waters," *Multinational Monitor* (April 1996): 23–25; Andrew Wheat, "NAFTA's Environmental Side Show," *Multinational Monitor* (January/February 1996): 35–38; Public Citizen, *The Border Betrayed* (Washington, D.C.: January 1996).

46. World Bank, *World Development Report 1997* (New York: Oxford University Press), 42.

47. Jessica Tuchman Mathews, "The Environment and International Security," in *World Security: Challenges for a New Century*, eds. Michael Klare and Daniel Thomas (New York: St. Martin's Press, 1994), 281.

48. United Nations Development Program, *Human Development Report 1994*, 36.

49. Saloman, "The Rise of the Nonprofit Sector," 116.

50. Mathews, "The Environment and International Security," 276.

51. Vicki L. Golich and Terry Forrest Young, "Debt-for-Nature-Swaps: Win-Win Solution or Environmental Imperialism," *Pew Case Studies in International Affairs* (Washington, D.C.: Georgetown University, Institute for the Study of Diplomacy, 1993), table one.

52. Richard Rosecrance, "The Rise of the Virtual State," *Foreign Affairs* 75 (July/August 1996): 46.

53. This theme is further developed in Chapter 12, "Beyond Sovereignty: Theory and Practice," in this book.

Institutions

Open markets, societies, and economies, and the transsovereign problems that accompany these trends, present challenges to foreign policy institutions. Existing foreign policy organizations, even multilateral ones, are generally state-based, while transsovereign threats go beyond sovereignty. States are hierarchically and bureaucratically organized, whereas many nonstate actors are not. NGOs as well as international crime organizations, such as drug, nuclear, and refugee smuggling and terrorist groups, often are organized as flatter, more fluid and less formal networks, which are less hierarchical and bureaucratic. State based institutions may need to improve coordination, communication, and facilitation functions across a wide variety of state and nonstate actors to combat transsovereign problems, but current institutions were not wired to do this. Besides incorporating the same new technologies that transsovereign actors use, institutions need to change their ways of thinking about themselves and their world if they are to serve as networks or clearinghouses for information and action.

Our survey of transsovereign problems shows that institutional change is necessary, as foreign policy organizations may be poorly equipped to handle post–Cold War challenges. Political scientists, though, are pessimistic about the prospects for change as they describe the many obstacles to institutional change. However, as NATO expansion shows, change is occurring, no matter how difficult. This chapter analyzes the challenges to, prospects for, and examples of institutional change to combat post–Cold War transsovereign issues.

The Challenge to Institutions

Maryann K. Cusimano

If the spate of fiftieth anniversary celebrations in recent years reminds us of anything, it is that existing foreign policy institutions were created in a far different era. The United Nations, the Organization of American States, the North Atlantic Treaty Organization, the World Bank, the International Monetary Fund (IMF), even U.S. foreign policy bureaucracies such as the Department of Defense and the Central Intelligence Agency—all of these institutions were shaped by their Cold War origins. While many of these institutions were used to promote open markets, open societies, and open technologies, their architects could not have imagined a world in which communism was (largely) dead, Russia was an ally, and open society, economy, and technology forces were pervasive enough to create transsovereign challenges. With the Cold War over, how are institutions changing to meet the new foreign policy challenges of transsovereign issues? This chapter will consider the difficulties encountered in changing foreign policy institutions, and the ways in which change can and ₤ being achieved.[1]

POLITICAL SCIENCE AND OBSTACLES TO ORGANIZATIONAL CHANGE

Institutions are a hot topic these days in political science. The end of the Cold War has brought about huge experiments in institution building. Internationally, existing institutions such as NATO and the UN are retooling, and new institutions, such as the World Trade Organization and the Partnership for Peace are being created. At the domestic level, the emphasis also is on institutions as states from Albania to South Africa establish constitutions, courts, parliaments, legal codes, police and law enforcement systems, capitalist financial institutions, etc., for the most part simultaneously and often from scratch. In the United States, think tanks are turning out a steady menu of suggestions for reorganizing the U.S. foreign policy agencies in a post–Cold War world, and a blue ribbon commission is devising recommendations for rewriting the National

Security Act of 1947 for the President to be inaugurated in January 2001. The tasks are daunting and exciting, and the political science academy is both a participant and an observer of this end-of-the-century focus on institutions.

The very term *institution* is quite broad, and can mean anything from "formal organizations, which have explicit rules and forms of administration and enforcement, to any stabilized pattern of human relationships and actions."[2] Thus, both generally agreed upon societal norms and specific treaties or organizations with a routine way of doing business may be referred to as institutions. The institutions we are considering in this chapter, however, are a much narrower group: the organizations charged with carrying out foreign policy. These organizations may be unilateral (based in one state, like the Russian Ministry of Atomic Energy or the U.S. Department of Energy), or multilateral, such as the UN or NATO. By taking a narrower focus, we can look at some of the more specific literature on bureaucratic organizations, as well as some of the literature on institutions writ large. Unlike the broader definition of institution (which can incorporate ideas, behavioral patterns, roles, or even ceremonies such as marriage), the institutions addressed in this chapter are specific in time and space; they have addresses. They are organizations which are generally arranged bureaucratically and hierarchically.

There are three main schools of thought in the political science literature on international institutions: the rationalists, the reflectivists, and the institutionalists.[3] Rationalists stress the utilitarian functions that institutions fulfill for states. They emphasize that states create institutions because it is in their interest to do so—states expect benefits will flow to them from the institutional arrangements that will be worth the cost. Because cooperation between states is difficult and can be uncertain, institutions are needed to make relations more stable and predictable, and to mitigate the costs of interaction. If cooperation was easy and the cost of interaction was low, institutions would be unnecessary. If the cost of forming institutions was too high, institutions might be unattainable.[4] In that middle ground of the expected costs and benefits, states find it in their interest to form institutions. These institutions reflect the power balances and resource distributions of states at the time of their creation. For example, the five permanent members of the UN Security Council are the only states with the veto power; these states were also the most powerful states to emerge from World War II. Germany and Japan were then defeated powers, and thus do not have the veto power or status as permanent members of the Security Council, even though today they are clearly major powers. The power, resources, and interests of states explain institutional structures. States create institutions and thus states can change institutions whenever they want, which usually occurs when the distribution of power or resources has changed.

Changes in the power environment may not directly or quickly translate into institutional changes, however, because of the power of sunk costs. States are attentive to how much time, attention, and resources they have already poured into an institution, and thus are not likely to change institutions quickly or lightly. So, although Germany and Japan are now more powerful states than they were fifty years ago, the composition of the UN Security Council has not adapted to reflect this development because changing the institution would impose costs on the other states that they do not perceive would be worth the benefit of a Security Council more in line with present-day realities.

Reflectivists criticize rationalists for their failure to take into account ideas, norms, values, culture, or history in their accounts of institutions. "Relationships are built not only on the distribution of capabilities but also on ideas, norms, and habits."[5] Thus, institutions cannot be reduced merely to the power structures and cost-benefit analysis which underlie organizational choices. For example, while the structure of the UN did represent the interests of the World War II victors, it also reflected the lessons learned from the failure of the League of Nations. The structure of NATO represented not only the interest of containing the USSR's power, but also ideas about promoting democracy in Western Europe and cooperation among democratic states. States are not billiard balls moved only by power dynamics; a state's history, culture, norms, ideology and identity matter and affect its institutions. Institutions, in turn, affect a state's interests and identity.

This observation of the reflectivists is especially important as democratization spreads around the globe. Democratic government is a lot of things, but efficient is *not* necessarily one of them. Democracy was never set up to be efficient. In the U.S. experience of democracy, Madison and the Founders thought that by having powers shared by separate institutions and by creating checks and balances among them, you might short circuit tyranny. By putting the government at each other's throats they thought it might stay off the people's backs. By making it difficult for government to respond too quickly to changes in the external environment, Madison and his colleagues thought that perspective and deliberation just might result. Of course, they didn't want the government to be so hog-tied by checks that it would be out of balance; this was the mistake of the government they had created under the Articles of Confederation that they were trying to remedy in the Constitution, and this is why they struggled long and hard with the powers of the presidency concerning foreign policy and war. They wanted a state that could defend itself against precipitous foreign invasion, but they were equally concerned that governments usually gorged themselves at the expense of the people via the rationale of foreign policy.

While the precise balance between executive efficiency and political deliberation, representation, and democratic accountability was never set down in the Constitution but has been battled out in practice ever since, it is important to remember that government efficiency was never the goal of the Constitution. You can say what you want about tyranny, but it can be quick and efficient; the government does what the ruler says, whether it is right, just, legal, or in the public interest. The Nazi government was chillingly efficient in its conduct of the Holocaust, systematically using industrial technology. Government becomes much more slow and bothersome when you have to consult others about what to do, and when you have to factor in civil rights and liberties and accountability to the law. In an era of e-mail, cell phones, and laptop computers, where the economy and technology place great value on speed and efficiency, we tend to forget that our democratic institutions were not built for speed. Opportunities for gridlock were built into our system by design; as de Toqueville noted, the miracle of the system is that it works at all. In the realm of foreign policy, where speed and efficiency are especially prized, we forget these lessons even more.

But if the reflectivists are right that ideas affect institutions, then the spread of democracy may carry with it the spread of institutions more concerned with process than with outcome, and more attentive to being representative or accountable to the law, to voters, or to interest groups than to being efficient in a narrow business sense. Some degree of slowness and inefficiency may be built in because of democratic ideals, and may not be responsive to organizational proposals to "reinvent government" to make it run more like a business.

Reflectivists believe that institutions are not just created to fulfill utilitarian functions such as reducing uncertainty and transaction costs. Institutions are created to reflect and give actors meaning and identity, and the institutions, in turn, affect and constrain actors' behavior. Actors often do not know exactly what they want, and institutions help shape and create their interests. Institutional change, therefore, will reflect changing values and ideas, and preferences will be effected and constrained by existing institutions.[6]

Institutionalists criticize both these previous approaches for insufficient attention to historical process and to the nature of change. Institutionalists stress the importance of path dependency. "Initial choices, often small and random, may determine future historical trajectories. Once a particular path is chosen, it precludes other paths, even if these alternatives might, in the long run, have proven to be more efficient or adaptive."[7] Thus, the emergence of the VHS video format over Beta, or the selection of Silicon Valley as the headquarters for many high-tech companies, may have more to do with small choices that were made early in the selection process than with the ultimate efficiency or desirability of the outcome. Early choices may achieve economies of scale with which later options have difficulty competing; for example, once a few high-tech firms had chosen Silicon Valley as their base, later firms did not have as extensive a choice of where to locate because the economy of scale had already been created. Changeover costs may wipe out any gains in cost or efficiency of switching to another option; thus, while there may be alternatives that offer higher quality or better resolution than VHS video, VHS endures because it would be too costly to switch to an alternative system. Alternatives may also be thinned out through gatekeeping or self-censorship. Once an initial path has been chosen the dominant form may actively work to keep out alternative forms, or alternatives may try to make themselves resemble the dominant form so that they will be accepted into the system. Both of these dynamics are evident with Microsoft's Windows operating system. Either Microsoft prevents competitors from entering the market, or competitors of their own accord mimic Microsoft in order to be compatible with and accepted by the dominant system.

According to institutionalists, power and identity are not the only important factors in institutional choices; historical chronology and chance also play roles. When considering institutional structures, actors do not have the entire universe of possible organizational varieties from which to choose. They must choose from the options which are available to them, and earlier selections likely winnowed down those options from many potential choices.

Krasner cites Stephen Jay Gould on evolution to illustrate the difficulty of institutional change. "Organisms are not putty before a molding environment or billiard balls before the pool cue of natural selection. Their inherited forms and behaviors constrain and push back; they cannot be quickly transformed to new optimality every time the environment alters."[8]

Thus, institutionalists criticize the rationalists' description of change as being too easy and adaptive; the real world doesn't work that way. They also criticize both schools for not paying enough attention to the historical process of change. Reflectivists don't have a great deal to say about what happens when ideas conflict, or how norms change. Similarly, rationalists don't have much to say about where change comes from in the distribution of power capabilities or interests.

For the institutionalists, evolution of institutions does not happen efficiently in logical response to changes in the international environment. Instead, change happens in fits and starts (punctuated equilibrium), and is constrained by the weight of existing organizational structures. People conceive of the world and themselves within present institutional frameworks (what was referred to in Chapter One as vertical linkages) and existing organizations have many standardized ways of doing business with other organizations (therefore changes in one organization require changes in others—horizontal linkages). Vertical and horizontal linkages allow institutional structures to persist even after the circumstances they were created to deal with have changed, and even when institutions are inefficient or outmoded. These links create formidable obstacles to institutional change. While Krasner does acknowledge that rapid change can occur unexpectedly, if "a stable structure is stressed beyond its buffering capacity to resist and absorb [change],"[9] he suggests that such examples are rare, since institutions actively influence the environment to promote their own survival.

More likely than the discarding of old institutions and the building of new institutions from scratch is the possibility of using existing institutional structures to do new tasks. Even though these structures in and of themselves may not be the most efficient or logical way to tackle a new problem, the existing structure has the advantage of being available. "Credit cards can be used to open doors."[10] The U.S. military may be used to fight famine in Somalia or stop an outbreak of cholera among Rwandan refugees. It is not what the military was created to do and it may not be the most efficient or effective way to deal with the problem, but the tool has the eminent advantage of being available. Having the tool may lead to its use.

All three of these perspectives are criticized for an insufficient attention to the role and impact of domestic politics and internal bureaucratic politics on institutional structures.[11] In addition, none of these approaches really tells us where change comes from, how it occurs or under what conditions it is more likely. Rationalists say little about where changes in power distributions or interests might come from, or how specifically these would translate into institutional changes. Reflectivists say little about how ideas and norms change, and what happens when norms conflict. Institutionalists suggest that organizations with weaker vertical or horizontal linkages will be more vulnerable to change, and that path dependency will constrain the alternatives for change, but otherwise this approach also says little about the sources and processes of change. Thus, we turn now to the literature on domestic bureaucratic organizations. Like the literature on international institutions, the domestic literature tends to emphasize the obstacles to changes in bureaucracies, organizations, and institutions.

Graham Allison, Morton Halperin, I. M. Destler, Francis Rourke,[12] and other writers on bureaucratic organizations are academics who have also intermittently held positions in government service. These authors describe bureaucratic organizations as semifeudal agencies, each fighting to protect their turf, to guard their missions, budgets, functions, personnel, resources, and autonomy. Internal conflicts may exist in organizations between bureaucratic chiefs and followers, but in general personnel are socialized (through training, standard operating procedures, and advancement incentives) into certain shared organizational viewpoints (what Krasner would call vertical linkages). This has been the most critiqued part of bureaucratic theory, the idea that "where you stand (on an issue) depends on where you sit (in which organization)."[13]

Bureaucratic organizations may engage in strategic bargains with others in order to provide a more stable environment over the long run (reminiscent of Krasner's discussions of horizontal linkages). Thus, bureaucratic theory does not posit that every interaction between agencies will be a to-the-death conflict with each agency going for the jugular. Agencies may give up subsidiary functions in order to protect primary ones. They may bow out of fights with more powerful agencies that they don't believe they can win in order to reserve resources and survive. But regardless of the specific strategy devised to fit the particular circumstance, this literature emphasizes that bureaucratic organizations will seek to promote their own survival, and change will come only slowly, in an incremental fashion, and when viewed as necessary to organizational survival. Change which is seen as threatening to the organization's missions, functions, budgets, autonomy, or personnel will likely be resisted.

This literature is criticized for being too focused on the minute details of organizations to offer much help looking at the larger picture of international politics. It is also criticized for not making precise predictions about which organizational strategy a given bureaucracy may pursue in any given instance. But it does have the advantage of focusing on characteristics of organizations which policymakers and practitioners believe are important; as politicians have long lamented, organizations can take on lives of their own and be unresponsive to political leaders. This meshes with Krasner's idea that institutions alter their environments in order to promote their own survival. It also dovetails with the reflectivists' view that institutions are not merely the creature of states but also exert an independent effect on states and foreign policy preferences. The bureaucratic account is contrary to the rationalist view, however, of institutions as being controlled and controllable by states, and as being efficient and adaptive to the outside environment.

James Q. Wilson shares Allison's concern with the ways bureaucratic organizations work to promote their own missions, functions, budgets, personnel, and autonomy, often at the expense of efficiency and openness to institutional change. He notes, however, that much of what is perceived as bureaucratic waste and inefficiency is actually attributable to organizations being given too many conflicting purposes. We have different expectations of public and private organizations. No one expects a private company to behave fairly or well, to use environmentally sensitive products, to search far and wide for contractors and products, giving every citizen an opportunity to apply. The contractor can hire a brother-in-law and no one will care as long as the product is delivered on time and within budget. As Milton Friedman put it, "the moral responsibility of business is to make a profit."[14]

We have different expectations of government organizations. We care about what they produce as well as how they produce it. In some cases, what is produced is so nebulous ("national security" for example) and hard to measure, that we place even greater emphasis and constraints on what we can see and measure—the process for producing it. We may not be entirely sure what we want the military to do or how it may best produce "national security," but we know a lot about how we expect the military to operate. For example, the U.S. military was under strict orders to integrate the armed services decades before the rest of U.S. society even attempted to clean up its racial record. We expect the marketplace to offer better treatment to those who can pay more. We expect the government to treat all citizens equally.

Because government bureaucracies face greater operational constraints than private bureaucracies, it is unrealistic to expect them to operate as efficiently as their private counterparts. Wilson is skeptical of trying to change organizations through additional regulations or external reorganization plans without parallel changes in internal incentives. If executives favor change, if they change the incentive structure (through training and promotion opportunities) to reward innovation and encourage the rank and file to innovate, organizations may change, but change will not be quick or easy.

Terry Moe is also pessimistic about the opportunities for organizational change. He emphasizes the obstacles to institutional change and to creating effective institutions by focusing on the interest group politics that underlie institutions. Foreign policy institutions in a democracy are inherently political animals. Organizational structures are not above politics; they are created by and answer to political pulling and hauling. Every organizational structure was created as a result of political negotiation enacted into law. Thus, every organization is based on the political coalitions that won out or the compromise that was reached in order to create an institutional structure. In this sense, Moe's account resembles the rationalists: institutions represent the interests of powerful actors. But the parallels end there, because Moe looks at substate, interest group actors, unlike the rationalists who see states as the main actors. Moe also believes powerful actors rarely get what they want, as institutional structures represent compromise and bargaining among groups. Additionally, Moe does not believe institutions are particularly adaptive or efficient in response to changes in the external environment. He agrees with Allison that bureaucratic actors can exert independent influences and will attempt to guard their own institutions and autonomy. But he does not believe bureaucratic actors overall are well-positioned to exert more than a marginal role. The real powers in the United States are the president, Congress, and interest groups, and the powers of bureaucratic organizations pale next to these players.

Moe does echo Krasner's focus on path dependency, however. He stresses that "the choices about structure that are made in the first period, when the agency is designed and empowered with a mandate, are normally far more enduring and consequential than those that will be made later . . . Most of the pushing and hauling in subsequent years is likely to produce only incremental change. This, obviously, is very much on everyone's minds in the first period."[15]

Structures may be quite ill-suited to organizational goals by design. In democracies, organizational structures were created by groups who wanted to address particular needs, curry favor with political constituents, or wrest power or functions from existing organizations. Controlling mechanisms were foisted on organizations either by opponents who did not want particular issue areas addressed or who did not want the new organization to succeed or become too powerful, or sometimes by proponents of the original organization who, fearful that political opponents would control the organization at some future point, wanted to limit the damage they could do.[16] Foreign policy organizations are political responses to political pressures more than they are rational responses to international pressures.

Changing institutions is therefore not about making more efficient structures, but about changing political balances. As Moe concludes, there are no easy answers (or they would have been implemented long ago). "It would be nice to say that there is an easy way out of all this, that the nation can have an effective public bureaucracy if only it wants one. But this is probably not so. A bureaucracy that is structurally unsuited for effective action is precisely the kind of bureaucracy that interest groups and politicians routinely and deliberately create . . . because they are forced to design bureaucracy through a democratic process, their structural choices turn out to be very different indeed from those intended to promote effective organization." Moe expects bureaucratic structures to be "grotesque" and "bizarre," not efficient or easily adapted.[17]

Ironically, this point seems lost on many inside-the-Beltway think tanks and groups suggesting organizational reform who should know better. Conferences, press releases, and studies are churned out at a prolific rate on how to reform specific foreign policy organizations from the CIA to the IMF for greater efficiency and effectiveness in a changed post–Cold War world, generally with little thought or attention to changing the political coalitions necessary to implement the suggested organizational changes. Since ideas alone cannot produce change, these studies often die on the vine, without the political support to bring them to fruition.

Another academic approach which may be helpful in understanding institutional change is the literature on political psychology. These authors also stress the difficulty of changing conceptual or belief systems, and the ways in which outmoded beliefs can persist despite changes in external circumstances. However, this literature also focuses on the importance of individual decisionmakers and small decision-making groups in international politics. People make policy and people create and lead institutions, therefore people can bring about change. Conceptual change is necessary for institutions to change, but it does not come easily or precipitously, because change in beliefs is "gradual and ragged."[18]

Deborah Larson studied the origins of containment: How specifically did President Truman and his advisors change their belief system from one in which the USSR was an ally (FDR's "grand design" idea of cooperation among the great powers) to one in which the focus was containing the Soviet Union by countervailing pressure, not cooperation (the Cold War "Containment Doctrine")? The change to the Cold War belief system coincided with the extensive institutional change begun with the National Security Act of 1947.

Larson describes an extended period in which policymakers themselves did not know what course of action to pursue and what to think about Soviet behavior and the nature of the new postwar world. They did not develop new beliefs in the abstract, on the basis of logical argumentation or rational analysis.

Instead, they were forced by circumstances to deal with the changed environment. They improvised and developed ad hoc policy responses, tinkering with a variety of sometimes contradictory approaches. Gradually out of their forced experimentation with the new environment, they began to develop new beliefs about how the world worked. Policymakers often knew their old ideas were inadequate, but they did not discard outdated concepts quickly because they had no replacement theory. According to Larson:

> Truman did not abandon FDR's "grand design" until almost two years after Germany's surrender. Throughout this period, Truman improvised, following no consistent policy toward the Soviet Union. It was already apparent . . . that FDR's vision of great power unity probably could not be realized . . . But Truman had no policy with which to replace Roosevelt's "grand design." Desperately, he tried a number of expedients . . . None was well-thought out or part of any consistent strategy.[19]

Decisionmakers were forced to act, and out of those actions they developed new beliefs, which they then used to justify their past and subsequent actions, and the creation of new organizations.

"Forged in the fires" of action and crisis then, "ideology leads to the development of policy doctrines that become institutionalized through the creation of bureaucracies. In particular, the Cold War ideology underlay a vast expansion of the power and resources of the executive branch of the U.S. government."[20] Thus, according to Larson's account, belief change made organizational change possible.

So the literature agrees that change is difficult. It will be resisted by bureaucracies that see change as threatening to their missions, functions, budgets, personnel, autonomy, or standard operating procedures. Peripheral tasks will be easier to change than core tasks. In democratic systems, change can be initiated by legislators, presidents, interest groups, or voters, but even externally imposed changes need some degree of internal support if the proposed changes are to be carried out in accordance with the spirit, and not just the letter, of the law. Beliefs may need to change before organizations can change, and beliefs may change only through hands-on experience grappling with a changed environment.

But what is often overlooked in the literature's emphasis on the obstacles to organizational change are the facts that (1) change does occur, and (2) sometimes the very characteristics of bureaucratic and organizational behavior cited as obstacles to change can be marshaled to promote institutional change.

Perhaps the only thing organizations fear and resist more than change is their own obsolescence or threats to their survival. If organizations are seen as ineffective, outdated anachronisms, organizations may have powerful incentives for reinventing themselves in order to survive with the changing times. It is not merely a matter of cosmetics, either. Organizations do not want to put their personnel or resources at risk; if older standard operating procedures are seen as no longer being able to protect personnel or resources, organizations will have powerful incentives to change the way they do business. As Vice President Gore put it when discussing changes to NATO, "everyone realizes that a military alliance, when faced with a fundamental change in the threat for which it was founded, either must define a convincing new rationale or become decrepit. Everyone knows that economic and political organizations tailored for a divided continent must now adapt to new circumstances—including acceptance of new members— or be exposed as mere bastions of privilege."[21]

Organizations do not want to appear outdated, not just because they want to convince political decisionmakers of their validity, necessity, and fiscal worth. While there may be some bureaucrats concerned only with maintaining their paychecks, there are many others who want to use their organizations to effectively perform tasks. Most bureaucrats consider themselves members of some profession, and their professional ethics prompt them to want to pursue effective action in their field. Thus, there will always be some advocates for change within institutions, people who see better ways to do their jobs or who want to improve their institution's abilities in a changed world. Once these agents for change begin interacting with the environment, the results may be unpredictable. Gorbachev did not set out to dismantle the USSR. He began trying to improve worker productivity and to cut down on alcohol abuse on the job, in an attempt to improve the performance of Soviet institutions. But the changes he unleashed had the eventual, unintended consequences of ending the Soviet empire.

Additionally, as people engage in the process of changing institutions, the process may have the effect of changing the people as well. Perhaps you can't always get what you want in institutional structure, as Moe suggests. But if Larson is correct about how people revise their belief systems, then you may not know what you want until you engage in the process and begin to learn from your own experiences. Thus, while action for change may come from individuals or political coalitions in alliance with reformers within institutions, the process may change as the institutions interact with the agents for change and vice versa.

SPECIFIC OBSTACLES TO INSTITUTIONAL CHANGE IN THE POST–COLD WAR ENVIRONMENT

Chapter One described many of the difficulties states have in responding to transsovereign problems. These issues blur the lines between domestic and foreign policy; they require multilateral and public-private sector cooperation; they often occur in areas where states have least control (be it in failed states or in the economic and social sectors where liberal states have less influence); and they require consideration of the negative ramifications of what are otherwise deemed positive international trends: open markets, societies, and technologies. All of these factors make institutional adaptation more difficult, because responses require coordination among a wider variety of actors, over a wider variety of issues, in areas where states are not well-positioned to act, and with impact on liberalizing trends Western states usually favor. Yet there are more pressing obstacles to institutional change.

It is difficult to adapt to a world we cannot even name. The fact that we identify the period after 1989–1991 only as the post–Cold War era shows how little we have advanced in our ways of conceptualizing the world since the end of the Soviet empire. The twentieth century was the bloodiest in history, and is marked in our minds and our history books by our wars: World War I, the interwar period, World War II, the Cold War, and now the post–Cold War period. But the post-Cold War period is not an era of international war between sovereign states, so it cannot be tagged as the "next war" period. Almost all of the major armed conflicts in the post–Cold War Era have been internal, not international, wars. The West has tried hard to plug new threats into the hole left by the old Soviet Union: Iraq, China, and rogue states. But there is no sovereign state challenger on a par with the old Soviet Union or the fascist right before it. While there are states which have poor relations with the West, none of them plans hegemonic forays guided by principle and bent on world domination à la Hitler and *Mein Kampf,* or the USSR and the *Communist Manifesto.*[22]

Threats are diffuse and decentralized. They cut across borders and issue areas, and are facilitated by open economy, society, and technology forces which existing institutions have promoted. There is little consensus about the nature of the post–Cold War world, making it difficult to marshal political and organizational consensus. Not only are institutions slow to change in general, but we are asking institutions to do what they are least able to do well: to innovate proactively against multiple, long-term, diffuse, indirect, decentralized threats without a specific name or face, in the absence of a catastrophe to mobilize public or political support, attention, and resources.

The last time wide-scale institutional change took place was in the aftermath of World War II. The environment then was more hospitable to institutional change, and consequently it was a period of great institutional dynamism. For example, the United States began an unprecedented period of foreign policy institution building. The armed forces were united into the Department of Defense (DOD) under a single civilian secretary of defense; the Air Force was created as an independent military department; and the missions, functions, and interservice mechanisms among the Army, Navy, Air Force, and Marines were set. For the first time in its history, the United States had a large, standing military in peacetime.[23] The CIA was created; this was also an important first in peacetime, especially for a country that had long held the view that "gentlemen don't read each other's mail."[24] The National Security Council (NSC) was formed to coordinate the myriad foreign policy advice that the president would now receive from this alphabet soup of foreign policy organizations.[25] The Department of Energy (DOE) was established to handle the new instrument of nuclear power, and to ensure civilian control over nuclear weapons. Later, the U.S. Information Agency (USIA),[26] the U.S. Agency for International Development (USAID),[27] and the Arms Control and Disarmament Agency (ACDA)[28] were also created to handle U.S. public diplomacy, foreign aid, and arms control needs.

Externally, the United States was instrumental in the creation of new regional and international organizations, such as the UN, the IMF, and the World Bank. Never before had the United States committed to a defensive, military alliance in peacetime; now it took the lead in creating several, including the North Atlantic Treaty Organization (NATO), the South East Asia Treaty Organization (SEATO), and the Organization of American States (OAS).

In a country flush with money (the U.S. economy dwarfed all others immediately after World War II), and still positive about the New Deal legacy, creating and funding new foreign policy organizations seemed a natural way to deal with changed international circumstances. Previous institutions had already been discredited by both world wars, and the extended period of warfare had created ad hoc institutional responses that led to a period of institutional flexibility and experimentation at World War II's end. The old coalitions behind previous institutional arrangements were so buffeted by the war that they were vulnerable to institutional challenges. The external threat was sufficiently high in the form of a communist, expansionist, and soon-to-be nuclear armed Soviet Union that internal opposition to change was able to be overcome.

Therefore, the last time wide-scale institutional change took place, previous institutional arrangements had been discredited, new threats were perceived as dire and immediate, money for new institutions abounded, and leaders were committed to changing institutions. Conceptual change was also made easier because the change from the World War II to the Cold War belief system was in some sense just a substitution of players. International politics was still about great power, state-to-state conflict, but instead of the enemy to democracy and free market capitalism being authoritarian fascism, totalitarian communism was now the enemy. There were other changes to the conceptual system which had to be accommodated—the end of colonial empires, the beginning of an atomic age—but the parameters of state-to-state conflict remained unchanged. The new coalitions around the new ideas created new legal structures authorizing new organizations. Thus, the last great change in the exterior international environment was met with fewer institutional, political, and conceptual challenges than this time around.

Now reorganization proposals abound, but political, institutional, and conceptual dynamics constrain fundamental rethinking efforts. The more politically viable reorganization proposals that exist are often based on an erroneous premise: that foreign policy organizations can and should be more like business organizations. These proposals focus more on downsizing, defunding, and privatizing the existing machine for budgetary purposes (less is more, by definition), and less on refocusing organizations for greater efficacy in a changed world.

For example, the United States has been debating reorganization of the UN and the elimination of ACDA, USIA, and USAID as independent agencies by downsizing them and folding them into the overall State Department structure. These debates are driven by concerns over cutting resources and personnel. While cost savings, organizational efficiency, or a simplified chain of command are all laudable goals, these reforms are not aimed at making the organization better able to meet transsovereign challenges, and it is too early to tell whether they will improve the organizations' bottom lines. But by focusing exclusively on cutting budgets and bodies, any such reforms enacted may actually hamper the State Department's and the UN's capacities to respond to new issues.

MACHIAVELLI WAS RIGHT

Despite all these obstacles to change, foreign policy organizations are changing, although perhaps not as quickly or efficiently as many would like. It seems after all these years that Machiavelli is still right; change is the only constant in politics. While an exhaustive description of the institutional changes to foreign policy organizations underway since the end of the Cold War is beyond the scope of this book, the sections that follow sketch recurring themes in organizational change in the post–Cold War era.

Reaching Out to the Private Sector

As this book has documented, many state-based institutions have turned to the private sector to mitigate transsovereign problems. They are forming new collaborative networks to help monitor, report, and share information on problems; contribute input into determining policy solutions; and implement policy toward transsovereign challenges.

For example, the UN is actively developing partnerships with private businesses. Worried about global warming and the impact that rising ocean levels and climactic change will have on property damage, insurance companies work with the UN Environment Programme. Together with NGOs, private sector actors played key roles in the UN conferences on global warming in Kyoto, Japan, and Rio de Janeiro, Brazil.

Private, multinational banks help the UN Development Programme establish microenterprises in developing countries. Information technology companies work with the UN Commission on Trade and Development (UNCTAD), "contributing technical assistance to an automated customs system developed by UNCTAD which has already improved trade efficiency in developing countries." The UN also works as an intermediary between business suppliers of technology and needy developing countries through the UN Industrial Development Organization, which "has brought over a billion dollars worth of investment and clean technologies to more than eighty countries in the last four years." UN activities benefit from private sector help, and businesses help to lay the groundwork in developing economies for future investment and customer loyalty to their company.[29]

In the fight against international crime, the UN and government agencies are increasing and institutionalizing private sector collaboration. Since international criminals rely on economic and transportation infrastructures in the private sector to move illicit profits, goods and operators, tracking and combating international crime is impossible without private sector support.

The private sector also helps the UN financially. The UN's budget comes from dues paid by member states, but $2.5 billion is currently owed to the UN by member states who have not paid their dues (two thirds of that amount—$1.6 billion—is owed by the United States). To make up for their budgetary shortfall, the UN has turned to private businesses and contributors, such as U.S. businessman Ted Turner, the founder of Cable News Network, who has pledged $1 billion over the next ten years to UN programs. In addition, "Rotary Clubs worldwide, backed heavily by the business community, have given more than $400 million to the World Health Organization's efforts to eradicate polio. Working with UNICEF's "Change for Good" project, major airlines such as British Airways are collecting and donating extra foreign currency from passengers returning from abroad. Since 1991 they have raised over $18 million for children."[30] Across a variety of issue areas, diverse foreign policy institutions are widening their contacts and partnerships with the private sector.

Forming Networks of Coordination and Communication

As the previous section indicates, institutions are developing new collaborative networks to exchange information and coordinate action among a wide variety of state and nonstate actors. Rather than creating entirely new state agencies to deal with transsovereign problems, existing institutions are seeking to develop new integrating and coordinating mechanisms that cross agency and public-private sector boundaries. For example, on May 22, 1998, President Clinton signed Presidential Decision Directives (PDDs) 62 and 63, which establish new coordinating mechanisms to combat terrorism and threats to critical infrastructure (anything from the highways to the electric grid to the Internet). The idea is that by systematizing interagency and public-private contacts, not only will international crime and terrorism be deterred (including cyber terrorism and cyber attacks on computer systems), but also suspicions among the actors will be diminished and cooperation will be encouraged. Government agencies often seek to protect their information, especially the "sources and methods" by which they collect their intelligence, and likewise private actors often jealously guard information that is proprietary.

While PDD 62 created a new "National Coordinator for Security, Infrastructure Protection, and Counterterrorism" within the NSC, PDD 63 created the National Infrastructure Protection Center (NIPC) at FBI headquarters in Washington, D.C. to serve as a coordinating entity on "national critical infrastructure threat assessment, warning, vulnerability, and law enforcement investigation and response." The NIPC aims to develop a more complete assessment of threats to the nation's infrastructure by developing two-way information sharing, communication, and consultation with the private sector and among government agencies at all levels.

> The NIPC requires the combined efforts of many different government agencies—federal, state, and local. And it requires the intensive involvement of the private sector. It is for this reason that the NIPC is founded on the notion of a partnership that will include representatives from the FBI, Department of Defense, the Intelligence Community, other federal departments and agencies, state and local law enforcement, and private industry. The NIPC Outreach effort is designed to establish and build strong relationships with its partners—the public and private owners and operators of the critical infrastructures, as well as with federal, state, and local government agencies. In addition, the Center will augment the physical presence of these representatives by establishing electronic connectivity to the many different entities in government and the private sector who might have—or need—information about threats to our infrastructures . . . The NIPC has been in existence for only a short period. We still have a lot of work to do in establishing the necessary liaison with other agencies and the private sector. This will take time. But the president, Department of Justice, and the FBI have taken an important first step in establishing this Center, in recognizing the need for an interagency and public-private partnership, and in realizing that the new challenges of the next century require new ways of thinking and new solutions.[31]

Borrowing ideas from the private sector and from computer technology about connectivity, institutions are not trying to create large, new federal bureaucracies that attempt to control activities and impose policy solutions from the top down (as was done after World War II). Instead, state institutions are trying to serve as better facilitators, coordinators, and integrators of information and action across a wide variety of actors and issues.

Networking may be difficult for government organizations, because they are organized as hierarchical bureaucracies, whereas NGOs and other nonstate actors may not be organized that way. State institutions' roles, missions, functions, procedures, authority, accountability, and chain of command are often more clearly demarcated than nonstate actors. NGOs often have flatter and looser organizations, and bureaucratic government organizations may find it difficult to determine "who's in charge here." When a bureaucratically organized institution attempts to coordinate and integrate information and action with a less hierarchically organized institution, they may "talk past each other." The bureaucratic organization wonders how anyone can function in such fluid chaos, without standardized ways of doing business; the non-bureaucratic organization wonders why the bureaucracy can't be more flexible to the nuances of the emerging situation. Differences in communication, culture, and organization make networking difficult, but not impossible. For example, the UN and the U.S. military have come a long way since initial relief operations in Somalia in 1992 in their relations with NGOs, even though they still have a long way to go.

BEYOND BUREAUCRACY?

These new types of collaborative foreign policy networks mirror ideas in organization studies about "postbureaucratic" organizations. These forms of organization stress integrative, interactive networks, based on ideas drawn from successful entrepreneurs and technologies.[32]

Often when government reformers talk of moving beyond bureaucracy and "reinventing government," what they really mean is cleaning up bureaucracy and making government more like a business: getting rid of excessive and unnecessary rules and layers of hierarchy, empowering the grassroots workers by giving them more discretion and incentives to make improvements, eliminating waste and inefficiency, and improving the bottom line.[33] Despite the grandiose language of a "paradigm shift,"[34] these reforms really do not demolish bureaucracy; instead they streamline and downsize overgrown and inefficient bureaucracy. For all the advantages of cost savings, this approach is limited in how far it can go, given the differences discussed earlier between businesses and governments.

But some of the current reforms break down or circumvent bureaucracy's formal, rule-bound structures based on clear demarcations of hierarchy and office (as described in the previous section). The National Infrastructure Protection Center, like the State Department's "Relief Net" which brings together government and private sector actors working on issues of complex humanitarian emergencies, share many characteristics of "postbureaucratic" institutionalized dialogue.

> In bureaucracies, consensus of a kind is created through acquiescence to authority, rules, or traditions. In the post-bureaucratic form it is created through institutionalized dialogue. Dialogue is defined by the use of influence rather than power: That is, people affect decisions based on their ability to persuade rather than their ability to command. The ability to persuade

is based on a number of factors, including knowledge of the issue, commitment to shared goals, and proven past effectiveness. It is not, however, based significantly [or solely] on official position . . . Influence depends initially on trust—on the belief by all members that others are seeking mutual benefit rather than maximizing personal gain . . . The major source of this kind of trust is interdependence: an understanding that the fortunes of all depend on combining the performances of all.[35]

These theorists do not believe bureaucracy is going away any time soon, and they have found no evidence of large organizations switching over entirely to post-bureaucratic forms. But they stress that alternative organizations are responding to rapid change in the external environment, and that even large bureaucratic organizations are using more integrative, active collaboration subsystems to deal with problems of interdependence and rapid change. The benefits to this type of structure are increased flexibility, increased information sharing regardless of rank or organizational affiliation, a greater emphasis on the job to be done than on bureaucratic rules or routines, and more fluid boundaries. These trends are facilitated by career patterns that no longer assume people will spend entire careers in one organization, and by information technologies that allow the building of "temporary networks. It is now possible for managers to put out a general message asking for help on a given project, or to collect a list of people who have knowledge and experience in the area: They can maintain contacts with people whom they never meet face to face . . . There is far more tolerance for outsiders coming in and for insiders going out."[36] This is also facilitated by the "growth of alliances and joint ventures among different firms" in recent years.

These institutional changes may help combat transsovereign problems. When the models of organization from business were large, cookie-cutter bureaucracies like IBM, and when the external threat was a stable, monolithic, universal, hegemonic Cold War threat, foreign policy organizations responded with large, bureaucratic, hierarchical structures that heavily emphasized stable routines, rules, and standard operating procedures. It makes sense now that business and technology offer models of diverse, collaborative, integrative networks, and external threats come from diffuse and decentralized networks such as terrorism and international crime, that the organizational response would include decentralized, interactive, coordinating networks.

OLD INSTITUTIONS LEARN NEW TRICKS

Why are existing institutions modified more frequently than new institutions are created? In part because, as Krasner observes, existing institutions, for all their flaws and baggage, have the decided advantage of availability. Rather than creating new foreign policy institutions from scratch, Western states are trying to teach Cold War institutions to do new tricks. Of course, many newly democratizing and liberalizing states are creating new foreign policy institutions, as they attempt to replace communist era institutions (secret police forces, etc.) with new, democratically accountable, bureaucratic organizations. Many are finding it difficult, however, to totally erase the vestiges and traditions of previous institutions, as expected by Krasner's theory of path dependency. Nevertheless, even the newly democratizing states are working to modify existing international foreign policy institutions, rather than lobbying to create entirely new institutions. Thus, new states did not want to disband NATO once the Cold War was over (and a key portion of NATO's founding purpose was obsolete); they wanted to join NATO.

NATO is a primary example of retrofitting old institutions to tackle new tasks. Many expected that the dissolution of the Soviet Union and the demise of the Warsaw Pact would end NATO, since NATO had been largely formed to combat the Soviet threat. Instead, the organization expanded.[37] In 1999, the Czech Republic, Hungary, and Poland formally entered NATO. The most contentious debates were not over whether NATO should disband or expand, but over how much to expand NATO; for example, should Romania or Slovakia also be allowed to join and how soon? The arguments in favor of expanding rather than disbanding NATO centered on the need for a cooperative security structure to stabilize a democratizing Europe.[38]

NATO forces undertook their first military action (outside of training exercises and war games) *not* fighting the Cold War or the Soviet empire, but responding to the bombing of a Sarajevo marketplace during the Bosnian war in March of 1994. Since then NATO troops have been used extensively to try to enforce peace accords in Bosnia and to bomb Kosovo. Like the previous institutions discussed, NATO is establishing collaborative and cooperative networks to help in its new tasks with a variety of actors: NGOs, IGOs, as well as various government agencies.

As NATO celebrates its fiftieth birthday, arguments continue about its future role. Though NATO was formed to fight the Cold War, some argue that its infrastructure provides unique capabilities that can now be turned toward transsovereign threats, such as the proliferation of weapons of mass destruction, and terrorism.[39] As German foreign minister Joschka Fischer put it, "NATO has never in the past imposed taboos on thinking. One of the alliance's special qualities has always been its ability to react flexibly to new situations. On the eve of the twenty-first century, we should ask ourselves if our instruments still match the changed security environment."[40]

Like NATO, the United Nations High Commission on Refugees (UNHCR) was created after World War II. Its mission was to help repatriate refugees, and it was thought that the organization would be temporary, that it would soon make itself obsolete by completing the relocation of that war's refugees. But with wars of colonial independence and the proxy battles of the Cold War, however, the UNHCR soon found itself ministering to the needs of permanent refugee populations displaced by conflicts in the Middle East, Vietnam, Cambodia, etc.[41]

By definition, refugees are people who have traveled outside their country of origin because of legitimate fears of political persecution at home. The UNHCR was not authorized to help displaced persons still within a war zone. With the end of the Cold War this changed. The UN secretary-general asked the UNHCR to assist the internally displaced within the war zone in Bosnia. This was done to try to prevent the Serbs from driving the non-Serbian populations away in their policy of ethnic cleansing, to aid a needy population who had not crossed an international border, and to thereby save the neighbors the cost of attending to large refugee flows. "For the first time, the UNHCR found itself coordinating relief not only for refugees and displaced persons, but also for the besieged population in the middle of a full-scale war. Moveover, the number of people requiring assistance skyrocketed."[42]

While the UNHCR did change to be able to assist refugees in the midst of post–Cold War conflicts, these changes are ad hoc, case-by-case, and contingent on the will of the UN General Assembly or secretary-general.

> Only in cases where the UN General Assembly or the UN secretary-general expand the UNHCR's mandate has the organization been able to aid the internally displaced or war affected populations. The expansion of the UNHCR's mandate applies exclusively to assistance, however. It is not possible for the organization to protect IDPs (internally displaced persons), or civilians trapped in war zones. Even more distressing, the delivery of assistance is dependent on the consent of the warring factions. Thus, UNHCR assistance to the internally displaced must rely on the goodwill of the groups who are forcing the displacement in the first place.[43]

Another example of an existing institution changing to deal with post–Cold War transsovereign threats is the U.S. Military's Cooperative Threat Reduction (CTR) program[44] to deal with the nuclear proliferation threat emerging from the break-up of the Soviet Union. As discussed in Chapter Three, the break-up of the Soviet Union unleashed an unprecedented threat of the proliferation of components of the former Soviet Union's (FSU) nuclear arsenal and infrastructure. Senators Sam Nunn and Richard Lugar championed the historic Nunn-Lugar legislation establishing the CTR program. The idea behind the program was that the U.S. government and the governments of the FSU states would cooperate to ensure the safe and swift destruction of nuclear weapons in accordance with the START treaties, and to safeguard, protect, control, and account for the nuclear materials, weapons, and scientists from the FSU's nuclear complex.

In practice, it was not easy to move from the legislative idea to changing bureaucratic and organizational practices. The Russian nuclear energy ministries MINATOM and GAN were deeply suspicious of the U.S. agencies they were assigned to work with (the Departments of Defense, Energy, and State), and the U.S. organizations were also skeptical of their Russian counterparts. These bureaucracies had just spent forty-five years armed and prepared to fight one another; their rivalries and hostilities would not disappear overnight with the stroke of a legislative pen. Initially there also were rivalries among U.S. bureaucracies for control of the program. DOD was tepid about its role because initially it received no additional Congressional funding outlays, meaning DOD was given the mandate without the means to implement the program. Funding CTR required raiding other DOD budgets and projects, which was unpopular and difficult to do. The program was also unpopular initially because it conflicted with many Pentagon employees' ideas of what DOD was supposed to do. If DOD's purpose historically was to fight the nation's wars, and to protect against the FSU armies, why were they now being asked to give the Russians military aid? The program was imposed by Congress without the support of President Bush, Secretary of Defense Dick Cheney, and Joint Chiefs of Staff Chairman Colin Powell.

CTR program implementation improved over time, however. As initial treaties and agreements were reached with FSU states, U.S. agencies could then step in and implement the programs. Organizational resistance broke down and the program began to achieve tremendous results when Congress allocated new funding for the projects; when roles and tasks were sorted out among Defense, State, and Energy; and when the Clinton administration came in with Pentagon officials firmly in favor of the program. Additionally, Secretary of Defense William Perry went to great lengths to reframe the program wholly within traditional defense department objectives. He called the novel program "defense by other means" and "preventive defense," stressing that every nuclear weapon CTR could safeguard or destroy was one less threat facing a U.S. soldier or citizen.[45] Under the new leadership and approach, DOD rallied behind the new program and tasks.

LESSONS LEARNED ABOUT INSTITUTIONAL CHANGE?

In each of these examples, a change in the external, international environment was not enough to produce institutional change. Most of these institutions took years to change to meet the changing circumstances. The Berlin Wall came down in 1989, the Soviet Union fell in 1991, war in Bosnia broke out in 1991, but NATO didn't change and intervene in Bosnia until 1994, which is also when CTR program implementation began in earnest. PDDs 62 and 63 were set down in 1998 and NATO expansion didn't occur until 1999. Institutional changes were not the direct or quick result of changes in the international environment, as rationalist theorists would expect.

Rationalist accounts also assume that state interests are stable and unproblematic, but in most of these cases, states were unsure of what they wanted. Determining interests was the product of fierce and contentious political battles among and within states, and that process was affected by existing institutional structures, as the reflectivists would stress. Ideas about the promotion of democratic cooperation were also key in many of these cases.

Sustained and sophisticated political leadership and pressure was able to overcome organizational inertia and bureaucratic intransigence. Sustained effort by Senator Jesse Helms was able to push UN downsizing and remove the autonomy of ACDA, USIA, and USAID. Activism by Anthony Lake was able to spearhead NATO expansion. Institutions resisted changes to their core missions and functions (as DOD initially gave CTR a lukewarm reception), but they embraced changes they saw as necessary to their survival, such as the UN's and the FBI's outreach to the private sector.

Drawing connections between an institution's new tasks and existing missions was the most successful way to produce organizational change, as when William Perry reframed CTR as "preventive defense," or when Anthony Lake and Madeleine Albright pressed NATO expansion as consistent with the traditional NATO goals of promoting a stable, free, and united Europe. Sometimes leaders go so far as to deny that the proposed changes really represent anything new. For example, Albright responded to criticisms about proposed NATO activities fighting terrorism or proliferation by saying, "I know that there are those who try to suggest that by assuming these new missions . . . we are somehow tinkering with the original intent of the North Atlantic Treaty. I've said it before; I will repeat it again today: this is hogwash . . . What we are doing is using the flexibility the Treaty always offered to adapt this Alliance to the realities of a new strategic environment and the challenges we must face together in the twenty-first century."[46]

Organizations where vertical or horizontal links are weak (in Krasner's terms), or without the backing of powerful interest groups (in Moe's terms) were less able to resist organizational changes. ACDA, USIA, and USAID had few powerful constituents. Their "customers" were primarily foreign governments and citizens, they provided few jobs or contracts in the United States, and they were largely headquartered in the District of Columbia, so they lacked even congressional representation to lobby on their behalf. They were sitting ducks for organizational change proposals. However, even organizations with strong vertical and horizontal links and strong constituent backing (such as DOD which spreads defense contracting dollars in every congressional district, and thus marshals considerable political support) will be subject to change when political leadership advocates for change, when internal leaders promote change, and when bureaucrats are motivated to change, as finally occurred in the CTR case.

The hardest part about changing organizations is changing beliefs about the world. One DOD official noted that the biggest obstacle to post–Cold War cooperation with Russia was the persistence of Cold War mindsets. "Cooperation with that chunk of land and capabilities was not a Bush administration priority. They were still skeptical, and treated it like the same old Soviet Union . . . The administration missed huge opportunities to engage the FSU, and the United States missed out on what could have been a longer honeymoon period with these states."[47] A career officer involved in the program, General William Burns, agreed. "We had to rid ourselves to some degree of Cold War mindsets and so did they [the Russians]. Then we had to pick up from basically a blank slate and devise a relationship so we could talk comfortably about nuclear weapons, something we could not talk comfortably about before."[48] In testimony before Congress explaining the slow start of the CTR program, DOD official Dr. Harold P. Smith, Jr., echoed the same theme, "arguing that mutual trust between the United States and former adversaries took time—much more than two years—to develop against a backdrop of fifty years of suspicion."[49]

This mindset is still evident now, years after the Soviet Union's collapse, according to a key Senate staffer. "The dynamic which seeks to attack Nunn-Lugar/CTR is not based in reality. It comes from people still caught up in a Cold Warrior ideology, who are completely lost when it comes to comprehending this kind of a program. They are still wondering, 'why are we helping *them*?'"[50] Thus, changes in organizational structures and operating procedures may be slow and incomplete unless attitudes can be changed as well.

CONCLUSIONS

Change is not easy, direct, or logical, and institutions created by democracies will not be efficient in the narrow economic sense. But these observations about the obstacles to change should not obscure the fact that change is occurring, even if it is hard-fought, long in coming, constrained by political parameters, and occurring unevenly in fits and starts.

In C. S. Lewis' classic story *Alice in Wonderland,* the white queen chastises Alice for an insufficient imagination, and tells her that expanding her imagination requires daily practice. "My dear, sometimes I think six impossible thoughts before breakfast."

Perhaps during the stability of the nearly fifty-year Cold War period, our imaginations atrophied. We didn't give our imaginations much practice, as indicated by an exchange in 1986 between then-director of the CIA Richard Gates and Senator Daniel Patrick Moynihan. The senator, a former professor, had noticed that all economic indicators from the Soviet Union seemed to be pointing to an end to the Soviet empire. No one in Washington agreed with Moynihan's analysis, as the Reagan administration and Congress were involved in unprecedented peacetime defense spending levels in order to combat the evil empire of the Soviet threat. Moynihan asked Gates in a Senate Intelligence Committee hearing what plans the agency was making for how to deal with a post-Soviet world.[51] Gates responded, ". . . my resources do not permit me the luxury of sort of just idly speculating on what a different kind of Soviet Union might look like."[52] He did not see the point of making plans for the impossible.

But today we find that the impossible has occurred and our thoughts have not caught up with it. Like Alice, we have not figured out how to think about the strange new world we have unexpectedly fallen into. Until we do, institutional change will likely be of the sort we have discussed here. Change will occur, but as Krasner suggests, it will be a tinkering with existing structures rather than creation of new structures from scratch as occurred after World War II. Of all the obstacles to organizational change, the biggest obstacle appears to be ourselves, and our limited ways of thinking about the changed world in which we find ourselves.

But if Larson is correct that we learn by doing and we change our beliefs about the world as a result of our actions in the world (not prior to our actions), then perhaps we will see greater conceptual change as a result of initial experiences in the post–Cold War environment. Perhaps these changed beliefs will then lead to more profound organizational change in the years to come.

At least this is how Dean Acheson described the way he and other members of the Truman administration changed beliefs and then institutions to fight the Cold War. He describes a period of smoke and confusion as to the nature of the true situation, followed by a period of probing and interaction with the new environment. As a result of those ad hoc actions, decisionmakers reevaluated their assumptions about the world, revised their ways of thinking about the world, and then revised or created new institutions to match their new ideas.

Eventually, important new institutions came out of the process. A similar period of institutional dynamism might yet emerge if initial experiences with the post–Cold War environment produce large-scale conceptual change. New organizations might then be built to enact new ideas. So far our ideas about diffuse computer networks and decentralized capitalist business networks are affecting our institutions, as we attempt to make our institutions more like the models we see in business and technology and as we set up strategic networks of communication, cooperation, and coordination among a wide variety of public and private actors. That trend will likely continue. An indicator that we are in store for more fundamental institutional change will be if leaders ever call this historical period something other than its present default name—the post–Cold War era. If that happens, buckle your seatbelts; we'll be in for a ride.

Notes

1. This chapter is drawn from Maryann K. Cusimano, *Unplugging the Cold War Machine: Rethinking U.S. Foreign Policy Institutions* (Thousand Oaks, Calif.: Sage Publications, forthcoming).
2. Jack Knight, *Institutions and Social Conflict* (Cambridge: Cambridge University Press, 1996), 2.
3. Robert Keohane, "International Institutions: Two Approaches," *International Studies Quarterly* 32 (1988): 379–396; Steven Weber, "Institutions and Change," in *New Thinking in International Relations Theory,* ed. Michael W. Doyle and G. John Ikenberry (Boulder, Colo.: Westview Press, 1997), 229–265; Stephen Krasner, "Sovereignty: An Institutional Perspective," *Comparative Political Studies* 21 (April 1988): 66–94.
4. Keohane, "International Institutions: Two Approaches," 386–387.
5. Weber, "Institutions and Change," 235.
6. Martha Finnemore, *National Interests in International Society* (Ithaca, N.Y.: Cornell University Press, 1996).
7. Krasner, "Sovereignty: An Institutional Perspective," 83.
8. Ibid., 66.
9. Ibid., 79.
10. Ibid., 80.
11. Keohane, "International Institutions: Two Approaches," 379–396; Weber, "Institutions and Change," 229–265; Krasner, "Sovereignty: An Institutional Perspective" 66–94.
12. Graham Allison and Philip Zelikow, *The Essence of Decision: Explaining the Cuban Missile Crisis* (New York: Addison, Wesley, Longman, 1999); I. M. Destler, *Presidents, Bureaucrats, and Foreign Policy* (Princeton: Princeton University Press, 1972); Francis Rourke, *Bureaucracy and Foreign Policy* (Baltimore: Johns Hopkins University Press, 1974); Morton Halperin, *Bureaucratic Politics and Foreign Policy* (Washington, D.C.: Brookings Institution), 1974.
13. A cottage industry has practically developed in critiquing this aspect of bureaucratic theory. But convincing as these studies are that issue positions are not determined by organizational membership alone, it is important to note that Allison never said this was the only determinant of an actor's position, but was one factor among many. Also, many of these studies mistakenly conclude when they see a lack of conflict among bureaucratic actors that therefore bureaucratic and organizational dynamics were not involved. If agencies often pursue strategic alliances, and especially if actors seek to reduce uncertainty and be sure in advance of a meeting that they will not be blind-sided, then a lack of conflict along agency lines at key meetings might not be evidence that bureaucratic politics theory has been disproved, but the phenomenon might actually be explicable according to the theory. Thus, the problem for Allison's theory is not that it has been proved wrong by numerous critical studies, but that it is too poorly specified to be proved wrong or right. Evidence of conflict among agencies or its absence can both be interpreted in light of the theory.
14. Charles Heckscher, "Defining the Post-Bureaucratic Type," *The Post-Bureaucratic Organization* (Thousand Oaks, Calif.: Sage Publications, 1994), 27.
15. Terry Moe, "The Politics of Bureaucratic Structure," in *Can the Government Govern?,* eds. John E. Chubb and Paul E. Peterson, (Washington, D.C.: Brookings Institution, 1989), 285.
16. Ibid.
17. Ibid., 329.

18. Deborah Larson, *The Origins of Containment: A Psychological Explanation* (Princeton, NJ: Princeton University Press, 1985), 341.
19. Ibid., 326.
20. Ibid., 349.
21. Vice President Al Gore, *U.S. Department of State Dispatch,* September 12, 1994, 597–598.
22. This has been a problem for the Bush and Clinton administrations; they would like to sell Saddam Hussein as the next Hitler, but while he is clearly a menace in his neighborhood, he has no *Mein Kampf.*
23. Peter D. Feaver and Kurt M. Campbell, "Rethinking Key West: Service Roles and Missions After the Cold War," in *The American Defense Annual 1993,* ed. Joseph Kruzel (New York: Lexington Books), 155–173.
24. Joshua Rosenbloom, *The CIA to 1961* (Harvard University, 1983); Bradley F. Smith, *The Shadow Warriors: O.S.S. and the Origins of the C.I.A.* (New York: Basic Books, 1983); James Sherr, "Cultures of Spying," *The National Interest* (Winter 1994/1995): 56–62.
25. John Prados, *Keepers of the Keys: A History of the National Security Council from Truman to Bush* (New York: William Morrow and Company, 1991).
26. Shawn Parry-Giles, "The Eisenhower Administration's Conceptualization of the USIA: The Development of Overt and Covert Propaganda Strategies," *Presidential Studies Quarterly* (Spring 1994): 263–276; United States Information Agency, *Telling America's Story to the World* (Washington, D.C.: Office of Public Liason, January 1993); Fitzhugh Green, *American Propaganda Abroad* (New York: Hippocrene Books, 1988).
27. Gary Posz, Bruce Janigian, and Jong Jun, "Redesigning U.S. Foreign Aid," *SAIS Review* (Fall 1994): 159–169; John W. Sewell, "Foreign Aid for a New World Order," in *U.S. Foreign Policy After the Cold War,* ed. Brad Roberts (Cambridge, Mass.: MIT Press, 1992), 181–191; Ian J. Bickerton, "Foreign Aid," in *American Foreign Policy: Studies of the Principal Movements and Ideas,* Vol. II, ed. Alexander DeConde (New York: Scribner's, 1978), 372–379.
28. Duncan L. Clarke, *The Politics of Arms Control* (New York: The Free Press, 1979); Bernard J. Firestone, *The Quest for Nuclear Stability* (Westport, Conn.: Greenhouse Press, 1986).
29. United Nations, "The UN and Business: A Global Partnership," October 29, 1998, 2.
30. Ibid.
31. Federal Bureau of Investigations, "NIPC Outreach," January 4, 1999, 1.
32. Charles Heckscher and Anne Donnellon, eds., *The Post Bureaucratic Organization: New Perspectives on Organizational Change* (Thousand Oaks, Calif.: Sage Publications, 1994); also there is a growing literature in sociology developing on diffuse networks—see Mary Durfee and Paul Lopes, eds., "Networks of Novelty: The Diffusion of Ideas and Things," *The Annals* (Philadelphia, PA.: American Academy of Political and Social Sciences, forthcoming November 1999).
33. Vice President Al Gore, *Common Sense Government: Works Better and Costs Less* (New York: Random House, 1995); Vice President Al Gore, "Report on the National Performance Review," White House press releases on July 14, 1994, September 14, 1994, October 13, 1994, December 5, 1994, and January 26, 1995; also see White House Documents, Office of the Press Secretary, "Gore Announces Initial Restructuring of Foreign Affairs Agencies," January 27, 1995; Donald F. Kettl, *Reinventing Government? Appraising the National Performance Review* (Washington, D.C.: Brookings Institution, August 19, 1994); Donald F. Kettl and John J. Dilulio, Jr., *Cutting Government* (Washington, D.C.: Brookings Institution, May 22, 1995); Ronald C. Moe, "The 'Reinventing

Government' Exercise: Misinterpreting the Problem, Misjudging the Consequences," *Public Administration Review* 54 (March/April 1994): 111–122; Gerald E. Caiden, "Administrative Reform—American Style," *Public Administration Review* 54 (March/April 1994): 123–128.

34. James P. Pinkerton, *What Comes Next: The End of Big Government and the New Paradigm Ahead* (New York: Hyperion, 1995).

35. Heckscher, "Defining the Post-Bureaucratic Type," 25.

36. Ibid., 27.

37. James M. Goldgeier, "NATO Expansion: The Anatomy of a Decision," *The Washington Quarterly* 21 (Winter 1998): 85–102; James M. Goldgeier, "U.S. Security Policy Toward the New Europe: How the Decision to Expand NATO Was Made" (paper delivered at the 1997 APSA annual meeting, Washington, D.C., August 28–31, 1997).

38. Secretary of State Madeleine K. Albright, "Statement on NATO Enlargement before the Senate Foreign Relations Committee," Washington, D.C., February 24, 1998; Secretary of State Madeleine K. Albright, "Statement before the House International Relations Committee," Office of the Spokesman, U.S. Department of State, Washington, D.C., February 12, 1998.

39. Secretary of State Madeleine K. Albright, "Statement to the North Atlantic Council," Brussels, Belgium, December 8, 1998; Secretary of State Madeleine K. Albright, "Press Conference at NATO Headquarters," Brussels, Belgium, December 8, 1998; William Drozdiak, "Albright Urges NATO to Take Broader Role," *Washington Post,* December 9, 1998, A1.

40. Joschka Fischer quoted in William Drozdiak, "Albright Urges NATO to Take Broader Role," A1.

41. Gil Loescher, *Beyond Charity: International Cooperation and the Global Refugee Crisis* (Oxford: Oxford University Press, 1993).

42. Jesse Kay Jolene, *Humanitarian Relief in the Midst of Conflict: The UN High Commissioner for Refugees in the Former Yugoslavia* (Washington, D.C.: Institute for the Study of Diplomacy Publications, Georgetown University Press, 1996), 1.

43. Ibid., 7.

44. Maryann K. Cusimano, "Bureaucratic Politics After the Cold War: The Cooperative Threat Reduction Program" (paper prepared for 1997 ISA meeting, March 19–23, 1997).

45. William Perry, as quoted in "U.S. - Perry Presents New Military Philosophy," *Army Times,* May 27, 1996.

46. Albright, "Statement to the North Atlantic Council"; Albright, "Press Conference at NATO Headquarters"; Drozdiak, "Albright Urges NATO to Take Broader Role," A1.

47. Interview with DOD official March 1997, quoted in Cusimano, "Bureaucratic Politics After the Cold War: The Cooperative Threat Reduction Program."

48. General William Burns, interview with Jack Mendelsohn and Dunbar Lockwood, *Arms Control Today,* September 1993, 3.

49. Dr. Harold P. Smith, Jr.'s testimony, as recounted by Jason D. Ellis, in "Cooperative Threat Reduction: Complex Decisionmaking and the Politics of Denuclearization" (doctoral diss., School of International Service, American University, August 1997), 226.

50. Interview with author, U.S. Senate, Washington D.C., August 7, 1997.

51. Daniel Patrick Moynihan, "Our Stupid but Permanent CIA: What Are We Going to Do About Reforming the Agency? Nothing," *Washington Post,* July 24, 1994, C3.

52. Richard Gates, as quoted in David M. Kennedy, *Sunshine and Shadow: The CIA and the Soviet Economy* (Cambridge, Mass.: Harvard University, 1991, case program), 18.

Chapter Twelve

Sovereignty's Future

The Ship of Theseus and Other Conclusions

Maryann K. Cusimano

UNINTENDED CONSEQUENCES

Much of this book has been about the impact of unintended consequences. States worked to build international markets, to create the political, economic, and technological infrastructure that made the global marketplace possible. States courted foreign direct investment, and technological advancement. They pursued these policies to increase economic development and prosperity, perhaps believing that wealthy states are strong states. Western states sought to promote open societies, believing that democratic states are more stable trade partners and are less likely to go to war with other democracies. States did not intend, however, to create the infrastructure for transsovereign problems to thrive. State governments did not realize that the new actors and dynamics created by the pursuit of open economy, society, and technology policies would drain autonomy, choice, and freedom of action away from states. Sovereignty is based on territory, yet the new economy and new actors' prosperity does not derive from territory, making them less beholden to states. How then can these new dynamics and actors be managed within a system of sovereign states?

THE POLICY PRESCRIPTIONS

Each of the authors in the preceding chapters offered their own set of policy prescriptions for dealing with transsovereign problems. Their suggestions can be divided into state-centric and nonstate-centric responses.

Steve Flynn argues that the war on drugs is going badly because our drug control regime rests almost entirely on the coercive arm of the state. It is a mistake to look to state law enforcement bodies to stop drug trafficking, because most of the world's illicit drug supply is cultivated within states that are weak or failing, and thus lack effective law enforcement bodies. Even in strong states, drug trade and consumption take place in the economic and social realms in which liberal democratic states have the least ability to intercede. Police cannot randomly break into people's homes or bedrooms to oust drug users; this would be an infringement of civil liberties. Likewise, interdiction efforts run directly counter to legal, market forces, making it increasingly difficult to find the needle of contraband from the growing haystack of legal goods, services, and people that now wash across state borders as a result of economic liberalization and privatization.

To turn around the war on drugs, Flynn argues, we must turn to the primary beneficiaries of open societies, open economies, and open technologies to redress the unintended consequences of globalization. Since states have a declining presence in the economic and social spheres where the drug trade thrives, ultimately nongovernmental organizations (NGOs), businesses, and community activists are best positioned to combat drug supply and demand. Nonstate actors must be enlisted to temper the forces that motivate and facilitate drug-related activities. This should be done, however, within an integrative context. For example, drug control programs in developing states should be part of overall economic development programs, to get at the root cause of the burgeoning drug trade in poor regions. Legal reform and standardization of drug codes internationally should be done in the context of promoting and strengthening democratic institutions.

The creation of Regional Drug Crime (RDC) Task Forces could help to create a more comprehensive response, integrating the activities of nonstate actors with those of state governments. These RDCs could spur movement toward a regional investment code to establish a common global data base on criminals and their activities, to work with the private sector to deter smuggling, and to improve cultural understanding and linguistic abilities in order to improve transsovereign law enforcement. Thus, while Flynn advocates increased coordination among state agencies involved in the war on drugs, his proposals are primarily aimed at the nonstate sector.

Pirages and Runci agree with Flynn that state-centric responses are increasingly limited. Emerging health threats require accurate surveillance, reporting, and response at both the national and international levels, but states may underreport disease. Additionally, developed states have been cutting the resources dispersed to this problem, while developing states are poorly equipped to respond to the threat. Instead, the authors suggest that a network of clinics, hospitals, and laboratories could fill the necessary tracking and response functions because "technology has placed real power in the hands of nongovernmental groups, enabling them to act swiftly to bridge gaps in existing government programs and political will." Since the state has withdrawn from some of its historic regulatory and oversight roles, private or market-based approaches relying on nonstate actors appear more attractive and effective, and circumvent government involvement and limitations.

Cusimano, Hensman, and Rodrigues echo the increased importance of the private sector in combating transsovereign problems and generally agree that nonstate actors can be powerful allies in battling transsovereign problems. However, because nonstate actors may be the source of transsovereign problems, such as multinational corporations (MNCs) with poor environmental records, it is not a straightforward case of relying on nonstate actors to perform in sectors where state power is declining. As states "contract out" to MNCs and NGOs, accountability may be lost in ways that adversely impact transsovereign problems.

Hal Kane agrees with Flynn about the futility of reactive policies by states, such as increased border controls and interdiction. Fundamental solutions to the refugee problem are proactive policies that will enable people to avoid flight in the first place. Spending on sanitation, public health, family planning technologies and education, preventive medicine, maintaining stable soils and waters for farming, and literacy can profoundly stabilize and mitigate push-and-pull factors. He suggests a mixture of nongovernmental and government spending to attack the underlying causes of economic and political instability that cause refugees to flee. While he believes that military responses to humanitarian crises "can make a huge difference in protecting and aiding refugees," such military action can never be a substitute for more fundamental and long-range solutions, and may actually drain resources away from more long-term and comprehensive preventive measures. He recommends developmental economic and social initiatives not normally considered relevant to refugees over ad hoc, reactive, crisis-driven state policies.

Similarly, David Wirth argues for adopting a more comprehensive approach to environmental concerns and turning to international institutions since "power has ebbed away from national governments." Wirth argues against compartmentalizing environmental policy in a zero-sum manner so that environmental protection is seen as coming at the expense of other important policy concerns (trade, development, etc.). Instead he points to efforts by the Conference on Security and Cooperation in Europe and its successor the Organization for Security and Cooperation in Europe (OSCE) to focus on overall stability, of which sustainable development, sustainable trade, and environmental protection are interwoven components. International organizations must integrate environmental concerns into their work across the gamut of specialized agencies such as the World Bank and World Trade Organization, rather than simply developing more environmental programs and bodies which are seen as separate from and sometimes opposed to the work of states and intergovernmental organizations (IGOs).

Tafe agrees that IGOs provide a logical forum for addressing transsovereign problems, but notes that until states properly fund IGOs, the effectiveness of IGOs will be restricted. Thus, where Wirth sees states losing power to IGOs, Tafe notes that states still restrict IGOs' activities and performance by restricting resources available to IGOs.

In contrast, James Ford and Rensselaer Lee argue for state-centric responses to nuclear smuggling, since IGOs and NGOs are limited in what assistance they can bring to bear on this problem. Increased private sector involvement in nuclear nonproliferation could conceivably have the unintended effect of fostering proliferation, by allowing nonnuclear powers in NGOs and IGOs access to nuclear information they otherwise would not have. Therefore, they suggest bilateral efforts by existing nuclear powers to stem the threat from the former Soviet Union. In another state-centric policy proposal, they advocate strengthening and stabilizing the Russian law enforcement and security communities to be able to more effectively interdict attempted smuggling. Even they believe, however, that efforts must be broadened from the current emphasis on containing thefts at nuclear facilities. The basic social and economic motivations underlying the nuclear trade must be better addressed, or else attempts at strengthening state institutions will be overcome by market dynamics that the state cannot easily control.

David E. Long sees international terrorism as requiring increased law enforcement efforts by states and international bodies. If terrorism could be depoliticized and treated predominantly as a criminal justice issue and less as a political issue (since terrorists conduct crimes such as murder, fraud, sabotage, theft, destruction of property, etc.), multinational cooperation and consensus might be improved.

Roy Godson and Phil Williams are concerned with how to increase law enforcement efforts against international crime. Most of their prescriptions focus on state-centric responses, such as increasing police training, strengthening state institutions, routing out corruption among state agents, increasing information and intelligence sharing among states, harmonizing legal and regulatory regimes so they are more standard and interoperable across state boundaries, generating new anticrime international conventions and norms, and strengthening international institutions. While Godson and Williams do not believe that the private sector can "solve" the international crime problem alone, they do believe private sector responses can aid and supplement state-centric responses. They advocate a comprehensive approach that includes the private sector in areas such as civic education, information sharing, development of international legal and regulatory norms, and increasing transparency.

The state-centric approach to transsovereign problems suggests that states strengthen law and order institutions and their control over borders, markets, and illegal activities. Open societies, economies, and technologies make it more difficult to protect against the flow of unwanted people, goods, or ideas at a time when overall movement across state borders is easier than ever before. But these state-centric policy responses emphasize that states should reexert control over borders, and establish better procedures for tracking and interdiction of unwanted people, goods, or ideas, by using new technologies, increasing state-to-state cooperation, and enlisting nonstate actors in service of the goals of the state regarding transsovereign problems. In essence, they are arguing that the same forces which facilitate transsovereign problems and undermine sovereignty (open technologies, economies, and societies) can be harnessed to fight transsovereign problems.

The nonstate-centric policy approach emphasizes the limitations of trying to work through the state for help in reining in activities that largely fall in the social and economic sectors, where the arms of liberal, capitalist states reach the least. Therefore, this approach emphasizes developing new responses and infrastructure that utilize nonstate actors such as NGOs and MNCs.

Many of the authors advocate a mixed response, using both state-centric and nonstate-centric prongs of attack to combat transsovereign problems. For example, Flynn talks about increasing the effectiveness of law and order institutions, especially in states transitioning to democracy and liberal economies, and simultaneously advocates a focus on nonstate actors and the social and economic spheres. While at first glance such a scattershot response might seem analytically and practically messy, a grab bag exercise in "everything-but-the-kitchen-sink" policy making, there is an underlying theoretical rationale that may justify the mixed response that most of the authors advocate.

Underlying these differences over responses to transsovereign problems are implicit assumptions about the future of the sovereign state. Is the sovereign state retreating, its power becoming more diffuse in a globalized economy? Susan Strange argues that power is moving sideways from states to markets, as states abdicate more functions either to nonstate actors or vacate certain functions altogether.[1] There is some evidence from the preceding chapters in favor of this view. Kane, Pirages, and Runci discuss how nonstate actors are increasingly assuming duties regarding refugees and disease that states used to fulfill. Wirth noted the importance of NGOs in international environmental negotiations. Cusimano, Hensman, and Rodrigues note that nonstate actors are increasingly taking on functions which used to be performed by states, even in the arms control arena. Flynn, Ford, and Lee argue that market dynamics in drug and nuclear smuggling are outstripping the state's power to respond. Additionally, debt-for-nature swaps in the environmental realm shows support for Strange's claims that states are losing their independent ability to chart economic development policies. IGOs, NGOs, and MNCs increasingly restrain the state's autonomy in choosing economic development policies. The debt-for-nature swaps example also supports Rosecrance's idea of the declining importance of territory relative to the rising importance of market forces.[2] If states are losing power to nonstate actors and market dynamics, then responses to transsovereign problems should be aimed at nonstate actors and market forces.

Other authors, such as Stephen Krasner[3] and Hendrik Spruyt[4] argue that the sovereign state is still the fundamental unit in the international system. While it is being challenged, sovereignty took centuries to develop and will not disappear in a few decades, and there are no well-developed alternative organizing units ready to replace sovereign states. The preceding chapters offer some evidence to support this view. Long argues that terrorists are primarily state "wannabes," fighting for a place in the state system, not trying to overthrow it. The methods terrorists use may undermine sovereignty, and the open society, open economy, and open technology forces that facilitate terrorism may make unilateral state responses more difficult. However, terrorism highlights that the state is still important enough to be worth fighting for. Likewise, Ford and Lee believe that states created nuclear weapons, and only state actions can effectively contain nuclear smuggling, and Godson and Williams believe that state responses will form the primary front against organized crime. If this is the case and state actors still reign supreme, then efforts to fight transsovereign problems should still be aimed at states and strengthening state institutions or perhaps at developing more cooperative ventures among states.

But there may be a third way. If sovereignty is denigrated but not dead, fighting transsovereign problems may necessitate a multipronged approach, in which a wide spectrum of policy responses are undertaken and coordinated, aimed at both state and nonstate sectors. If we are in a period of transition, or what James Rosenau terms turbulence,[5] in which a changed economic system has created new actors and dissipated the power of states in crucial economic and social sectors, but in which state actors are still important (for example, in nuclear security sectors), then a wide scatter approach is not the result of analytical "adhocary," but necessity. Just as new interstate highways are often built alongside old, existing two lane highways, new networks using new actors must be built at the same time that the old state actors are still functioning.

If a wide-angle policy approach is to be pursued, coordination, communication, and cooperation among various policy responses and players becomes key. It is also problematic because existing institutional structures and bureaucratic dynamics can make coordination, communication, cooperation, prioritization, and accountability difficult to achieve in practice, as discussed in Chapter 11.

Pursuing a multipronged approach also necessitates vigilance for threshold effects and unintended consequences. For example, policy responses may need a certain level of funding for a protracted period of time before a program can yield results. But if policy responses are split over a variety of state and nonstate venues, resources may be diluted or a plan of attack may be pursued for too short a period, never reaching the threshold necessary for effective action. Likewise, unintended consequences are not unique to a multipronged approach, but since action must be coordinated among a wider variety of players, it may be more difficult to anticipate the full ramifications of a wider array of actions. For example, combating organized crime or drug trafficking in one sector or one region may merely drive it into another area. Funneling attention and funding to nonstate actors and sectors could further undermine state actors and sectors. As new highways are built, sometimes the old roadways fall into disuse. Continued monitoring and attention to coordination, prioritization, and accountability are necessary in undertaking a multipronged response to transsovereign issues.

DOES SOVEREIGNTY STILL REIGN?

If state-centric responses are still necessary, along with other approaches, in dealing with transsovereign problems, does this mean that Krasner and Spruyt are right? Is there no competitor to the sovereign state out there right now, so sovereignty still reigns by default? Not exactly, because sovereignty is changing in significant ways. Vertical and horizontal linkages may still be anchoring sovereignty in place, but they are each breaking down in fundamental ways. The anchor is becoming dislodged.

It is instructive to remember Hendrik Spruyt's story of how fundamental change came about the last time, ushering in the sovereign state: the economy changed; new elites were created who benefitted from the new economic system and needed a new form of political organization to better accommodate them and their economic practices; ideas changed; new organizational forms emerged and competed, and after centuries of flux the sovereign state eventually won out.

There are a number of parallels today. The economy has changed. The new economic system is based on information, technology, and services, which is less dependent on the control of territory. The means of production, capital, and labor are mobile, not fixed. Players who make use of modern information, communication, transportation, and financial technologies reap the benefits of increasingly open borders and economies. Political systems that make room for the new economic system reap the profit in foreign direct investment, and so regime types as distinct as the Chinese communist system, the Australian parliamentary system, and the Iranian theocracy are all simultaneously undertaking reforms to make themselves more attractive to investors' capital and technology flows.

New elites are emerging who profit from the new economic system. Typified by George Soros, Bill Gates, and Ted Turner, these business investors increasingly follow no flag. They are passionate about expanding technologies and markets, and they are frustrated by what they see as anachronistic state barriers to investment and trade flows. The international business information classes attend the same schools, fly the same airlines, vacation at the same resorts, eat at the same restaurants, and watch the same movies and television shows. Independent of national identities, these elites mobilize to try to make states facilitate market dynamics. Political scientist Samuel Huntington calls it the "Davos culture,"[6] after the annual World Economic Summit that meets in that Swiss luxury resort. Sociologist Peter Berger calls it the "yuppie internationale,"[7] typified by the scene in a Buddhist temple in Hong Kong of "a middle aged man wearing a dark business suit over stocking feet. He was burning incense and at the same time talking on his cellular phone."[8] He believes these commonalities in culture have made peace talks in South Africa, Northern Ireland, and the Middle East go more smoothly. "Whether one is edified by this spectacle or not, it may be that commonalities in taste make it easier to find common ground politically."[9] Can it be that leaders who all shop at the Gap and Bennetton and eat at McDonald's find political antagonisms quaint and unnecessary? Even though clearly there are many economically underpriviledged around the world who do not partake of this lifestyle, Berger argues that the values of this new elite percolate into the rest of society as people mimic the behavior of the elites and as they strive to better their economic situations to one day rise into the wealthier classes.

Ideas are changing (including ideas of authority, identity, and organization), facilitated by the new information technologies and changes in the economy. Never before in human history have we been able to spread ideas so quickly and widely. Modern communication technologies allow an increasingly wide swath of the planet to be tuned in to the same advertisements, the same television shows, and thereby, to some of the same ideas about consumerism and personal freedoms. Identity is becoming less tied to territory. If identity and authority do not stem from geography, what is our new church, our new religion? In the Middle Ages identity came from Christendom, the church, while authority stemmed from spiritual connections. In the modern era identity was tied up with the nation-state; authority corresponded with geography.

Now authority and identity are increasingly contested. As Strange puts it, "If indeed we have now, not a system of global governance by any stretch of the imagination, but rather a ramshackle assembly of conflicting sources of authority . . . Where do allegiance, loyalty, identity lie? Not always in the same direction."[10] She believes we now have Pinocchio's problem: the strings of state control, authority, and identity have been cut, but no new strings have been fastened. States no longer are the supreme recipient of individual loyalties, especially as states no longer fulfill basic services and functions, and other actors step into the gap. Firms, professions, families, social movements have all significantly challenged the state's territorial and security-based claim to individual loyalty. We are left to choose among competing sources of allegiance, authority and identity, with no strings to bind us like puppets to one source of authority, and with more freedom to let our conscience be our guide.

Certainly the new economy would like identity to be formed around consumer products—you are what you wear, what you consume. Advertisers spend billions to imprint brand loyalty at an early age, and all the advertising of Planet Reebok, I'd-like-to-buy-the-world-a-Coke, and Microsoft's One World Internet Explorer icon share a common theme, that identity stems not from national borders but from consumer products. Identity is therefore just as mobile as the economy; you are not born with it, you can buy it. Alternatively, authors such as Susan Strange and James Rosenau, see identity as increasingly flowing from professions and firms—you are what you do, and your commitment is to your profession rather than a specific nation-state. Rosecrance also supports this view, as he encourages people to pursue their best economic futures internationally, to follow the jobs not a particular flag.

As Rosecrance describes it, "Today and for the foreseeable future, the only international civilization worthy of the name is the governing economic culture of the world market."[11] Benjamin Barber refers to this popular, consumer market culture as "McWorld."[12] As market values permeate various cultures, certain ideas emerge as prized: the value of change, mobility, flexibility, adaptability, speed, and information. As capitalism becomes our creed, with technology as our guide, distinct national and religious cultures are becoming permeated with common market values.

Ideas of organization are also changing, and are based on models from the marketplace and technology: the computer, the Internet, and the market are diffuse, decentralized, loosely connected networks with a few central organizing parameters but strong ties to the activities of individual entrepreneurs. As discussed in Chapter 11, foreign policy organizations are in some instances going beyond bureaucracy, creating flexible, innovative, coordinating networks among public and private sector actors, with an emphasis on integrating information, persuasion, and interdependence, rather than on formal, top-down, hierarchical controls.

For example, even in the arena of U.S. nuclear weapons, privatization efforts are under way. The Energy Enrichment Corporation of Bethesda, Maryland, is a federally owned corporation responsible for enriching uranium to the highly concentrated level needed in nuclear warheads. With the end of the Cold War, enriched uranium is no longer in demand since no new nuclear weapons are being built. Instead, the disintegration of the Soviet Union, and the dismantling of nuclear weapons in accord with the INF and START treaties, has increased concerns over the glut of bomb-grade material now stockpiled in the United States and former Soviet Union.

Since 1992, the Enrichment Corporation has been charged with reversing the process; instead of enriching uranium to make it bomb-grade, they have been charged with diluting bomb-grade uranium to make it suitable for use in civilian nuclear power reactors. In an effort to stop the alarming post–Cold War smuggling of nuclear materials from the former Soviet Union into the international nuclear black market, the U.S. government struck a creative deal with Russia. The Bush administration began, and the Clinton administration concluded, an agreement in which Russia would sell five hundred metric tons of bomb-grade uranium to the United States over the next twenty years, in exchange for $12 billion in desperately needed hard currency. [13]

The agreement was expected to stem the threat of the proliferation of fissile materials to nuclear rogues or terrorists; reduce the risks of nuclear accidents and theft in the impoverished Russian nuclear complex; help strengthen disarmament efforts; and aid Russia's attempts to create a stable, free-market economy. To top it all off, it was hoped that all these benefits would cost U.S. taxpayers almost nothing: The Enrichment Corporation would buy the uranium from Russia, recycle it to civilian grade, and then recoup their expenses through the sale of the civilian reactor fuel to nuclear power plants.

While this gem of a nuclear agreement was good for the U.S. government at almost any price, the per unit fuel price was a crucial variable for the Enrichment Corporation's profits.[14] Eager to ensure an attractive bottom line as the company entered the market in 1996, the Enrichment Corporation's profit concerns nearly derailed the agreement. While top level negotiations between Vice President Gore and Russian Prime Minister Chernomyrdrin resuscitated the agreement,[15] the episode points out some of the difficulties inherent in privatizing the foreign policy machinery. As Energy Enrichment Corporation President Timbers said, "I don't conduct national security here. I actually run a business."

Creative public-private partnerships are definitely the wave of the future in solving transsovereign problems, especially because these issues often manifest themselves in the areas where the arm of the state reaches least. Rather than trying to become draconian, "big brother" states (which would conflict with open society, open economy, open technology goals) it makes sense for governments to look toward civil society for help in combating transsovereign problems. If drug traffickers and international criminals develop flexible, strategic networks, it seems prudent that states respond in kind. But states must be aware of the costs of contracting out. In privatizing, not only do governments lose some control over policy, but additionally, private entities may present obstacles to the government's agenda as profit motives conflict with important policy goals.[16] Although privatization and moving beyond bureaucracy are popular buzzwords in today's budget-conscious political climate,[17] changes in state architecture have consequences for how we think about political authority, identity, and organization.

Perhaps, as in Spruyt's analysis of the late Middle Ages, ideas drawn from the new economic system are helping to shape new ideas of political organization. A resurgence of IGOs simultaneous with an increased attention to local governance may not seem at all strange to a civilization used to surfing the Net, using a system that is simultaneously globally connected but only as good as your local link.

Rosenau believes that as individuals become more analytically skillful, that the nature of authority is shifting. People no longer uncritically accept traditional criteria of state authority based on historical, legal, or customary claims of legitimacy. Instead, authority and legitimacy are increasingly based upon performance criteria, in that "the readiness of individuals to comply with governing directives (are) very much a function of their assessment of the performances of the authorities."[18] Kane's description of the huge increase in refugees and migrants seems to give credence to Rosenau's claim. People are increasingly voting with their feet, offering allegiance and desire to live in a particular area not based on state loyalty, nationalism, ethnic, religious, language, cultural, or traditional bonds, but rather based on personal standard of living, on performance based loyalty. Thus, while scholars disagree about the sources of identity and authority in the emerging era, they agree that these ideas are changing.

Finally, Spruyt acknowledges that new forms of political organization are beginning to emerge, as evidenced by the European Union and the increasing roles and profile of IGOs. Thus, even if, as Spruyt maintains, the sovereign state is still supreme, three out of four of his indicators of fundamental change are with us: change in economy, elites, and ideas are in evidence, and while no new form of political organization has unseated the sovereign state, new forms are beginning to emerge around the sovereign state that are chipping away at functions previously performed by the state and changing the role of the state.

To put it in Krasner's terms, the vertical linkages that maintain sovereignty—identification with citizenship, loyalty, and socialization to the nation-state—are breaking down, in favor of new forms of identity and socialization unleashed by market dynamics that are loyal to no particular flag or territory. Horizontal linkages are also breaking down, as elites find political organization along territorial lines impedes the market flow of goods, labor, services, technology, information, and investment across state borders.

GOING GLOBAL VERSUS GOING LOCAL

Are new forms of political organization emerging to accompany these changes? Many commentators have noted the irony that the globalizing forces of open markets, open technologies, and open societies are spreading and deepening at the same time as virulent forms of nationalism are evident in internal wars. There are a number of reasons why this is not surprising. First of all, scholars on nationalism note that ties to ethnic or national groups increase under threat.[19] Therefore, it makes sense that at precisely the time when globalizing forces threaten local identities, this brings about resurgent attention to local ways of life. It is only when movement toward the European Economic Union and single European currency threatens the French Franc and the English pound that citizens wax eloquent about these symbols and their importance to society.

Threat is only one piece of the puzzle, however. Transitions to liberal economic and political forms are very destabilizing. As societies undergo fundamental and difficult transitions brought on by open society, open technology, and open economy forces, virulent nationalisms can be resuscitated as a means of finding a scapegoat for tough times. The fact that there once was a violent form of nationalism does not mean that future conflicts will break out along national or ethnic lines. Many of the most highly developed states today once endured bloody civil wars—the United Kingdom, the United States, and France. Previous conflict by itself is neither an indicator nor an explanation for later conflict. This is where the case of Bosnia becomes critical. Most journalists and pundits peg the cause of conflict in the Balkans as "ancient ethnic hatreds." But this no more explains the conflict than does noting that the sun rose before the fighting took place, and since A came before B, therefore A caused B. Poland and Czechoslovakia also experienced "ancient ethnic hostilities," yet violent nationalisms did not plunge these societies into internal war as occurred in the former Yugoslavia. Susan Woodward believes that economics was a pivotal trigger in bringing violent nationalism to Yugoslavia, while Poland and Czechoslovakia had gentler transitions from communism. As the economic situation deteriorated in Yugoslavia, politicians sought to protect their own national groups, and leaders exploited nationalist tensions to explain away economic woes and distance themselves from their communist pasts.[20] Michael Brown notes that bad leaders, bad neighbors, bad internal problems, and bad neighborhoods can also fire nationalism into internal conflict.[21] The point is that there is no straight causal line between violent nationalism in the past and violent nationalism in the future. However, states undergoing difficult transitions to open society, open economy, and open technology forces, can be more vulnerable to violent forms of nationalism. Globalizing forces can (in combination with other factors) resuscitate attention to local identities.

Going global and going local are connected in another way as well. A recent preliminary study of twelve states over the past twenty years showed a correlation between indicators of open societies, open economies, and open technologies and government decentralization. States that increased in openness over the time period also increased in government decentralization (the amount of money and decision-making power that went to the local government level as opposed to the central government). States that stayed closed in the same time period did not experience government decentralization. Correlation is not causation, and so open economy, open technology, and open society forces and government decentralization might be caused by some third factor (the IMF, for example, as international investors pressure states both to decentralize governments and to privatize markets). But initial evidence does show that there are "simultaneous trends in globalization and decentralization;"[22] decentralization and open society, open market, open technology forces go together.

By this view it is not an accident that the highly centralized states of the communist Soviet Union and Eastern Europe, the apartheid state of South Africa, the military regimes in Argentina, and the social-welfare states of the United Kingdom and the United States are undergoing decentralization simultaneously. As U.S. President Bill Clinton put it, the era of big government is dead, but not just in the United States.[23] Big government is being downsized all over the planet, and power is increasingly moving to local governments in federated systems, and to nonstate actors. Sometimes the central state government retains authority over certain functions but no longer performs the functions themselves, as when states turn the operation of prisons or schools over to private actors or to local governments.

> When a country's political, economic, and development activities become globalized, the national government may no longer be the dominant entity; transnational cooperations emerge at all levels of government (national and subnational) and among all types of organizations (public organizations, multinational organizations, and NGOs). Linkages between global and local socioeconomic, political, and administrative organizations are webs of organized networks and human interactions. Global changes occurring today are creating new, complex, and decentralized systems of networks that are radically different from the old centralized systems of governance which controlled the process of international activities and decision making. Global changes influence the functions and actions of local administrators. And as local administrators become more conscious of global information, they become prepared to take innovative actions without the supervision of the national government.[24]

Government decentralization makes sense given the views of scholars; Rosenau noted that open technologies such as faxes, personal computers, hand-held video cameras, etc., empower individuals and small groups such as NGOs. Likewise, open economies allow individuals power over their economic futures, as Rosecrance and Strange note, and open societies take away the arbitrary power of strong central governments in favor of protection of individual liberties and rights. All these factors would facilitate government at the local level, and make control at the central level more difficult. The state, it would appear, is not going away; the state is contracting out.

How can it be that local government is making a comeback all over the globe at the same time that IGOs are becoming more important? The state is contracting out functions to a number of actors simultaneously: to IGOs, NGOs,

MNCs, and local governments. The strong central governments of the twentieth century—the fascist states, the communist states, and even the Roosevelt social security state and the Cold War national security state—are receding. Thus, while Krasner and Spruyt may be right that at the dawn of the twenty-first century the sovereign state remains, this is not the state that we drove into this century in; this is not your father's Oldsmobile.

THE SPEED OF CHANGE

If the sovereign state is changing and new forms of political organization are emerging, will change take centuries this time around? In Spruyt's story of the emergence of sovereignty, competing political forms coexisted for centuries before feudalism receded and the sovereign state emerged as the standard. Krasner and Spruyt imply that it will take a similarly long time before current changes in economic or social structures mount a fundamental challenge to the sovereign state system, in part because those who benefit from the existing state system will fight to keep it around. But the end of feudalism and the rise of sovereignty took place in an era when the modes of transportation and communication were horseback and slow-moving ships. Might change occur more quickly in an era of jet planes, the Internet, faxes, e-mail, personal computers, and cell phones?

Susan Strange argues that the sovereign state's authority over society and economy is eroding and becoming more diffuse, but she also believes the rate of change is different than it used to be. "What is new and unusual is that all—or nearly all—states should undergo substantial change of roughly the same kind within the same short period of twenty or thirty years. The last time that anything like this happened was in Europe when states based on a feudal system of agricultural production geared to local subsistence, gave way to states based on a capitalist system of industrial production for the market. The process of change was spread over two or three centuries at the very least and in parts of eastern and southern Europe is only now taking shape. In the latter part of the twentieth century, the shift has not been confined to Europe and has taken place with bewildering rapidity."[25]

Ideas are spread instantaneously in an era of satellite television and Internet connections. The "one world" advertising themes of Nike, IBM, and the United Parcel Service may contain a grain of truth in highlighting the ramifications of a wired planet in which many of us are plugged in. In an era of open technologies, mass advertising, television, and pop culture, new ideas are disseminated much more quickly than in an era of Gutenberg printing presses and wooden ships.

As discussed in Chapter 11, Stephen Krasner introduces the idea of punctuated equilibrium from evolutionary biology to draw the analogy that institutional change may occur rapidly over a limited period of time in unexpected ways. Rather than the Darwinian idea of change as slow, steady, continuous, and gradual, punctuated equilibrium stresses that change is "usually accomplished rapidly when a stable structure is stressed beyond its buffering capacity to resist and absorb . . . These evolutionary shifts can be quirky and unpredictable as the potentials for complexity are vast."[26]

One question this raises is whether the fast rate of change that open economy, society, and technology forces have unleashed is comparable to the rate of change of sovereign states to keep up with new environmental circumstances. This is particularly important as more states become democratic, since democratic state institutions are often slow to act, with opportunities for gridlock and delay built right into the state structure. If the rate of external change vastly supercedes the institution's ability to respond, will sovereign institutions be stressed beyond their ability to evolve and adapt? Buffeted by external blows, sovereignty continues to limp along, but as the speed of technological change outpaces the sovereign state's ability to hobble and hotwire responses, the limp may become more pronounced and perhaps—though no time soon—eventually fatal to the sovereign state.

Krasner emphasizes that changes can occur in unintended ways, and can occur rapidly when threshold effects are reached. Just as "credit cards can be used to open doors," structures that developed for one reason may later be put to very different uses. So even though Krasner concludes that the sovereign state "will not be dislodged easily, regardless of changed circumstances in the material environment," and that sovereignty is so entrenched that "[i]t is now difficult to even conceive of alternatives," he acknowledges that in evolution, surprises are possible.[27]

CONCLUSION: THE SHIP OF THESEUS

At what point do we have a new ship of state? International relations scholars agree that change is occurring. The authors discussed here agree that the sovereign state is not obsolete, and will continue to play a role along with other actors on the international scene. The theorists disagree, however, about whether sovereignty is being replaced or will be replaced or fundamentally changed, and about how fast change is occurring and whether it will eventually add up to enough to dethrone the sovereign state. We are in a period of transition—of smoke and confusion—and we do not know yet whether the state can be retrofitted to weather the storms of changes in economy, elites, and ideas, or whether these changes will someday bring about new forms of political organization.

The situation is analogous to a famous puzzle in the study of philosophy, the ship of Theseus. There are three different ways the ship of Theseus problem is discussed. The first stems from its origins in Greek mythology. Theseus was the son of Aegeus, the king of Athens. Theseus sailed away to fight a heroic battle, but after slaying the Minotaur he forgot to change the sails to indicate the victory to his father. Sailing in the same old sails unwittingly brought about tragedy, as his father did not realize the battle had been won because the changed situation was not immediately apparent by viewing his son's ship. In a fit of despair Theseus' father committed suicide, throwing himself from a cliff into the sea.[28] The analogy here is to the discussion in Chapter 11 about institutions. Many of our foreign policy institutions were built to fight the Cold War. Now the Cold War battle is over and won, but we have not changed our institutional sails to signify the new situation, and we may be flirting with disaster by traveling with our old sails.

The more pressing analogy, however, concerns the other two ways in which the ship of Theseus problem is discussed, questioning the nature of change and identity. If the planks of a ship are removed one by one over intervals of time, and each time an old plank is removed it is replaced by a new plank, is it a new vessel, and at what point did it reach critical mass to call it something new?[29]

This is the question we now face in considering the sovereign state. In Chapter 1 we considered ten functions of states that Susan Strange believes are either no longer performing or at least are sharing with other, nonstate actors. Scholar William Zartman posts his own list. In discussing failed or weak states that are collapsing, he lists five basic functions states perform: the state as the decision-making center of government; the state as a symbol of identity; the state as controller of territory and guarantor of security; the state as authoritative, legitimate political institution; and the state as a system of socioeconomic organization, the target of citizen demands for providing supplies or services.[30] Although Zartman offers this list as a litmus test for when weak states are failing because basic state functions are no longer being performed, many of these functions correspond with Strange's and other authors' observations of roles all states—weak and strong—used to undertake but no longer fulfill. Strange, Rosecrance, and Rosenau argue that states are no longer the sole decision-making center; MNCs, IGOs, and NGOs increasingly make decisions about matters which were traditionally handled by states. Economic decisions increasingly take place in corporate board rooms, on the floors of international stock exchanges, and in the conference rooms of the IMF, and states increasingly react to rather than generate these key decisions. The authors, as discussed earlier in this chapter, note that states are being challenged as the symbol of identity and as authoritative, legitimate political institution, as citizens increasingly place their loyalties elsewhere. In the discussions of transsovereign problems in this book, the authors illustrate that states no longer can unilaterally control territory or borders, or secure territory from external threats. Finally, many of the authors discuss alternative institutions, be they MNCs, NGOs, IGOs, or other nonstate actors, as increasingly being the target of citizen demands for services or supplies which citizens do not believe the state can supply. If the sovereign state is no longer performing the basic functions associated with sovereign states, at what point does sovereignty cease?

Hendrik Spruyt maintains that the primary innovation of the sovereign state was its connection of authority to territory, but Richard Rosecrance argues that the sovereign state's connection to territory is being severed, and that states no longer derive authority or power from territory. Rosenau agrees that authority is no longer automatically conferred to the traditional sources on the basis of customary legitimacy claims, be they legal or geographic, but that people are instead judging legitimacy and authority on the basis of performance. If sovereignty is no longer about territory, what is it about? If territory is at the heart of sovereignty and territory is removed, is what's left still sovereignty? How many planks must be pulled for us to recognize it as something different?

The difference between the case of sovereignty and the changes that occurred to the ship of Theseus was that the ship's planks were replaced exactly, in the same manner and fulfilling the same functions. The planks were not altered to turn the ship into a biplane; the ship was not retrofitted to serve as a cruise liner or a tugboat. In the case of sovereignty, however, materials are not only changing to slowly give the vessel a facelift. Such changes might be correlated to the changes in regime and administrative type between the authoritarian regimes and regimes with strong central government functions of the twentieth century, as compared with the decentralized, capitalist, democratic regimes of the century's end. However, the changes this volume discusses are not just changes in sovereignty's face or outward appearance, but changes in its very nature. Unlike the ship of Theseus, the ship of state is changing the very functions it performs and how it performs those functions. If sovereignty is as sovereignty does, and what sovereignty does is changing, is what sovereignty *is* changing?

The final analogy with the ship concerns the nature of change. Some philosophers argue for foundationalism, that sound principles need to be laid out first for new concepts to be built and based upon. But Otto Neurath argues that we seldom have the luxury of changing our ideas in a pristine vacuum, starting from scratch. Instead he argues that "we are like sailors who must rebuild their ship on the open sea, never able to dismantle it in dry dock and to reconstruct it there out of the best materials."[31] Certainly this is analogous to the changes now occurring to sovereignty. The ship's wheel is being replaced while the ship is still in operation; new planks are added and old functions are jettisoned while we are underway. New nonstate actors are cropping up and assuming functions that states used to perform; new policies toward transsovereign problems are evolving, utilizing nonstate sectors, at the same time that state responses are being fine-tuned. We are not dry-docked awaiting the emergence of a new ship of political organization, but we must go forward while we are in the midst of major construction.

Sovereignty is changing in real and fundamental ways. Sovereignty is evolving away from its Westphalian origins, but the sovereign state will not become obsolete, and no single replacement organizational unit will arise, anytime soon. For the immediate future, sovereignty will be first among competing forms, but there will be a "return to history" in the sense of a return to cross-cutting, non-hierarchical, ad hoc, and relative forms of order and organization. The state is alive, but is increasingly contracting out; and a decentralized state less connected to territory and to traditional state functions is something different than the sovereign states we have known in the twentieth century, although it is something less than the wholesale eviction of the idea of sovereignty. Sovereignty is here for our lifetime, but it is morphing in ways that need to be monitored, with an eye both toward recognizing (inductively) and theorizing about (deductively) emerging alternatives to sovereignty.

The problem with our ability to track changes in the sovereign state is that we are so used to the system, we are not good at even contemplating what alternatives to sovereignty might look like—we are truly conceptual prisoners. The problem with this is that outdated ideas can kill. As Krasner notes, when the Spanish conquistadores arrived in Mexico, the local inhabitants had no categories to ascribe to their new visitors. Lacking new concepts to fit the new situation, the conquistadores were categorized as gods within the existing belief framework. The consequences of this error were catastrophic for the local populations, who were decimated by the diseases and the firepower that the newcomers brought.[32] Urgently needed are new thoughts on how we might organize humans, as well as more specific ideas about the organizational shapes into which sovereignty might morph, or that might rival or replace sovereignty at some unknown future point. It is likely that these ideas will develop out of our experiences of economic or technological change, as our ideas about organization are informed by the new organizational structures we see modeled in the marketplace and on the Internet.

In the meantime we confront an international system where the state increasingly "contracts out." Along with states, more actors play more roles on a variety of transsovereign issues to which states cannot effectively respond unilaterally. Sovereignty is not going away, but it is evolving, decentralizing, and contracting out.

The upshot of these changes is that states will increasingly have to coordinate policy among a wider variety of public and private actors. Richard Neustadt describes an American political system in which, although the president is more powerful than other political actors, he rarely has the ability to command or compel; instead he must persuade others to pursue his preferred outcomes.[33]

The state is entering a similar position. While it may be the more powerful actor vis-à-vis NGOs, IGOs, MNCs, etc. (depending on the case and the situation), it rarely has the power to command or compel outcomes on transsovereign problems. Instead states have to assume new roles as coordinators, facilitators, initiators, and persuaders in order to engineer action on transsovereign problems. This places burdens on state institutions, requiring organizational changes and adding more functions for states to undertake though not necessarily control. This is precisely the situation Neustadt considered when he noted that an increase in duties did not equate to an increase in power or in the capacity to fulfill new duties, and that more duties without means is equivalent to being a glorified clerk, not a power entity. In diffuse, decentralized systems, policy is more complex, and the lines of accountability for policy more blurred, than under the old system. However, integrating action among a wider variety of players also opens new opportunities for policy, and offers greater possibilities for effectively tackling transsovereign issues than old-style unilateral responses. International political problems have gone beyond sovereignty. We must also go beyond sovereignty in theory and in practice, changing our ideas and our actions in order to sail ahead of the waves of change and more successfully respond to transsovereign challenges.

Notes

1. Susan Strange, *The Retreat of the State: The Diffusion of Power in the World Economy* (Cambridge: Cambridge University Press, 1996), 189.
2. Richard Rosecrance, "The Rise of the Virtual State," *Foreign Affairs* (July/August 1996): 59–60.
3. Stephen D. Krasner, "Sovereignty: An Institutional Perspective," *Comparative Political Studies* 21 (April 1988): 74.
4. Hendrik Spruyt, *The Sovereign State and Its Competitors* (Princeton, N.J.: Princeton University Press, 1994) 62, 75.
5. James N. Rosenau, *Turbulence in World Politics* (Princeton, N.J.: Princeton University Press, 1990).
6. Samuel Huntington, *The Clash of Civilizations and the Remaking of World Order* (New York: Simon & Schuster, 1996).
7. Peter L. Berger, "Four Faces of Global Culture," *The National Interest* (Fall 1997): 24.
8. Ibid.
9. Ibid.
10. Strange, *The Retreat of the State*, 199.
11. Rosecrance, "The Rise of the Virtual State," 59–60.
12. Benjamin R. Barber, *Jihad vs. McWorld* (New York: Ballantine Books, 1996).
13. William J. Broad, "Deal for U.S. to Buy Fuel from Russia Said to Be in Peril," *New York Times,* June 12, 1995; "An Endangered Nuclear Bargain," *New York Times,* June 13, 1995; Josef Hebert, "Disputes Slow U.S.-Russian Uranium Deal," *Washington Post,* June 14, 1995; William J. Broad, "Senate Panel Seeks to Save Russian Atom-Arms-for-Peace Deal," *New York Times,* June 14, 1995.

14. The deal called for the Russians to be paid $82 per separative work unit for the uranium, which the Enrichment Corporation could then sell for $120 per separative work unit to utility companies. However, the Enrichment Corporation believed this profit margin was not high enough, and sought to drive the Russian price down to $68 per unit, which insulted the Russians. There is no real comparable "market price" for this good; since the Enrichment Corporation has a virtual monopoly on this work in the United States, there is no other company that could enter a bid. Also complicating the agreement were Commerce Department anti-dumping restrictions against importing Russian uranium ore (Ibid.).

15. Thomas W. Lippman, "U.S. Vows Faster Payment to Russia in Uranium Deal," *Washington Post,* July 6, 1995; "U.S. and Russia Narrow Differences on Uranium Sale, but Not Iranian Pact," *Wall Street Journal,* July 3, 1995.

16. Peter Passell, "U.S. Goals at Odds in a Plan to Sell Off Nuclear Operation," *New York Times,* July 25, 1995, A1.

17. David E. Sanger, "Money-Savers and Risks Mix in Plan to Privatize Agencies," *New York Times,* December 25, 1994, A1.

18. Interestingly, Rosenau's thesis would explain why President Clinton's approval ratings have not diminished and have even improved during his impeachment hearings. The media and conservative thinkers have been at a loss to explain why the U.S. public has not been more exercised about President Clinton's extramarital affair, its moral implications, and its effects on the dignity of the presidential office. But if the public judges legitimacy and authority by performance criteria, not by appeals to tradition or moral authority, then breaches of tradition and morality would not affect the public's perception of Clinton's legitimacy or authority. If performance criteria are all that matters, then Clinton's poll ratings make sense given the low unemployment rate and strong performance of the U.S. economy, especially while European and Asian economic growth rates have been flat or declining. According to Rosenau, it would seem that political leaders can "get away with" quite a bit as long as it does not poorly affect their record of concrete achievements.

19. Ted Robert Gurr, "Minorities, Nationalists, and Ethnopolitical Conflict," in *Managing Global Chaos,* eds. Chester Crocker, Fen Osler Hampson, and Pamela Aall (Washington: U.S. Institute of Peace, 1996), 53–78; David Little, "Religious Militancy," in *Managing Global Chaos,* 79–92; Ernest Gellner, "Nations and Nationalism," in *Conflict After the Cold War: Arguments on the Causes of War and Peace,* ed. Richard Betts (New York: Macmillan Publishing Company, 1994), 280–292; Louis Kriesberg, "Regional Conflicts in the Post–Cold War Era: Causes, Dynamics, and Modes of Resolution," in *World Security: Challenges for a New Century,* eds. Michael Klare and Daniel Thomas (New York: St. Martin's Press, 1994), 155–174; Donald L. Horowitz, "Ethnic and Nationalist Conflict," in *World Security: Challenges for a New Century,* 175–187; Michael Shuman and Hal Harvey, "Conflict Resolution," *Security Without War: A Post-Cold War Foreign Policy* (Boulder, Colo.: Westview Press, 1993), 143–161.

20. Susan Woodward, *Balkan Tragedy* (Washington, D.C.: Brookings Institution, 1995).

21. Michael Brown, *The International Dimensions of Internal Conflict* (Cambridge, Mass.: MIT Press, 1996), 579.

22. Jong S. Jun and Deil S. Wright, *Globalization and Decentralization: Institutional Contexts, Policy Issues, and Intergovernmental Relations in Japan and the U.S.* (Washington, D.C.: Georgetown University Press, 1996), 1.

23. President Clinton was referring to the end of welfare as we knew it and reforms that have downsized the federal government to the smallest it has been since the Kennedy administration.

24. Ibid., 3–4.
25. Strange, *The Retreat of the State,* 87.
26. Krasner, "Sovereignty: An Institutional Perspective," 79.
27. Ibid., 80.
28. Robert E. Bell, *Dictionary of Classical Mythology: Symbols, Attributes and Associations* (Santa Barbara, Calif.: ABC-Clio Publisher, 1982), 207.
29. Rodrick M. Chisholm, *Person and Object: A Metaphysical Study* (LaSalle, Ill.: Open Court Publishers, 1976), 89–92.
30. Zartman, *Collapsed States,* 5.
31. Otto Neurath quoted in A. J. Ayer, ed., *Logical Positivism* (Glenco, Ill.: Free Press, 1959). This is sometimes referred to as Neurath's ship.
32. Krasner, "Sovereignty: An Institutional Perspective," 80.
33. Richard E. Neustadt, *Presidential Power and the Modern Presidents: The Politics of Leadership from Roosevelt to Reagan* (New York: Free Press, 1990).